APPLIED DATABASE LOGIC I: Fundamental Database Issues

Barry E. Jacobs
Senior Research Computer Scientist
National Space Science Data Center
Goddard Space Flight Center
National Aeronautics and Space Administration
Greenbelt, Maryland 20771

PRENTICE-HALL, INC., Englewood Cliffs, New Jersey 07632

Library of Congress Cataloging in Publication Data
Jacobs, Barry E., 1947–
Applied database logic I.

Includes bibliographies and index.
1. Data base management. I. Title. II. Title:
Applied database logic 1. III. Title: Applied
database logic one.
QA76.9.D3J33 1985 001.64 85-3499
ISBN 0-13-040205-2

Editorial/production supervision and
interior design: Fred Dahl
Manufacturing buyer: Gordon Osbourne

Printed in the United States of America
10 9 8 7 6 5 4 3 2 1

ISBN 0-13-040205-2 01

Prentice-Hall International (UK) Limited, *London*
Prentice-Hall of Australia Pty. Limited, *Sydney*
Editora Prentice-Hall do Brasil, Ltda., *Rio de Janeiro*
Prentice-Hall Canada Inc., *Toronto*
Prentice-Hall Hispanoamericana, S.A., *Mexico*
Prentice-Hall of India Private Limited, *New Delhi*
Prentice-Hall of Japan, Inc., *Tokyo*
Prentice-Hall of Southeast Asia Pte. Ltd., *Singapore*
Whitehall Books Limited, *Wellington, New Zealand*

This book is dedicated to the memory of my father,
David Jacobs (1907–1981),
who taught me that it is more important to follow the heart
than to follow the crowd.

CONTENTS

PREFACE

Data can be represented in a number of ways in a database. For example, there are the three major methodologies: relational, hierarchical, and network. Further, even for a particular methodology, there are different implementations from which to choose. For instance, in the relational approach there are Oracle, Ingres, dBase II, and so on. In the network case, although CODASYL is intended to be a standard, there are many variations among existing CODASYL systems.

This abundance has resulted in two significant problems. First, because of the diversity of approaches, a database professional often finds that reading the literature requires tedious translation between terminology with which the professional is familiar and that which appears in, say, a journal article. Second, database users wanting to access data in a database type other than their own have to learn new rules and operations for manipulating the data. Consequently, this has created an "it's too much trouble to do" attitude. As a result, a tremendous proliferation and repetition of database research papers and databases has developed.

Database logic, the focal point of this book, is a proposed remedy for this situation. In very simple terms, database logic can be thought of as a uniform layer that can be placed on top of heterogeneous databases (i.e., relational, hierarchical, and network). Consequently, it can provide a uniform paradigm for communicating results of database research. In addition, database logic can be used as a way of looking at heterogeneous databases so that user access is facilitated.

More precisely, database logic is to the heterogeneous cases what first-order logic is to the relational approach. In this book, which presumes no previous background in logic, we show how database logic can be used to deal with many important database issues. These include

1. External-to-conceptual mapping
2. View update
3. View integration
4. Database conversion and query processing
5. Automatic program conversion
6. External axiomatization

These issues are all seen to be related using the notion of "interpretation."

Many of the ideas to be presented have come from our experience on the Distributed Access View Integrated Database (DAVID) project funded by National Aeronautics and Space Administration (NASA). The objective of this project is the development of an easy-to-use system with which people in the federal government can uniformly access distributed heterogeneous databases. Basically, DAVID is a database management system which is built on top of already existing database and file management systems. The front end of the DAVID system is database logic.

This book is unique in several ways. First, it is the first text that contains a treatment of all the above-mentioned issues. Second, it presents a unified approach, namely, interpretations, for dealing with all these issues. Third, many of the results in this book are new and have not yet appeared in the literature. Fourth, it presents a complete treatise of the recently developed tool of database logic. Fifth, it provides a vehicle through which computer science students can learn mathematical logic and discover how it can be applied to important database issues.

This book is the first in a series. The main theme throughout is the demonstration of how database logic may be used as a uniform tool for addressing many important database issues. This book deals with the fundamental issues mentioned above and shows how the notion of interpretation can tie them all together. The second book will deal with query processing over a set of heterogeneous distributed databases. The third book will deal with expert systems that are built on top of databases. Other books will deal with machine learning, transaction processing, database machine architecture, and theoretical issues concerning database logic. Our *modus operandi* is simple: We generalize database technology from the relational to the heterogeneous case using database logic as the framework.

The development of this book and the material within would not have been possible without the help of a number of people. Alan R. Aronson, Dehe Cao, Upen S. Chakravarthy, John Grant, Cindy Walczak, and Jack Welch have all contributed, in many ways, to the material that is presented in this book. Milt Halem and Paul H. Smith of NASA have provided the support, both technical and moral, for the DAVID project which resulted in this endeavor. Michael Anshel, Phillip Bernstein, John Berbert, Marco Casanova, Seymour Ginsburg, Keith Harrow, Stephen Hegner, David

Hsiao, Jack Minker, Ray Reiter, Ira Sack, Ed Sibley, and Moshe Vardi have provided direction and reassurance.

There are a number of individuals who helped to test and proofread the manuscript. These are Joseph Aulino, Kenneth Baum, Nancy Broderick, Isadore Brodsky, Edmund D'souza, Jennifer Elgot, Hsin Fang, Liang Fang, Elizabeth Fineman, James Finucane, Hsiao-Fang Hu, Kyu-Hyun Hwang, Adel Gharib, Diana Gordon, Kim Haynes, George Kertz, Thomas Jacobs, Susan Mittelman, David Moraff, Karen Roberts, Gompa Raghuramaih, Michael Shapiro, Duc Tran, John Waclawsky, and Karen Weiss.

I wish to also express my deepest thanks to a number of people at Prentice-Hall who helped me through various stages of this book. These are Lynn Frankel, Rhoda Haas, Barb Klink, Leon Liguori, Nancy Milnamow, and Gordon Osbourne. Special thanks also to Ira Shore of PPI Inc. who gave me a course in computer typesetting; to Barbara Palumbo of Prentice-Hall, who taught me so much about book production; and Fred Dahl, who coordinated the editing, production, and design of this book.

I am tremendously grateful to Karl Karlstrom at Prentice-Hall, one of the true giants in the computer science publishing industry, for his unwavering support of this project. I also thank Raymond Yeh at the University of Maryland for his help in initiating the publication of this series. Most of all, I wish to express my gratitude to my wife, Susan, who walked with me through every step on the oftentimes rocky and frustrating road to this point. I love her dearly for it.

BARRY E. JACOBS

HOW TO READ THIS BOOK

In this section we provide the reader with helpful suggestions for reading this text. The way in which one goes through the material will depend on one's background and the topics of interest.

1. The Introduction should be read in its entirety. Its purpose is to provide the reader with some preliminary background as well as an overall view of the material in the book. As in all chapters in the book, doing the exercises at the end of each section is strongly encouraged.

2. Chapters 1 and 2 should be read in their entirety. They form the foundation for the rest of the book. Unfortunately, they will be the hardest parts to get through. This is because the notation and concepts will probably be foreign to most readers. The reader should spend more time on understanding the examples than in trying to figure out the nuances of the definitions. After completing the first two chapters, the reader will be able to proceed faster through the rest of the book.

Chapter 1 shows how database logic can be used to represent heterogeneous databases. In Section 1.1 we cover the special case in which first-order logic represents relational databases. This section is particularly useful for readers without any background in logic. In Section 1.2 the notions of Section 1.1 are generalized to the heterogeneous case in database logic. In Section 1.3 the ideas of the first two sections are illustrated by defining a data manipulation language based on database logic.

After finishing Chapter 1, the reader is not expected to be a proficient "logician." Instead, it is expected that the reader will be comfortable with database logic view definitions as exemplified by Figures 1.3 and 1.8. There are formal definitions of database logic in Chapter 3. These should be looked at while reading Chapter 1 only if the reader feels uncomfortable with the presentation.

Chapter 2 shows how the notion of "interpretation" can be used as a vehicle to relate two different databases. In Section 2.1 we cover the special case in which both databases are relational. In Section 2.2 we generalize the material of Section 2.1 to the heterogeneous case. In Section 2.3 we show how programs can be converted from one database to another.

After finishing Chapter 2, the reader should be comfortable with the interpretation definition as exemplified by Figures 2.3 and 2.11. Also, it is expected that the reader will be familiar with the two mappings produced by the interpretation and the "Flipper Theorem." Again, the reader should consult the formal material in Chapter 3 only if uncomfortable with the presentation in Chapter 2.

3. Chapter 3 contains the formal definitions of database logic. Section 3.1 presents a discussion of how the important issues mentioned in the Introduction can be framed using the concepts from Chapters 1 and 2. This section should be read in its entirety. Sections 3.2 and 3.3 contain the formal material. The reader can skim through them and move on in the book.

4. The reader can now choose to read any of the remaining chapters in the book. Chapter 4 should be read before Chapter 5; otherwise, the reader can jump around as he or she chooses. There are cases in which material occurring in one chapter is referred to in other chapters. For example, logical optimization of Chapter 8 is mentioned in Chapter 7. However, these situations do not occur too often, and when they do, the material can still be pretty well digested.

5. The general mode of presentation in this book is that issues are first covered for the relational case and then generalized to the heterogeneous case. If one is concerned only with the relational case, then one can study only those chapters and sections pertaining to it. In all cases, proofs are provided for the heterogeneous case. However, a relational reader can still follow the arguments simply by pretending that only the relational case is dealt with.

B.E.J.

INTRODUCTION

0.1 DATABASES

Roughly speaking, a *database* is a collection of data and operations that represents some aspects of the real world. For example, a university database can be regarded as representing parts of a university environment. Hence, one may regard a database as a "model" of that part of reality in which one is interested. Consequently, when we use a database, questions about the real world are reduced to questions about the model.

There are three major types of databases: relational, hierarchical, and network. The differences between them are based on the way in which data in the database appear to the user. Illustrations of the three types are given below. A *database management system* is a large-scale computer program that is responsible for supporting many databases. Depending on the type of databases it maintains, a database management system is called relational, hierarchical, or network.

Relational Databases

Relational databases are databases in which data appear to the user in one or more separate tables. These tables, called *relations,* have rows that are called *records.* For example, Figure 0.1 contains an instance of a relational database. The database represents student transcript information at a university. The relation TRANSCRIPT has records that indicate the student id#, student name, semester, year, department, course#, section#, course title, grade, and credits. The relation STUDENT has records which have student id#, student name, and date of admission.

TRANSCRIPT									
STUDID	STUDNAME	SEMESTER	YEAR	DEPT	COURSE #	SEC #	TITLE	GRADE	CREDITS
123456789	SMITH ROBERT J.	FALL	1979	COMPSCI	103	001	INTRO	B	3
123456789	SMITH ROBERT J.	FALL	1979	MATH	103	001	CALC	B	3
123456789	SMITH ROBERT J.	FALL	1979	ART	101	001	INTRO	B	3
123456789	SMITH ROBERT J.	FALL	1979	HIST	102	001	AM HIST	C	3
123456789	SMITH ROBERT J.	SPRING	1980	COMPSCI	220	001	DISCR STRUCT	B	3
123456789	SMITH ROBERT J.	SPRING	1980	MATH	104	001	CALC	B	4
123456789	SMITH ROBERT J.	SPRING	1980	ECON	101	001	INTRO	C	3
123456789	SMITH ROBERT J.	SPRING	1980	ENG	105	001	COMPOS	A	3
361258823	JONES MARY T.	SPRING	1980	MATH	104	001	CALC	A	4
361258823	JONES MARY T.	SPRING	1980	ECON	101	001	INTRO	C	3
361258823	JONES MARY T.	SPRING	1980	PHYSICS	102	001	INTRO	D	4
361258823	JONES MARY T.	SPRING	1980	ENG	105	001	COMPOS	I	3

STUDENT		
ID#	NAMES	DATEADM
123456789	SMITH ROBERT J.	SEPT 2 1979
361258823	JONES MARY T.	FEB 1 1980

Figure 0.1 Relational database.

There are also semantic properties attached to a relational database, called *integrity constraints.* The most common type of integrity constraint is the *dependency constraint.* It is defined as a collection of fields in a record that uniquely determines other fields in a record. For example, in the TRANSCRIPT relation, STUDID determines STUDNAME, and DEPT and COURSE# determine TITLE and CREDITS. In STUDENT, ID# determines NAME and DATEADM.

When a set of fields determines the rest of the fields in the row, that set is called a *key.* For example, ID# is a key for STUDENT. Also, the reader can check that STUDID, SEMESTER, YEAR, DEPT, and COURSE# is a key for TRANSCRIPT.

Hierarchical Databases

In a *hierarchical database* data appear to the user as "hierarchies" of records. For example, Figure 0.2 contains an instance of a hierarchical database. The database represents registration information at a university. Each REGISTRAR record has two fields, SEMESTER and YEAR. Below each instance of a REGISTRAR record are instances of COURSE records that contain DEPT and COURSE# values. Below each COURSE record are SECTION records that contain SEC#, INSTRUCT, LOCAT, and TIMES corresponding to the section. Finally, below each SECTION record are STUDENT records that contain STUDID, STUDNAME, and GRADE values. In addition, there are STUDINFO records that contain ID#, STUDNAME, BIRTHDATE, and DATEADM values.

In a hierarchy, a specific record can have sets of records below it called "children." Each of the children can themselves have sets of records below them as their children. A special characteristic of a hierarchical database is that once a record name is used at some level of the hierarchy, the same record name cannot be used anywhere else in the hierarchy.

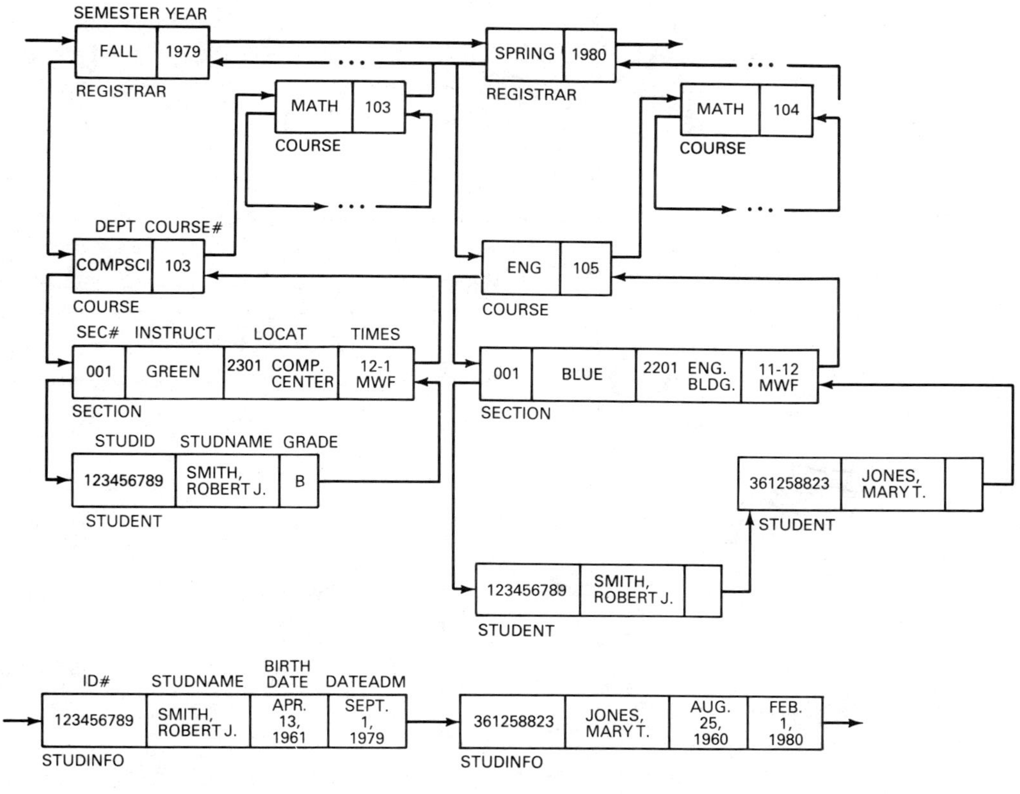

Figure 0.2 Hierarchical database.

Hierarchical databases also have integrity constraints. For example, in the REGISTRAR record, {SEMESTER, YEAR} is a key. That means that no two different REGISTRAR records in the entire database can have the same SEMESTER, YEAR pair. In the COURSE record, DEPT, COURSE# is a key. This means that below a particular REGISTRAR record (i.e., identified by a particular SEMESTER, YEAR) no two COURSE records can have the same DEPT, COURSE# pair. Similarly, in the SECTION, STUDENT, and STUDINFO records, SEC#, STUDID, and ID# are, respectively, also keys.

Network Databases

In a *network database,* data appear to the user as sets of records where each record instance may have many children and itself be the child of many parents. Whereas in the hierarchical approach, a child record can have only one parent, in the network approach, a child record can have many parents. In the hierarchical approach, a record type can appear only once in its ancestral tree. In the network, this restriction disappears.

For example, Figure 0.3 contains an instance of a network database. The database represents catalogue information for courses at a university. The record type CATALOGUE contains fields DEPT, COURSE#, TITLE, CREDITS, and DESCR (description). Each CATALOGUE record has below it (called a CATALOGUE-LINK "set") a single occurrence of a LINK record with no data. Below each LINK record (in a LINK-CATALOGUE set) are other occurrences of the CATALOGUE record. The lower-level CATALOGUE records indicate the courses that are prerequisites for the courses in the CATALOGUE records at the upper level.

Although network systems allow the same record type to occur several places in the ancestral structure (e.g., CATALOGUE), many do not allow both parent and child to be of the same type. This is the reason for the existence of the intermediary LINK record in our example. As in the relational and hierarchical cases, network databases can also have integrity constraints on the data. For example, in CATALOGUE, the fields DEPT and COURSE# form a key. Since LINK has no data, it has no key.

Exercises

1. Construct a relational version of the hierarchical database of Figure 0.2.
2. Construct a relational version of the network database of Figure 0.3.
3. Construct a hierarchical version of the relational database of Figure 0.1.
4. Construct a hierarchical version of the network database of Figure 0.3.

0.2 MULTI DATABASE ISSUES

In this section we will discuss several important database issues. The study of these makes up the bulk of this text. The reader will observe that there is a fundamental

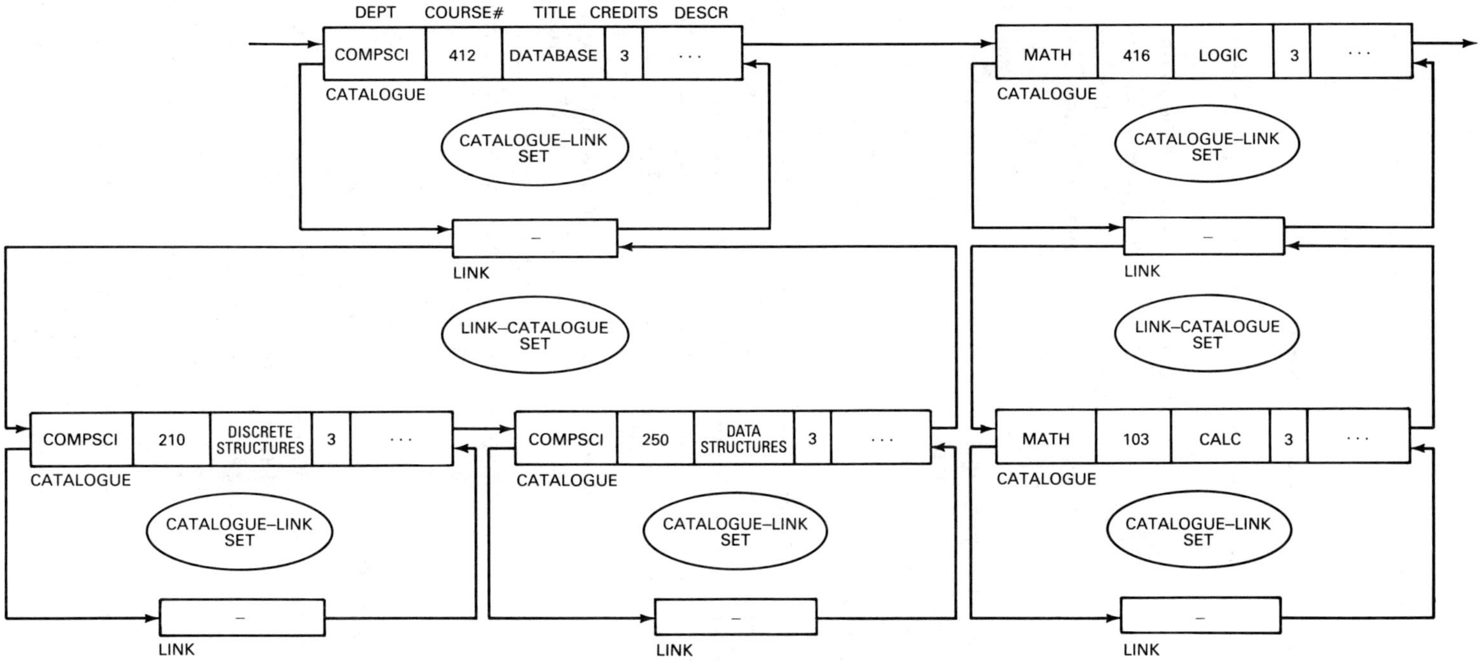

Figure 0.3 Network database.

theme linking all these issues; namely, they all involve two or more different databases.

External-to-Conceptual Mapping

Suppose that a university maintains the hierarchical database of Figure 0.2. Suppose also that a group of students prefer to see the data in terms of the relational database of Figure 0.1. A solution is to build the relational database as an outside or "external" view of the underlying "conceptual" hierarchical database. That is, the students can pretend that the database is relational even though, in fact, it is hierarchical.

The *external-to-conceptual mapping problem* is as follows. How can one precisely express the relationship between two databases so that one can be maintained as an "external" view of a second "conceptual" database? The mapping should provide a mechanism by which programs at the external level can be transformed into programs at the conceptual level. It should also provide a means by which data can be transferred back and forth between levels.

View Update

Suppose that, in some way, the student's relational database was maintained as an external view of the hierarchical database. Then, as far as the students are concerned, there is only one database, the relational one. Suppose that a student wants to insert a new row into the TRANSCRIPT table. Since the TRANSCRIPT table does not exist physically, this insertion has to be "simulated" on the underlying hierarchical database.

The *view update problem* is that of determining how updates (e.g., insertions, deletions, etc.) on an external view can be simulated "correctly" on the underlying conceptual database. Constraints also play a role in the view update problem. For example, suppose that an update is desired at the external level which would violate an external constraint (e.g., a key constraint). Then the update simulation at the conceptual level should, in some way, catch the violation and prevent it from occurring.

View Integration

Suppose that a university database is being planned or designed. Suppose also that in the analysis it is discovered that there are three classes of users: the registrar, who wants a hierarchical database like that of Figure 0.2; the students, who want a relational database like that of Figure 0.1; and the departments, which want a network database like that of Figure 0.3. The problem is how to build a database that will satisfy the needs of all these potential users.

The *view integration problem* is as follows. Given a collection of views, how can one construct a conceptual database that will support all of them as external views? The choice of underlying database should be such that the most frequent users incur the least overhead in the translation between external and conceptual levels. The view integration problem is often a major component in a design methodology in which external views are first extracted from a community of potential users and then integrated into a conceptual database.

Database Conversion and Query Processing

Suppose that the university designs its database so that the underlying conceptual database is the hierarchy of Figure 0.2 plus the network of Figure 0.3. Thus, the registrar, the students, and the departments all have their own views established. Suppose that the students no longer want to pay the price of the overhead of translation into the conceptual hierarchy. A solution is to build another copy of the database in the form of the relational view (Figure 0.1) that they use. Thus, one is giving up centrality of the data for improved performance for a class of users.

The *database conversion problem* is that of finding a methodology by which already existing databases can be used to construct new databases. The result of processing a query is often a "table" of values that satisfy the query. The problem of *query processing* is actually a special case of the database conversion problem. This is because in query processing, we are constructing new "relational" databases from other databases.

Automatic Program Conversion

Suppose that in time, the students decide to change their relational database to the hierarchical database of Figure 0.2. During the period that they used their relational database, they collected a large (and costly) amount of software. Unfortunately, the old software refers to the old database (i.e., TRANSCRIPT and STUDENT tables), hence cannot be used on the new hierarchical database. Consequently, all the old software has to be discarded and new software has to be written.

The *automatic program conversion problem* is that of deriving, from the old and new database descriptions, a mechanical means of transforming old application programs to programs on the new database. The process not only involves translation from the old to the new, but also optimization of the resultant programs. Furthermore, in some cases, the language in which the old programs are written is different from the language of the new database. This would, indeed, be the case if the old and new databases are in different database management systems.

External Axiomatization

Suppose that the student's relational database of Figure 0.1 is maintained as an external view of the hierarchical database of Figure 0.2. Thus, every instance of the conceptual database "produces" an instance of the external relational database. Furthermore, the constraints on the data in the conceptual database (e.g., DEPT, COURSE# determines TITLE and CREDITS in CATALOGUE) reflect the properties of the data in the produced external database (e.g., DEPT, COURSE# determine TITLE and CREDITS in TRANSCRIPT).

The *external axiomatization problem* is that of finding a characterization of all possible external databases. Such a characterization is important, especially if updating on the external view is permitted. Consequently, an external user can know beforehand if the results of an external update are within the range of possible external databases.

Hidden Databases

The notion of one database "hidden" in a second database is an important commonality between all the issues mentioned in the preceding section. For example, in the external-to-conceptual mapping problem, the question is how to "hide" the external database within the conceptual database. In view update, the problem is how to simulate updates on the hidden external database by "correct" operations on the conceptual database. In view integration, the problem is how to choose a single database that can hide a set of different databases.

In database conversion, the problem is how to construct a database that is hidden within the old database. In automatic program conversion, the old database is thought of as being hidden in the new database. The problem then is how to convert programs to the new database so that they will have the same effect as the old programs have on the hidden database. In external axiomatization, the problem is to characterize the class of all databases that are hidden within instances of the conceptual databases.

Exercises

Suppose that there is a correspondence between the relational database of Figure 0.1 and the hierarchical and network databases of Figures 0.2 and 0.3. Namely, there is a row in the TRANSCRIPT table:

(STUDID, STUDNAME, SEMESTER, YEAR, DEPT, COURSE#,
SEC#, TITLE, GRADE, CREDITS)

whenever there is a path of REGISTRAR, COURSE, SECTION, STUDENT records:

(SEMESTER, YEAR),
(DEPT, COURSE#),
(SEC#, INSTRUCT, LOCAT, TIMES),
(STUDID, STUDNAME, GRADE),

a record in STUDINFO:

(STUDID, STUDNAME, BIRTHDATE, DATEADM),

and a CATALOGUE record:

(DEPT, COURSE#, TITLE, CREDITS).

1. Suppose that the following query is asked on the relational database of Figure 0.1:

> Get all the rows in TRANSCRIPT which have SEMESTER = FALL, YEAR = 1979, DEPT = COMPSCI, COURSE# = 103, and GRADE = B.

How would such a query be translated into the underlying databases of Figures 0.2 and 0.3 according to the correspondence above?

2. Suggest a way that one can simulate the deletion of Robert Smith's Computer Science 103 course taken during the fall 1979 semester according to the correspondence above.

3. How would the following constraints on the underlying databases be reflected on the relational database according to the correspondence above?

(a) In STUDINFO: ID# determines STUDNAME, BIRTHDATE, DATE-ADM.

(b) In the REGISTRAR, COURSE, SECTION, STUDENT path, and CATALOGUE records: DEPT, COURSE# determines TITLE and CREDITS.

(c) In the REGISTRAR, COURSE, SECTION, STUDENT path: STUDID, SEMESTER, YEAR, DEPT, COURSE# determines SEC#.

0.3 LOGIC AND DATABASES

One of the benefits of working with the relational approach to databases is that it can be couched within the formalism of first-order predicate logic. As a result a mathematical foundation is available for dealing with database issues when databases are all relational.

Relational Databases in First-Order Logic

By a *first-order theory,* we mean a set of formulas or statements in some formal language. For example, recall the constraint on the database of Figure 0.1, which says that in the STUDENT table, ID# determines NAME and DATEADM. This is expressed in first-order logic by the following statement:

(STUDENT(ID#:1,NAME:1,DATEADM:1)
&STUDENT(ID#:1,NAME:2,DATEADM:2))
→(NAME:1 = NAME:2 & DATEADM:1 = DATEADM:2).

That is, if two rows appear in the STUDENT table with the same ID#, they will also have the same values for NAME and DATEADM.

As another example, recall the constraint which says that in the TRANSCRIPT table, STUDID determines STUDNAME. This is expressed in first-order logic as

((TRANSCRIPT(STUDID:1,STUDNAME:1,SEMESTER:1,...,CREDITS:1)
&TRANSCRIPT(STUDID:1,STUDNAME:2,SEMESTER:2,...,CREDITS:2))
→(STUDNAME:1 = STUDNAME:2).

A theory that represents the database of Figure 0.1 would consist of all statements, like the above, which represent constraints on the data.

By a *first-order structure,* we mean a mathematical entity which has (1) a universe of objects, (2) a set of predicates (i.e., each of which evaluates to true or false), and (3) a set of functions on the universe. For example, a first-order structure corresponding to the relational database in Figure 0.1 is as follows. A universe would be comprised of objects such as EBCDIC DECIMAL (9) values for STUDID plus EBCDIC CHAR(20) values for STUDNAME, etc.

Two predicates would correspond to the TRANSCRIPT and STUDENT tables. For example,

STUDENT(123456789,SMITH ROBERT J.,SEPT 2 1979)

is "true" because this row is in the STUDENT table in Figure 0.1. A function TOTCREDITS would be one that inputs a studid, semester, and year and returns the total number of credits taken by that student during that semester year; for example, according to Figure 0.1,

TOTALCREDITS(123456789,FALL,1979) = 12.

By a *model* of a first-order theory we mean a first-order structure that satisfies all the statements in the theory. At any moment of time, a relational database can be regarded as a model of a first-order theory, namely, its constraints. For example, the instance of the relational database pictured in Figure 0.1 does not violate any of the constraints in the theory described above. Hence, the instance is a model of that theory.

In Section 0.2, several issues were discussed which involved two or more databases. From the above we see that a relational database can be represented as a theory in first-order logic. Consequently, these issues reduce to, in the relational case, issues between two or more theories. To get a grip on such problems, let us see how multiple theories are handled in first-order logic.

Interpretations in First-Order Logic

In ordinary first-order logic, whenever two or more theories are contrasted, the usual comparison operator is the "interpretation." This notion will play a fundamental role throughout this book. The concept of an interpretation can be illustrated by considering an interpretation I(R;C) of the theory of real numbers R in the theory of the complex numbers C.

First, we associate with every real number in R a complex number, called its "code" in C. For example, we code the real number 3.5 by the complex number 3.5 + 0i. Second, we associate with predicates and functions in R representative predicates and functions in C that work on the codes. For instance, we represent real equality "a = b" by the complex equality on codes "(a + 0i) = (b + 0i)." Also, we associate with real addition "a + b" the complex addition on codes "(a + 0i) + (b + 0i) = (a + b) + 0i." Third, each of the axioms of the theory of the real numbers is "implied" from the axioms of the theory of the complex numbers. For example, the commutativity of complex addition [e.g., (a + bi) + (c + di) = (c + di) + (a + bi)] implies the commutativity of addition on the codes [e.g., (a + 0i) +(b + 0i) = (b + 0i) + (a + 0i)].

When one theory is interpreted in a second, any model of the second theory has "hidden" inside it a model of the first. For example, in the interpretation I(R;C) of R in C given above, the model of the real numbers is hidden inside the model of the complex numbers. First, the set of real numbers is hidden inside the set of complex numbers. Namely, each real number "a" is hidden as the complex number "a + 0i." Second, the real predicates and functions are hidden inside complex predicates and functions. For example, the real equality predicate "a = b" is represented by the complex equality predicate as "(a + 0i) = (b + 0i)." Also, the real addition function "a+b" is hidden inside the complex addition function as "(a + 0i) + (b + 0i) = (a + b) + 0i." Third, since each of the axioms of R is "implied" by the axioms of C, the hidden reals will also be a model of the axioms in R.

Database Logic: Views and Interpretations

In this book, we use the formal system called *database logic.* Database logic is to the relational, hierarchical, and network approaches as first-order logic is to the relational approach. That is, it provides a mathematical foundation for the study of databases. This book is relatively self-contained. Consequently, little previous knowledge of logic (first-order or database) is required for understanding this presentation.

The notion of a first-order theory generalizes to the notion of a *database view* in database logic. The notion of a first-order structure generalizes to the notion of a *database structure.* At any instant of time, a database (relational, hierarchical, or network) is regarded as a database structure that is a model of the view. Since the notion of database view subsumes that of first-order theory, any result obtained using database views gives us, as a special case, a result about relational databases.

The notion of an interpretation in first-order logic generalizes to the notion of *interpretation of database views* in database logic. Roughly speaking, an interpretation of one database view in a second is a correspondence between the objects (i.e., data, functions, predicates, etc.) of the first view and those of the second. In addition, the constraints in the first view are "implied" from the constraints in the second view. Since the notion of database view interpretation subsumes that of first-order interpretation, any result we obtain using view interpretations gives us, as a special case, a result about relational databases.

Exercises

1. Express in first-order logic the constraint that in STUDENT: NAME determines ID# and DATEADM.
2. Express in first-order logic the constraint that in TRANSCRIPT: DEPT, COURSE# determines TITLE and CREDITS.
3. Express in first-order logic the constraint that in TRANSCRIPT: STUDID, SEMESTER, YEAR, DEPT, COURSE# determines SEC#.

4. Express in first-order logic the constraint that in TRANSCRIPT: STUDID, SEMESTER, YEAR, DEPT, COURSE#, SEC# determines GRADE.

0.4 RELATED READING

DATE, C. J., *An Introduction to Database Systems,* Vol. I, 3rd ed., Addison-Wesley, Reading, MA, 1983.

KROENKE, D., *Database Processing,* Science Research Associates, Chicago, 1977.

MARTIN, J., *Computer Data-Base Organizations,* Prentice-Hall, Englewood Cliffs, N.J., 1975.

SIBLEY, E., (ed.), "Data-Base Management Systems," *ACM Computing Surveys,* **8**, Mar. 1976.

ULLMAN, J. D., *Principles of Database Systems,* 2nd ed., Computer Science Press, Rockville, MD, 1982.

1

DATABASE LOGIC

In Chapter 1 we informally introduce the reader to database logic. Formal definitions are given in Chapter 3. In Section 1.1 we show how relational databases can be represented within ordinary first-order logic. In Section 1.2 we demonstrate how hierarchical databases can be represented in database logic. (In Chapter 2 it is seen how network databases can also be represented by database logic.) In Section 1.3 we show how database logic may be used to define a generalized calculus data manipulation language.

1.1 RELATIONAL DATABASES IN FIRST-ORDER LOGIC

A relational database is represented in first-order logic by a "relational view" which is comprised of a "relational schema," "relational language," and "relational constraints." The idea is that at any instant of time a database is regarded as a "relational structure" which satisfies the integrity constraints of the view. We also see how these notions can be used to define a relational calculus data manipulation language.

Example

Throughout this section we use a relational database Rext illustrated in Figures 1.1 and 1.2. The database is intended to represent student transcripts at a university. The DOMAIN declarations SIDTPE, NAMTPE, ..., CRDSTPE of Figure 1.1 define the

```
DOMAIN SIDTPE EBCDIC DEC(9)
DOMAIN NAMTPE EBCDIC CHAR(20)
DOMAIN SEMTPE EBCDIC CHAR(4)
DOMAIN YRTPE  EBCDIC DEC(4)
DOMAIN DEPTPE EBCDIC CHAR(10)
DOMAIN CS#TPE EBCDIC DEC(3)
DOMAIN SEC#TPE EBCDIC DEC(3)
DOMAIN TTLTPE EBCDIC CHAR(25)
DOMAIN GRDTPE EBCDIC CHAR(1)
DOMAIN DATPE EBCDIC CHAR(15)
DOMAIN CRDSTPE EBCDIC DEC(2)

RELATION TRANSCRIPT
 (STUDID DOMAIN SIDTPE,
  STUDNAME DOMAIN NAMTPE,
  SEMESTER DOMAIN SEMTPE,
  YEAR DOMAIN YRTPE,
  DEPT DOMAIN DEPTPE,
  COURSE# DOMAIN CS#TPE,
  SEC# DOMAIN SEC#TPE,
  TITLE DOMAIN TTLTPE,
  GRADE DOMAIN GRDTPE,
  CREDITS DOMAIN CRDSTPE)
KEY(STUDID,SEMESTER,YEAR,DEPT,COURSE#);

RELATION STUDENT
 (ID# DOMAIN SIDTPE,
  NAME DOMAIN NAMTPE,
  DATEADM DOMAIN DATPE);
KEY(ID#)

CONSTRAINTS
  FD: TRANSCRIPT:STUDID → STUDNAME
  FD: TRANSCRIPT:DEPT,COURSE# → TITLE,CREDITS
```

Figure 1.1 Relational data definition language (DDL) definition of database Rext.

sets of atomic data elements that are to appear in the tables. The RELATION declaration for the table TRANSCRIPT defines its column names STUDID, STUDNAME, ..., CREDITS and the domains over which these columns will range. Similar remarks apply for the RELATION declaration for STUDENT.

The relation TRANSCRIPT has three integrity constraints which are *functional dependencies.* For example, the functional dependency

TRANSCRIPT:STUDID,SEMESTER,YEAR,DEPT,COURSE#
→STUDNAME,SEC#,TITLE,CREDITS,GRADE

means that in any two rows of the TRANSCRIPT table, if the two rows agree on STUDID, SEMESTER, YEAR, DEPT, COURSE# values, they will also agree on their STUDNAME, SEC#, TITLE, CREDITS, and GRADE values. This functional

TRANSCRIPT									
STUDID	STUDNAME	SEMESTER	YEAR	DEPT	COURSE #	SEC #	TITLE	GRADE	CREDITS
123456789	SMITH ROBERT J.	FALL	1979	COMPSCI	103	001	INTRO	B	3
123456789	SMITH ROBERT J.	FALL	1979	MATH	103	001	CALC	B	3
123456789	SMITH ROBERT J.	FALL	1979	ART	101	001	INTRO	B	3
123456789	SMITH ROBERT J.	FALL	1979	HIST	102	001	AM HIST	C	3
123456789	SMITH ROBERT J.	SPRING	1980	COMPSCI	220	001	DISCR STRUCT	B	3
123456789	SMITH ROBERT J.	SPRING	1980	MATH	104	001	CALC	B	4
123456789	SMITH ROBERT J.	SPRING	1980	ECON	101	001	INTRO	C	3
123456789	SMITH ROBERT J.	SPRING	1980	ENG	105	001	COMPOS	A	3
361258823	JONES MARY T.	SPRING	1980	MATH	104	001	CALC	A	4
361258823	JONES MARY T.	SPRING	1980	ECON	101	001	INTRO	C	3
361258823	JONES MARY T.	SPRING	1980	PHYSICS	102	001	INTRO	D	4
361258823	JONES MARY T.	SPRING	1980	ENG	105	001	COMPOS	I	3

STUDENT		
ID#	NAMES	DATEADM
123456789	SMITH ROBERT J.	SEPT 2 1979
361258823	JONES MARY T.	FEB 1 1980

Figure 1.2 Instance of the relational database Rext.

dependency is declared in Figure 1.1 by the declaration KEY(STUDID, SEMESTER, YEAR, DEPT, COURSE#). Other functional dependencies for TRANSCRIPT are

TRANSCRIPT:STUDID → STUDNAME

and

TRANSCRIPT:DEPT,COURSE# → TITLE,CREDITS.

declared in the two FD clauses in the CONSTRAINTS section. For the relation STUDENT, the only functional dependency given is

STUDENT:ID# → NAME,DATEADM,

which is denoted by KEY(ID#).

Relational Views

A *relational view* is comprised of a relational schema, which tells the structure of the tables; a relational language, which is a language for making assertions about the database; and a set of relational constraints, which are assertions in the relational language that every instance of the database must obey. These are explained below. The relational view definition of Figure 1.3 corresponds to the relational database Rext of Figure 1.1. **The reader is strongly advised to refer often to Figure 1.3 while reading this section.**

A *relational schema* S is a finite collection of rules of the form

S = { ...,R0 = (R1,...,Rn),... }.

The objects Ri, i=0,1, ..., n, are called *names. Relation* names appear on the left side of rules; *atomic* names appear only on the right side of rules. A rule with the name R0 on its left side is called an *R0 rule.*

The relational schema S(Rext) of Figure 1.3 is the set of rules

{TRANSCRIPT = (STUDID,STUDNAME,SEMESTER,YEAR,DEPT,
COURSE#,SEC#,TITLE,GRADE,CREDITS),
STUDENT = (ID#,NAME,DATEADM)}.

The relation names are TRANSCRIPT and STUDENT; the atomic names are STUDID, SEMESTER, ..., DATEADM.

Let S be a relational schema. A *relational language* L *for* S is comprised of three parts: a typing, a set of nonlogical symbols, and a set of logical symbols. The purpose of a language L is to make assertions about the database. It can also be used as the basis for a query language.

By a *typing* T *of the schema* S we mean a collection of sets of atomic names {T1, ..., Tk} such that at each atomic name Ri of the schema S appears in one and only one set Tj. The set Tj that contains the name Ri is called the *type* of Ri. In the relational schema of Figure 1.3, the typing T(Rext) is the set {SIDTPE, NAMTPE, ..., CRDSTPE}. The idea is that names within the same type all range over the same values.

By a *nonlogical symbol,* we mean either a *typed predicate* symbol, a *typed function* symbol, or a *typed constant* symbol. The assertions made in the language will be made using these predicate, function, and constant symbols. These are called nonlogical since they are not always a part of any language L.

```
V(Rext): VIEW DEFINITION
  S(Rext): SCHEMA DEFINITION
    TABLE TRANSCRIPT = (STUDID,STUDNAME,SEMESTER,YEAR,DEPT,
                        COURSE#,SEC#,TITLE,GRADE,CREDITS)

 TABLE STUDENT = (ID#,NAME,DATEADM)

  L(Rext): LANGUAGE DEFINITION
  T(Rext): TYPING DEFINITION
    TYPE SIDTPE   = {ID#,STUDID} EBCDIC CHAR(9)
    TYPE NAMTPE   = {NAME,STUDNAME} EBCDIC CHAR(20)
    TYPE DATPE    = {DATEADM} EBCDIC CHAR(15)
    TYPE SEMTPE   = {SEMESTER} EBCDIC CHAR(8)
    TYPE YRTPE    = {YEAR} EBCDIC DEC(4)
    TYPE DEPTPE   = {DEPT} EBCDIC CHAR(8)
    TYPE CS#TPE   = {COURSE#} EBCDIC DEC(4)
    TYPE SEC#TPE  = {SEC#} EBCDIC CHAR(10)
    TYPE TTLTPE   = {TITLE} EBCDIC CHAR(25)
    TYPE GRDTPE   = {GRADE} EBCDIC CHAR(1)
    TYPE CRDSTPE  = {CREDITS} EBCDIC DEC(2)

  NONLOGICAL SYMBOLS DEFINITION
    PREDICATES
      TRANSCRIPT:(SIDTPE,NAMTPE,SEMTPE,YRTPE,
        DEPTPE,CS#TPE,SEC#TPE,TTLTPE,GRDTPE,
        CRDSTPE) PREDICATE
      STUDENT: (SIDTPE,NAMTPE,DATPE) PREDICATE
      ≤:(YRTPE,YRTPE) PREDICATE
    FUNCTIONS
      TOTCREDITS:(SIDTPE,SEMTPE,YRTPE;CRDSTPE) FUNCTION

  C(Rext): CONSTRAINTS DEFINITION
   C(Rext,1):CONSTRAINT TRANSCRIPT:
     STUDID,SEMESTER,YEAR,DEPT,COURSE#,SEC#
       → STUDNAME,TITLE,GRADE,CREDITS
   C(Rext,2):CONSTRAINT TRANSCRIPT:STUDID → STUDNAME
   C(Rext,3):CONSTRAINT TRANSCRIPT:DEPT,COURSE#
     → TITLE,CREDITS
   C(Rext,4):CONSTRAINT STUDENT:ID# → NAME,DATEADM
```

Figure 1.3 Database logic DDL definition of view V(Rext).

For example, the typed predicate symbols of L(Rext) are

TRANSCRIPT, an (SIDTPE, NAMTPE, SEMTPE, YRTPE,
DEPTPE, CS#TPE, SEC#TPE, TTLTPE, GRDTPE,
CRDSTPE) predicate symbol, and
STUDENT, an (SIDTPE, NAMTPE, DATPE) predicate symbol,
≤E a (YRTPE, YRTPE) predicate symbol.

Notice that the description above indicates the types of the arguments used, hence the label "typed."

The only typed function symbol of L(Rext) is

TOTCREDITS, an (SIDTPE, SEMTPE, YRTPE; CRDSTPE) function symbol.

The notation indicates that TOTCREDITS maps objects of type SIDTPE, SEMTPE, YRTPE into objects of type CRDSTPE. The constant symbols of L(Rext) are

{e(SIDTPE):i} = {x|x is an EBCDIC decimal string of length 9},
{e(NAMTPE):i} = {x|x is an EBCDIC character string of length 20},

.
.
.

{e(CRDSTPE):i} = {x|x is an EBCDIC decimal string of length 2}.

The predicate symbols TRANSCRIPT and STUDENT represent the two tables in the relational database. The predicate symbol $\leq$ is intended to denote the "less than or equal to" relationship on type YRTPE. The function symbol TOTCREDITS denotes a function which, given a student id, semester, and year, returns the total number of credits taken by that student during that term. The constant symbols in the language L(Rext) are identical to the EBCDIC strings that are used to represent them internally.

By a *logical symbol* we mean either an *atomic variable,* a *typed equality symbol,* or one of the special symbols

$$E, A, \&, V, \sim, \rightarrow, \longleftrightarrow, (\ ,\ ).$$

The symbols E and A are called *existential* and *universal quantifiers,* respectively. The symbols &, V, $\sim$, $\rightarrow$ and $\longleftrightarrow$ are called *connectives.* These symbols are called "logical" since they are always part of any language L.

For example, the atomic variables in L(Rext) are

{ID#:1,ID#:2,...}, {NAME:1,NAME:2,...},..., {CREDITS:1,CREDITS:2,...} .

The typed equality symbols in L(Rext) are

=(SIDTPE), =(NAMETPE), ..., =(CRDSTPE).

We will often just use the symbol = when type Tj is clear.

Remark. Logical symbols are not indicated in a definition such as that of Figure 1.3. This is because the logical symbols can be derived from the other information given in the definition.

The notion of a *well-formed formula* (wff) in a language L is defined in the usual way; namely, by induction on the length of the formula. The formal definition of wff for database logic, and for the special case of first-order logic, will be given in Chapter 3. However, the reader should be able to grasp the notion of wff without referring to the definition.

An example of a wff in the language L(Rext) is

C(Rext,1)
= (TRANSCRIPT(STUDID:1,STUDNAME:1,SEMESTER:1,YEAR:1,DEPT:1,
COURSE#:1,SEC#:1,TITLE:1,GRADE:1,CREDITS:1)
& TRANSCRIPT(STUDID:1,STUDNAME:2,SEMESTER:1,YEAR:1,DEPT:1,
COURSE#:1,SEC#:1,TITLE:2,GRADE:2,CREDITS:2)) →
(STUDNAME:1 = STUDNAME:2 & TITLE:1 = TITLE:2
& GRADE:1 = GRADE:2 & CREDITS:1 = CREDITS:2).

This wff says that in any TRANSCRIPT table the STUDID, SEMESTER, YEAR, DEPT, and COURSE# values determine the rest of the values in the row. In other words, C(Rext,1) is a first-order representation of the functional dependency constraint

TRANSCRIPT: STUDID, SEMESTER, YEAR, DEPT, COURSE#, SEC#
→ STUDNAME, TITLE, GRADE, CREDITS.

Examples of other wffs in L(Rext) are as follows:

C(Rext,2) = TRANSCRIPT: STUDID → STUDNAME
= (TRANSCRIPT(STUDID:1,STUDNAME:1,SEMESTER:1,YEAR:1,
DEPT:1,COURSE#:1,SEC#:1,TITLE:1,GRADE:1, CREDITS:1)
& TRANSCRIPT(STUDID:1,STUDNAME:2,SEMESTER:2,YEAR:2,
DEPT:2,COURSE#:2,SEC#:2,TITLE:2,GRADE:2,CREDITS:2))
→ STUDNAME:1 = STUDNAME:2,
C(Rext,3) = TRANSCRIPT: DEPT,COURSE# → TITLE,CREDITS
= (TRANSCRIPT(STUDID:1,STUDNAME:1,SEMESTER:1,YEAR:1,
DEPT:1, COURSE#:1,SEC#:1,TITLE:1,GRADE:1,CREDITS:1)
& TRANSCRIPT(STUDID:2,STUDNAME:2,SEMESTER:2,YEAR:2,
DEPT:1,COURSE#:1,SEC#:2,TITLE:2,GRADE:2,CREDITS:2))
→ (TITLE:1 = TITLE:2 & CREDITS:1 = CREDITS:2) ,

and

C(Rext,4) = STUDENT: ID# → NAME, DATEADM
= (STUDENT(ID#:1,NAME:1,DATEADM:1)
& STUDENT(ID#:1,NAME:2,DATEADM:2))
→ (NAME:1 = NAME:2 & DATEADM:1 = DATEADM:2)

As mentioned above, a *relational view* is a triple of the form V = <S,L,C>, where S is a relational schema, L is a relational language for S, and C is a set of formulas of L called the *constraints* or *axioms* of the view. An example of a relational view is

V(Rext) = < S(Rext),L(Rext),C(Rext) >

where S(Rext), L(Rext) and C(Rext) = {C(Rext,1), ..., C(Rext,4)} are given above.

Relational Structures

Let L be a relational language for some schema S. A *relational structure* M *for* L is a quadruple

$$M = \langle U', \{p'\}, \{f'\}, \{e'\} \rangle$$

where

$$U' = \underset{Tj \text{ in } T}{\text{UNION}} \text{ dom}(Tj)$$

where dom(Tj) is the set of values, one for each constant symbol of type Tj, p′ is a (typed) predicate over U′ which is the meaning of the predicate symbol p, f′ is a (typed) function on U′ which is the meaning of the function symbol f, and e′ is an element of U′ which is the meaning of the constant symbol e. The idea is that at any instant of time a relational database is represented by a relational structure.

For example, let L(Rext) be the relational language above. Then at any instant a database for Rext is regarded as a relational structure M(Rext) for L(Rext) defined as follows:

The universe U′ is the union of the sets

dom(SIDTPE) = {x|x is an EBCDIC decimal string of size 9},
dom(NAMTPE) = {x|x is an EBCDIC character string of size 20},

.
.
.

dom(CRDSTPE) = {x|x is an EBCDIC decimal string of size 2}.

Notice that the constant symbols are identified with the objects they represent.

The meaning of the predicate symbol TRANSCRIPT is the relational table designated by the relation TRANSCRIPT (see Figure 1.2); similar remarks apply for STUDENT. The meaning of the predicate symbol ≤ is the usual "less than or equal to" predicate defined on the Cartesian product dom(YRTPE) × dom(YRTPE). The meaning of the equality symbols are the usual typed equality predicates. The meaning of the function symbol TOTCREDITS is the function that returns the total number of credits (CRDSTPE) taken by the student during a term for values of student id (SIDTPE), semester (SEMTPE), and year (YRTPE). The meaning of each constant symbol is itself.

Notice that as the database gets updated, the corresponding relational structures differ only in the meanings of the symbols TRANSCRIPT, STUDENT, and TOTCREDITS. The latter changes since its values are determined by the entries in the tables.

Let L be a language for relational schema S and Q a wff of L. Let M be a relational structure for L. The notion of *truth* of Q in M, denoted $M \models Q$, will be formally defined in Chapter 3. (The notation $\not\models$ means that $\models$ does not hold.) Without referring to the formal definition, the reader should be able to check that the wffs

{C(Rext,1), ... , C(Rext,4)} are all true in the relational structure M(Rext) represented in Figure 1.2. In such a case, we say that M(Rext) is a *model* of the wffs {C(Rext,1), ..., C(Rext,4)} and denote this by

$$M(Rext) \models \{C(Rext,1),\ldots,C(Rext,4)\}.$$

Relational CALC DML

We illustrate the above by showing how a data manipulation language, relational CALC, may be defined in terms of the notions above. Let V = <S,L,C> be a relational view and M be some relational structure representing the database at some instant of time.

A query on a relational database corresponding to V has the form

GET W(<R>):Q(<R>);

where <R> is a set of variables in L, Q is a wff of L with nonquantified variables <R> and W is a workspace. The execution of this query results in the set of *constant symbols*

$$\{ \langle e \rangle \mid M \models Q(\langle e \rangle)\}$$

being placed into W. That is, the query returns the collection of constant symbols <e> such that the wff Q(<e>) is "true" in the relational structure denoting the relational database at the time of execution.

Example 1.1.1.

Find the id#'s and names of all those students who took Math 103 during the fall 1979 semester and earned the grade of B.

Solution

```
GET W (STUDID:1,STUDNAME:1):
  (E)SEC#:1(E)TITLE:1(E)CREDITS:1
  TRANSCRIPT(STUDID:1,STUDNAME:1,FALL,1979,
                MATH,103,SEC#:1,TITLE:1,B,CREDITS:1);
```

The execution of this query on the relational structure M(Rext) of Figure 1.2 results in the placement of the EBCDIC strings {(123456789, SMITH ROBERT J.)} into workspace W. Notice that with the exception of the "target" variables STUDID:1, STUDNAME:1, all the other variables are existentially (E) quantified.

An insertion operation has the form

INSERT(R)(W);

where R is a relation name and W contains tuples of constants of the language L. Let M be the relational structure representing the database just prior to the execution of the insert operation. This execution results in another relational structure M′ of L denoting the database after update. The relational structure M′ is the same as the relational structure M except that

1. M′ ⊨ R(<e>) for <e> in W.
2. Other predicates and/or functions may have their meanings changed (e.g., the function TOTCREDITS depends on the contents of TRANSCRIPT).

However, if the relational structure M′ is not a model of C, there is no change to M.

Example 1.1.2.

Add the information that Robert J. Smith, id# 123456789, took Biology 103, Introduction section 101, during the fall 1979 semester and earned the grade of B for 3 credits.

Solution

```
MOVE {(123456789,SMITH ROBERT J.,FALL,1979,BIO,
        103,101,INTRO,B,3)} TO W;
INSERT(TRANSCRIPT)(W);
```

The effect of these instructions is the insertion of the row (123456789,SMITH ROBERT J.,FALL,1979,BIO,103,101,INTRO,B,3) into the table TRANSCRIPT. Alternatively, we can regard this as producing a new relational structure M′(Rext) where

M′(Rext) ⊨ TRANSCRIPT(123456789,SMITH ROBERT J.,FALL,
1979,BIO, 103,101,INTRO,B,3)

as long as M′(Rext) still satisfies the constraints in C(Rext).

Analogous definitions hold for DELETE and UPDATE.

Exercises

The following exercises refer to the relational database BIOG-REG in Figures 1.4 and 1.5.

1. Formulate the schema S(BIOG-REG) that corresponds to Figures 1.4 and 1.5.
2. Formulate the language L(BIOG-REG) corresponding to Figures 1.4 and 1.5. Assume no functions and only the usual predicates.
3. Determine the integrity constraints corresponding to Figures 1.4 and 1.5. Express the integrity constraints as well-formed formulas in first-order logic.
4. Express the view definition V(BIOG-REG) corresponding to the above in a format similar to that of Figure 1.3.
5. Formulate the following query in relational CALC for view V(BIOG-REG):

   Find the names, id#'s, and addresses of all registered mathematics majors.

   What would be the results of executing the query on the relational structure given in Figure 1.5?

```
DOMAIN NAME EBCDIC CHAR(20)
DOMAIN ADDR EBCDIC CHAR(30)
DOMAIN ID EBCDIC DEC(6)
DOMAIN MAJOR EBCDIC CHAR(7)
DOMAIN COURSE EBCDIC CHAR(15)

RELATION BIOG
 (SNAME DOMAIN NAME,
  SADDR DOMAIN ADDR,
  SID DOMAIN ID)
KEY(SNAME)

RELATION REG
 (SID DOMAIN ID,
  SMAJOR DOMAIN MAJOR,
  SCOURSE DOMAIN COURSE)
KEY(SID,SCOURSE)
  CONSTRAINTS
    FD REG:SID → SMAJOR
```

Figure 1.4 Relational DDL definition of database BIOG-REG hierarchical database.

BIOG		
SNAME	SADDR	SID
MARY SMITH	104 MAIN ST.	1234
JOHN DOE	6 GREEN AVE.	6731
JULIE BAKER	10 E. GRAND	0097

REG		
SID	SMAJOR	SCOURSE
1234	MATH	MATH 306
1234	MATH	ENGLISH 201
0097	HISTORY	HISTORY 480
6731	ENGLISH	ENGLISH 412
6731	ENGLISH	CHEM 305
1234	MATH	MATH 455

Figure 1.5 Instance of the relational database BIOG-REG.

6. Formulate the following operations in relational CALC for view V(BIOG-REG):

> Insert a new student Julie Baker who lives at 13 Elm St. and has id# 2371. Also, insert the information that she is a computer science major and is currently taking Computer Science 220 and Math 306.

What are the results of executing the above on the relational structure in Figure 1.5?

1.2 HETEROGENEOUS DATABASES IN DATABASE LOGIC

In this section we generalize the definitions given in Section 1.1 to database logic. A "database view" is comprised of a "database schema," "database language," and "database constraints." The idea is that at any instant of time a database is regarded as a "database structure" which satisfies the constraints in the view.

Example

Throughout this section we use the hierarchical database illustrated in Figure 1.6. The database is intended to represent student transcripts of a university and is a hierarchical version of the relational database of Section 1.1. The database has three "segment" or "record" types: TRANSCRIPT, RECORD, and COURSES. The TRANSCRIPT

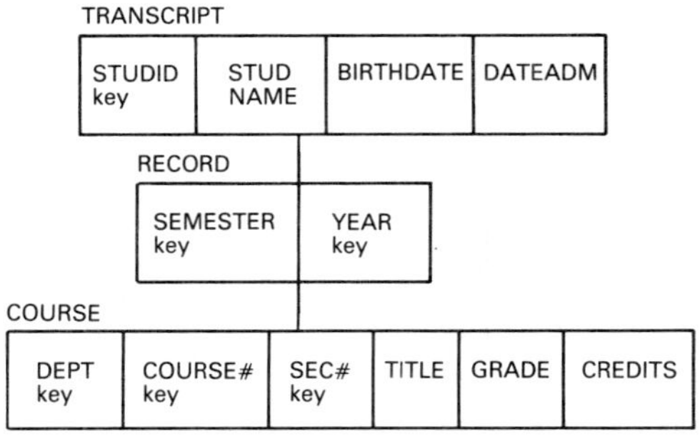

(a)

```
DBD   NAME=DEXT
SEGM  NAME=TRANSCRIPT,BYTES=50
FIELD NAME=(STUDID,SEQ) BYTES=9,START=1
FIELD NAME=STUDNAME,BYTES=20,START=10
FIELD NAME=BIRTHDATE,BYTES=15,START=30
FIELD NAME=DATEADM,BYTES=15,START=45
SEGM  NAME=RECORD,PARENT=TRANSCRIPT,BYTES=11
FIELD NAME=(SEMESTER,SEQ,M),BYTES=6,START=1
FIELD NAME=(YEAR,SEQ,M),BYTES=4,START=7
SEGM  NAME=COURSES,PARENT=RECORD,BYTES=49
FIELD NAME=(DEPT,SEQ,M),BYTES=10,START=1
FIELD NAME=(COURSE#,SEQ,M),BYTES=3,START=11
FIELD NAME=SEC#,BYTES=3,START=14
FIELD NAME=TITLE,BYTES=30,START=17
FIELD NAME=GRADE,BYTES=1,START=47
FIELD NAME=CREDITS,BYTES=1,START=48
```

(b)

Figure 1.6 Database schema Dext: (a) pictorial representation of the scheme Dext; (b) IMS DDL definition for database Dext.

record contains STUDID, STUDNAME, BIRTHDATE, and DATEADM (date admitted) fields. Each TRANSCRIPT record has several RECORD records, each containing SEMESTER and YEAR fields. Each RECORD record has several COURSES records, each having a DEPT, COURSE#, SEC#, TITLE, GRADE, and CREDITS fields. The record TRANSCRIPT has key STUDID; the record RECORD has key SEMESTER, YEAR; and the record COURSES has key DEPT, COURSE#, SEC#.

The IMS (Information Management System) Data Definition Language Schema is given in Figure 1.6 (b). The DBD line gives the name of the database DEXT. Each segment or record definition gives the name of the segment (NAME =), the length in bytes (BYTES =), and the name of the parent segment (PARENT =) if there is a parent. For each field within the segment the name (NAME =), size (BYTES =), and the starting position in the segment (START =) are given. Segment instances are physically stored by fields labeled SEQ. Figure 1.7 provides an instance of the hierarchical database.

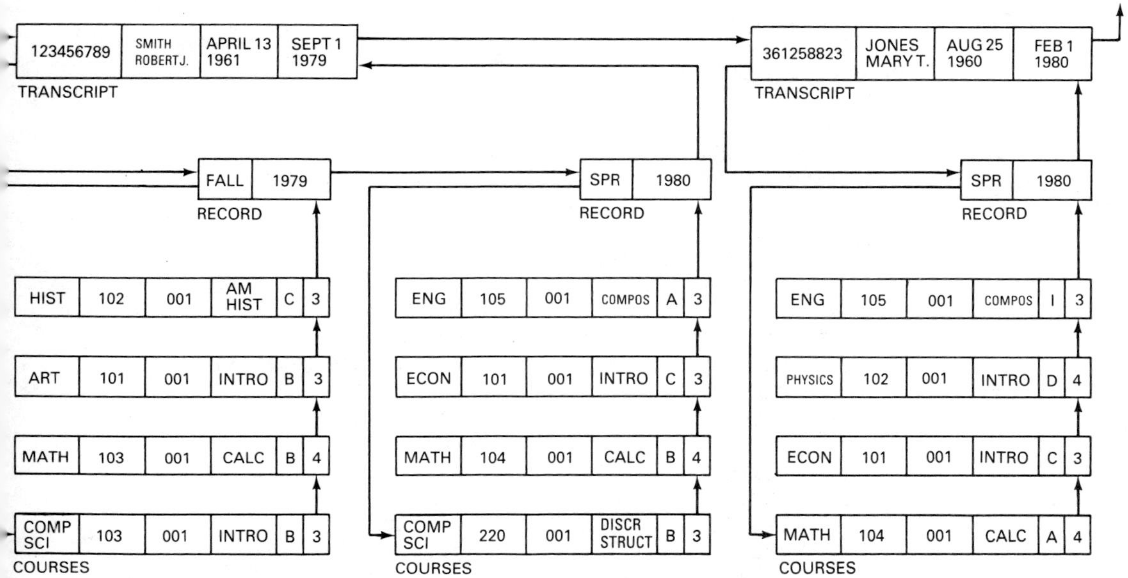

Figure 1.7 Instance of the hierarchical database Dext.

Remark. IMS has no explicit means for supporting key constraints or other types of dependencies. However, we will assume that these integrity contraints are maintained as users input data into the database.

Database Views

A *database view* is comprised of a database schema, which describes the data in the database; a database language, which is a language for making assertions about the database; and a set of database constraints, which are assertions in the database language that every instance of the database must obey. These are explained below. The database view definition of Figure 1.8 corresponds to the hierarchical database in Figure 1.6. **The reader is strongly advised to refer often to Figure 1.8 while reading this section.**

In database logic, we regard databases in terms of "tables," and "rows" in tables. For example, the instance of the database in Figure 1.7 is represented in database logic as in Figure 1.9. Notice there is one large TRANSCRIPT table in which there are rows made up of STUDID, STUDNAME, BIRTHDATE, and DATEADM values and a RECORD table. Each RECORD table is made up of rows comprised of SEMESTER and YEAR values and a COURSES table. Each COURSES table has rows comprised of DEPT, COURSE#, SEC#, TITLE, GRADE and CREDITS values.

```
V(Dext): VIEW DEFINITION
 S(Dext): SCHEMA DEFINITION
  TABLE TRANSCRIPT = (STUDID,STUDNAME,BIRTHDATE,
                      DATEADM,RECORD)
  TABLE RECORD = (SEMESTER,YEAR,COURSES)
  TABLE COURSES = (DEPT,COURSE#,SEC#,TITLE,GRADE,
                   CREDITS)

L(Dext): LANGUAGE DEFINITION
 T(Dext): TYPING DEFINITION
  TYPE SIDTPE   = {STUDID} EBCDIC CHAR(9)
  TYPE NAMTPE   = {STUDNAME} EBCDIC CHAR(20)
  TYPE DATPE    = {BIRTHDATE,DATEADM} EBCDIC CHAR(15)
  TYPE SEMTPE   = {SEMESTER} EBCDIC CHAR(6)
  TYPE YRTPE    = {YEAR} EBCDIC DEC(4)
  TYPE DEPTPE   = {DEPT} EBCDIC CHAR(8)
  TYPE CS#TPE   = {COURSE#} EBCDIC DEC(3)
  TYPE SEC#TPE  = {SEC#} EBCDIC CHAR (10)
  TYPE TTLTPE   = {TITLE} EBCDIC CHAR(25)
  TYPE GRDTPE   = {GRADE} EBCDIC CHAR(1)
  TYPE CRDSTPE  = {CREDITS} EBCDIC DEC(2)

NONLOGICAL SYMBOLS DEFINITION
 PREDICATES
  TRANSCRIPT-RECORD-COURSES:
    (SIDTPE,NAMTPE,DATPE,DATPE,RECORD,SEMTPE,
    YRTPE,COURSES,DEPTPE,CS#TPE,SEC#TPE,TTLTPE,
    GRDTPE,CRDSTPE) PREDICATE
  TRANSCRIPT-RECORD:
    (SIDTPE,NAMTPE,DATPE,DATPE,RECORD,SEMTPE,
    YRTPE,COURSES) PREDICATE
  TRANSCRIPT:
    (SIDTPE,NAMTPE,DATPE,DATPE,RECORD)
      PREDICATE
  ≤: (YRTPE,YRTPE) PREDICATE
 FUNCTIONS
  TOTCREDITS:(SIDTPE,SEMTPE,YRTPE;
    CRDSTPE) FUNCTION
C(Dext): CONSTRAINTS DEFINITION
 C(Dext,1) CONSTRAINT TRANSCRIPT:
  STUDID → STUDNAME,BIRTHDATE,DATEADM,RECORD
 C(Dext,2):CONSTRAINT TRANSCRIPT-RECORD:
  STUDID,SEMESTER,YEAR → COURSES
 C(Dext,3):CONSTRAINT TRANSCRIPT-RECORD-COURSES:
 STUDID,SEMESTER,YEAR,DEPT,COURSE#,SEC#
  → TITLE,GRADE,CREDITS
```

Figure 1.8 Database logic DDL definition of view V(Dext).

TRANSCRIPT											
				RECORD							
						COURSES					
STUDID	STUDNAME	BIRTHDATE	DATEADM	SEMESTER	YEAR	DEPT	COURSE#	SEC#	TITLE	GRADE	CREDITS
				RECORD (e(RECORD):1)							
							COURSES (e(COURSES):1)				
23456789	SMITH ROBERT J.	APRIL 13 1961	SEPT 1 1979	FALL	1979	COMPSCI	103	001	INTRO	B	3
						MATH	103	001	CALC	B	3
						ART	101	001	INTRO	B	3
						HIST	102	001	AM HIST	C	3
						COURSES (e(COURSES):2)					
				SPRING	1980	COMPSCI	220	001	DISCR STRUCT	B	3
						MATH	104	001	CALC	B	4
						ECON	101	001	INTRO	C	3
						ENG	105	001	COMPOS	A	3
				RECORD (e(RECORD):2)							
						COURSES (e(COURSES):3)					
81258823	JONES MARY T.	AUG 25 1960	FEB 1 1980	SPRING	1980	MATH	104	001	CALC	A	4
						ECON	101	001	INTRO	C	3
						PHYSICS	102	001	INTRO	D	4
						ENG	105	001	COMPOS	I	3

Figure 1.9 Database structure M(Dext) for V(Dext) corresponding to Figure 1.7.

A database schema describes the format of the tables. Specifically, a *database schema* S is a finite collection of rules of the form

$$S=\{\ldots,R0 = (R1,\ldots,Rn),\ldots\}.$$

The objects Ri, i = 0,1,...,n, are called *names. Higher-order* names appear on the left sides of rules; *zero-order* names appear only on the right sides of rules. A rule with the name R0 on its left side is called an *R0 rule.*

The database schema S(Dext) in Figure 1.8 is the set of rules

{ TRANSCRIPT = (STUDID,STUDNAME,BIRTHDATE,DATEADM,RECORD),
RECORD = (SEMESTER,YEAR,COURSES),
COURSES = (DEPT,COURSE#,SEC#,TITLE,GRADE,CREDITS) }.

The higher-order names are TRANSCRIPT, RECORD, and COURSES; the zero-order names are STUDID, STUDNAME, ... , CREDITS.

Remark. By placing various restrictions on the rules in schema S, one can obtain "relational," "hierarchical," and "network" schemas. More will be said on this point in Chapter 3.

Let S be a database schema. A *database language* L *for* S is comprised of three parts: a typing, a set of nonlogical symbols, and a set of logical symbols. The purpose of a language L is to be able to make assertions about the database. It can also be used as the basis for a query language.

By a *typing* T *of the schema* S we mean a set {T1, ..., Tk} where for each j = 1,...,k either (1) Tj is a higher-order name of S, or (2) Tj is a set of zero-order names. Further, every higher-order name of S is listed in T and every zero-order name is contained in exactly one set Tj. Each member of the typing T is called a *higher-order type* or *zero-order type* depending on whether it falls under condition (1) or (2) above. In particular, if Ri is a zero-order name contained in Tj, then Tj is called the *type for* Ri.

For example, one such typing for the schema S(Dext) is given as follows:

T(Dext)
= {TRANSCRIPT,SIDTPE,NAMTPE,DATTPE,RECORD,SEMTPE,
YRTPE,COURSES,DEPTPE,CS#TPE,SEC#TPE,TTLTPE,
GRDTPE,CRDSTPE},

where SIDTPE, NAMTPE, ..., CRDSTPE are defined in Figure 1.8. As in the relational case, all the zero-order names within the same type range over the same (atomic) data values. However, every higher-order name, itself, uniquely defines its own type.

By a *nonlogical symbol,* we mean either a *typed predicate* symbol, a *typed function* symbol, or a *typed constant* symbol. Assertions made in the language will be made using these predicate, function, and constant symbols.

For example, the typed predicate symbols of L(Dext) are

TRANSCRIPT-RECORD-COURSES, a
(SIDTPE,NAMTPE,DATPE,DATPE,RECORD,SEMTPE,YRTPE,
COURSES,DEPTPE,CS#TPE,SEC#TPE,TTLTPE,GRDTPE,
CRDSTPE) predicate symbol,

TRANSCRIPT-RECORD, a
(SIDTPE,NAMTPE,DATPE,DATPE,RECORD,SEMTPE,YRTPE,
COURSES) predicate symbol,

TRANSCRIPT, a
(SIDTPE,NAMTPE,DATPE,DATPE,RECORD)
predicate symbol, and

$\leq$, a (YRTPE,YRTPE) predicate symbol.

The only typed function symbol of L(Dext) is

TOTCREDITS, a (SIDTPE,SEMTPE,YRTPE; CRDSTPE) function symbol.

The constant symbols of L(Dext) are

{TRANSCRIPT},{e(RECORD):i},{e(COURSES):i},
{e(SIDTPE):i} = {x| x is an EBCDIC decimal string of length 9},
{e(NAMTPE):i} = {x| x is an EBCDIC character string of length 20},

.
.
.

{e(CRDSTPE):i} = {x| x is an EBCDIC decimal string of length 1}.

The first three nonlogical predicate symbols above are called *clusters,* and will be defined below. The fourth denotes the "less than or equal to" relationship on type YRTPE. Function symbol TOTCREDITS denotes a function that computes the sum of the credits taken by a student during a semester and year. Notice that there are constant symbols for all zero-order (atomic) type objects as well as constant symbols for the higher-order (table) types.

By a *logical symbol* we mean either a name variable, a typed equality symbol, or one of the special symbols

E ,A , & , V , ~, → , ⟷ , (or) .

In addition, there are typed row predicates which represent questions about whether or not a row is in a given table.

For example, the name variables in L(Dext) are

{RECORD:1,,RECORD:2,...},{COURSES:1,COURSES:2,...},
{STUDID:1,STUDID:2,...},...,{CREDITS:1, CREDITS:2,...}.

Notice that there are variables for both higher-order and zero-order names, since in database logic we are able to quantify over tables as well as atomic values. The typed equality symbols in L(Dext) are

{=(RECORD), =(COURSES), =(SIDTPE), =(NAMTPE), ..., =(CRDSTPE)}.

Also notice that in database logic we are permitted to ask if two tables (e.g., RECORD, COURSES) are equal. We will often just use the symbol = when the type Tj is clear.

Some examples of typed row predicates are

TRANSCRIPT(STUDID:1,STUDNAME:1,BIRTHDATE:1,DATEADM:1,RECORD:1),

RECORD:1(SEMESTER:1,YEAR:1,COURSES:1), and

COURSES:1(DEPT:1,COURSE#:1,SEC#:1,TITLE:1,GRADE:1,CREDITS:1).

These ask, respectively, if a row is in the TRANSCRIPT table, if a row is in the RECORD table RECORD:1, and if a row is in the COURSES table COURSES:1.

The formal definition of *well-formed formula* (*wff*) of a database language L is given in Chapter 3. The reader should be able to grasp the notion of wff without referring to the definition. Several examples of wffs in L(Dext) are given below.

TRANSCRIPT-RECORD-COURSES(STUDID:1,STUDNAME:1,
BIRTHDATE:1,DATEADM:1,RECORD:1,SEMESTER:1,YEAR:1,
COURSES:1,DEPT:1,COURSE#:1,SEC#:1,TITLE:1,GRADE:1,
CREDITS:1)

⟷TRANSCRIPT(STUDID:1,STUDNAME:1,BIRTHDATE:1,DATEADM:1,
RECORD:1)
&RECORD:1(SEMESTER:1,YEAR:1,COURSES:1)
&COURSES:1(DEPT:1,COURSE#:1,SEC#:1,TITLE:1,GRADE:1,CREDITS:1)

and

TRANSCRIPT-RECORD(STUDID:1,STUDNAME:1,BIRTHDATE:1,
DATEADM:1,RECORD:1,SEMESTER:1,YEAR:1, COURSES:1)
⟷TRANSCRIPT(STUDID:1,STUDNAME:1,BIRTHDATE:1,DATEADM:1,
RECORD:1)
&RECORD:1(SEMESTER:1,YEAR:1,COURSES:1).

These wffs define the cluster symbols TRANSCRIPT-RECORD-COURSES and TRANSCRIPT-RECORD. Notice again that in database logic, variables can be both zero-order (e.g., STUDID:1) and higher-order (e.g., RECORD:1, RECORD:2).

Remark. Clusters cannot only be "paths," as illustrated in this example, but can also be "hierarchical trees" and "networks." An illustration of the former is given in Exercises 1 to 5 of this section. Illustrations of the latter are given in the next chapter, both in the text and in Exercises 9 and 10 of Section 2.2.

Remark. Clusters TRANSCRIPT-RECORD and TRANSCRIPT are parts or *subclusters* of the full cluster TRANSCRIPT-RECORD-COURSES. Notice that the subclusters can be derived from the full cluster by removing various parts from it. In the view definitions, we will usually indicate only the full clusters in the NONLOGICAL SYMBOLS DEFINITION and omit the derivable subclusters. (The precise method of obtaining subclusters from clusters is given in Section 2.2.)

Other examples of wffs are given by the constraints in C(Dext).

C(Dext,1)
= TRANSCRIPT:STUDID → STUDNAME,BIRTHDATE,DATEADM,RECORD

= (TRANSCRIPT(STUDID:1,STUDNAME:1,BIRTHDATE:1,DATADM:1,
RECORD:1)
& TRANSCRIPT(STUDID:1,STUDNAME:2,BIRTHDATE:2,DATADM:2,
RECORD:2))
→ (STUDNAME:1 = STUDNAME:2 & BIRTHDATE:1 = BIRTHDATE:2
& DATADM:1 = DATADM:2 & RECORD:1 = RECORD:2)

This wff says that in the TRANSCRIPT table, STUDID functionally determines STUDNAME, BIRTHDATE, DATEADM, and RECORD (i.e., STUDID is a key in TRANSCRIPT).

C(Dext,2)
= TRANSCRIPT-RECORD:STUDID,SEMESTER,YEAR → COURSES

= TRANSCRIPT-RECORD(STUDID:1,STUDNAME:1,BIRTHDATE:1,
DATEADM:1,RECORD:1,SEMESTER:1,YEAR:1, COURSES:1)
& TRANSCRIPT-RECORD(STUDID:1,STUDNAME:2,BIRTHDATE:2,
DATEADM:2,RECORD:2,SEMESTER:1,YEAR:1, COURSES:2)
→ COURSES:1 = COURSES:2.

This wff says that in the TRANSCRIPT-RECORD cluster, STUDID, SEMESTER, and YEAR functionally determine COURSES.

C(Dext,3)
= TRANSCRIPT-RECORD-COURSES:
STUDID,SEMESTER,YEAR,DEPT,COURSE#
→ SEC#,TITLE,GRADE,CREDITS

= TRANSCRIPT-RECORD-COURSES
(STUDID:1,STUDNAME:1,BIRTHDATE:1,DATEADM:1,
RECORD:1,SEMESTER:1,YEAR:1,COURSES:1,DEPT:1,
COURSE#:1,SEC#:1,TITLE:1,GRADE:1,CREDITS:1)
& TRANSCRIPT-RECORD-COURSES
(STUDID:1,STUDNAME:2,BIRTHDATE:2,DATEADM:2,
RECORD:2,SEMESTER:1,YEAR:1, COURSES:2,DEPT:1,
COURSE#:1,SEC#:2,TITLE:2,GRADE:2,CREDITS:2)
→(SEC#:1 = SEC#:2 & TITLE:1 = TITLE:2
& GRADE:1 = GRADE:2 & CREDITS:1 = CREDITS:2).

This wff says that in TRANSCRIPT-RECORD-COURSES, clusters STUDID, SEMESTER, YEAR, DEPT, and COURSE# functionally determine SEC#, TITLE, GRADE, and CREDITS.

Recall that a *database view* is a triple of the form V = <S,L,C>, where S is a database schema, L is a database language for S, and C is a set of formulas of L called the *constraints* or *axioms* of the view. An example of a database view is

V(Dext) = <S(Dext),L(Dext),C(Dext)>

where S(Dext), L(Dext), and C(Dext) = {C(Dext,1), ..., C(Dext,3)} are given above.

Database Structures

Let L be a database language for some schema S. A *database structure* M *for* L is a quadruple

$$M = \langle U', \{p'\}, \{f'\}, \{e'\} \rangle$$

where

$$U' = \underset{Tj \text{ in } T}{\text{UNION}} \text{dom}(Tj)$$

where dom(Tj) is a set of values, one for each constant symbol of type Tj, p′ is a (typed) predicate over U′ which is the meaning of the predicate symbol p, f′ is a (typed) function on U′ which is the meaning of the function symbol f, and e′ is the individual of U′ which is the meaning of the constant symbol e. The idea is that at any instant of time a database is represented by a database structure.

For example, let L(Dext) be the database language above. Then at any instant a database for Dext is regarded as a database structure M(Dext) for L(Dext) defined as follows.

The universe U′ is the union of the sets

dom(TRANSCRIPT), dom(RECORD), dom(COURSES),
dom(SIDTPE) = {x|x is an EBCDIC decimal value of length 9},
dom(NAMTPE) = {x|x is an EBCDIC character string of length 20}

.
.
.

dom(CRDSTPE) = {x|x is an EBCDIC decimal string of length 1}.

Here dom(TRANSCRIPT) is a set that contains a single TRANSCRIPT table, for example, the one in Figure 1.9. The set dom(RECORD) contains a corresponding RECORD table for each constant symbol e(RECORD):i. For example, corresponding to Figure 1.9, there would be two nonempty RECORD tables associated with the nonempty tables in the picture plus all the empty tables that are not in the picture; and similarly, for dom(COURSES).

The meanings of the nonlogical cluster symbols TRANSCRIPT-RECORD-COURSES, TRANSCRIPT-RECORD, and TRANSCRIPT are represented by the picture in Figure 1.9. For example,

TRANSCRIPT-RECORD-COURSES
(123456789,SMITH ROBERT J.,APR.13 1961,
SEPT.1 1979,e(RECORD):1,FALL,1979,e(COURSES):1,
MATH,103,001,CALC,B,3)

is true according to the Figure 1.9 because the following is true in the figure:

TRANSCRIPT(123456789,SMITH ROBERT J.,APR.13 1961,
SEPT 1 1979,e(RECORD):1)
& e(RECORD):1(FALL,1979,e(COURSES):1)
& e(COURSES):1(MATH,103,001,CALC,B,3).

The meaning of the predicate symbol $\leq$ is the familiar "less than or equal to" predicate on the set dom(YRTPE) $\times$ dom(YRTPE). The meanings of the equality symbols are the usual typed equality predicates. The meaning of the function symbol TOTCREDITS is a function which, if given SIDTPE, SEMTPE, YRTPE values, returns the sum of all the credits taken by that student during that semester year. The meaning of each atomic constant symbol is itself; the meaning of each higher-order constant symbol is the table it denotes in the database.

When a relational database structure gets updated, the new relational structure differs from the old in the meaning of the updated tables as well as the related functions and/or predicates. No changes ever occur to the meanings of the atomic constant symbols. However, when a database structure is updated, the new database structure may differ from the old one in several other ways. Namely, if Ti is higher-order (e.g., TRANSCRIPT, RECORD, COURSES) and a Ti table named by e(Tj) is updated, then changes will occur to the meaning of the constant symbol e(Tj). Also, the set dom(Tj) as well as related functions and/or predicates can change.

Let L be a database language for schema S and let Q be a wff of L. Let M be a database structure for L. The formal definition of "truth" of a wff Q in a database structure M, denoted $M \models Q$, is given in Chapter 3. (The notation $\not\models$ means that $\models$ does not hold.) Without referring to the formal definitions, the reader can check that the wffs {C(Dext,1), ..., C(Dext,3)} are true in the database structure represented in Figure 1.9.

Exercises

The following exercises refer to the hierarchical database EDUCDB in Figures 1.10 and 1.11.

1. Formulate the schema S(EDUCDB) corresponding to the definition in Figure 1.10.
2. Formulate the language L(EDUCDB) corresponding to the definition in Figure 1.10. Assume no functions and only the usual cluster predicates. **Hint:** Use

   COURSE-PREREQ-OFFERING-TEACHER-STUDENT

   as the full cluster.
3. Express the integrity constraints corresponding to the declaration in Figure 1.10. Express the integrity constraints as well-formed formulas in database logic.
4. Express the view definition V(EDUCDB) corresponding to the declaration in Figure 1.10 in a format similar to that of Figure 1.8.
5. Draw a database structure (like Figure 1.9) for V(EDUCDB) corresponding to the instance of the database given in Figure 1.11.

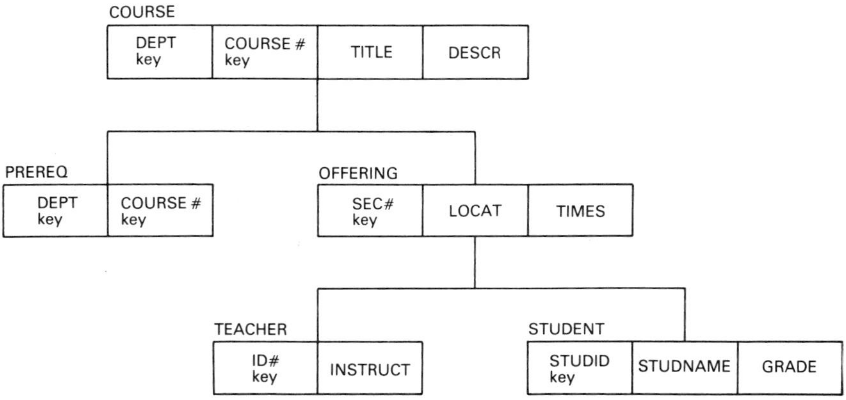

(a)

```
DBD   NAME=EDUCDBD
SEGM  NAME=COURSE,BYTES=86
FIELD NAME=(DEPT,SEQ) BYTES=8, START=1
FIELD NAME=(COURSE#,SEQ) BYTES=3,START=9
FIELD NAME=TITLE,BYTES=25,START=12
FIELD NAME=DESCR, BYTES=50,START=37
SEGM  NAME=PREREQ,PARENT=COURSE,BYTES=11
FIELD NAME=(DEPT,SEQ),BYTES=8,START=1
FIELD NAME=(COURSE#,SEQ),BYTES=3,START=9
SEGM  NAME=OFFERING,PARENT=COURSE,BYTES=53
FIELD NAME=(SEC#,SEQ),BYTES=3,START=1
FIELD NAME=LOCAT,BYTES=30,START=4
FIELD NAME=TIMES,BYTES=20,START=34
SEGM  NAME=TEACHER,PARENT=OFFERING,BYTES=29
FIELD NAME=(ID#,SEQ),BYTES=9,START=1
FIELD NAME=INSTRUCT,BYTES=20,START=10
SEGM  NAME=STUDENT,PARENT=OFFERING,BYTES=30
FIELD NAME=(STUDID,SEQ),BYTES=9,START=1
FIELD NAME=STUDNAME,BYTES=20,START=10
FIELD NAME=GRADE,BYTES=1,START=30
```

(b)

Figure 1.10 Database schema EDUCDB, hierarchical database: (a) pictorial representation of the scheme EDUCDB; (b) IMS DDL definition for database EDUCDB.

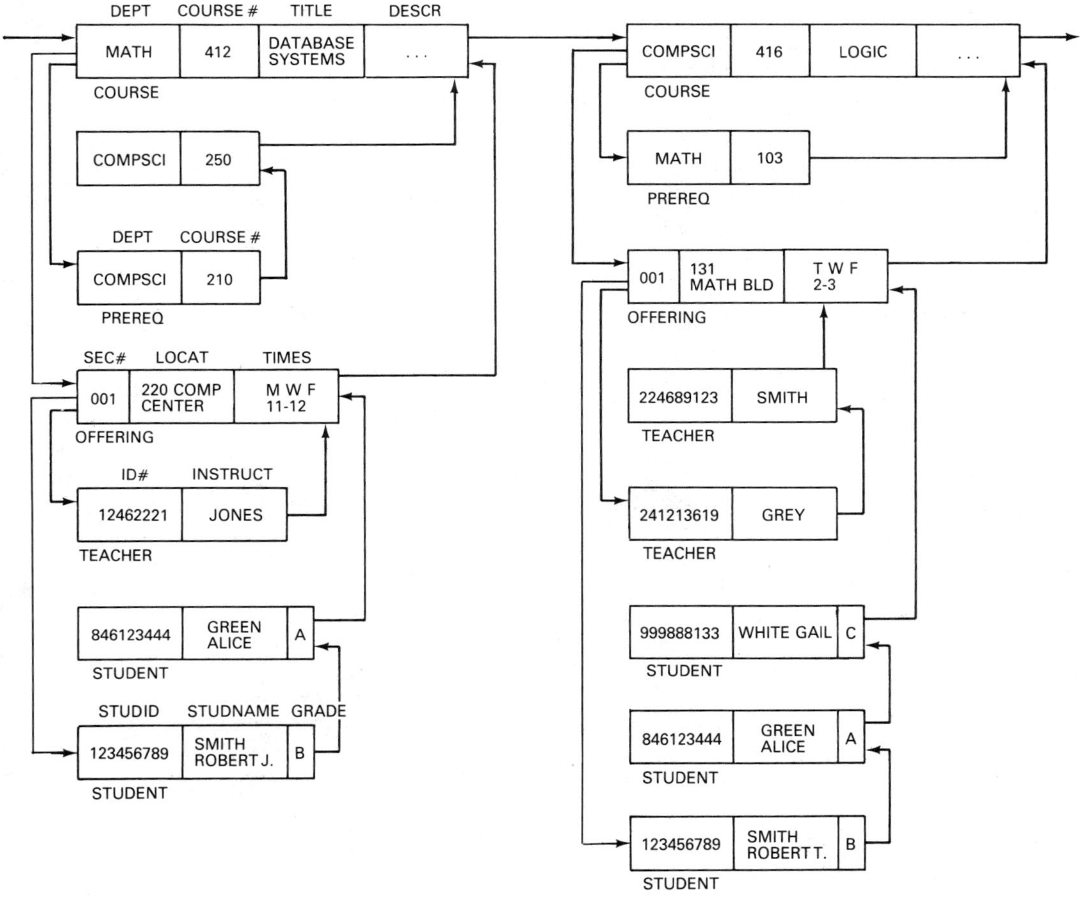

Figure 1.11 Instance of the hierarchical database EDUCPDB.

1.3 GCALC DATA MANIPULATION LANGUAGE

In this section we introduce a generalization of relational CALC of Section 1.1, generalized CALC DML (GCALC), based on the definitions of database logic. The instruction set is comprised of four types of operations: GET, INSERT, DELETE, and UPDATE. All four operations use the database structure denoting the current database. We also see how GCALC may be used to define formally the semantics of other data manipulation languages.

Let V = <S,L,C> be a database view, and suppose that M is a "meta-variable" that corresponds to a database structure for L which represents the current database.

Queries

The general form for this type of instruction is

GET W(<R>):Q(<R>);

where W is a workspace, <R> are variables in L, and Q(<R>) is a wff of L with nonquantified variables <R>. The effect of this operation is to place into W tuples of *constant symbols* (<e>) of L such that

M ⊨ Q(<e>) ;

that is, such that the formula obtained by replacing the variables <R> by the constants <e> is "true" in the database structure M.

For example, let V(Dext) = <S(Dext),L(Dext),C(Dext)> be the database view in Section 1.2.

Example 1.3.1.

Find the student id# and name of each student who took Math 103 and earned the grade of B during the fall of 1979.

Solution

```
GET W (STUDID:1,STUDNAME:1): (E)BIRTHDATE:1
  (E)DATEADM:1(E)RECORD:1(E)COURSES:1(E)SEC:1
  (E)TITLE:1(E)CREDITS:1
  TRANSCRIPT-RECORD-COURSES(STUDID:1,STUDNAME:1,
     BIRTHDATE:1,DATEADM:1,RECORD:1,FALL,1979,
     COURSES:1,MATH,103,SEC:1,TITLE:1,B,CREDITS:1);
```

or in terms of the definition of the cluster TRANSCRIPT-RECORD-COURSES

```
GET W (STUDID:1,STUDNAME:1): (E)BIRTHDATE:1
  (E)DATEADM:1(E)RECORD:1(E)COURSES:1(E)SEC:1
  (E)TITLE:1(E)CREDITS:1
  TRANSCRIPT(STUDID:1,STUDNAME:1,BIRTHDATE:1,
     DATEADM:1,RECORD:1)
& RECORD:1(FALL,1979,COURSES:1)
& COURSES:1(MATH,103,SEC:1,TITLE:1,B,CREDITS:1);
```

If these queries were run on the database structure of Figure 1.9, the result in W would be the set of constant (EBCDIC) symbols {(123456789, SMITH ROBERT J.)}.

Insertions

The general form for this type of instruction is

INSERT(R0)(W);

where R0 is a higher-order name of S with rule R0=(R1,...,Rk) and W is an n × (k

+ 1) array. Each row of W [i.e., W(i).R0, W(i).R1, ..., W(i).Rk] contains constant symbols ei0, ei1, ..., eik. The idea is that the database structure M representing the current database is changed to a new database structure. The change is effected by having the rows named by (ei1,...,eik) inserted into the R0 table named by ei0, i = 1, ..., n, as long as the constraints C are not violated. If they are, the database structure in M remains unchanged.

Example 1.3.2.

Insert the information that Robert J. Smith, id# 123456789, took Biology 103, Introduction, section 101, during the fall 1979 semester and earned the grade of B for 3 credits.

Solution

```
GET W (COURSES:1): (E)BIRTHDATE:1(E)DATEADM:1(E)RECORD:1
  TRANSCRIPT-RECORD(123456789,SMITH ROBERT J.,
   BIRTHDATE:1,DATEADM:1,RECORD:1,FALL,1979,COURSES:1);
IF LENGTH(W) ≠ 1 THEN GO TO ERROR-ROUTINE;
MOVE({W(1).COURSES,BIO,103,101,INTRO,B,3}) TO W1(1);
INSERT(COURSES)(W1);
```

The GET instruction finds the name of the COURSES table which contains Robert J. Smith's courses for the fall 1979 term. If a single COURSE table is not found, an error routine is invoked. In M(Dext) of Figure 1.9, this results in the placement of the constant symbol e(COURSES):1 into workspace W [actually, W(1).COURSES]. Next, we move to workspace W1 the contents of W(1).COURSES, BIO and 103, 101, INTRO, B, and 3. The last instruction inserts into the table named in W1(1).COURSES the row named in W1(1).DEPT, W1(1).COURSE#, ..., W1(1).CREDITS. The effect of these instructions on the database structure of Figure 1.9 is given in Figure 1.12(a).

Deletions

The general form for this type of instruction is

DELETE(R0)(W);

where R0 is a higher-order name of S with rule R0=(R1,...,Rk) and W is an $n \times (k + 1)$ array. Each row of W [i.e., W(i).R0, W(i).R1 ,..., W(i).Rk] contains constant symbols ei0, ei1, ..., eik. The idea is that the database structure M representing the current database structure is changed to a new database structure. The change is effected by having the row named by (ei1, ..., eik) deleted from the R0 table named by ei0, i = 1 ,..., n, as long as the new database structure also satisfies the constraints of C. If not, the database structure in M remains unchanged.

Example 1.3.3.

Delete all information about the courses that Robert J. Smith, student id# 123456789, took during his college career.

<table>
<tr><td rowspan="12">123456789</td><td rowspan="12">SMITH
ROBERT J.</td><td rowspan="12">APR 13
1961</td><td rowspan="12">SEPT 1
1979</td><td colspan="8">RECORD (e(RECORD):1)</td></tr>
<tr><td rowspan="6">FALL</td><td rowspan="6">1979</td><td colspan="6">COURSES (e(COURSES):1)</td></tr>
<tr><td>COMP SCI</td><td>103</td><td>001</td><td>INTRO</td><td>B</td><td>3</td></tr>
<tr><td>MATH</td><td>103</td><td>001</td><td>CALC</td><td>B</td><td>3</td></tr>
<tr><td>ART</td><td>101</td><td>001</td><td>INTRO</td><td>B</td><td>3</td></tr>
<tr><td>HIST</td><td>102</td><td>001</td><td>AM HIST</td><td>C</td><td>3</td></tr>
<tr><td>BIO</td><td>103</td><td>101</td><td>INTRO</td><td>D</td><td>3</td></tr>
<tr><td rowspan="5">SPRING</td><td rowspan="5">1980</td><td colspan="6">COURSES (e(COURSES):2)</td></tr>
<tr><td>COMP SCI</td><td>230</td><td>001</td><td>DISCR
STRUCT</td><td>B</td><td>3</td></tr>
<tr><td>MATH</td><td>104</td><td>001</td><td>CALC</td><td>B</td><td>3</td></tr>
<tr><td>ECON</td><td>101</td><td>001</td><td>INTRO</td><td>C</td><td>4</td></tr>
<tr><td>ENG</td><td>105</td><td>001</td><td>COMPOS</td><td>A</td><td>3</td></tr>
</table>

(a)

<table>
<tr><td rowspan="2">123456789</td><td rowspan="2">SMITH
ROBERT J.</td><td rowspan="2">APR 13
1961</td><td rowspan="2">SEPT 1
1979</td><td>RECORD (e(RECORD):1)</td></tr>
<tr><td>╳</td></tr>
</table>

(b)

<table>
<tr><td rowspan="6">161258823</td><td rowspan="6">JONES
MARY T.</td><td rowspan="6">AUG 25
1960</td><td rowspan="6">FEB 1
1980</td><td colspan="8">RECORD (e(RECORD):2)</td></tr>
<tr><td rowspan="5">SPRING</td><td rowspan="5">1980</td><td colspan="6">COURSES (e(COURSES):3)</td></tr>
<tr><td>MATH</td><td>104</td><td>001</td><td>CALC</td><td>A</td><td>4</td></tr>
<tr><td>ECON</td><td>101</td><td>001</td><td>INTRO</td><td>C</td><td>3</td></tr>
<tr><td>PHYSICS</td><td>102</td><td>001</td><td>INTRO</td><td>A</td><td>4</td></tr>
<tr><td>ENG</td><td>103</td><td>001</td><td>COMPOS</td><td>I</td><td>3</td></tr>
</table>

(c)

Figure 1.12 Results of the calculus operations on M(Dext) of Figure 1.9: (a) first row of M(Dext) of (Figure 1.9) following execution of instructions in Example 1.3.2; (b) first row of M(Dext) of (Figure 1.9) following execution of instructions in Example 1.3.3; (c) second row of M(Dext) of (Figure 1.9) following execution of instructions in Example 1.3.4.

Solution

```
GET W (RECORD:1,SEMESTER:1,YEAR:1,COURSES:1):
  (E)BIRTHDATE:1(E)DATEADM:1
  TRANSCRIPT-RECORD(123456789,SMITH ROBERT J.,BIRTHDATE:1,
    DATEADM:1,RECORD:1,SEMESTER:1,YEAR:1,COURSES:1);
IF LENGTH(W) = 0 THEN GO TO ERROR-ROUTINE;
DELETE(RECORD)(W);
```

The GET instruction finds the name of the RECORD table for Robert J. Smith. It also finds the SEMESTER and YEAR values and the COURSES-table which comprise all rows picked out. In M(Dext) of Figure 1.9, this results in the placement of

{(e(RECORD):1, FALL, 1979, e(COURSES):1),
(e(RECORD):1, SPRING, 1980, e(COURSES):2)}

into workspace W. If nothing is returned to W, an error routine is called. Otherwise, for each i, i = 1 ,..., LENGTH(W), the tuple (W(i).SEMESTER, W(i).YEAR, W(i). COURSES) is removed from the RECORD table named in W(i).RECORD. The effect of these instructions on the database structure of Figure 1.9 is given in Figure 1.12(b).

Updates

The general form for this type of instruction is

UPDATE(R0)(W);

where R0 is a higher-order name of S with rule R0=(R1,...,Rk) and W is an $n \times (2k + 1)$ array. Each row W(i) of W has three parts: W(i).R0, W(i).W1, and W(i).W2. W(i).R0, W(i).W1.R1, ..., W(i).W1.Rk, W(i).W2.R1, ..., W(i).W2.Rk contains constant symbols ei0, ei1, ..., eik, e′i1, ..., e′ik. The idea is that the database structure M representing the current database is changed to a new database structure. The change is effected by having the row named by (ei1, ..., eik) deleted from the R0 table named by ei0, and replaced by the row named by (e′i1,...,e′ik), i = 1, ..., n, as long as the new constraints C are not violated. If they are, the database structure in M remains unchanged.

Example 1.3.4.

Change the grade that Mary T. Jones, student id# 361258823, earned in Physics 102 during the spring 1980 semester from whatever is recorded to a grade of A.

Solution

```
GET W (COURSES:1,SEC#:1,TITLE:1,GRADE:1,CREDITS:1):
  (E)BIRTHDATE:1(E)DATEADM:1(E)RECORD:1
  TRANSCRIPT-RECORD-COURSES(361258823,JONES MARY T,
      BIRTHDATE:1,DATEADM:1,RECORD:1,SPRING,1980,COURSES:1,
      PHYSICS,102,SEC#:1,TITLE:1,GRADE:1,CREDITS:1);
```

```
IF LENGTH(W) ≠ 1 THEN GO TO ERROR-ROUTINE;
MOVE (W(1).COURSES,{PHYSICS,102,W(1).SEC#,W(1).TITLE,
    W(1).GRADE, W(1).CREDITS},{PHYSICS,102,W(1).SEC#,
    W(1).TITLE,A.,W(1).CREDITS}) TO W1(1);
UPDATE(COURSES)(W1);
```

The GET instruction finds the name of Mary T. Jones' COURSES table which contains Physics 102. It also finds the SEC#, TITLE, GRADE, and CREDITS values, which are, respectively, the third, fourth, fifth, and sixth components of that row. In M(Dext) of Figure 1.9, this results in the placement of

{(e(COURSES):3,001,INTRO,D,4)}

into W(1). If LENGTH(W) is 1, the COURSES table named in W(1).COURSES is updated so that the Physics 102 row has a GRADE component of A instead of D. The effect of these instructions on the database of Figure 1.9 is given in Figure 1.12(c).

Other DML Conversions

GCALC DML can be used to define the semantics of other more user-friendly data manipulation languages. That is, other DMLs can be formally defined in terms of some GCALC DML equivalent. One such language is Generalized SQL (GSQL) DML [Cao and Jacobs], which generalizes the well-known relational SQL DML [Astrahan, et. al.]. GSQL will be studied in more detail in Chapter 8 when we consider the problem of automatic program conversion. Another such language is Generalized Query-By-Example (GQBE) [Jacobs and Walczak], which generalizes the well-known relational Query-By-Example [Zloof].

Recall the query in Example 1.1.1 on V(Rext). The relational SQL (and GSQL) solution is given by the following:

```
SET INTO W
 SELECT UNIQUE STUDID,STUDNAME
 FROM TRANSCRIPT
 WHERE SEMESTER = FALL
     AND YEAR = 1979
     AND DEPT = MATH
     AND COURSE# = 103
     AND GRADE = B;
```

The relational QBE (and GQBE) solution to this query is given in Figure 1.13(a). In both cases the queries select all occurrences of the "row" TRANSCRIPT in which the SEMESTER, YEAR, DEPT, COURSE#, and GRADE values are, respectively, FALL, 1979, MATH, 103, and B. For each occurrence found, the STUDID and STUDNAME values are extracted. The formal semantics for the SQL and QBE queries is precisely the solution given above for Example 1.1.1.

TRANSCRIPT									
P. STUDID	P. STUDNAME	SEMESTER = FALL	YEAR = 1979	DEPT = MATH	COURSE # = 103	SEC#	TITLE	GRADE = B	CREDIT

(a)

TRANSCRIPT											
STUDID	P. STUDNAME	BIRTHDATE	DATEADM	RECORD							
				SEMESTER = FALL	YEAR = 1979	COURSES					
						DEPT = MATH	COURSE# = 103	SEC#	TITLE	GRADE = B	CREDITS

(b)

I. TRANSCRIPT									
STUDID	STUDNAME	SEMESTER	YEAR	DEPT	COURSE#	SEC #	TITLE	GRADE	CREDIT
123456789	SMITH ROBERT J.	FALL	1979	BIO	103	101	INTRO	B	3

(c)

TRANSCRIPT						
DID 23456789	STUDNAME = SMITH ROBERT J.	BIRTHDATE	DATE ADM	D. RECORD		
				SEMESTER	YEAR	COURSES

(d)

Figure 1.13 Some Generalized Query-By-Example operations: (a) GQBE solution for the query of Example 1.1.1; (b) GQBE solution for the query of Example 1.3.1; (c) GQBE solution for the insertion of Example 1.1.2; (d) GQBE solution for the deletion of Example 1.3.3.

Recall the query in Example 1.3.1 on V(Dext). The GSQL solution is given by the following:

```
SET INTO W
  SELECT UNIQUE STUDID,STUDNAME
  FROM TRANSCRIPT-RECORD-COURSES
  WHERE SEMESTER = FALL
       AND YEAR = 1979
       AND DEPT = MATH
       AND COURSE# = 103
       AND GRADE = B;
```

The GQBE solution to this query is given in Figure 1.13(b). In both cases the queries select all occurrences of the "cluster" TRANSCRIPT-RECORD-COURSES in which the SEMESTER, YEAR, DEPT, COURSE#, and GRADE values are, respectively, FALL, 1979, MATH, 103, and B. For each occurrence found, the STUDID and STUDNAME values are extracted. The formal semantics for the GSQL and GQBE queries is precisely the solution given above for Example 1.3.1.

Recall the insertion of Example 1.1.2 on V(Rext). The relational SQL (and GSQL) solution is given by

```
INSERT INTO TRANSCRIPT
{(123456789,SMITH ROBERT J.,FALL,1979,BIO,103,101,INTRO,B,3)};
```

The relational QBE (and GQBE) solution is given in Figure 1.13(c). In both cases, the effects of these operations will be the placement of the tuple into the TRANSCRIPT table. The formal semantics for both of these is the solution given by Example 1.1.2.

Recall the deletion of Example 1.3.3. The GSQL solution is given by

```
DELETE TRANSCRIPT-RECORD
 WHERE STUDID = 123456789
   AND STUDNAME = SMITH ROBERT J.
```

The GQBE solution is given in Figure 1.13(d). In both cases the effects of these operations may be regarded as the searching of all the RECORD tables on a TRANSCRIPT-RECORD cluster where the STUDID and STUDNAME values of the TRANSCRIPT records are 123456789 and SMITH ROBERT J., respectively. When all such RECORD tables are found, all the rows in them are deleted. The formal semantics for both of these is the solution given by Example 1.3.3.

In Chapter 2 we investigate the external-to-conceptual mapping problem using database logic. As a result, using external-to-conceptual mappings, one can translate GCALC DML from the external level to the conceptual level. Since GSQL and GQBE can both be defined in terms of GCALC, the results there can also be used to convert GSQL and GQBE into GCALC at the conceptual level.

Exercises

The following operations refer to the database logic view V(Dext) in Figure 1.8. For each of these, express it in GCALC and describe the results of execution on the database structure in Figure 1.9.

1. Find the names and id numbers of all the students who ever took Calculus.
2. Find all of the courses and final grades for courses taken by Robert J. Smith during the spring 1980 semester.
3. Find the names and id numbers of all the students who were in the same section of Math 104 during the spring 1980 semester.
4. Insert for Mary T. Jones an empty (NULL) COURSES table for the fall 1979 semester.
5. Insert the fact that Mary T. Jones took Computer Science 220, Introduction to Logic, section 001, and earned a grade of B for 3 credits during the spring semester of 1980.
6. Delete all Math courses from Robert J. Smith's record.
7. Change the name of the Computer Science Department from COMPSCI to CMSC.

1.4 RELATED READING

ASTRAHAN, M. M., et al., "System R: Relational Approach to Database Management," *ACM Transactions on Database Systems,* **1,** (2) June 1976, pp. 97-137.

BACHMAN, C. W., "Data Structure Diagrams," *Data Base* (journal of ACM SIGBDP), **1,** (2), Summer 1969.

BRADLEY, J., "An Extended Owner-Coupled Set Data Model and Predicate Calculus for Database Management," *ACM Transactions on Database Systems,* **3,** (4) Dec. 1978, pp. 385-416.

CAO, D., AND JACOBS, B. E., "A Generalized Structured English Data Manipulation Language Based on Database Logic," Department of Computer Science Technical Report, University of Maryland, College Park, June 1983.

CHEN, P. C., "The Entity-Relationship Model—Toward a Unified View of Data," *ACM Transactions on Database Systems,* **1,** (1), Mar. 1979, pp. 9–36.

CHILDS, D. L., "Feasibility of a Set-Theoretical Data Structure—A General Structure Based on a Reconstituted Definition of a Relation," *Proceedings IFIP Congress,* North-Holland, Amsterdam, 1968, pp.162-172.

CODD, E. F., "A Relational Model of Data for Large Shared Data Banks," *Communications of the ACM,* **13,** (6), June 1970, pp. 377-387.

DATE, C. J., "An Introduction to the Unified Database Language (UDL)," *Proceedings Sixth International Conference on Very Large Databases,* Oct. 1980.

GALLAIRE, H., AND MINKER, J. (eds.), *Logic and Databases.* Plenum, New York, 1979.

GALLAIRE, H., MINKER, J., AND NICOLAS, J. M. (eds.), *Advances in Database Theory,* Vol. 1, Plenum, New York, 1980.

HAMILTON, A. G., *Logic for Mathematicians,* Cambridge University Press, Cambridge, 1978.

HAMMER, M., AND MCLEOD, D., "Database Description with SDM: A Semantic Database Model," *ACM Transactions on Database Systems,* **6,** (3) Sept. 1981, pp. 351-386.

IBM Corporation, *Information Management System/Virtual Storage Utilities Reference Manual,* IBM Form SH20-9029.

JACOBS, B. E., "On Database Logic," *Journal of the ACM,* **29,** Apr. 1982, pp.310-332.

JACOBS, B. E., AND WALCZAK C. A., "A Generalized Query-By-Example Data Manipulation Language Based on Database Logic," *IEEE Transactions on Software Engineering,* **SE-9,** (1), January 1983, pp. 40-57.

MCGEE, W. C., "On the Evaluation of Data Models," *ACM Transactions on Database Systems,* **1,** (4), Dec. 1976, pp. 370-387.

MENDELSON, E., "Introduction to Mathematical Logic," (2nd ed.), Van Nostrand, Reinhold, New York, 1980.

NICOLAS, J. M., "First-Order Logic Formalization for Functional, Multivalued and Mutual Dependencies," *Proceedings ACM SIGMOD Conference,* 1978, pp. 40-46.

SHIPMAN, D. W., "The Functional Data Model and the Data Language DAPLEX," *ACM Transactions on Database Systems,* **6** (1) Mar. 1981, pp. 140-173.

SHOENFIELD, J., *Mathematical Logic,* Addison-Wesley, Reading, Mass., 1967.

SIBLEY, E. H., "On the Equivalence of Data Based Systems," *Proceedings ACM SIGMOD Workshop on Data Description, Access and Control,* Vol. 2, May 1974.

SMITH, J. M., AND SMITH, D. C. P., "Database Abstractions: Aggregation and Generalization," *ACM Transactions on Database Systems,* **2,** (2), 1977, pp. 105-133.

STONEBRAKER, M., WONG, E., KREPS, P., AND HELD, G., "The Design and Implementation of INGRES," *ACM Transactions on Database Systems,* **1** (3), Sept. 1976, pp. 189-223.

TSICHRITZIS, D. C., AND LOCHVOSKY, F. H., *Data Models*, Prentice-Hall, Englewood Cliffs, N.J., 1982.

ZLOFF, M. M. "Query-By-Example: A Database Language," *IBM Systems Journal*, **16** (4), Dec. 1977, pp. 324–343.

2

EXTERNAL-TO-CONCEPTUAL MAPPING

In Chapter 2 we provide a methodology for the construction of external-to-conceptual mappings that will support one database as an external view of a second conceptual database. In Section 2.1 we demonstrate the method when external and conceptual levels are both relational. In Section 2.2 we generalize the situation to the case where both levels are heterogeneous. In Section 2.3 we show how programs at the external level can be mechanically converted into corresponding programs at the conceptual level.

2.1 MAPPINGS BETWEEN RELATIONAL VIEWS

In this section we see how to construct an external-to-conceptual mapping when both the external and conceptual views are relational. The mapping is made up of (1) an "interpretation" of the external relational view into the conceptual relational view, and (2) a set of operation simulators that translate insertions, deletions, and updates from the external level to the conceptual level. In Section 2.2 these ideas are generalized from the relational to the heterogeneous case.

Example

We illustrate the external-to-conceptual mapping process using view V(Rext) of Chapter 1 as an external view. The relational database Rcon used as the conceptual database is given in Figures 2.1 and 2.2. Figure 2.1 contains the database logic DDL for the view and Figure 2.2 contains an instance of the database. Notice that while the

```
V(Rcon): VIEW DEFINITION
S(Rcon): SCHEMA DEFINITION
  TABLE STUDENT = (ID#,STUDNAME,BIRTHDATE,DATEADM)
  TABLE REGISTRAR = (SEMESTER,YEAR,DEPT,COURSE#,
    SEC#,INSTRUCT,LOCAT,TIMES,STUDID,GRADE)
  TABLE CATALOGUE = (DEPT,COURSE#,TITLE,CREDITS,
    DESCR,PREDEPT,PRECOURSE#)

L(Rcon): LANGUAGE DEFINITION
  T(Rcon): TYPING DEFINITION
    TYPE IDTPE = {ID#,STUDID> ASCII CHAR(9)
    TYPE NAMTPE = {STUDNAME,INSTRUCT} ASCII CHAR(20)
    TYPE DATPE = {BIRTHDATE,DATEADM} ASCII CHAR(15)
    TYPE SEMTPE = {SEMESTER} ASCII CHAR(8)
    TYPE YRTPE = {YEAR} ASCII DEC(4)
    TYPE DEPTPE = {DEPT,PREDEPT} ASCII CHAR(10)
    TYPE CS#TPE = {COURSE#,PRECOURSE#} ASCII DEC(3)
    TYPE SEC#TPE = {SEC#} ASCII CHAR(3)
    TYPE LOCTPE = {LOCAT} ASCII CHAR(30)
    TYPE TIMTPE = {TIMES} ASCII CHAR(20)
    TYPE GRDTPE = {GRADE} ASCII CHAR(1)
    TYPE TTLTPE = {TITLE} ASCII CHAR(25)
    TYPE CRDSTPE = {CREDITS} ASCII DEC(2)
    TYPE DESCR = {DESCR} ASCII CHAR(50)

NONLOGICAL SYMBOLS DEFINITION
  PREDICATES
    STUDENT: (IDTPE,NAMTPE,DATPE,DATPE)
      PREDICATE
    REGISTRAR: (SEMTPE,YRTPE,DEPTPE,CS#TPE,
        SEC#TPE,NAMTPE,LOCTPE,TIMTPE,IDTPE,
        GRDTPE) PREDICATE
    CATALOGUE: (DEPTPE,CS#TPE,TTLTPE,CRDSTPE,
        DESCTPE,DEPTPE,CS#TPE) PREDICATE
    ≤:(YRTPE,YRTPE) PREDICATE
  FUNCTIONS
    TOTALCREDITS:(IDTPE,SEMTPE,YRTPE;
      CRDSTPE) FUNCTION

C(Rcon): CONSTRAINTS DEFINITION
  C(Rcon,1):CONSTRAINT STUDENT: ID# → STUDNAME,
    BIRTHDATE,DATEADM
  C(Rcon,2):CONSTRAINT REGISTRAR:SEMESTER,YEAR,DEPT,
    COURSE#,SEC# → INSTRUCT,LOCAT,TIMES
  C(Rcon,3):CONSTRAINT REGISTRAR:SEMESTER,YEAR,DEPT,
    COURSE#,SEC#,STUDID → GRADE
  C(Rcon,4):CONSTRAINT CATALOGUE:DEPT,COURSE#
    → TITLE,CREDITS,DESCR
  C(Rcon,5):CONSTRAINT REGISTRAR:SEMESTER,YEAR,
    DEPT,COURSE#,STUDID → SEC#
```

Figure 2.1 Part of a database logic DDL definition of view V(Rcon).

REGISTRAR

SEMESTER	YEAR	DEPT	COURSE #	SEC #	INSTRUCT	LOCAT	TIMES	STUDID	GRADE
FALL	1979	ART	103	001	BLUE	2100 ART BLDG	2-3 MWF	123456789	B
FALL	1979	COMP SCI	103	001	GREEN	2301 COMP CENTER	12-1 MWF	123456789	B
FALL	1979	HIST	101	001	YELLOW	3600 SOC SCI	8-9 MWF	123456789	B
FALL	1979	MATH	103	001	WHITE	4303 SCI	9-1 MWF	123456789	B
FALL	1979	BIO	103	001	PINK	4102 SCI	9-12 MWF		
SPRING	1980	COMP SCI	220	001	GREEN	4612 COMP CENTER	8-9 MWF	123456789	B
SPRING	1980	MATH	104	001	WHITE	4201 SCI	10-11 MWF	123456789	B
SPRING	1980	ECON	101	001	RED	3200 SOCSCI	1-3 MWF	123456789	C
SPRING	1980	ENG	105	001	PINK	4200 HUMANITIES	3-4 MWF	23456789	A
SPRING	1980	MATH	104	001	WHITE	4201 SCI	10-11 MWF	361258823	A
SPRING	1980	ECON	101	001	RED	3200 SOCSCI	1-3 MWF	361258823	C
SPRING	1980	PHYSICS	102	001	WHITE	3600 SCI	8-9 MWF	361258823	D
SPRING	1980	ENG	105	001	PINK	4200 HUMANITIES	3-4 MWF	361258823	I

STUDENT

ID#	STUDNAME	BIRTHDATE	DATEADM
123456789	SMITH ROBERT J.	APR 13 1961	SEPT 1 1979
361258823	JONES MARY T.	AUG 25 1960	FEB 1 1980

CATALOGUE

DEPT	COURSE#	TITLE	CREDITS	DESCR	PREDEPT	PRECOURSE#
COMP SCI	412	DATABASE SYSTEMS	3	. . .	COMP SCI	220
COMP SCI	412	DATABASE SYSTEMS	3	. . .	COMP SCI	250
COMP SCI	220	DISCRETE STRUCTURES	3	. . .	COMP SCI	103
COMP SCI	250	INTRO	3	. . .	---	---
COMP SCI	103	LOGIC	3	. . .	---	---
MATH	416	CALC	3	. . .	MATH	103
MATH	103	INTRO	3	. . .	---	---
BIO	103	INTRO	3	. . .	---	---

Figure 2.2 Part of a database structure M(Rcon) for V(Rcon).

atomic data values in Rext of Chapter 1 are EBCDIC, the atomic values in Rcon are ASCII.

The database represented in Figures 2.1 and 2.2 is a reorganization of the information in V(Rext). Namely, there are three tables: STUDENT, REGISTRAR, and CATALOGUE—which have, respectively, student, registration, and course information. The semantics of V(Rcon) should be apparent to the reader.

Language Interpretations

Let V(E) = <S(E),L(E),C(E)> represent a relational external view and let V(C) = <S(C),L(C),C(C)> represent a relational conceptual view. The first part of a relational external-to-conceptual mapping is an *interpretation of the language* L(E) in the language L(C). Figure 2.3 contains an interpretation I(Rext;Rcon) of the language L(Rext) of view V(Rext) into the language L(Rcon) of view V(Rcon). **The reader is strongly advised to refer often to Figure 2.3 while reading this section.** The components of an interpretation, namely, coding section, defining formula section, and constant transformation section, are defined below.

1. Coding Section. For each atomic type in Tj in L(E), we provide a sequence of atomic types <Tj;> of L(C) called the *code* for type Tj. The idea is that a Tj value in the external database is represented by a sequence of <Tj;> values in the conceptual database.

For example, the code for SIDTPE in L(Rext) is IDTPE; in L(Rcon). This is because any EBCDIC CHAR(9) value [i.e., SIDTPE in L(Rext)] in the view can be represented in the conceptual level V(Rcon) by a corresponding ASCII CHAR(9) value [i.e., IDTPE in L(Rcon)]. The other codings in Figure 2.3 are self-explanatory.

A simplistic way of thinking of coding is that when an external user names a data object (e.g., an EBCDIC id number) on a terminal screen, there is a little man "behind the screen" that glues on the corresponding code (e.g., the ASCII id number). This is because only codes exist at the conceptual level. The reader will see in Section 2.2 that the notion of "coding" can be used not only for simple atomic types, as in this scenario, but also to code higher-order types such as tables in nonrelational databases.

Remark. Other differences may also exist between the atomic data between different views. For example, one view may require measurement in feet and pounds, while another requires meters and kilograms. Throughout this book EBCDIC-to-ASCII conversions between atomic data items will be used to represent such situations.

Remark. For most examples in this book, an atomic type is coded by a single atomic type. However, there may be cases where several atomic types are needed to code a single atomic type. For example, a conceptual database may have three types, MONTHTPE, DAYTPE, and YRTPE, while in the external database there may be one type, DATPE. Hence, the code for DATPE would be MONTHTPE, DAYTPE,YRTPE;, since all three are needed to form a date.

```
I(Rext;Rcon): INTERPRETATION DEFINITION
  EXTERNAL VIEW IS V(Rext) = <S(Rext),L(Rext),C(Rext)>
  CONCEPTUAL VIEW IS V(Rcon) = <S(Rcon),L(Rcon),C(Rcon)>

  CODING SECTION
    CODE FOR SIDTPE IS IDTPE;
    CODE FOR NAMTPE IS NAMTPE;
    CODE FOR DATPE  IS DATPE;
    CODE FOR SEMTPE IS SEMTPE;
    CODE FOR YRTPE  IS YRTPE;
    CODE FOR DEPTPE IS DEPTPE;
    CODE FOR CS#TPE IS CS#TPE;
    CODE FOR SEC#TPE IS SEC#TPE;
    CODE FOR TTLTPE IS TTLTPE;
    CODE FOR GRDTPE IS GRDTPE;
    CODE FOR CRDSTPE IS CRDSTPE;

  DEFINING FORMULA SECTION

    PREDICATE: TRANSCRIPT
    ARGUMENTS ARE: (STUDID:1;,STUDNAME:1;,
      SEMESTER:1;,YEAR:1;,DEPT:1;,COURSE#:1;,SEC#:1;,
      TITLE:1;,GRADE:1;,CREDITS:1;)
    IS DEFINED BY:(E)BIRTHDATE:1(E)DATEADM:1
      (E)INSTRUCT:1(E)LOCAT:1(E)TIMES:1(E)DESCR:1
      (E)PREDEPT:1(E)PRECOURSE#:1
    STUDENT(STUDID:1,STUDNAME:1,BIRTHDATE:1,DATEADM:1)
    & REGISTRAR(SEMESTER:1,YEAR:1,DEPT:1,COURSE#:1,
    SEC#:1,INSTRUCT:1,LOCAT:1,TIMES:1,STUDID:1,GRADE:1)
      & CATALOGUE(DEPT:1,COURSE#:1,TITLE:1,CREDITS:1,DESCR:1,
        PREDEPT:1,PRECOURSE#:1)

    PREDICATE: STUDENT
    ARGUMENTS ARE: (ID#:1;,NAME:1;,DATEADM:1;)
    IS DEFINED BY:(E)BIRTHDATE:1
      STUDENT(STUDID:1,STUDNAME:1,BIRTHDATE:1,DATEADM:1)

    PREDICATE: ≤
    ARGUMENTS ARE:(YEAR:1;,YEAR:2;)
    IS DEFINED BY: YEAR:1≤ YEAR:2

    FUNCTION: TOTCREDITS
    ARGUMENTS ARE: (ID#:1;,SEMESTER:1;,YEAR:1;;CREDITS:1;)
    IS DEFINED BY: TOTALCREDITS(ID#:1,SEMESTER:1,
      YEAR:1) = CREDITS:1

  CONSTANT TRANSFORMATION SECTION
    PROC CODE(SIDTPE)(STUDID:1) RETURNS(ID#:1;);
      .
```

(continued)

(continued)

```
   .
   .
END;

PROC DECODE(SIDTPE)(ID#:1;) RETURNS(STUDID:1);
   .
   .
   .
END;
   .
   .
   .
```

Figure 2.3 Interpretation I(Rext;Rcon) of L(Rext) in L(Rcon).

2. Defining Formula Section

2.1. For each (T1,...,Tn) predicate symbol p of L(E) we provide a formula

Q(<R1;>,..., <Rn;>)

of L(C) called the *defining formula* of p. Here <Rj;> denotes variables which range over the code for Tj. The idea is that a question about p in L(E) is reduced to questions about codes in L(C).

For example, in Figure 2.3 the defining formula for the (SIDTPE, NAMTPE, SEMTPE, YRTPE, DEPTPE, CS#TPE, SEC#TPE, TTLTPE, GRDTPE, CRDSTPE) predicate symbol TRANSCRIPT of L(Rext) has arguments

(STUDID:1;,STUDNAME:1;,SEMESTER:1;,YEAR:1;,DEPT:1;,
COURSE#:1;,SEC#:1;,TITLE:1;,GRADE:1;,CREDITS:1;)

and has defining formula

(E)BIRTHDATE:1(E)DATEADM:1 ... (E)PRECOURSE#:1
STUDENT(STUDID:1,STUDNAME:1,BIRTHDATE:1,DATEADM:1)
& REGISTRAR(SEMESTER:1,YEAR:1,DEPT:1,COURSE#:1,
SEC#:1,INSTRUCT:1,LOCAT:1,TIMES:1,STUDID:1,GRADE:1)
& CATALOGUE(DEPT:1,COURSE#:1,TITLE:1,CREDITS:1,DESCR:1,
PREDEPT:1,PRECOURSE#:1).

Notice that a question in L(Rext) about whether or not a row is in the TRANSCRIPT table reduces to questions about rows in the STUDENT, REGISTRAR, and CATALOGUE tables in L(Rcon). The defining formulas for the predicates STUDENT and $\leq$ are clear from Figure 2.3.

The defining formula for type Tj equality is =(Tj), the componentwise equality for its code. For example, the defining formula for equality predicate =(NAMTPE) on L(Rext) is the formula

STUDNAME:1 =(NAMTPE) STUDNAME:2

in L(Rcon). This rule holds not just for I(Rext;Rcon), but for any interpretation between relational languages L(Rext) and L(Rcon).

2.2. For each (T1,...,Tn;T0) function symbol f of L(E), we provide a formula

Q(< R1; > ,..., < Rn; > ; < R0; >)

of L(C) called the *defining formula* of f . Here < Rj; > denotes variables that range over the code for Tj. The idea is that a question about f in L(E) is reduced to questions about codes in L(C).

For example, in Figure 2.3 the defining formula for the (SIDTPE, SEMTPE, YRTPE;CRDSTPE) function symbol TOTCREDITS of L(Rext) has arguments

(STUDID:1;,SEMESTER:1;,YEAR:1;;CREDITS:1;)

and has defining formula

TOTALCREDITS(STUDID:1,SEMESTER:1,YEAR:1) = CREDITS:1.

3. Constant Transformation Section. For each type Tj of L(E) and code < Tj; > of L(C) we have a procedure CODE(Tj)(-) which inputs a Tj constant e(Tj):i and returns the constants < e(Tj):i; > , which is its code. Also, for each type Tj of L(E) and code < Tj; > of L(C) we have a procedure DECODE(Tj)(-) which inputs < e(Tj):i; > , which is a code, and returns the constant in L(E) that it codes. In other words, CODE(Tj)(-) and DECODE(Tj)(-) are inverse mappings.

For example, in the interpretation of Figure 2.3, CODE(SIDTPE)(-) returns for an input EBCDIC DEC(9) string the corresponding ASCII DEC(9) string. Similarly, DECODE(NAMTPE)(-) returns for an input ASCII CHAR(20) string the corresponding EBCDIC CHAR(20) string. The values of the CODE(Tj)(-) and DECODE(Tj)(-) procedures may be obtained by computation or by a table look-up. If the constants at both levels are identical (e.g., both ASCII or EBCDIC), the procedures represent the identity map.

We will denote the interpretation I(Rext;Rcon) of L(Rext) in L(Rcon) as I′.

Two Mappings

The three parts above comprise the definition of an interpretation I of relational language L(E) in relational language L(C). As a result, we now have an automatic means of translating any wff Q of the language L(E) into a wff I(Q) of the language L(C) called the *interpretation of* Q *in* L(E) *via* I. Essentially, to get I(Q) from Q we replace variables and constants by their codes, and predicates and functions by their defining formulas. Formal details of the translation process are given in Chapter 3.

For example, recall the second constraint of V(Rext) given in Figure 1.3,

C(Rext,2)
= TRANSCRIPT:STUDID → STUDNAME

=TRANSCRIPT(STUDID:1,STUDNAME:1,SEMESTER:1,YEAR:1,
DEPT:1,COURSE#:1,SEC#:1,TITLE:1,GRADE:1,CREDITS:1)
& TRANSCRIPT(STUDID:1,STUDNAME:2,SEMESTER:2,YEAR:2,
DEPT:2,COURSE#:2,SEC#:2,TITLE:2,GRADE:2,CREDITS:2))
→ STUDNAME:1 = STUDNAME:2.

Then the interpretation of C(Rext,2) under I′,

I′(C(Rext,2))
= ((E)BIRTHDATE:1(E)DATEADM:1...(E)PRECOURSE#:1
STUDENT(STUDID:1,STUDNAME:1,BIRTHDATE:1,DATEADM:1)
&REGISTRAR(SEMESTER:1,YEAR:1,DEPT:1,COURSE#:1,
SEC#:1,INSTRUCT:2,LOCAT:2,TIMES:2,STUDID:1,GRADE:1)
&CATALOGUE(DEPT:1,COURSE#:1,TITLE:1,CREDITS:1,
DESCR:1,PREDEPT:1,PRECOURSE#:1))

&((E)BIRTHDATE:1(E)DATEADM:1...(E)PRECOURSE#:1
STUDENT(STUDID:1,STUDNAME:2,BIRTHDATE:1,
DATEADM:1)
&REGISTRAR(SEMESTER:2,YEAR:2,DEPT:2,COURSE#:2,
SEC#:2,INSTRUCT:2,LOCAT:2,TIMES:2,STUDID:1,
GRADE:2)
&CATALOGUE(DEPT:2,COURSE#:2,TITLE:2,CREDITS:2,
DESCR:1,PREDEPT:1,PRECOURSE#:1))
→ STUDNAME:1 = STUDNAME:2.

The interpretations of the wffs C(Rext,1), C(Rext,3) and C(Rext,4) under I′ will be left as exercises at the end of this section.

As a second consequence of the interpretation I, we have a mapping of any relational structure M(C) of L(C) into a relational structure, I[M(C)], of L(E) called the *relational structure induced from* M(C) *via* I. To illustrate, consider the defining formula for TRANSCRIPT given in Figure 2.3. We can regard this as saying that the row coded by

(STUDID:1;,STUDNAME:1;,SEMESTER:1;,YEAR:1;,
DEPT:1;,COURSE#:1;,SEC#:1;,TITLE:1;,GRADE:1;,
CREDITS:1;)

is in the table TRANSCRIPT of I′[M(Rcon)] precisely when the right-hand side of the defining formula is true in M(Rcon). Thus, a relational structure M(C) of L(C) together with an interpretation I "induces" a relational structure for L(E).

For example, consider the relational structure M(Rcon) given in Figure 2.2. The row

(123456789;,SMITH ROBERT J.;,FALL;,1979;,COMPSCI;,103;,001;,LOGIC;,B;,3;)

is in the TRANSCRIPT table in I′[M(Rcon)] because

(E)BIRTHDATE:1(E)DATEADM:1...(E)PRECOURSE#:1
STUDENT(123456789,SMITH ROBERT J.,BIRTHDATE:1,DATEADM:1)

& REGISTRAR(FALL,1979,COMPSCI,103,001,INSTRUCT:1,LOCAT:1
TIMES:1,123456789,B)
& CATALOGUE(COMPSCI,103,LOGIC,3,...,-,-,)

is true in M(Rcon). Part of the relational structure I′[M(Rcon)] induced by M(Rcon) via I′ is given in Figure 2.4. Notice that every atomic object in the induced relational structure is in EBCDIC but is named by some ASCII code from the relational structure M(Rcon).

An important link between the notions of interpreted formula and induced relational structure is given by the following.

Theorem 2.1.1. *Let* L(E) *and* L(C) *be two relational languages and* I *an interpretation of* L(E) *in* L(C). *Then for any relational structure* M(C) *for* L(C) *and any wff* Q *of* L(E)

$$I[M(C)] \models Q \quad \text{iff} \quad M(C) \models I(Q).$$

Theorem 2.1.1 tells us that the wffs of L(E) that are true in an induced relational structure are precisely those whose interpretations are true in the inducing relational structure. We refer to Theorem 2.1.1 as the "Flipper Theorem" since it tells us that I "flips" from M(C) to Q. The proof of Theorem 2.1.1 will be found in Chapter 3.

Induced relational structures play a central role in our methodology for external-to-conceptual view mapping. Intuitively, one thinks of the external database as being "hidden" somewhere in the conceptual database. The external database does not physically exist by itself. In our approach, the "hidden" or "external database" is precisely the relational structure induced from the conceptual relational structure via the interpretation.

View Interpretations

Let M(C) be a relational structure for L(C) which satisfies the constraints C(C) of view V(C) and let I be an interpretation of L(E) in L(C). Although I and M(C) induce a hidden external relational structure I[M(C)] for L(E), it might not be the case that I[M(C)] satisfies the constraints C(E) of the view V(E). It may also happen that for **no** relational structure M(C) for L(C) does **any** induced I[M(C)] satisfy the constraints in C(E). To eliminate these difficulties, we define the notion of a "view interpretation."

Let X and Y be sets of wffs in the same relational language L. We say that X *logically implies* Y *in* L if every relational structure M of L that is a model of X is also a model of Y. We also say that Y is a *logical consequence of* X. As a special case, if Y is the singleton set {Q}, then we say that X *logically implies* Q *in* L.

For example, recall I′(C(Rext,2)), the interpretation of C(Rext,2) above. The reader can easily check that {I′(C(Rext,2)) } is logically implied in L(Rcon) by {C(Rcon,1)}. This is because any relational structure M(Rcon) for L(Rcon) which satisfies the constraint C(Rcon,1) must necessarily satisfy the wff I′(C(Rext,2)).

Let V(E) = <S(E),L(E),C(E)> and V(C) = <S(C),L(C),C(C)> be two rela-

TRANSCRIPT									
STUDID	STUDNAME	SEMESTER	YEAR	DEPT	COURSE #	SEC #	TITLE	GRADE	CREDITS
123456789 (123456789;)	SMITH ROBERT J. (SMITH ROBERT J.;	FALL (FALL;)	1979 (1979;)	COMPSCI (COMPSCI;)	103 (103;)	001 (001;)	LOGIC (LOGIC;)	B (B;)	3 (3;)
123456789 (123456789;)	SMITH ROBERT J. (SMITH ROBERT J.;)	FALL (FALL)	1979 (1979;)	MATH (MATH;)	103 (103;)	001 (001;)	INTRO (INTRO;)	B (B;)	3 (3;)
123456789 (123456789;)	SMITH ROBERT J. (SMITH ROBERT J.;)	FALL (FALL;)	1979 (1979;)	ART (ART;)	103 (103;)	001 (001;)	INTRO (INTRO;)	B (B;)	3 (3;)
123456789 (123456789;)	SMITH ROBERT J. (SMITH ROBERT J.;)	FALL (FALL;)	1979 (1979;)	HIST (HIST;)	101 (101;)	001 (001;)	AM HIST (AM HIST;)	B (B;)	3 (3;)
123456789 (123456789;)	SMITH ROBERT J. (SMITH ROBERT J.;)	SPRING (SPRING;)	1980 (1980;)	COMPSCI (COMPSCI;)	220 (220;)	001 (001;)	DISCRETE STRUCT (DISCRETE STRUCT;)	B (B;)	3 (3;)
123456789 (123456789;)	SMITH ROBERT J. (SMITH ROBERT J.;)	SPRING (SPRING;)	1980 (1980;)	MATH (MATH;)	104 (104;)	001 (001;)	CALC (CALC;)	B (B;)	4 (4;)
123456789 (123456789;)	SMITH ROBERT J. (SMITH ROBERT J.;)	SPRING (SPRING;)	1980 (1980;)	ECON (ECON;)	101 (101;)	001 (001;)	INTRO (INTRO;)	C (C;)	3 (3;)
123456789 (123456789;)	SMITH ROBERT J. (SMITH ROBERT J.;)	SPRING (SPRING)	1980 (1980;)	ENG (ENG;)	105 (105;)	001 (001;)	COMPOS (COMPOS;)	A (A;)	3 (3;)
361258823 (361258823;)	JONES MARY T. (JONES MARY T.;)	SPRING (SPRING;)	1980 (1980;)	MATH (MATH;)	104 (104;)	001 (001;)	CALC (CALC;)	A (A;)	4 (4;)
361258823 (361258823;)	JONES MARY T. (JONES MARY T.:)	SPRING (SPRING;)	1980 (1980;)	ECON (ECON;)	101 (101;)	001 (001;)	INTRO (INTRO;)	C (C;)	3 (3;)
361258823 (361258823;)	JONES MARY T. (JONES MARY T.;)	SPRING (SPRING;)	1980 (1980;)	PHYSICS (PHYSICS;)	102 (102;)	001 (001;)	INTRO (INTRO;)	D (D;)	4 (4;)
361258823 (361258823;)	JONES MARY T. (JONES MARY T.;)	SPRING (SPRING;)	1980 (1980;)	ENG (ENG;)	105 (105;)	001 (001;)	COMPOS (COMPOS;)	E (E;)	3 (3;)

NOTE: The upper values are EBCDIC;
The lower values are ASCII.

STUDENT		
ID	NAME	DATEADM
123456789 (123456789;)	SMITH ROBERT T. (SMITH ROBERT T.;)	SEPT 2, 1979 (SEPT 2, 1979;)
361258823 (361258823;)	JONES MARY T. (JONES MARY T.;)	FEB 1, 1980 (FEB 1, 1980;)

Figure 2.4 Induced database structure I(Rext;Rcon)[M(Rcon)].

tional views. Let I be an interpretation of L(E) in L(C). By I(C(E)) we mean the set of wffs obtained by interpreting all the wffs of C(E).

Definition. We call I an *interpretation of view* V(E) *in view* V(C) if I(C(E)) is a logical consequence of the set of wffs C(C) in V(C).

By the remarks above we know that I′(C(Rext,2)) is a logical consequence of the set of wffs C(Rcon) in L(Rcon). It will be left as an exercise to show that I′(C(Rext,i)), i = 1, 3 and 4, are all logical consequences of the wffs C(Rcon) in L(Rcon). As a result, I′ is an interpretation of V(Rext) in V(Rcon).

An important consequence of view interpretations is given by the following result.

Theorem 2.1.2 *Let* V(E) *and* V(C) *be any two relational views and let* I *be an interpretation of view* V(E) *in view* V(C). *Then for any relational structure* M(C) *for* L(C),

$$M(C) \models C(C) \quad \text{implies} \quad I[M(C)] \models C(E).$$

In other words, if I is an interpretation of V(E) in V(C) and M(C) is any model of C(C), the induced database I[M(C)] is a model of V(E).

Proof. Suppose that $M(C) \models C(C)$. Since V(E) is interpretable in V(C), then I(C(E)) is a logical consequence of C(C). Since $M(C) \models C(C)$, we have $M(C) \models I[C(E)]$. By Theorem 2.1.1, $I[M(C)] \models C(E)$.

This result has significance in the case when there are many external relational views supported by a single conceptual view. Namely, let V(Ei) = <S(Ei),L(Ei),C(Ei)>, i = 1, ...,n, and V(C) = <S(C),L(C),C(C)> be a collection of relational views, and let I(Ei;C) be an interpretation of view V(Ei) in V(C), i = 1, ...,n. Whenever an update occurs (see below) it will be manifested in the conceptual database. Consequently, constraint checking will occur only at the conceptual level. Since updates will be done only as long as constraints C(C) are not violated, at any instance the conceptual database will be a model of C(C). Since all interpretations I(Ei;C) are view interpretations, by Theorem 2.1.2, each induced database I(Ei;C)[M(C)] will be a model of its constraints C(Ei), i = 1, ...,n.

Operation Simulators

Recall from Section 1.1 that operation INSERT(TRANSCRIPT)(W), on view V(Rext), adds to the TRANSCRIPT table of a relational structure M(Rext) the rows given in the array W as long as the constraints C(Rext) are not violated. If V(Rext) is an external view, the insertion takes place in the "external database" I′[M(Rcon)]. Since the external database does not exist, the insertion has to be "simulated" on the conceptual database. A program that simulates such an operation on the conceptual database is called a *simulator.*

```
PROC SIM(INSERT(TRANSCRIPT))(CW);

  /* CW is an array of codes where:
    CW(i).STUDID = an SIDTPE code
                 = an ASCII DEC(9) value (IDTPE;),
    CW(i).STUDNAME = a  NAMTPE code
                 = an ASCII CHAR(20) value (NAMTPE;),
    CW(i).SEMESTER = a SEMTPE code
                 = an ASCII CHAR(8) value (SEMTPE;),
    CW(i).YEAR   = a YRTPE code
                 = an ASCII DEC(4) value (YRTPE;),
    CW(i).DEPT   = a DEPTPE code
                 = an ASCII CHAR(10) value (DEPTPE;),
    CW(i).COURSE# = a CS#TPE code
                 = an ASCII DEC(3) value (CS#TPE;),
    CW(i).SEC#   = a SEC#TPE code
                 = an ASCII DEC(3) value (SEC#TPE;),
    CW(i).TITLE= a TTLTPE code
                 = an ASCII CHAR(25) value (TTLTPE;),
    CW(i).GRADE = a GRDTPE code
                 = an ASCII DEC(9) value (GRDTPE;),
    CW(i).CREDITS= a CRDSTPE code
                 = an ASCII DEC(1) value (CRDSTPE;),

      i = 1,...,length(CW) */

    ESTABLISH CHECKPOINT;

  /* If the simulation should fail [e.g., the resultant conceptual database is
not a model of C(Rcon)], we can use this checkpoint to reestablish the old database
instance.*/

    FOR i = 1 TO LENGTH(CW);

  /* For each row of CW perform the following operations.*/

    GET W (CW(i).STUDID): (E)BIRTHDATE:1(E)DATEADM:1(E)DESCR:1
      (E)PREDEPT:1(E)PRECOURSE#:1
     STUDENT(CW(i).STUDID,CW(i).STUDNAME,BIRTHDATE:1,DATEADM:1)
    & CATALOGUE(CW(i).DEPT,CW(i).COURSE#,CW(i).TITLE,CW(i).CREDITS,
        DESCR:1,PREDEPT:1,PRECOURSE#:1);

    IF LENGTH(W) = 0 THEN GO TO L1;
  /* If there is no row in STUDENT with ID# = CW(i).STUDID or if course
CW(i).DEPT, CW(i).COURSE# is not listed in CATALOGUE, roll back to the last
checkpoint.*/

    INSERT(REGISTRAR)({(CW(i).SEMESTER,CW(i).YEAR,CW(i).DEPT,
      CW(i).COURSE#,CW(i).SEC#,null,null,null,CW(i).STUDID,
        CW(i).GRADE)};

  /* Insert into REGISTRAR data pertaining to the student in the i-th
row of CW; fill in "null" values for INSTRUCT, LOCAT, and TIMES.*/
```

(continued)

```
        END i;
         IF M(Rcon) ⊨ C(Rcon) THEN RETURN;

    L1: RESTORE TO LAST CHECKPOINT;

    /* If the current conceptual database instance is a model of C(Rcon) then
exit; otherwise, we roll back to the instance of the conceptual database prior to
execution.*/

        END SIM(INSERT(TRANSCRIPT));
```

Figure 2.5 Operation simulator SIM(INSERT(TRANSCRIPT)).

For example, a simulator for the operation INSERT (TRANSCRIPT)(W) is the program SIM(INSERT (TRANSCRIPT)) (CODE(W)) given in Figure 2.5. The input to the program are the "codes" for the inputs to the names in W. The execution of the simulator SIM(INSERT(TRANSCRIPT)) works as follows.

First, a "checkpoint" is made just prior to the beginning of execution. This is done so that in case the simulation is to be canceled [e.g., insertions violate the conceptual constraints C(Rcon)], the database can be "rolled back" to its status just prior to the execution of this simulation.

Next, for each row of the input, insertions are made into the conceptual database. The insertions are done so that the defining formula of the atom TRANSCRIPT in the interpretation I′ becomes "true" in the conceptual database. By Theorem 2.1.2 this will automatically make the row appear in TRANSCRIPT in the induced external database I′[M(Rcon)].

When all the simulations are completed for all the rows in W, the simulator checks to see if the conceptual constraints still hold. If they do, SIM(INSERT-(TRANSCRIPT)) exits; otherwise, it rolls back to the point just prior to execution before exiting.

Recall the execution of INSERT(TRANSCRIPT)(W) of Example 1.1.2 when W was the array

{(123456789, SMITH ROBERT J., FALL,
1979, BIO, 103, 101, INTRO, B, 3)}.

The array CODE(W) is the same as W except that the atomic values are now ASCII instead of EBCDIC. The effect of the execution of SIM(INSERT(TRANSCRIPT)) (CODE(W)) on the database structure M(Rcon) of Figure 2.2 is given in Figure 2.6(a). The effect of the execution of SIM(INSERT(TRANSCRIPT)) on the induced external database I′[M(Rcon)] is given in Figure 2.6(b).

Simulators for deletion and updating are constructed in a way similar to that of SIM(INSERT(TRANSCRIPT)) except that in the case of deletion, the simulator makes "false" the defining formula and in the case of update the simulator makes

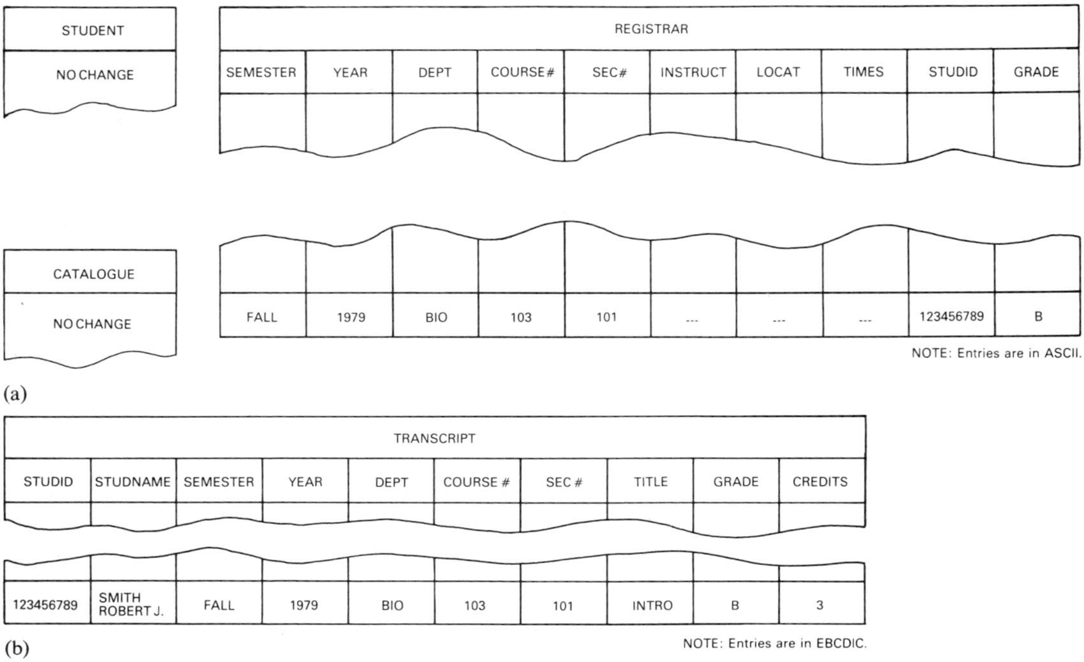

Figure 2.6 Effects of simulator: (a) on M(Rcon); (b) on I′[M(Rcon)].

"false" half the input row and "true" for the other half. In the next section, simulators are extended to the heterogeneous cases. In Chapters 4 and 5 simulator "correctness" is investigated in detail.

Exercises

1. Find the interpretation of C(Rext,1) of V(Rext) in L(Rcon) via I′.
2. Find the interpretation of C(Rext,3) and C(Rext,4) of V(Rext) in L(Rcon) via I′.
3. Show that the wffs of L(Rcon) obtained from Exercises 1 and 2 are logical consequences of the wffs C(Rcon) in L(Rcon).
4. What would be the effect of the execution of the simulator SIM(INSERT(TRANSCRIPT)) of Figure 2.5 on M(Rcon) of Figure 2.2 and I′[M(Rcon)] of Figure 2.4 when CODE(W) is the set

   {(361258823;,EVANS GRACE J;,FALL;,1979;,MATH;,103;,INTRO;,B;,3;)} ?

   The following represents an algebraic mapping of the database V(BIOG-REG) (Exercises 1 to 4 of Section 1.1):

```
DEFINE
  BIOREG (BRNAME,BRADDR,BRID,BRMAJOR,BRCOURSE)
  AS
  SELECT UNIQUE SNAME,SADDR,SID,SMAJOR,SCOURSE
```

FROM BIOG,REG
WHERE BIOG.SID = REG.SID.

The new database, call it BIOREG, is obtained by "joining" the BIOG and REG tables over fields ID. UNIQUE means that the duplicate rows are compressed.

5. Specify, in a format similar to that of Figure 2.1, the schema S(BIOREG) and the language L(BIOREG) corresponding to this new relational database.
6. Specify, in a format similar to that of Figure 2.3, the interpretation I(BIOREG;BIOG-REG) of language L(BIOREG) in language L(BIOG-REG).
7. Is the interpretation of the functional dependency BIOREG:NAME → MAJOR under I(BIOREG;BIOG-REG) a logical consequence of C(BIOG-REG) in L(BIOG-REG)?
8. Is the interpretation of the functional dependency BIOREG:NAME → COURSE under I(BIOREG;BIOG-REG) a logical consequence of C(BIOG-REG) in L(BIOG-REG)?
9. Is the interpretation of the "multivalued dependency" BIOREG:NAME → → COURSE under I(BIOREG;BIOG-REG) a logical consequence of C(BIOG-REG) in L(BIOG-REG)? **Hint:** the multivalued dependency is expressible in L(BIOREG) as

   (BIOREG(NAME:1,ADDR:1,ID:1,MAJOR:1,COURSE:1)
   & BIOREG(NAME:1,ADDR:2,ID:2,MAJOR:2,COURSE:2))
   → BIOREG(NAME:1,ADDR:1,ID:1,MAJOR:1,COURSE:2).

10. Let M(BIOG-REG) be the database structure for L(BIOG-REG) given in Figure 1.5. Construct the induced relational structure I(BIOREG;BIOG-REG)[M(BIOG-REG)].
11. Construct an operation simulator SIM(DELETE(BIOREG)) for the operation DELETE-(BIOREG) of L(BIOREG). What would be the effect of executing it on M(BIOG-REG) of Figure 1.5 and the induced relational structure of Exercise 10 when the input is CODE(W) is the set

   {(MARY SMITH;,104 MAIN ST;,1234;,MATH;,MATH 306;)} ?

2.2 MAPPINGS BETWEEN HETEROGENEOUS VIEWS

In this section we extend the external-to-conceptual mapping of Section 2.1 to the case where both the external and conceptual views are heterogeneous. The mapping consists of (1) an "interpretation" of the external database view into the conceptual database view, and (2) a set of operation "simulators" that translate insertions, deletions, and updates from the external level to the conceptual level.

Example

We illustrate the external-to-conceptual mapping process using view V(Dext) of Chapter 1 as an external view. The network database Dcon that will be used as the conceptual database is given in Figures 2.7 and 2.8. Figure 2.7 contains the CODASYL (network) DDL definition and Figure 2.8 contains an instance of the database. An explanation of the CODASYL definition is given below. Figure 2.9 contains the data-

```
SCHEMA NAME IS DCON.

RECORD NAME IS SYSTEM

RECORD NAME IS REGISTRAR

    DUPLICATES ARE NOT ALLOWED
    FOR SEMESTER,YEAR IN REGISTRAR.
      SEMESTER   ; TYPE IS ASCII CHAR(8).
      YEAR       ; TYPE IS ASCII DEC(4)

RECORD NAME IS COURSE
    DEPT         ; TYPE IS ASCII CHAR(10)
    COURSE#      ; TYPE IS ASCII DEC(3)

RECORD NAME IS SECTION
    SEC#         ; TYPE IS ASCII DEC(3)
    INSTRUCT     ; TYPE IS ASCII CHAR(20)
    LOCAT        ; TYPE IS ASCII CHAR(30)
    TIMES        ; TYPE IS ASCII CHAR(20)

RECORD NAME IS STUDENT
    STUDID      ; TYPE IS ASCII DEC(9)
    STUDNAME    ; TYPE IS ASCII CHAR(20)
    GRADE       ; TYPE IS ASCII CHAR(1)

RECORD NAME IS STUDINFO
    DUPLICATES ARE NOT ALLOWED
    FOR ID# IN STUDINFO
    ID#        ; TYPE IS ASCII DEC(9)
    STUDNAME   ; TYPE IS ASCII CHAR(20)
    BIRTHDATE  ; TYPE IS ASCII CHAR(15)
    DATEADM    ; TYPE IS ASCII CHAR(15)

RECORD NAME IS CATALOGUE
    DEPT      ; TYPE IS ASCII CHAR(10)
    COURSE#   ; TYPE IS ASCII DEC(3)
    TITLE     ; TYPE IS ASCII CHAR(25)
    CREDITS   ; TYPE IS ASCII DEC(2)
    DESCR     ; TYPE IS ASCII CHAR(50)

RECORD NAME IS LINK
    FILLER    ; TYPE IS ASCII CHAR(0)

SET NAME IS SYSTEM-REGISTRAR
    OWNER IS SYSTEM
    ORDER IS SORTED BY DEFINED KEYS
      DUPLICATES ARE NOT ALLOWED
    MEMBER IS REGISTRAR
      INSERTION IS AUTOMATIC
      RETENTION IS FIXED
      KEY IS ASCENDING SEMESTER,YEAR IN REGISTRAR
      SET SELECTION IS BY SYSTEM
```

Figure 2.7 *(cont. next page)*

(continued)

```
SET NAME IS REGISTRAR-COURSE
    OWNER IS REGISTRAR
    ORDER IS SORTED BY DEFINED KEYS
      DUPLICATES ARE NOT ALLOWED
    MEMBER IS COURSE
      INSERTION IS MANUAL
      RETENTION IS OPTIONAL
      KEY IS ASCENDING DEPT,COURSE# IN COURSE
      SET SELECTION IS BY APPLICATION

SET NAME IS COURSE-SECTION
    OWNER IS COURSE
    ORDER IS SORTED BY DEFINED KEYS
      DUPLICATES ARE NOT ALLOWED
    MEMBER IS SECTION
      INSERTION IS MANUAL
      RETENTION IS OPTIONAL
      KEY IS ASCENDING SEC# IN SECTION
      SET SELECTION IS BY APPLICATION

SET NAME IS SECTION-STUDENT
    OWNER IS SECTION
    ORDER IS SORTED BY DEFINED KEYS
      DUPLICATES ARE NOT ALLOWED
    MEMBER IS STUDENT
      INSERTION IS MANUAL
      RETENTION IS OPTIONAL
      KEY IS ASCENDING STUDID IN STUDENT
      SET SELECTION IS BY APPLICATION

SET NAME IS SYSTEM-STUDINFO
    OWNER IS SYSTEM
    ORDER IS SORTED BY DEFINED KEYS
      DUPLICATES ARE NOT ALLOWED
    MEMBER IS STUDINFO
      INSERTION IS AUTOMATIC
      RETENTION IS FIXED
      KEY IS ASCENDING ID# IN STUDINFO
      SET SELECTION IS BY SYSTEM

SET NAME IS SYSTEM-CATALOGUE
    OWNER IS SYSTEM
    ORDER IS SORTED BY DEFINED KEYS
      DUPLICATES ARE NOT ALLOWED
    MEMBER IS CATALOGUE
      INSERTION IS AUTOMATIC
      RETENTION IS FIXED
      KEY IS ASCENDING DEPT,COURSE# IN CATALOGUE
      SET SELECTION IS BY SYSTEM
```

Figure 2.7 *(cont. next page)*

(continued)

```
SET NAME IS CATALOGUE-LINK
    OWNER IS CATALOGUE
    ORDER IS SORTED BY DEFINED KEYS
      DUPLICATES ARE NOT ALLOWED
    MEMBER IS LINK
      INSERTION IS MANUAL
      RETENTION IS OPTIONAL
      KEY IS ASCENDING FILLER IN LINK
      SET SELECTION IS BY APPLICATION

SET NAME IS LINK-CATALOGUE
    OWNER IS LINK
    ORDER IS SORTED BY DEFINED KEYS
      DUPLICATES ARE NOT ALLOWED
    MEMBER IS CATALOGUE
      INSERTION IS MANUAL
      RETENTION IS OPTIONAL
      KEY IS ASCENDING DEPT,COURSE# IN CATALOGUE
      SET SELECTION IS BY APPLICATION
```

Figure 2.7 Codasyl DDL definition for view V(Dcon).

base logic DDL view definition V(Dcon) and Figure 2.10 contains the database structure corresponding to the instance in Figure 2.8.

The CODASYL DDL of Figure 2.7 declares the name of the schema to be Dcon. The database has "record" types SYSTEM, REGISTRAR, COURSE, SECTION, STUDENT, STUDINFO, CATALOGUE, and LINK. The SYSTEM record is unique and serves as the "top" of the database. The REGISTRAR declaration indicates two fields, SEMESTER and YEAR. The DUPLICATES ARE NOT ALLOWED clause declares that for the stored set of REGISTRAR records the fields SEMESTER and YEAR are unique. Similar comments hold for the records COURSE, SECTION, STUDENT, STUDINFO, CATALOGUE, and LINK.

The CODASYL definition also defines several "set" types: SYSTEM-REGISTRAR, REGISTRAR-COURSE, COURSE-SECTION, SECTION-STUDENT, SYSTEM-STUDINFO, SYSTEM-CATALOGUE, CATALOGUE-LINK, and LINK- CATALOGUE. In the SYSTEM-REGISTRAR set the "owner" is the unique record SYSTEM and its "members" are REGISTRAR records. The physical ordering of the member REGISTRAR records is by the defined keys—namely, SEMESTER, YEAR. The DUPLICATES ARE NOT ALLOWED clause indicates that within this unique set occurrence, no two REGISTRAR records can have the same SEMESTER, YEAR values.

The MEMBERSHIP clause for the SYSTEM-REGISTRAR set indicates that INSERTION is AUTOMATIC. This means that whenever a REGISTRAR-record instance is placed into the database, it is automatically linked into the (unique) SYSTEM-REGISTRAR set in its proper position. For other sets, INSERTION is MANUAL means that it is the programmer's responsibilty to place the record into the appropriate set occurrence whenever a new record is inserted into the database. The RETENTION is FIXED means that the only way that a REGISTRAR record can be

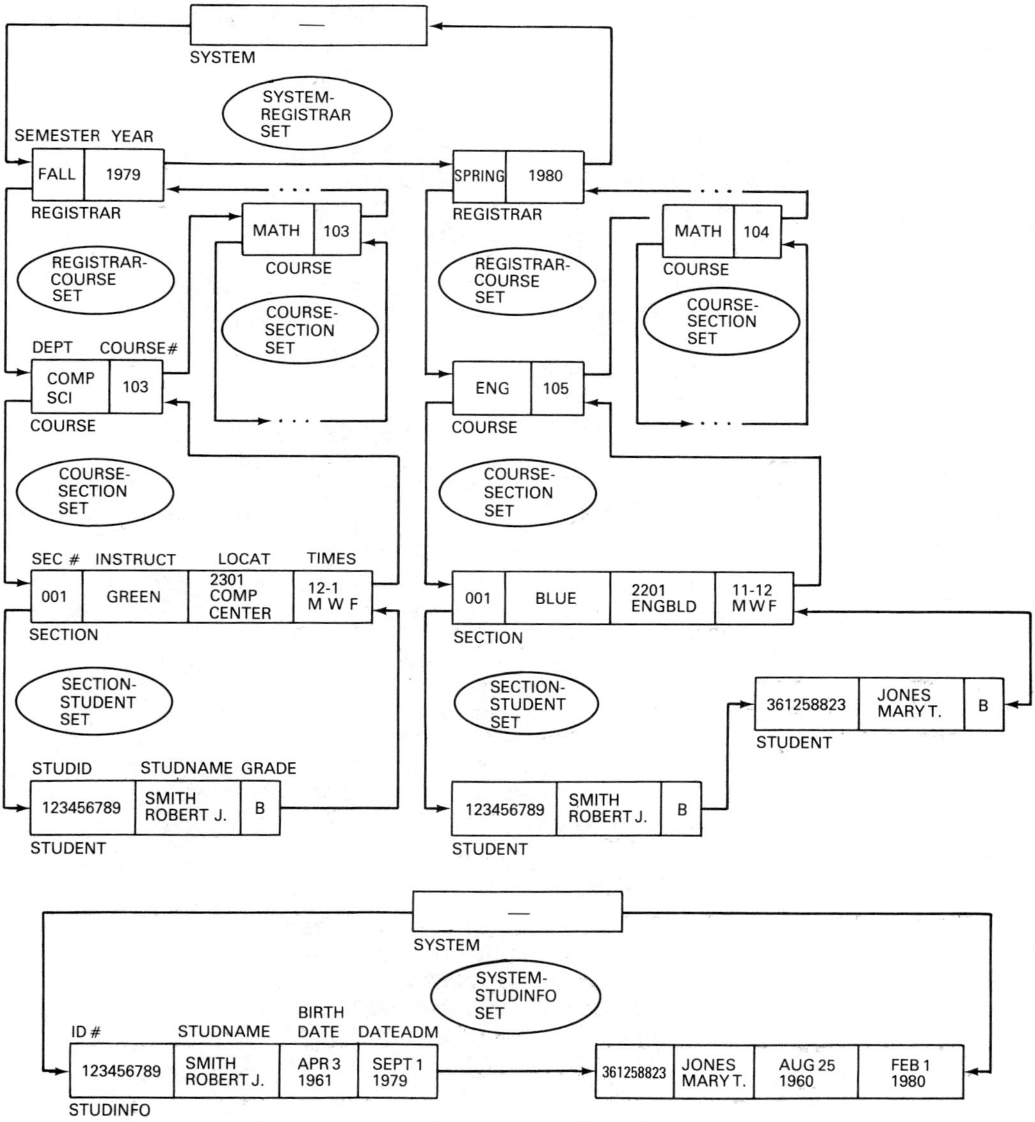

Figure 2.8 Instance of the Codasyl database Dcon.

removed from the SYSTEM-REGISTRAR set is by removing it totally from the database. For other sets, RETENTION is OPTIONAL means that records can be removed from the set occurrence without being taken out of the database.

In this database there will be only one occurrence of the sets SYSTEM-REGISTRAR, SYSTEM-STUDINFO, and SYSTEM-CATALOGUE. Hence, the particular occurrences of these sets will be uniquely determined or "SELECTED" by the SYSTEM record. In other defined sets (e.g., REGISTRAR-COURSE) there may be mul-

```
V(Dcon): VIEW DEFINITION
         S(Dcon): SCHEMA DEFINITION
           TABLE SYSTEM = (REGISTRAR,STUDINFO,CATALOGUE)
           TABLE REGISTRAR = (SEMESTER,YEAR,COURSE)
           TABLE COURSE = (DEPT,COURSE#,SECTION)
           TABLE SECTION = (SEC#,INSTRUCT,LOCAT,TIMES,STUDENT)
           TABLE STUDENT = (STUDID,STUDNAME,GRADE)
           TABLE STUDINFO = (ID#,STUDNAME,BIRTHDATE,DATEADM)
           TABLE CATALOGUE = (DEPT,COURSE#,TITLE,CREDITS,DESCR,
                              LINK)
           TABLE LINK = (CATALOGUE)

         L(Dcon): LANGUAGE DEFINITION
           T(Dcon): TYPING DEFINITION
             TYPE SEMTPE = {SEMESTER} ASCII CHAR(8)
             TYPE YRTPE = {YEAR} ASCII DEC(4)
             TYPE DEPTPE = {DEPT} ASCII CHAR(10)
             TYPE CS#TPE = {COURSE#} ASCII DEC(3)
             TYPE TTLTPE = {TITLE} ASCII CHAR(25)
             TYPE CRDSTPE = {CREDITS} ASCII DEC(2)
             TYPE SEC#TPE = {SEC#} ASCII CHAR(10)
             TYPE NAMTPE = {STUDNAME, INSTRUCT} ASCII CHAR(20)
             TYPE LOCTPE = {LOCAT} ASCII CHAR(30)
             TYPE TIMTPE = {TIMES} ASCII CHAR(20)
             TYPE IDTPE = {STUDID,ID#} ASCII CHAR(9)
             TYPE GRDTPE = {GRADE} ASCII CHAR(1)
             TYPE DATPE = {BIRTHDATE,DATEADM} ASCII CHAR(15)
             TYPE DESCTPE = {DESCR} ASCII CHAR(50)

         NONLOGICAL SYMBOLS DEFINITION
           PREDICATES
             SYSTEM-REGISTRAR-COURSE-SECTION-STUDENT:
               (SEMTPE,YRTPE,COURSE,DEPTPE,CS#TPE,SECTION,
               SEC#TPE,NAMTPE,LOCTPE,TIMTPE,STUDENT,IDTPE,
               NAMTPE,GRDTPE) FULL CLUSTER PREDICATE
             SYSTEM-STUDINFO:
               (IDTPE,NAMTPE,DATPE,DATPE) FULL CLUSTER PREDICATE
             SYSTEM-CATALOGUE-LINK-CATALOGUE:
               (DEPTPE,CS#TPE,TTLTPE,CRDSTPE,DESCTPE,LINK,
               CATALOGUE,DEPTPE,CS#TPE,TTLTPE,CRDSTPE,DESCTPE,
               LINK) FULL CLUSTER PREDICATE
             ≤:(YRTPE,YRTPE) PREDICATE
           FUNCTIONS
             TOTALCREDITS:(IDTPE,SEMTPE,YRTPE;
             CRDSTPE) FUNCTION

         C(Dcon): CONSTRAINTS DEFINITION
           C(Dcon,1):CONSTRAINT SYSTEM-REGISTRAR:SEMESTER,
             YEAR → COURSE
           C(Dcon,2):CONSTRAINT SYSTEM-REGISTRAR-COURSE:
             SEMESTER,YEAR,DEPT,COURSE# → SECTION
```

Figure 2.9 *(cont. next page)*

(continued)

```
C(Dcon,3):CONSTRAINT SYSTEM-REGISTRAR-COURSE-
  SECTION:SEMESTER,YEAR,DEPT,COURSE#,SEC#
  → INSTRUCT,LOCAT,TIMES,STUDENT
C(Dcon,4):CONSTRAINT SYSTEM-REGISTRAR-COURSE-
  SECTION-STUDENT:
    SEMESTER,YEAR,DEPT,COURSE#,SEC#,STUDID
    → STUDNAME,GRADE
C(Dcon,5):CONSTRAINT SYSTEM-STUDINFO:
  ID# → STUDNAME,BIRTHDATE,DATEADM
C(Dcon,6):CONSTRAINT SYSTEM-CATALOGUE:
  DEPT,COURSE# → TITLE,CREDITS,DESCR,LINK
C(Dcon,7):CONSTRAINT SYSTEM-REGISTRAR-
  COURSE-SECTION-STUDENT:
  SEMESTER,YEAR,DEPT,COURSE#,STUDID → SEC#
```

Figure 2.9 Database logic DDL definition for V(Dcon).

tiple set occurrences. In these cases set occurrences have to be determined by the "APPLICATION" program.

Language Interpretations

Let V(E) = <S(E),L(E),C(E)> represent an external database view and let V(C) = <S(C),L(C),C(C)> represent a conceptual database view. The first part of a database external-to-conceptual mapping is an "interpretation" of the language L(E) in the language L(C). Figure 2.11 contains an interpretation I(Dext;Dcon) of the language L(Dext) of view V(Dext) into the language L(Dcon) of view V(Dcon). **The reader is strongly advised to refer often to Figure 2.11 while reading this section.** The components of an interpretation, namely, the coding section, defining formula section, and constant transformation section, will now be defined.

1. Coding section. For each data type Tj, either atomic or higher-order in L(E), we provide a sequence of atomic types <Tj;> of L(C), called the *code* for type Tj. The idea is that a Tj value in the external database is represented by a sequence of <Tj;> values in the conceptual database.

For example, the code for atomic type SIDTPE in L(Dext) is IDTPE; in L(Dcon). This is because in the external view any EBCDIC NUM(9) value [i.e., SIDTPE in L(Dext)] can be represented at the conceptual level V(Dcon) by a corresponding ASCII NUM(9) value [i.e., IDTPE in L(Dcon)]. The codings for the other atomic types in L(Dext) in Figure 2.11 are self-explanatory.

Each higher-order (table) type Tj is coded by a sequence of atomic types <Tj;> of L(Dcon). For example, the code for COURSES in V(Dext) is the sequence IDTPE, SEMTPE,YRTPE;. This is because in the external database V(Dext), a COURSE table is uniquely determined by the id# (IDTPE) of the student and the semester, year (SEMTPE,YRTPE) that the courses in COURSES were taken. Any triple of values of type IDTPE, SEMTPE, YRTPE can be used to represent a particular COURSES ta-

SYSTEM		
REGISTRAR	STUD INFO	CATALOGUE

STUDINFO			
ID #	STUDNAME	BIRTHDATE	DATEADM
123456789	SMITH ROBERT J.	APR 13 1961	SEPT 1 1970
361258823	JONES MARY T.	AUG 25 1960	FEB 1 1980

(a)

Figure 2.10 Part of a database structure M(Dcon) for V(Dcon).

REGISTRAR										
SEMESTER	YEAR	COURSE								
		DEPT	COURSE	SECTION						
				SEC #	INSTRUCT	LOCAT	TIMES	STUDENT		
								STUDID	STUDNAME	GRADE
FALL	1979	COURSE (e)COURSES):1)								
		ART	103	SECTION (e(SECTION):1)						
				001	BLUE	2100 ART BLDG	2-3 M W F	STUDENT (e(STUDENT):1)		
								123456789	SMITH ROBERT J.	B
		COMP SCI	103	SECTION (e(SECTION):2)						
				001	GREEN	2301 COMP CENTER	12-1 M W F	STUDENT (e(STUDENT):2)		
								123456789	SMITH ROBERT J.	B
		HIST	101	SECTION (e(SECTION):3)						
				001	YELLOW	3600 SOC SCI	8-9 M W F	STUDENT (e(STUDENT):3)		
								123456789	SMITH ROBERT J.	B
		MATH	103	SECTION (e(SECTION):4)						
				001	PINK	4102 SCI	9-12 M W F	STUDENT (e(STUDENT):4)		
								123456789	SMITH ROBERT J.	B
SPRING	1980									

(b)

Figure 2.10 *(cont. next page)*

<table>
<tr><td colspan="16">CATALOGUE</td></tr>
<tr><td rowspan="5">DEPT</td><td rowspan="5">COURSE #</td><td rowspan="5">TITLE</td><td rowspan="5">CREDITS</td><td rowspan="5">DESCR</td><td colspan="11">LINK</td></tr>
<tr><td colspan="11"></td></tr>
<tr><td rowspan="3">DEPT</td><td rowspan="3">COURSE #</td><td rowspan="3">TITLE</td><td rowspan="3">CREDITS</td><td rowspan="3">DESCR</td><td colspan="6">LINK</td></tr>
<tr><td colspan="6">CATALOGUE</td></tr>
<tr><td>DEPT</td><td>COURSE #</td><td>TITLE</td><td>CREDITS</td><td>DESCR</td><td>LINK</td></tr>
<tr><td rowspan="8">COMP SCI</td><td rowspan="8">412</td><td rowspan="8">DATABASE SYSTEMS</td><td rowspan="8">3</td><td rowspan="8">. . .</td><td colspan="11">LINK (e(LINK):1)</td></tr>
<tr><td colspan="11">CATALOGUE (e(CATALOGUE):2)</td></tr>
<tr><td rowspan="4">COMP SCI</td><td rowspan="4">210</td><td rowspan="4">DISCRETE STRUCTURES</td><td rowspan="4">3</td><td rowspan="4">. . .</td><td colspan="6">LINK (e(LINK):2)</td></tr>
<tr><td colspan="6">CATALOGUE (e(CATALOGUE):4)</td></tr>
<tr><td rowspan="2">COMP SCI</td><td rowspan="2">103</td><td rowspan="2">INTRO</td><td rowspan="2">3</td><td rowspan="2">. . .</td><td>LINK (e(LINK):3)</td></tr>
<tr><td></td></tr>
<tr><td rowspan="2">COMP SCI</td><td rowspan="2">250</td><td rowspan="2">DATA STRUCTURES</td><td rowspan="2">3</td><td rowspan="2">. . .</td><td colspan="6">LINK (e(LINK):4)</td></tr>
<tr><td colspan="6"></td></tr>
<tr><td rowspan="4">MATH</td><td rowspan="4">416</td><td rowspan="4">LOGIC</td><td rowspan="4">3</td><td rowspan="4">. . .</td><td colspan="11">LINK (e(LINK):5)</td></tr>
<tr><td colspan="11">CATALOGUE (e(CATALOGUE):3)</td></tr>
<tr><td rowspan="2">MATH</td><td rowspan="2">103</td><td rowspan="2">CALC</td><td rowspan="2">3</td><td rowspan="2">. . .</td><td colspan="6">LINK (e(LINK):6)</td></tr>
<tr><td colspan="6"></td></tr>
<tr><td rowspan="2">BIO</td><td rowspan="2">103</td><td rowspan="2">INTRO</td><td rowspan="2">3</td><td rowspan="2">. . .</td><td colspan="11">LINK (e(LINK):7)</td></tr>
<tr><td colspan="11"></td></tr>
</table>

```
I(Dext;Dcon): INTERPRETATION DEFINITION
  EXTERNAL VIEW IS V(Dext) = <S(Dext),L(Dext),C(Dext)>
  CONCEPTUAL VIEW IS V(Dcon) = <S(Dcon),L(Dcon),C(Dcon)>

CODING SECTION
  CODE FOR SIDTPE IS IDTPE;
  CODE FOR NAMTPE IS NAMTPE;
  CODE FOR DATPE  IS DATPE;
  CODE FOR SEMTPE IS SEMTPE;
  CODE FOR YRTPE  IS YRTPE;
  CODE FOR DEPTPE IS DEPTPE;
  CODE FOR CS#TPE IS CS#TPE;
  CODE FOR SEC#TPE IS SEC#TPE;
  CODE FOR TTLTPE IS TTLTPE;
  CODE FOR GRDTPE IS GRDTPE;
  CODE FOR CRDSTPE IS CRDSTPE;
  CODE FOR RECORD IS IDTPE;
  CODE FOR COURSES IS IDTPE,SEMTPE,YRTPE;

  DEFINING FORMULA SECTION

  PREDICATE: COURSES
  ARGUMENTS ARE:(STUDID:1,SEMESTER:1,YEAR:1;,DEPT:1;,
    COURSE#:1;,SEC#:1;,TITLE:1;,GRADE:1;,
    CREDITS:1;)
  IS DEFINED BY:(E)STUDNAME:1(E)BIRTHDATE:1,
    (E)DATEADM:1(E)COURSE:1(E)SECTION:1
    (E)INSTRUCT:1(E)LOCAT:1(E)TIMES:1(E)STUDENT:1
    (E)DESCR:1(E)LINK:1
    SYSTEM-REGISTRAR-COURSE-SECTION-STUDENT
     (SEMESTER:1,YEAR:1,COURSE:1,DEPT:1,COURSE#:1,SECTION:1,
     SEC#:1,INSTRUCT:1,LOCAT:1,TIMES:1,STUDENT:1,STUDID:1,
     STUDNAME:1,GRADE:1)
  & SYSTEM-CATALOGUE
    (DEPT:1,COURSE#:1,TITLE:1,CREDITS:1,DESCR:1,LINK:1)
  & SYSTEM-STUDINFO
    (STUDID:1,STUDNAME:1,BIRTHDATE:1,DATEADM:1)

  PREDICATE:RECORD
  ARGUMENTS ARE:(STUDID:1;,SEMESTER:1;,YEAR:1;,
    STUDID:1,SEMESTER:1,YEAR:1;)
  IS DEFINED BY:
    (E)STUDNAME:1(E)BIRTHDATE:1
    (E)DATEADM:1(E)DEPT:1(E)COURSE#:1
    (E)SEC#:1(E)GRADE:1(E)COURSE:1(E)SECTION:1
    (E)INSTRUCT:1(E)LOCAT:1(E)TIMES:1(E)STUDENT:1
    SYSTEM-REGISTRAR-COURSE-SECTION-STUDENT
      (SEMESTER:1,YEAR:1,COURSE:1,DEPT:1,COURSE#:1,SECTION:1,
      SEC#:1,INSTRUCT:1,LOCAT:1,TIMES:1,STUDENT:1,STUDID:1,
      STUDNAME:1,GRADE:1)
  & SYSTEM-STUDINFO
  (STUDID:1,STUDNAME:1,BIRTHDATE:1,DATEADM:1)
```

Figure 2.11 *(cont. next page)*

(continued)

```
PREDICATE:TRANSCRIPT
ARGUMENTS ARE: (STUDID:1;,STUDNAME:1;,BIRTHDATE:1;,
  DATEADM:1;,STUDID:1;)
IS DEFINED BY:
  SYSTEM-STUDINFO
  (STUDID:1,STUDNAME:1,BIRTHDATE:1,DATEADM:1)

PREDICATE:TRANSCRIPT-RECORD-COURSES
ARGUMENTS ARE: (STUDID:1;,STUDNAME:1;,BIRTHDATE:1,
  DATEADM:1;,STUDID:1;,SEMESTER:1,YEAR:1;,
  STUDID:1,SEMESTER:1,YEAR:1;,DEPT:1;,
  COURSE#:1;,SEC#:1;,TITLE:1;,GRADE:1;,
  CREDITS:1;)
IS DEFINED BY:(E)COURSE:1(E)SECTION:1
  (E)INSTRUCT:1(E)LOCAT:1(E)TIMES:1(E)STUDENT:1
  (E)LINK:1(E)DESCR:1
  SYSTEM-REGISTRAR-COURSE-SECTION-STUDENT
    (SEMESTER:1,YEAR:1,COURSE:1,DEPT:1,COURSE#:1,SECTION:1,
    SEC#:1,INSTRUCT:1,LOCAT:1,TIMES:1,STUDENT:1,STUDID:1,
    STUDNAME:1,GRADE:1)
& SYSTEM-CATALOGUE
    (DEPT:1,COURSE#:1,TITLE:1,CREDITS:1,DESCR:1,LINK:1)
& SYSTEM-STUDINFO
    (STUDID:1,STUDNAME:1,BIRTHDATE:1,DATEADM:1)

PREDICATE:TRANSCRIPT-RECORD
ARGUMENTS ARE: (STUDID:1;,STUDNAME:1;,BIRTHDATE:1,
  DATEADM:1;,STUDID:1;,SEMESTER:1,YEAR:1;,
  STUDID:1,SEMESTER:1,YEAR:1;)
IS DEFINED BY:
  (E)DEPT:1(E)COURSE#:1(E)SEC#:1(E)GRADE:1
  (E)CREDITS:1;)(E)COURSE:1(E)SECTION:1(E)INSTRUCT:1
  (E)LOCAT:1(E)TIMES:1(E)STUDENT:1
SYSTEM-REGISTRAR-COURSE-SECTION-STUDENT
    (SEMESTER:1,YEAR:1,COURSE:1,DEPT:1,COURSE#:1,SECTION:1,
    SEC#:1,INSTRUCT:1,LOCAT:1,TIMES:1,STUDENT:1,STUDID:1,
    STUDNAME:1,GRADE:1)
& SYSTEM-STUDINFO
    (STUDID:1,STUDNAME:1,BIRTHDATE:1,DATEADM:1)

PREDICATE: ≤
ARGUMENTS ARE:(YEAR:1;,YEAR:2;)
IS DEFINED BY: YEAR:1 ≤ YEAR:2

FUNCTION: TOTCREDITS
ARGUMENTS ARE: (ID#:1;,SEMESTER:1;,YEAR:1;,CREDITS:1;)
IS DEFINED BY: TOTALCREDITS(ID#:1,SEMESTER:1,
YEAR:1) = CREDITS:1

CONSTANT TRANSFORMATION SECTION
```

Figure 2.11 (*cont. next page*)

(continued)

```
PROC CODE(SIDTPE)(STUDID:1) RETURNS(ID#;);
.
.
.
END;

PROC DECODE(SIDTPE)(ID#:1;) RETURNS(STUDID:1);
.
.
.
END;
.
.
.
```

Figure 2.11 Interpretation I(Dext;Dcon) of view V(Dext) in V(Dcon).

ble. In the case of a triple where either the student with that id# is not in the database, or has not taken courses during that semester and year, the corresponding COURSES table will be empty. A similar discussion holds for codings for the RECORD table (IDTPE;). Since there is only one TRANSCRIPT table in V(Dext), no code for TRANSCRIPT is necessary.

2. Defining formula section

2.1. For each (T0,T1,...,Tn) row predicate R0(R1,...,Rn) of L(E) we provide a formula

Q(<R0;>, <R1;>,..., <Rn;>)

of L(C) called the *defining formula* of R0(R1,...,Rn). Here <Rj;> denotes some sequence of variables that range over the code for Tj. The idea is that a question about whether or not a row is in a table in L(E) reduces to questions about codes in L(C).

For example, consider the (COURSES, DEPTPE, CS#TPE, SEC#TPE, TTLTPE, GRDTPE, CRDSTPE) row predicate of L(Dext):

COURSES:1(DEPT:1,COURSE#:1,SEC#:1,TITLE:1,GRADE:1,CREDITS:1).

The defining formula for it in Figure 2.11 has arguments

(STUDID:1,SEMESTER:1,YEAR:1;,DEPT:1;,
COURSE#:1;,SEC#:1;,TITLE:1;,GRADE:1;,CREDITS:1;).

Notice how the variables of L(Dcon) correspond to the codes for the original variables in L(Dext). The defining formula for this row predicate in Figure 2.11 is

(E)STUDNAME:1...(E)LINK:1
SYSTEM-REGISTRAR-COURSE-SECTION-STUDENT

(SEMESTER:1,YEAR:1,COURSE:1,DEPT:1,COURSE#:1,SECTION:1,
SEC#:1,INSTRUCT:1,LOCAT:1,TIMES:1,STUDENT:1,STUDID:1,
STUDNAME:1,GRADE:1)
& SYSTEM-CATALOGUE
(DEPT:1,COURSE#:1,TITLE:1,CREDITS:1,DESCR:1,LINK:1)
& SYSTEM-STUDINFO
(STUDID:1,STUDNAME:1,BIRTHDATE:1,DATEADM:1).

The defining formulas for the row predicates RECORD:1( ) and TRANSCRIPT( ) are also given in Figure 2.11. Notice that since there is only one TRANSCRIPT table, its row predicate can also be regarded as a nonlogical predicate symbol.

2.2. For each (T1,...,Tn) predicate symbol p of L(E) we provide a formula

$$Q(<R1;>,\ldots,<Rn;>)$$

of L(C) called the *defining formula* of p. Here $<Rj;>$ denotes some sequence of variables which range over the code for Tj. The idea is that a question about p in L(E) is reduced to questions about codes in L(C).

The defining formula for the (SIDTPE, NAMTPE, DATPE, DATPE, RECORD, SEMTPE, YRTPE, COURSES, DEPTPE, CS#TPE, SEC#TPE, TTLTPE, GRDTPE, CRDSTPE) predicate symbol TRANSCRIPT-RECORD-COURSES of L(Dext) is given in Figure 2.11. How the defining formulas for the subcluster TRANSCRIPT-RECORD and TRANSCRIPT are obtained from this will be explained below. The defining formula for the (YRTPE,YRTPE) predicate symbol $\leq$ in Figure 2.11 should be clear to the reader.

The defining formulas for equality depend on whether the type Tj is zero- or higher-order. This holds for any interpretation between database languages. If Tj is zero-order, the defining formula is equality for its code. This is identical to the pure relational situation in Section 2.1. If Tj is higher-order, we are dealing with "sets" and the defining formula is a bit more complex.

To illustrate, recall the defining formula for the row predicate COURSES:1(-) given in Figure 2.11. Denote it by

DEF(COURSES)(STUDID:1,SEMESTER:1,YEAR:1;,DEPT:1;,
COURSE#:1;,SEC#:1;,TITLE:1;,GRADE:1;,CREDITS:1;).

The defining formula for =(COURSES) has arguments

(STUDID:1,SEMESTER:1,YEAR:1;,
STUDID:2,SEMESTER:2,YEAR:2;).

This is because each argument represents a code for a COURSE table in L(Dext). The defining formula for =(COURSES) is

DEF(COURSES)(STUDID:1,SEMESTER:1,YEAR:1;,DEPT:1;,
COURSE#:1;,SEC#:1;,TITLE:1;,GRADE:1;,CREDITS:1;).

↔ DEF(COURSES)(STUDID:2,SEMESTER:2,YEAR:2;,DEPT:1;,
COURSE#:1;,SEC#:1;,TITLE:1;,GRADE:1;,CREDITS:1;).

That is, two COURSES tables are equal if and only if they have the same set of rows.

Similar comments hold for the defining formulas for =(RECORD). Notice that since there is only one TRANSCRIPT table, there is no need for =(TRANSCRIPT) or its defining formula.

2.3. For each (T1,...,Tn;T0) function symbol f of L(E), we provide a formula

Q(< R1; > ,..., < Rn; > ; < R0; >)

of L(C) called the *defining formula* of f . Here < Rj; > denotes some sequence of variables which range over the code for Tj. The idea is that a question about f in L(E) is reduced to questions about codes in L(C).

For example, in Figure 2.11 the defining formula for the (ID#TPE, SEMTPE, YRTPE; CRDSTPE) function symbol TOTCREDITS of L(Dext) has arguments

(STUDID:1;,SEMESTER:1;,YEAR:1;;CREDITS:1;)

and has defining formula

TOTALCREDITS(STUDID:1,SEMESTER:1,YEAR:1) = CREDITS:1.

3. Constant transformation section. For each type Tj of L(E) and code < Tj; > of L(C) we have a procedure CODE(Tj)(-) which inputs a Tj constant e(Tj):i and returns the sequence of constants < e(Tj):i; > , which forms its code. Also, for each type Tj of L(E) and code < Tj; > of L(C), we have a procedure DECODE(Tj)(-) which inputs a sequence of constants < e(Tj):i; > , which is a code, and returns the constant e(Tj):i in L(E) coded by the sequence. In other words, CODE(Tj)(-) and DECODE(Tj)(-) are inverse mappings.

For example, in the interpretation of Figure 2.11, CODE(SIDTPE)(-) returns for an input EBCDIC DEC(9) string, the corresponding ASCII DEC(9) string. Similarly, DECODE(NAMTPE)(-) returns for an input ASCII CHAR(20) string the corresponding EBCDIC CHAR(20) string.

The CODE, DECODE mappings also convert constants coding higher-order tables. For example, the name of Robert J. Smith's COURSES table for fall 1979 is e(COURSES):1. Its code would be the triple 123456789, FALL, 1979;. Thus, the value of

CODE(COURSE)("e(COURSES):1")
= "123456789,FALL,1979;."

Conversely, the value of

DECODE(COURSE)("123456789,FALL,1979;")
= "e(COURSES):1."

The values of the CODE(Tj)(-) and DECODE(Tj)(-) procedures may be obtained by either computation or table look-up. If the constants at both levels are identical (e.g., both ASCII or EBCDIC), the procedures represent the identity map.

Cluster Interpretations

An interpretation (e.g., Figure 2.11) contains defining formulas for row predicates and cluster predicates. A *cluster* interpretation (e.g., Figure 2.12) contains defining formulas for clusters but none for row predicates. From a cluster interpretation, we can get defining formulas for row and subcluster predicates. This is explained below.

Cluster TRANSCRIPT-RECORD-COURSES has "subparts" that are the subcluster TRANSCRIPT-RECORD and the atomic predicates TRANSCRIPT, RECORD, and COURSES. A defining formula for a subpart is obtained from the defining formula of the cluster in two steps. First, we keep only those free variables that are used in the subpart and existentially quantify those that are not. Second, we remove irrelevant predicates and quantification. That is, we remove predicates that do not use any free variables of the subpart and are not above (in a data structure) any predicates that are not removable. We also omit no-longer-used quantification.

As an example, the defining formula for the atomic predicate COURSES may be obtained from the defining formula for cluster TRANSCRIPT-RECORD-COURSES. Following the first step, we have

```
PREDICATE:COURSES
ARGUMENTS ARE: (STUDID:1,SEMESTER:1,YEAR:1;,DEPT:1;,
    COURSE#:1;,SEC#:1;,TITLE:1;,GRADE:1;,CREDITS:1;)
IS DEFINED BY:
   (E)STUDNAME:1(E)BIRTHDATE:1 (E)DATEADM:1(E)COURSE:1
   (E)SECTION:1(E)INSTRUCT:1(E)LOCAT:1(E)TIMES:1(E)STUDENT:1
   (E)LINK:1(E)DESCR:1
SYSTEM-REGISTRAR-COURSE-SECTION-STUDENT
   (SEMESTER:1,YEAR:1,COURSE:1,DEPT:1,COURSE#:1,SECTION:1,
   SEC#:1,INSTRUCT:1,LOCAT:1,TIMES:1,STUDENT:1,STUDID:1,
   STUDNAME:1,GRADE:1)
& SYSTEM-CATALOGUE
     (DEPT:1,COURSE#:1,TITLE:1,CREDITS:1,DESCR:1,LINK:1)
& SYSTEM-STUDINFO
     (STUDID:1,STUDNAME:1,BIRTHDATE:1,DATEADM:1)
```

The variables used for COURSES are STUDID:1, SEMESTER:1, and YEAR:1;, for the code for the COURSES table and DEPT:1;, COURSE#:1;, SEC#:1;, TITLE:1;, GRADE:1;, and CREDITS:1;, which codes the row. All the other variables are existentially quantified within the actual formula. In this illustration there are no removals from the defining formula since all the free variables are used in all the clusters in the definition.

```
I(Dext;Dcon): INTERPRETATION DEFINITION
  EXTERNAL VIEW IS V(Dext) = <S(Dext),L(Dext),C(Dext)>
  CONCEPTUAL VIEW IS V(Dcon) = <S(Dcon),L(Dcon),C(Dcon)>

  CODING SECTION
    CODE FOR SIDTPE IS IDTPE;
    CODE FOR NAMTPE IS NAMTPE;
    CODE FOR DATPE  IS DATPE;
    CODE FOR SEMTPE IS SEMTPE;
    CODE FOR YRTPE  IS YRTPE;
    CODE FOR DEPTPE IS DEPTPE;
    CODE FOR CS#TPE IS CS#TPE;
    CODE FOR SEC#TPE IS SEC#TPE;
    CODE FOR TTLTPE IS TTLTPE;
    CODE FOR GRDTPE IS GRDTPE;
    CODE FOR CRDSTPE IS CRDSTPE;
    CODE FOR RECORD IS IDTPE;
    CODE FOR COURSES IS IDTPE,SEMTPE,YRTPE;

  DEFINING FORMULA SECTION

  PREDICATE:TRANSCRIPT-RECORD-COURSES
  ARGUMENTS ARE: (STUDID:1;,STUDNAME:1;,BIRTHDATE:1;,
    DATEADM:1;,STUDID:1;,SEMESTER:1,YEAR:1;,
    STUDID:1,SEMESTER:1,YEAR:1;,DEPT:1;,
    COURSE#:1;,SEC#:1;,TITLE:1;,GRADE:1;,
    CREDITS:1;)
  IS DEFINED BY:(E)COURSE:1(E)SECTION:1
    (E)INSTRUCT:1(E)LOCAT:1(E)TIMES:1(E)STUDENT:1
    (E)LINK:1(E)DESCR:1
      SYSTEM-REGISTRAR-COURSE-SECTION-STUDENT
      (SEMESTER:1,YEAR:1,COURSE:1,DEPT:1,COURSE#:1,SECTION:1,
      SEC#:1,INSTRUCT:1,LOCAT:1,TIMES:1,STUDENT:1,STUDID:1,
      STUDNAME:1,GRADE:1)
    & SYSTEM-CATALOGUE
      (DEPT:1,COURSE#:1,TITLE:1,CREDITS:1,DESCR:1,LINK:1)
    & SYSTEM-STUDINFO
      (STUDID:1,STUDNAME:1,BIRTHDATE:1,DATEADM:1)

  PREDICATE:TRANSCRIPT
  ARGUMENTS ARE: (STUDID:1;,STUDNAME:1;,BIRTHDATE:1,
    DATEADM:1;,STUDID:1;)
  IS DEFINED BY:
    SYSTEM-STUDINFO
    (STUDID:1,STUDNAME:1,BIRTHDATE:1,DATEADM:1)

  PREDICATE: ≤
  ARGUMENTS ARE:(YEAR:1;,YEAR:2;)
  IS DEFINED BY: YEAR:1 ≤ YEAR:2
```

Figure 2.12 *(cont. next page)*

(continued)

```
FUNCTION: TOTCREDITS
ARGUMENTS ARE: (ID#:1;,SEMESTER:1;,YEAR:1;,CREDITS:1;)
IS DEFINED BY: TOTALCREDITS(ID#:1,SEMESTER:1,YEAR:1)
    = CREDITS:1

CONSTANT TRANSFORMATION SECTION

PROC CODE(SIDTPE)(STUDID:1) RETURNS(ID#1);
  .
  .
  .
  END;

PROC DECODE(SIDTPE)(ID#:1;) RETURNS(STUDID:1);
  .
  .
  .
  END;
  .
  .
  .
```

Figure 2.12 Cluster interpretation I(Dext;Dcon) of L(Dext) in L(Dcon).

As a second example, consider the subcluster TRANSCRIPT-RECORD. Following the first step we get

```
PREDICATE:TRANSCRIPT-RECORD
ARGUMENTS ARE: (STUDID:1;,STUDNAME:1;,BIRTHDATE:1;,
  DATEADM:1;,STUDID:1;,SEMESTER:1;,YEAR:1;,
  STUDID:1,SEMESTER:1,YEAR:1;)
IS DEFINED BY:
   (E)DEPT:1(E)COURSE#:1(E)SEC#:1(E)TITLE:1(E)GRADE:1
   (E)CREDITS:1(E)COURSE:1(E)SECTION:1(E)INSTRUCT:1
   (E)LOCAT:1(E)TIMES:1(E)STUDENT:1(E)LINK:1(E)DESCR:1
    SYSTEM-REGISTRAR-COURSE-SECTION-STUDENT
      (SEMESTER:1,YEAR:1,COURSE:1,DEPT:1,COURSE#:1,SECTION:1,
      SEC#:1,INSTRUCT:1,LOCAT:1,TIMES:1,STUDENT:1,STUDID:1,
      STUDNAME:1,GRADE:1)
 & SYSTEM-CATALOGUE (DEPT:1,COURSE#:1,TITLE:1,CREDITS:1)
 & SYSTEM-STUDINFO (STUDID:1,STUDNAME:1,BIRTHDATE:1)
```

Here the variables used are STUDID:1;, STUDNAME:1;, BIRTHDATE:1;, DATEADM:1;, STUDID:1;, SEMESTER:1;,YEAR:1;, and STUDID:1, SEMESTER:1, YEAR:1;. If we remove the irrelevant predicates and quantifications, we get

```
PREDICATE:TRANSCRIPT-RECORD
ARGUMENTS ARE: (STUDID:1;,STUDNAME:1;,BIRTHDATE:1,
  DATEADM:1;,STUDID:1;,SEMESTER:1,YEAR:1;,
  STUDID:1,SEMESTER:1,YEAR:1;)
```

```
 IS DEFINED BY:
(E)DEPT:1(E)COURSE#:1(E)SEC#:1(E)GRADE:1
(E)CREDITS:1;)(E)COURSE:1(E)SECTION:1(E)INSTRUCT:1
(E)LOCAT:1(E)TIMES:1(E)STUDENT:1
 SYSTEM-REGISTRAR-COURSE-SECTION-STUDENT
 (SEMESTER:1,YEAR:1,COURSE:1,DEPT:1,COURSE#:1,SECTION:1,
 SEC#:1,INSTRUCT:1,LOCAT:1,TIMES:1,STUDENT:1,STUDID:1,
 STUDNAME:1,GRADE:1)
& SYSTEM-STUDINFO
    (STUDID:1,STUDNAME:1,BIRTHDATE:1,DATEADM:1).
```

In this case we removed the cluster SYSTEM-CATALOGUE since all the variables DEPT:1, COURSE#:1, TITLE:1, CREDITS:1, DESCR:1, and LINK:1 in the predicate are existentially quantified.

As a third example, consider the subcluster TRANSCRIPT. Following the first step, we get

```
PREDICATE:TRANSCRIPT
ARGUMENTS ARE: (STUDID:1;,STUDNAME:1;,BIRTHDATE:1;,
  DATEADM:1;,STUDID:1;)
IS DEFINED BY:
  (E)SEMESTER:1(E)YEAR:1(E)DEPT:1(E)COURSE#:1
  (E)SEC#:1(E)TITLE:1(E)GRADE:1(E)CREDITS:1;)
  (E)COURSE:1(E)SECTION:1(E)INSTRUCT:1(E)LOCAT:1
  (E)TIMES:1(E)STUDENT:1(E)LINK:1(E)DESCR:1
   SYSTEM-REGISTRAR-COURSE-SECTION-STUDENT
       (SEMESTER:1,YEAR:1,COURSE:1,DEPT:1,COURSE#:1,SECTION:1,
       SEC#:1,INSTRUCT:1,LOCAT:1,TIMES:1,STUDENT:1,STUDID:1,
       STUDNAME:1,GRADE:1)
       (DEPT:1,COURSE#:1,TITLE:1,CREDITS:1,DESCR:1,LINK:1)
& SYSTEM-STUDINFO
    (STUDID:1,STUDNAME:1,BIRTHDATE:1,DATEADM:1) .
```

Here the variables used are STUDID:1, STUDNAME:1, BIRTHDATE:1, and DATEADM:1. If we remove the irrelevant predicates and quantifications, we get

```
PREDICATE:TRANSCRIPT
ARGUMENTS ARE: (STUDID:1;,STUDNAME:1;,BIRTHDATE:1;,
  DATEADM:1;,STUDID:1;)
IS DEFINED BY:
  (E)SEMESTER:1(E)YEAR:1(E)DEPT:1(E)COURSE#:1
  (E)SEC#:1(E)GRADE:1(E)COURSE:1(E)SECTION:1
  (E)INSTRUCT:1(E)LOCAT:1(E)TIMES:1(E)STUDENT:1
  SYSTEM-REGISTRAR-COURSE-SECTION-STUDENT
    (SEMESTER:1,YEAR:1,COURSE:1,DEPT:1,COURSE#:1,SECTION:1,
      SEC#:1,INSTRUCT:1,LOCAT:1,TIMES:1,STUDENT:1,STUDID:1,
      STUDNAME:1,GRADE:1)
& SYSTEM-STUDINFO
    (STUDID:1,STUDNAME:1,BIRTHDATE:1,DATEADM:1) .
```

This would be what the algorithm above yields from the definition of TRANSCRIPT-RECORD-COURSES. However, if we wanted another definition for TRANSCRIPT, namely,

PREDICATE:TRANSCRIPT
ARGUMENTS ARE: (STUDID:1;,STUDNAME:1;,BIRTHDATE:1,
  DATEADM:1;,STUDID:1;)
IS DEFINED BY:
    SYSTEM-STUDINFO
    (STUDID:1,STUDNAME:1,BIRTHDATE:1,DATEADM:1) ,

then we have to include this in our interpretation definition. This is, in fact, what we do in Figures 2.11 and 2.12.

The reader can also check that the interpretation obtained from the cluster interpretation in Figure 2.12 is the interpretation in Figure 2.11. We will refer to both of these as I″.

It is easy to see that in the relational case, the two notions of interpretation coincide. Throughout the remainder of this book all our interpretations, relational and heterogeneous, are expressed as cluster interpretations. In the heterogeneous case, we will leave it to the reader to make the necessary changes to obtain defining formulas for subclusters and row predicates.

Two Mappings

The above comprises the definition of an interpretation I of database language L(E) in database language L(C). As a result, we have an automatic means of translating any wff Q of the language L(E) into a wff I(Q) of the language L(C), called the *interpretation of* Q *in* L(E) *via* I. Essentially, replace variables and constants by their codes and predicates and functions by their defining formulas. Formal details of the translation process are given in Chapter 3.

For example, recall the third constraint of V(Dext) of Figure 1.8.

C(Dext,3)
= TRANSCRIPT-RECORD-COURSES:
  STUDID,SEMESTER,YEAR,DEPT,COURSE#
    → SEC#,TITLE,GRADE,CREDITS
= TRANSCRIPT-RECORD-COURSES(STUDID:1,STUDNAME:1,
    BIRTHDATE:1,DATEADM:1,RECORD:1,SEMESTER:1,YEAR:1,
    COURSES:1,DEPT:1,COURSE#:1,SEC#:1,TITLE:1,GRADE:1,
    CREDITS:1)
& TRANSCRIPT-RECORD-COURSES(STUDID:1,STUDNAME:2,
    BIRTHDATE:2,DATEADM:2,RECORD:2,SEMESTER:1,YEAR:1,
    COURSES:2,DEPT:1,COURSE#:1,SEC#:2,TITLE:2,GRADE:2,
    CREDITS:2)
→ (SEC#:1 = SEC#:2 & TITLE:1 = TITLE:2
& GRADE:1 = GRADE:2 & CREDITS:1 = CREDITS:2).

The interpretation of C(Dext,3) in L(Dcon) via I″, with variables renamed, is

```
( (E)COURSE:1(E)SECTION:1...(E)DESCR:1
  SYSTEM-REGISTRAR-COURSE-SECTION-STUDENT
    (SEMESTER:1,YEAR:1,COURSE:1,DEPT:1,COURSE#:1,
    SECTION:1,SEC#:1,INSTRUCT:1,LOCAT:1,TIMES:1,
    STUDENT:1,STUDID:1,STUDNAME:1,GRADE:1)
& SYSTEM-CATALOGUE
    (DEPT:1,COURSE#:1,TITLE:1,CREDITS:1,DESCR:1, LINK:1)
& SYSTEM-STUDINFO
    (STUDID:1,STUDNAME:1,BIRTHDATE:1,DATEADM:1))
& ( (E)COURSE:2(E)SECTION:2...(E)DESCR:2
  SYSTEM-REGISTRAR-COURSE-SECTION-STUDENT
    (SEMESTER:1,YEAR:1,COURSE:2,DEPT:1,COURSE#:1,
    SECTION:2,SEC#:2,INSTRUCT:2,LOCAT:2,TIMES:2,
    STUDENT:2,STUDID:1,STUDNAME:2,GRADE:2)
& SYSTEM-CATALOGUE
    (DEPT:1,COURSE#:1,TITLE:2,CREDITS:2,DESCR:2,
    LINK:2)
& SYSTEM-STUDINFO
    (STUDID:1,STUDNAME:2,BIRTHDATE:2,DATEADM:2))
→ (SEC#:1 = SEC#:2 & TITLE:1 = TITLE:2
& GRADE:1 = GRADE:2 & CREDITS:1 = CREDITS:2)
```

As a second consequence of the interpretation I, we have a mapping of any database structure M of L(C) into a database structure I[M] of L(E) called the *database structure induced from* M *via* I. For example, consider the defining formula for TRANSCRIPT-RECORD-COURSES discussed above. We can regard this as saying that the TRANSCRIPT-RECORD-COURSES cluster coded by

```
(STUDID:1;,STUDNAME:1;,BIRTHDATE:1;,DATEADM:1;,STUDID:1;,
SEMESTER:1,YEAR:1;,STUDID:1,SEMESTER:1,YEAR:1;,DEPT:1;,
COURSE#:1;,SEC#:1;,TITLE:1;,GRADE:1;,CREDITS:1;)
```

holds when the right-hand side of the defining formula for TRANSCRIPT-RECORD-COURSES is true in M(Dcon). Thus, a database structure M(C) together with I(E;C) "induces" a database structure for L(E). Precise details of this process are given in Chapter 3.

As an illustration consider the database structure M(Dcon) in Figure 2.10. The database structure I″[M(Dcon)] induced by M(Dcon) via I″ is given in Figure 2.13. Notice that every object in the induced structure is named by some code from the database structure M(Dcon).

External users see the database along the lines of some external database view V(E). Given a fixed instance of the conceptual database M(C), the database structure I(E;C)[M(C)] induced from the conceptual database M(C) and the interpretation I(E;C) is (modulo the change in codes) the user's external database.

TRANSCRIPT											
				RECORD							
						COURSES					
TUDID	STUDNAME	BIRTHDATE	DATEADM	SEMESTER	YEAR	DEPT	COURSE #	SEC #	TITLE	GRADE	CREDITS
				RECORD[CODE(e(RECORD):1) = 123456789;]							
						COURSES[CODE(e(COURSES):1 = 123456789, FALL, 1979;]					
456789 (456789;)	SMITH ROBERT J. (SMITH ROBERT J.;)	APRIL 13 1961 (APRIL 13 1961;)	SEPT 1 1979 (SEPT 1 1979;)	FALL (FALL;)	1979 (1979;)	COMPSCI (COMPSCI;)	103 (103;)	001 (001;)	INTRO (INTRO;)	B (B;)	3 (3;)
						MATH (MATH;)	103 (103;)	001 (001;)	CALC (CALC;)	B (B;)	3 (3;)
						ART (ART;)	101 (101;)	001 (001;)	INTRO (INTRO;)	B (B;)	3 (3;)
						HIST (HIST;)	101 (101;)	001 (00l;)	AM HIST (AM HIST;)	B (B;)	3 (3);
						COURSES[CODE(e(COURSES):2) = 123456789, SPRING, 1980;]					
				SPRING (SPRING;)	1980 (1980;)	COMPSCI (COMPSCI;)	220 (220;)	001 (001;)	DISCR STRUCT (DISCR STRUCT;)	B (B;)	3 (3;)
						MATH (MATH;)	104 (104;)	001 (001;)	CALC (CALC;)	B (B;)	3 (3;)
						ECON (ECON;)	101 (101;)	001 (001;)	INTRO (INTRO;)	C (C;)	3 (3;)
						ENG (ENG;)	105 (105;)	001 (001;)	COMPOS (COMPOS;)	A (A;)	3 (3;)
				RECORD[CODE(e(RECORD):2) = 361258823;]							
						COURSES[CODE(e(COURSES):3) = 361258823,SPRING, 1980;]					
258823 (258823;)	JONES MARY T. (JONES MARY T.;)	AUG 25 1960 (AUG 25 1960;)	FEB 1 1980 (FEB 1 1980;)	SPRING (SPRING;)	1980 (1980;)	MATH (MATH;)	104 (104;)	001 (001;)	CALC (CALC;)	A (A;)	4 (4;)
						ECON (ECON;)	101 (101;)	001 (001;)	INTRO (INTRO;)	C (C;)	3 (3;)
						PHYSICS (PHYSICS:)	102 (102;)	001 (001;)	INTRO (INTRO;)	D (D;)	4 (4;)
						ENG (ENG;)	105 (105;)	001 (101;)	COMPOS (COMPOS;)	D (D;)	3 (3;)

Figure 2.13 Induced database structure I(Dext;Dcon)[M(Dcon)].

Theorem 2.2.1. *Let* L(E) *and* L(C) *be two database languages. Let* I *be an interpretation of* L(E) *in* L(C). *Then for any database structure* M(C) *for* L(C) *and any wff* Q *of* L(E)

$$I[M(C)] \models Q \quad \text{iff} \quad M(C) \models I(Q).$$

Flipper Theorem 2.2.1 tells us that the wffs of L(E) that are true in an induced database structure are precisely those whose interpretations are true in the inducing database structure. Theorem 2.2.1 is an obvious generalization to the heterogeneous case of Theorem 2.1.1. The proof of Theorem 2.2.1 is given in Chapter 3.

View Interpretations

Let M(C) be a database structure for L(C) which satisfies the constraints C(C) of view V(C) and let I be an interpretation of L(E) in L(C). Although I and M(C) induce a hidden external database structure I[M(C)] for L(E), it might not be the case that I[M(C)] satisfies the constraints C(E) of the view V(E). It may also happen that for **no** database structure M(C) for L(C) does **any** induced I[M(C)] satisfy the constraints in C(E). To eliminate these difficulties, we define the notion of a "view interpretation."

Let X and Y be sets of wffs in some database language L. We say that X *logically implies* Y *in* L if for every database structure M of L, if M is a model of X, then M is also a model of Y. We also say that Y is a *logical consequence of* X *in* L. As a special case, if Y is the singleton set {Q}, then we say that X *logically implies* Q *in* L.

For example, recall interpretation I″(C(Dext,3)) above. The reader can check that I″(C(Dext,3)) is a logical consequence of the set of wffs

$$\{C(Dcon,4), C(Dcon,6), C(Dcon,7)\}.$$

This is because C(Dcon,6) is used to establish that TITLE:1 = TITLE:2 and CREDITS:1 = CREDITS:2. C(Dcon,7) is used to get SEC#:1 = SEC#:2. Then C(Dcon,4) can be used to establish that GRADE:1 = GRADE:2.

Let $V(E) = \langle S(E),L(E),C(E) \rangle$ and $V(C) = \langle S(C),L(C),C(C) \rangle$ be two database views. Let I be an interpretation of L(E) in L(C). By I(C(E)) we mean the set of wffs obtained by interpreting all the wffs of C(E).

Definition. I is an *interpretation of view* V(E) *in view* V(C) if I(C(E)) is a logical consequence of the set of wffs C(C) in L(C).

From the above, I″(C(Dext,3)) is a logical consequence of C(Dcon). In Exercises 1 and 2, the reader is asked to show that I″(C(Dext,1)) and I″(C(Dext,2)) are also logical consequences of C(Dcon).

Theorem 2.2.2. *Let* V(E) *and* V(C) *be any two database views and let I be an interpretation of view* V(E) *in view* V(C). *Then for any database structure* M(C) *for* L(C),

$$M(C) \models C(C) \text{ implies } I[M(C)] \models C(E).$$

In other words, if I is an interpretation of V(E) in V(C) and M(C) is any model of C(C), then the induced database I[M(C)] is a model of V(E).

Proof. Similar to the proof of Theorem 2.1.2.

This result also has significance in the case where there are many heterogeneous external views supported by a single conceptual view. The situation here is analogous to the one discussed in Section 2.1.

Operation Simulators

Recall from Section 1.3 that operation INSERT(COURSES)(W) on view V(Dext) adds to the COURSES tables of a database structure M(Dext) the rows given in the array W as long as the constraints C(Dext) are not violated. If V(Dext) were an external view, the insertion is to take place on the external database I″ [M(Dcon)]. Since the external database does not exist, the insertion has to be simulated on the conceptual database. A program that simulates such an operation on the conceptual database is called a *simulator.*

For example, a simulator for the INSERT(COURSES)(W) operation is the program SIM(INSERT(COURSES))(CODE(W)) given in Figure 2.14. The inputs to the program are the "codes" for the inputs to the names in W. The execution of the simulator SIM(INSERT(COURSES)) works as follows.

First, a "checkpoint" is made just prior to the beginning of the execution. This is done so that in the case the simulation has to be canceled [e.g., insertions violate the conceptual constraints C(Dcon)], the database can be "rolled back" to its status just prior to the execution of this simulation.

Next, for each row of the input, insertions are done into the conceptual database. The insertions are done so that the defining formula of the row predicate for COURSES in the interpretation I″ becomes "true" in the conceptual database. By Theorem 2.2.1, this will automatically make the row appear in the COURSES tables

Figure 2.14

```
PROC SIM(INSERT(COURSES))(CW);
  /* CW is a an array of codes where:
     CW(i).COURSES.STUDID
                  = an ASCII DEC(9) value (IDTPE),
     CW(i).COURSES.SEMESTER
                  = an ASCII CHAR(8) value (SEMTPE)
     CW(i).COURSES.YEAR
                  = an ASCII DEC(4) value (YRTPE)
     CW(i).COURSES = a COURSES code

     CW(i).DEPT = a  DEPTPE code
                  = an ASCII CHAR(10) value (DEPTPE;),
     CW(i).COURSE# = a CS#TPE code
                  = an ASCII CHAR(3) value (CS#TPE;),
     CW(i).SEC#    = a SEC# code
                  = an ASCII DEC(3) value (SEC#;),
     CW(i).TITLE = a TTLTPE code
                  = an ASCII CHAR(25) value (TTLTPE;),
```

(cont. next page)

(continued)

```
     CW(i).GRADE    = a GRDTPE code
                    = an ASCII CHAR(1) value (GRDTPE;),
     CW(i).CREDITS= a CRDSTPE code
                    = an ASCII DEC(2) value (CRDSTPE;),
i = 1,...,length(CW) */

     ESTABLISH CHECKPOINT;
  /* If the simulation should fail [e.g., the resultant conceptual database is
not a model of C(Dcon)], we can use this checkpoint to reestablish the old database
instance.*/

     FOR i = 1 TO LENGTH(CW);

  /* For each row of CW perform the following operations.*/

  GET W (STUDENT:1,STUDNAME:1):
            (E)BIRTHDATE:1(E)DATEADM:1(E)COURSE:1
           (E)SECTION:1(E)INSTRUCT:1(E)LOCAT:1
           (E)TIMES:1(E)LINK:1(E)DESCR:1
        SYSTEM-REGISTRAR-COURSE-SECTION
           (CW(i).COURSES.SEMESTER,CW(i).COURSES.YEAR,COURSE:1,
           CW(i).DEPT,CW(i).COURSE#,SECTION:1,
           CW(i).SEC#,INSTRUCT:1,LOCAT:1,TIMES:1,STUDENT:1)
       & SYSTEM-CATALOGUE
           (CW(i).DEPT:1,CW(i).COURSE#,CW(i).TITLE,
           CW(i).CREDITS,DESCR:1,LINK:1)
       & SYSTEM-STUDINFO
           (CW(i).COURSES.STUDID,STUDNAME:1,BIRTHDATE:1,DATEADM:1)

  /* We look for a STUDENT table corresponding to the class in which the student is
     enrolled. We also find the name of the student. */


      IF LENGTH(W) = 0 THEN GO TO L1;

      INSERT(STUDENT)({(W(1).STUDENT,CW(i).COURSES.STUDID,
               W(1).STUDNAME,CW(i).GRADE)});

  /* If no such STUDENT table of NAME value is found, we go to L1 and restore the
old database instance. Otherwise, we insert a row into that STUDENT table.*/

      END i;
     IF M(Dcon) ⊨ C(Dcon) THEN RETURN;

L1: RESTORE TO LAST CHECKPOINT;

  /* If the current conceptual database instance is a model of C(Dcon), then exit;
otherwise, we roll back to the instance of the conceptual database prior to execu-
tion.*/
     END SIM(INSERT(COURSES));
```

Figure 2.14 Operation simulator SIM(INSERT(COURSES)).

[coded by the first entries in the CODE(W) array] in the induced external database I″[M(Dcon)].

When all the simulations are completed for each of the rows in W, the simulator checks to see if the conceptual constraints still hold. If they do, SIM(INSERT-(COURSES)) exits; otherwise, it rolls back to the point just prior to execution and then exits.

Recall the execution of INSERT(COURSES)(W1) of Example 1.3.2 when W1 was the array

$$\{(e(COURSES){:}1,BIO,103,101,INTRO,B,3)\}.$$

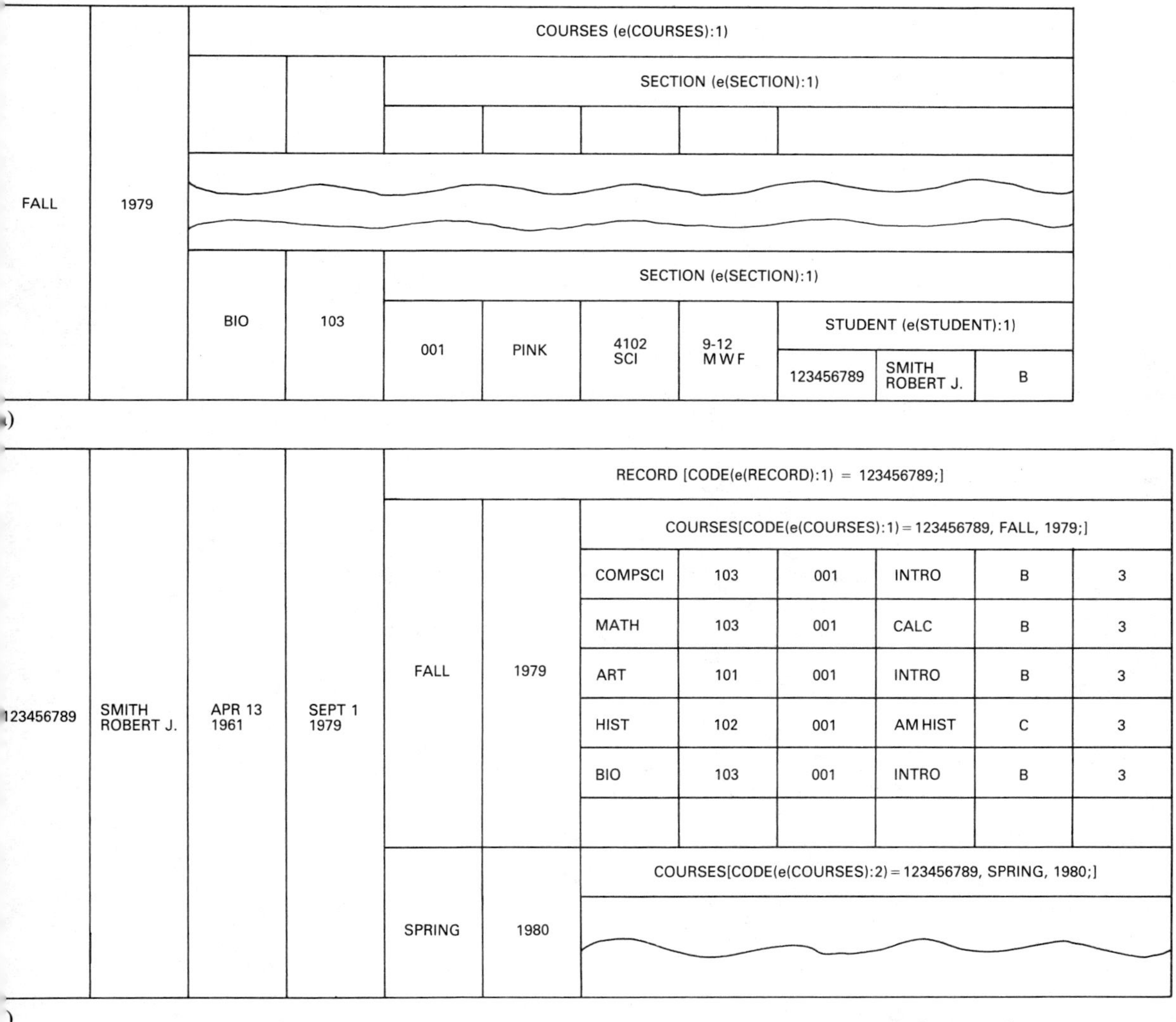

Figure 2.15 Effects of simulator SIM(INSERT(COURSES)): (a) on M(Dcon); (b) I″[M(Dcon)].

The array CODE(W1) is the same as W1 except that the atomic values are now ASCII instead of EBCDIC and the first component is "123456789,FALL,1979;", the code for the COURSES table e(COURSES):1. The effect of the execution of SIM(INSERT(COURSES))(CODE(W1)) on the database structure M(Dcon) of Figure 2.10 is given in Figure 2.15(a). The effect of the execution of SIM(INSERT(COURSES-))(CODE(W1)) on the induced external database I″[M(Dcon)] is given in Figure 2.15(b).

Simulators for deletion and updating are constructed in a way similar to that of SIM(INSERT(COURSE)) except that in the case of deletion the simulator makes the defining formula "false" and in the case of update the simulator makes half the input row "false" and the other half "true." In Chapters 4 and 5 simulator correctness is investigated in detail.

Exercises

1. Find the interpretation of C(Dext,1) via I″. Show that it is a logical consequence of the set C(Dcon) in L(Con).
2. Find the interpretation of C(Dext,2) via I″. Show that it is a logical consequence of C(Dcon) in L(Con).
3. What would be the effect of the execution of the simulator SIM(INSERT(COURSES)) of Figure 2.14 on M(Dcon) of Figure 2.10 and I″[M(Dcon)] of Figure 2.12 when CODE(W) is the set

{(123456789,FALL,1979;,MATH;,103;,001;,LOGIC;,B;,3;)}.

The following problems refer to V(Dext′) of Figure 2.16 and V(Dcon) of Figure 2.9.

```
V(Dext′): VIEW DEFINITION
  S(Dext′): SCHEMA DEFINITION
      TABLE TRANSCRIPT = (STUDID,STUDNAME,BIRTHDATE,DATEADM,RECORD)
      TABLE RECORD = (SEMESTER,YEAR,COURSES)
      TABLE COURSES = DEPT,COURSE#,SEC#,TITLE,GRADE,CREDITS)
      TABLE SCHEDULE = (SEMESTER,YEAR,DEPTSCHED)
      TABLE DEPTSCHED = (DEPT,COURSE#,CLASSCHED)
      TABLE CLASSCHED = (SEC#,INSTRUCT,LOCAT,TIMES)
      TABLE CATALOGUE = (DEPT,COURSE#,TITLE,CREDITS,DESCR,
                          LINK)
      TABLE LINK = (CATALOGUE)

  L(Dext′): LANGUAGE DEFINITION
    T(Dext′): TYPING DEFINITION
      TYPE SIDTPE = {STUDID} EBCDIC CHAR(9)
      TYPE NAMTPE = {STUDNAME,INSTRUCT} EBCDIC CHAR(20)
      TYPE DATPE = {BIRTHDATE,DATEADM} EBCDIC CHAR(15)
      TYPE SEMTPE = {SEMESTER} EBCDIC CHAR(6)
      TYPE YRTPE = {YEAR} EBCDIC DEC(4)
      TYPE DEPTPE = {DEPT} EBCDIC CHAR(8)
      TYPE CS#TPE = {COURSE#} EBCDIC DEC(3)
      TYPE SEC#TPE = {SEC#} EBCDIC CHAR(10)
```

(cont. next page)

(continued)

```
    TYPE TTLTPE = {TITLE} EBCDIC CHAR(25)
    TYPE GRDTPE = {GRADE} EBCDIC CHAR(1)
    TYPE CRDSTPE = {CREDITS} EBCDIC DEC(2)
    TYPE DESTPE = {DESCR} EBCDIC CHAR(50)
    TYPE LOCTPE = {LOCAT} EBCDIC CHAR(30)
    TYPE TIMTPE = {TIMES} EBCDIC CHAR(20)

       NONLOGICAL SYMBOLS DEFINITION
        PREDICATES

        TRANSCRIPT-RECORD-COURSES:
        (SIDTPE,NAMTPE,DATPE,DATPE,RECORD,SEMTPE,
        YRTPE,COURSES,DEPTPE,CS#TPE,SEC#TPE,TTLTPE,
        GRDTPE,CRDSTPE) FULL CLUSTER PREDICATE

        SCHEDULE-DEPTSCHED-CLASSCHED:
        (SEMTPE,YRTPE,DEPTSCHED,DEPTPE,CS#TPE,CLASSCHED,
        SEC#TPE,NAMTPE,LOCTPE,TTLTPE,TIMTPE) FULL
        CLUSTER PREDICATE

       CATALOGUE-LINK-CATALOGUE:
       (DEPTPE,CS#TPE,TTLTPE,CRDSTPE,DESCTPE,LINK,
       CATALOGUE,DEPTPE,CS#TPE,TTLTPE,CRDSTPE,DESCTPE,
       LINK) FULL CLUSTER PREDICATE
    ≤: (YRTPE,YRTPE)-PREDICATE

       FUNCTIONS
        TOTCREDITS:(SIDTPE,SEMTPE,YRTPE;
        CRDSTPE) FUNCTION

C(Dext'): CONSTRAINTS DEFINITION
  C(Dext',1) CONSTRAINT TRANSCRIPT:
  STUDID → STUDNAME,BIRTHDATE,DATEADM,RECORD

  C(Dext',2):CONSTRAINT TRANSCRIPT-RECORD:
  STUDID,SEMESTER,YEAR → COURSES

  C(Dext',3):CONSTRAINT TRANSCRIPT-RECORD-COURSES:
  STUDID,SEMESTER,YEAR,DEPT,COURSE#
  → SEC#,TITLE,CREDITS,GRADE

  C(Dext',4):CONSTRAINT SCHEDULE:SEMESTER,YEAR → DEPTSCHED
  C(Dext',5):CONSTRAINT SCHEDULE-DEPTSCHED:
  SEMESTER,YEAR,DEPT,COURSE# → CLASSCHED

  C(Dext',6):CONSTRAINT SCHEDULE-DEPTSCHED-CLASSCHED:
  SEMESTER,YEAR,DEPT,COURSE#,SEC#
  → LOCAT,TITLE:1,TIME:1

  C(Dext',7):CONSTRAINT CATALOGUE:DEPT,COURSE#-
  → TITLE,CREDITS,DESCR,LINK
```

Figure 2.16 Database logic DDL view definition for V(Dext').

```
SCHEMA NAME IS CODREG.

RECORD NAME IS SYSTEM

RECORD NAME IS REGISTRAR
   DUPLICATES ARE NOT ALLOWED
   FOR SEMESTER,YEAR IN REGISTRAR.
    SEMESTER  ; TYPE IS ASCII CHAR(8).
    YEAR      ; TYPE IS ASCII DEC(4)
    DEPT      ; TYPE IS ASCII CHAR(10)
    COURSE#   ; TYPE IS ASCII DEC(3)
    SEC#      ; TYPE IS ASCII DEC(3)
    INSTRUCT  ; TYPE IS ASCII CHAR(20)
    LOCAT     ; TYPE IS ASCII CHAR(30)
    TIMES     ; TYPE IS ASCII CHAR(20)
    STUDID    ; TYPE IS ASCII DEC(9)
    GRADE     ; TYPE IS ASCII CHAR(1)

RECORD NAME IS SYIDINDEX
   DUPLICATES ARE NOT ALLOWED
   FOR STUDID,SEMESTER,YEAR IN SYSIDINDEX.
    STUDID    ; TYPE IS ASCII DEC(9)
    SEMESTER  ; TYPE IS ASCII CHAR(8).
    YEAR      ; TYPE IS ASCII DEC(4)

RECORD NAME IS SYDCSINDEX
   DUPLICATES ARE NOT ALLOWED
   FOR SEMESTER,YEAR,DEPT.COURSE#,SEC# IN SYDSCINDEX.
    SEMESTER  ; TYPE IS ASCII CHAR(8).
    YEAR      ; TYPE IS ASCII DEC(4)
    DEPT      ; TYPE IS ASCII CHAR(10)
    COURSE#   ; TYPE IS ASCII DEC(3)
    SEC#      ; TYPE IS ASCII DEC(3)

SET NAME IS SYSTEM-SYIDINDEX
    OWNER IS SYSTEM
    ORDER IS SORTED BY DEFINED KEYS
      DUPLICATES ARE NOT ALLOWED
    MEMBER IS SYIDINDEX
      INSERTION IS AUTOMATIC
      RETENTION IS FIXED
      KEY IS ASCENDING STUDID,SEMESTER,YEAR IN SYSIDINDEX.
      SET SELECTION IS BY SYSTEM

SET NAME IS SYSTEM-SYDSCINDEX
    OWNER IS SYSTEM
    ORDER IS SORTED BY DEFINED KEYS
      DUPLICATES ARE NOT ALLOWED
    MEMBER IS SYDSCINDEX
      INSERTION IS AUTOMATIC
      RETENTION IS FIXED
      KEY IS ASCENDING SEMESTER,YEAR,DEPT.COURSE#,SEC# SYDSCINDEX IN
    SET SELECTION IS BY SYSTEM
```

Figure 2.17 *(cont. next page)*

(continued)

```
SET NAME IS SYIDINDEX-REGISTRAR
    OWNER IS SYIDINDEX
    ORDER IS SORTED BY DEFINED KEYS
      DUPLICATES ARE NOT ALLOWED
    MEMBER IS REGISTRAR
      INSERTION IS MANUAL
      RETENTION IS OPTIONAL
      KEY IS ASCENDING SEMESTER,YEAR,DEPT,COURSE#,SEC#,
          STUDID IN REGISTRAR
    SET SELECTION IS BY APPLICATION

SET NAME IS SYDCSINDEX-REGISTRAR
    OWNER IS SYDCSINDEX
    ORDER IS SORTED BY DEFINED KEYS
      DUPLICATES ARE NOT ALLOWED
    MEMBER IS REGISTRAR
      INSERTION IS MANUAL
      RETENTION IS OPTIONAL
    KEY IS ASCENDING SEMESTER,YEAR,DEPT,COURSE#,SEC#,
      STUDID IN REGISTRAR
    SET SELECTION IS BY APPLICATION
```

Figure 2.17 CODASYL DDL definition for CODREG.

4. Construct a cluster interpretation I(Dcon;Dext′) of database language L(Dcon) in database language L(Dext′).
5. Use the cluster interpretation of Exercise 4 to construct the defining formula for the row predicates and subcluster predicates.
6. Find the interpretations of the constraints C(Dcon) under the interpretation I(Dcon;Dext′).
7. Determine which of the wffs of Exercise 6 are logical consequences of the wffs in C(Dext′).
8. Construct a simulator SIM(INSERT(STUDENT)) .

The following exercises refer to the CODASYL database CODREG in Figures 2.17 and 2.18.

9. Express the view definition V(CODREG) corresponding to the declaration in Figure 2.17 in a format similar to that of Figure 2.9. **Hint:** Use

SYSTEM-SYSINDEX-REGISTRAR-SYDCSINDEX

as the full cluster.

10. Draw a database structure for V(CODREG) corresponding to the instance of the database given in Figure 2.18.

2.3 AUTOMATIC PROGRAM CONVERSION

In this section we show how to make use of the constructions of Sections 2.1 and 2.2 to convert GCALC DML from the external level to the conceptual level. The method is comprised of two steps. The first step involves the transformation of queries (i.e.,

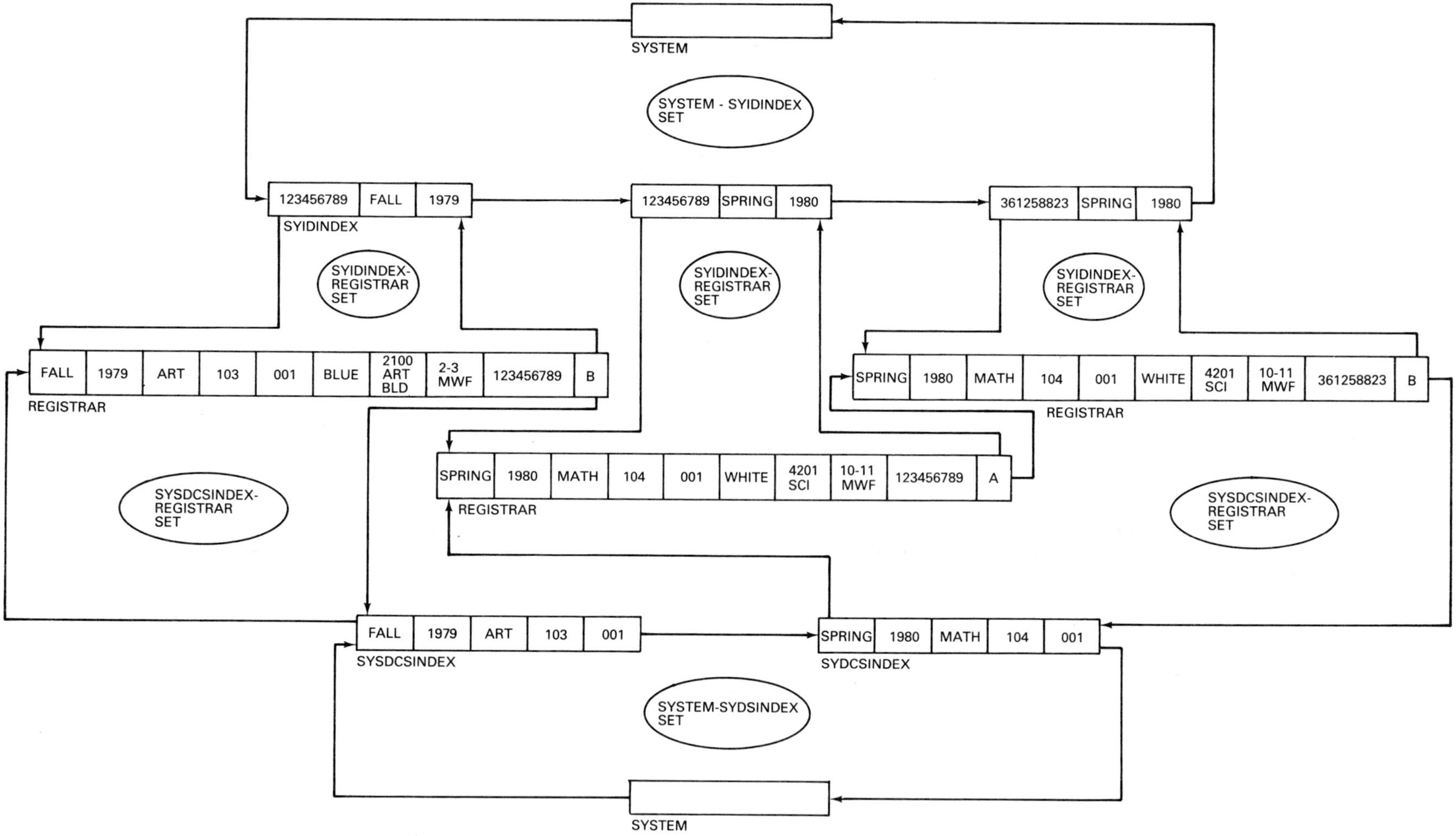

Figure 2.18 Instance of the network CODREG.

GET). The second concerns the transformation of INSERT, DELETE, and UPDATE operations. A discussion of query transformation correctness is given here, while a discusssion of correctness of the other operations is given in Chapters 4 and 5.

Let V(E) = <S(E),L(E),C(E)> and V(C) = <S(C),L(C),C(C)> represent, respectively, external and conceptual views of a database. Let ETC(E;C) = <I,SIM> be an external-to-conceptual mapping of view V(E) in V(C), where I is an interpretation of V(E) in V(C), and SIM a set of operation simulators.

Query Conversion

To transform queries from V(E) to V(C) replace all instructions of the form

(*) GET W (<R>): Q(<R>);

by

(**) GET W (DECODE(<R;>): I(Q(<R;>));

where <R;> are variables which are codes for the variables <R> and DECODE(<R;>) "decodes" the codes in <R;>. Furthermore, any constant symbol c in the wff Q is replaced in I(Q(<R;>)) by CODE(Ri)(c) (i.e., the "coding" of the constant c).

We remark that the resulting GET instruction is not strictly in the format described in Chapter 1, since it has the DECODE functions applied to the "target" or "output" variables <Ri;>. However, this means that after each set of satisfying constants is collected [i.e., { <c;> | M(C) ⊨ I(Q(<c;>)) }], it is immediately decoded into constants in L(E).

As an example, consider the query on V(Rext) given in Example 1.1.1:

```
GET W (STUDID:1,STUDNAME:1):
   (E)SEC#:1(E)TITLE:1(E)CREDITS:1
  TRANSCRIPT(STUDID:1,STUDNAME:1,FALL,1979,
     MATH,103,SEC#:1,TITLE:1,B,CREDITS:1);.
```

This query returns the id#'s and names of all students who earned the grade of B in Math 103 during the fall 1979 semester. The result of executing this query on the induced external database of Figure 2.4 is the placement of the set {(123456789, ROBERT J. SMITH)} into workspace W.

Now suppose that this instruction is transformed according to the process described above. Here we are using I′ of Figure 2.3. The result is

```
GET W (DECODE(SIDTPE)(STUDID:1;),
     DECODE(NAMTPE)(STUDNAME:1;)):
  (E)SEC#:1 ... (E)PRECOURSE#:1
  STUDENT(STUDID:1,STUDNAME:1,BIRTHDATE:1,DATEADM:1)
& REGISTRAR(FALL,1979,MATH,103,SEC#:1,INSTRUCT:1,
     LOCAT:1,TIMES:1,STUDID:1,B)
& CATALOGUE(MATH,103,TITLE:1,CREDITS:1,DESCR:1,
     PREDEPT:1,PRECOURSE:1);
```

The reader is invited to check that the result of executing the above on the database structure in Figure 2.2 is the placement of

```
{(123456789,SMITH ROBERT J.)}
  = {(DECODE(SIDTPE)(123456789;),
      DECODE(NAMTPE)(SMITH ROBERT J.;) )}
```

into workspace W. In the above, the top set contains EBCDIC strings and the bottom contains ASCII strings.

Remark. In addition to translating from the external language to the conceptual language, an optimization step is often needed. That is, after we have translated, we try to find a "smaller" but equivalent GCALC query. A last process called "logical optimization" is discussed further in Chapter 8.

As a second example, consider the query on V(Dext) given in Example 1.3.1.

```
GET W (STUDID:1,STUDNAME:1):
  (E)BIRTHDATE:1 ... (E)CREDITS:1
  TRANSCRIPT-RECORD-COURSES
    (STUDID:1,STUDNAME:1,BIRTHDATE:1,DATEADM:1,
    RECORD:1,FALL,1979,COURSE:1,MATH,103,SEC#:1,
    TITLE:1,B,CREDITS:1);
```

This is the same query as above, but it refers to the hierarchical view V(Dext). The effect of executing this instruction on the database structure I″[M(Dcon)] of Figure 2.13 is to place the set {(123456789, SMITH ROBERT J.)} into workspace W.

Now suppose that this instruction is transformed according to the process described above. Here we are using the interpretation I″ of Figure 2.11. The result is

```
GET W (DECODE(SIDTPE)(STUDID:1;),
      DECODE(NAMTPE)(STUDNAME:1;)):
    (E)BIRTHDATE:1 ... (E)LINK:1
    SYSTEM-REGISTRAR-COURSE-SECTION-STUDENT
      (FALL,1979,COURSE:1,MATH,103,SECTION:1,
      SEC#:1,INSTRUCT:1,LOCAT:1,TIMES:1,STUDENT:1,
      STUDID:1,STUDNAME:1,B)
  & SYSTEM-CATALOGUE:1
      (MATH,103,TITLE:1,CREDITS:1,DESCR:1,LINK:1)
  & SYSTEM-STUDINFO
      (STUDID:1,STUDNAME:1,BIRTHDATE:1,DATEADM:1).
```

The reader can check that the result of executing the above on the database structure in Figure 2.10 is also the placement of {(123456789, SMITH ROBERT J.)} into workspace W.

That these two transformed queries yield the same results on the conceptual structures (Figures 2.2 and 2.10, respectively) as the original queries did on the external structures (Figures 2.4 and 2.13, respectively) is no coincidence. Our transformation process generates instructions which **exactly** simulate the original queries. In other words, suppose that (*) is a query on database view V(E) and I[M(C)] is any induced or external database structure for V(E). Then the result of executing (*) on I[M(C)] gives precisely the same results as those of executing (**) on M(C). This result is a consequence of the Flipper Theorem and the facts that CODE( ) and DECODE( ) are (one-to-one, onto) inverses.

Update Conversion

To convert update operations from V(E) to V(C), we do the following. Replace all instructions of the form

```
(+) O(Ri)(W);
```

by

```
(+) SIM(O(Ri))(CODE(W));
```

where OP is in {INSERT,DELETE,UPDATE}, Ri is a table name in S(E), SIM(OP(Ri)) is a simulator for OP(Ri), and CODE(W) translates the constant symbols in W into their codes.

As an illustration, consider the operation on V(Rext) given in Example 1.1.2.

```
MOVE (123456789,SMITH ROBERT J.,FALL,1979,BIO,103,
      001,INTRO,B,3) TO W;
INSERT(TRANSCRIPT)(W);
```

The effect of these instructions is to insert the information that Robert J. Smith took Biology 103 during the fall 1979 semester and earned the grade of B in the TRANSCRIPT table.

The translation of the results above (note that non-DML instructions are left unchanged) is

```
MOVE (123456789,SMITH ROBERT J,FALL,1979,
      BIO,103,101,INTRO,B,3) TO W;
SIM(INSERT(TRANSCRIPT))(CODE(W));
```

where CODE(W) contains the row

```
(123456789;,SMITH ROBERT J.;,FALL;,
1979;,BIO;,103;,101;,INTRO;,B;,3;)
```

and SIM(INSERT(TRANSCRIPT)) is given in Figure 2.5. Suppose that these instructions are executed on the relational structure M(Rcon) of Figure 2.2. The effect of such was given in Figure 2.6(a). The effect on the induced external relational structure I'[M(Rcon)] was given in Figure 2.6(b).

As a second illustration, consider the operations of V(Dext) given in Example 1.3.2.

```
GET W (COURSES:1):
  (E)BIRTHDATE:1(E)DATEADM:1(E)RECORD:1
```

```
  TRANSCRIPT-RECORD(123456789,SMITH ROBERT J.,BIRTHDATE:1,
     DATEADM:1,RECORD:1,FALL,1979,COURSES:1);
IF LENGTH(W) ≠ 1 THEN GO TO ERROR-ROUTINE;
MOVE ({W(1).COURSES,BIO,103,101,INTRO,B,3}) TO W1;
INSERT(COURSES)(W1);
```

Recall that the effect of executing the GET instruction was to find Robert J. Smith's COURSES table for the fall 1979 semester. If no table name is returned, an error routine is called; otherwise, the row (BIO, 103, 101, INTRO, B, 3) is inserted into the COURSES table.

The translation of the GET instruction to V(Dcon) is

```
GET W (DECODE(COURSES)(123456789,FALL,1979;)):
  (E)BIRTHDATE:1 ... (E)LINK:1
  SYSTEM-REGISTRAR-COURSE-SECTION-STUDENT
   (FALL,1979,COURSE:1,DEPT:1,COURSE#:1,SECTION:1,
   SEC#:1,INSTRUCT:1,LOCAT:1,TIMES:1,STUDENT:1,
   123456789.SMITH ROBERT J.,GRADE:1)
& SYSTEM-STUDINFO
      (123456789,SMITH ROBERT J.,BIRTHDATE:1,DATEADM:1)
```

The reader can check that the results of executing the foregoing query on M(Dcon) of Figure 2.10 results in the placement of

e(COURSES):1 = DECODE(COURSES)(123456789,FALL,1979;)

into workspace W. Notice that this is the same result as the original query in the external database I″[M(Dcon)] of Figure 2.13.

The transformation of the fourth instruction is given by

SIM(INSERT(COURSES))(CODE(W1));

where SIM(INSERT(COURSES)) is given in Figure 2.14 and CODE(W1) contains the set

{(123456789,FALL,1979;,BIO;,103;,101;,INTRO;,B;,3;)}.

The effect of the above on the database structure M(Dcon) was given in Figure 2.15(a). The effect on the induced database structure I″[M(Dcon)] was seen in Figure 2.15(b).

As with queries, we would like to ensure that simulations of inserts, deletions, and updates on the conceptual view are correct. In Chapters 4 and 5, four formulations of correctness—weak, consistent, independent, and strong are defined and studied. It is seen that for some interpretations I and operations OP(Ri), OP in {INSERT, DELETE, UPDATE}, **no** simulator exists which is strongly correct.

Other DML Conversions

As mentioned at the end of Section 1.3, other more user-friendly DMLs can be defined in terms of GCALC. For example, generalized SQL (GSQL) and generalized

QBE (GQBE) operations can be converted into GCALC equivalents. Consequently, commands on the external view using these user-friendly DMLs can be tranformed into commands at the conceptual view by first converting to GCALC and then performing the external-to-conceptual transformation as prescribed in this section.

For example, recall the GSQL query on the view V(Dext) for Example 1.3.1:

```
SET INTO W
 SELECT UNIQUE STUDID,STUDNAME
 FROM TRANSCRIPT-RECORD-COURSES
 WHERE SEMESTER = FALL
     AND YEAR = 1979
     AND DEPT = MATH
     AND COURSE# = 103
     AND GRADE = B;
```

The GCALC equivalent of this was given above in the second example of query transformation. Its conversion to view V(Dcon) is then the conversion of the GCALC equivalent also given above.

Exercises

Convert each of the following from V(Dext) to V(Dcon) using I″ as the basis. Also, with each of the operations describe the effect of execution on the database structures in Figures 2.10 and 2.13.

1. Find the names and id numbers of all the students who ever took Calculus.
2. Find all of the courses and final grades for courses taken by Robert J. Smith during the spring 1980 semester.
3. Find the names and id numbers of all the students that were in the same section of Math 104 during the spring 1980 semester.
4. Insert the fact that Mary T. Jones took Computer Science 220, Introduction to Logic, section 001, and earned a grade of B for 3 credits during the spring semester of 1980.

2.4 RELATED READING

ADIBA, M., *Derived Relations: A Unified Mechanism for Views, Snapshots and Distributed Data,* IBM Technical Report RJ2881, IBM Corp., San Jose, Calif., 1980.

CLEMONS, E. K., "Design of an External Schema Facility to Define and Process Recursive Structures," *ACM Transactions on Database Systems,* **6** (2), June 1981, pp. 295-311.

DATE, C. J., AND HOPEWELL, P. "File Definition and Logical Data Independence," *Proceedings ACM SIGFIDET Workshop on Data Description, Access and Control,* 1971.

JACOBS, B. E., "On Interpretations in Database Logic and Its Applications," Department of Computer Science Technical Report TR 815, University of Maryland, College Park, Sept. 1979.

JACOBS, B. E., ARONSON, A. R., AND KLUG, A. C., "On Interpretations of Relational Languages and Solutions to the Implied Constraint Problem," *ACM Transactions on Database Systems,* **7**, (2) June 1982, pp. 291-318.

KAY, M. H., "An Assessment of the CODASYL DDL for Use with a Relational Subschema," in *Data Base Description* (ed., B. C. M. Douque and G. M. Nijssen), Proceedings IFIP TC-2 Working Conference on Data Base Description, Jan. 1975, North-Holland, Amsterdam, 1975.

MERCZ, L. A., "Issues in Building a Relational Interface on a CODASYL DBMS," in *Data Base Architecture* (ed. G. Bracchi and G. M. Nijssen), Proceedings IFIP TC-2 Working Conference on Data Base Architecture, June 1979, North-Holland, Amsterdam, 1979.

OLLE, T. W., *The CODASYL Approach to Data Base Management,* Wiley Interscience, New York, 1978.

PAOLINI, F. P., AND PELAGATTI, G., "Formal Definitions of Mappings in a Database," *Proceedings ACM SIGMOD International Symposium on Management of Data,* 1977, pp. 40-46.

STONEBRAKER, M. "Implementation of Integrity Constraints and Views by Query Modification," *Proceedings ACM SIGMOD International Symposium on Management of Data,* 1975, pp. 65-78.

TSICHRITZIS, D., AND KLUG, A. (eds.), "The ANSI/X3/SPARC DBMS Framework: Report of the Study Group on Database Management Systems," *Information Systems,* **3,** 1978.

ZANIOLO, C. A., "Multimodel External Schemas for CODASYL Data Base Management Systems," in *Data Base Architecture* (ed. G. Bracchi and G. M. Nijssen), Proceedings IFIP TC-2 Working Conference on Data Base Architecture, June 1979, North-Holland, Amsterdam, 1979.

3

FORMAL DATABASE LOGIC

In Chapter 3 we give a more precise treatment of the notions that were used in Chapters 1 and 2. In Section 3.1 we present an overview of the remainder of the book; namely, how the fundamental issues discussed in the introduction can be framed in terms of database logic and, in particular, interpretations in database logic. In Section 3.2 we deal with database schema, database languages, and database structures. Section 3.3 covers interpretations of database languages, interpreted wffs, induced database structures, and the Flipper Theorem. The material in Section 3.1 may be read with the knowledge obtained from Chapters 1 and 2. Sections 3.2 and 3.3 may be skimmed and referred back to later.

3.1 A SURVEY OF APPLICATIONS

In this section we outline how many of the important issues considered in this book can be framed within database logic and, in particular, interpretations.

External-to Conceptual Mapping

The external-to-conceptual mapping problem asks how we can precisely express the relationship between two databases so that one can be maintained as an external view of the second. The mapping should provide a mechanism by which programs at the external level can be transformed into programs at the conceptual level. It should also provide a means by which data can be transferred back and forth between levels.

In Chapter 2 we provided a solution to the external-to-conceptual mapping problem by treating the two levels as database logic views. The mapping was comprised of an interpretation of the external view in the conceptual view and a set of operation simulators. This mapping was used to transform GCALC programs from the external to the conceptual level. Since other DMLs (e.g., GSQL and GQBE) can be compiled into equivalent GCALC, they can also be transformed into GCALC at the conceptual level. The use of "codes" enables data to be transferred between levels.

View Update

The view update problem is that of determining how updates on an external view can be simulated "correctly" on an underlying conceptual view. There are several subproblems here. First, how are simulator programs constructed? Second, how is the notion of a correct simulation defined? Third, how is a simulator checked for "correctness"? Fourth, how is a "canonical" simulator built for commonly used views?

As seen in Chapter 2, our basic strategy in constructing a simulator is to perform operations that either make true or false a right-hand side of the defining formula for a row predicate in an interpretation. If the simulation causes a violation of the conceptual constraints, we abandon the simulation and "roll back" to the prior state of the conceptual database. If there is no violation, we leave normally.

In Chapter 4 we consider the view update problem strictly for the relational case. In Chapter 5 we generalize these results to the heterogeneous case. In both chapters we study four criteria for simulator correctness: weak, consistent, independent, and strong. We also establish tools that can be used to test correctness for arbitrary operation simulators. In Chapter 4 we show how to build canonical simulators for commonly used relational views (i.e., by projection, join, selection, and their combinations). We also use our tools to provide sufficient conditions that will ensure that these canonical simulators are correct.

View Integration

The view integration problem is as follows. Given a collection of databases, how can one construct a conceptual database that will support all of them as external databases? The view integration problem is often a major component in a design methodology in which external views are first extracted from a community of potential users and then integrated into a conceptual database.

In Chapter 6 we study the view integration problem in terms of the database logic concepts studied in Chapters 1 and 2. We provide a methodology that inputs a sequence of database logic views V(Ei), i = 1,...,k, in order of importance. Our process takes each of the external views V(Ei), one at a time, and integrates them into a temporary conceptual view V(Ci). When all the views have been integrated we have a final conceptual view V(C) together with k external-to-conceptual mappings.

Our integration methodology enables us to discover conflicts between candidate views. It also provides a series of possible remedies that can be used to alleviate these conflicts. This method also ensures that for each view the respective constraints are always maintained. This is because we build interpretations of each of the external views in the underlying conceptual view. By Theorem 2.2.2, each instance of the induced external databases satisfies its own constraints.

Our methodology also ensures that the most frequently used external views have external-to-conceptual mappings with minimum overhead. This is because our methodology begins with the first temporary conceptual views being close in structure to the most frequently used external views. Consequently, interpretations for the most frequently used views are as close as possible to the "identity" interpretation. Also, our method allows the incorporation of new external views by "adding" to the temporary conceptual views.

Database Conversion and Query Processing

The database conversion problem is as follows: Given an instance of a database, how can we construct a new database from it? This problem is closely related to the program conversion problem of the next chapter. For once we construct a new database from an old one, we can use the methodology of Chapter 8 to convert old programs mechanically to the new database.

In Chapter 7 we attack the database conversion problem by constructing an interpretation of the new database in the old database. We then take the interpretation and "execute" it as if it were a GCALC query. As we will see in Chapter 8, automatic program conversion methodology requires an interpretation of the old database into the new one. Consequently, to perform both steps, we need interpretations in both directions.

Our conversion methodology involves several steps. First, there is translation of the external-to-conceptual interpretation, in the case where the old database is itself an external view of some underlying conceptual database. Second, there is a decomposition, in order to determine the "best" strategy for evaluating the interpretation. Third, there is the problem of assembling the results obtained from the execution. Fourth, we have to load the results of the evaluation into the new database.

Our methodology is a generalization, to the heterogeneous case, of query processing on relational databases. Relational databases are comprised of tables and the results of executing queries are also tables. Thus, we can also regard relational query processing as particular solutions to the database conversion problem. In database logic, queries generalize to interpretations, and consequently, database conversion becomes "interpretation" processing.

Automatic Program Conversion

An important issue is that of automatic conversion of database application programs following a significant restructuring of a database. Database programs strongly reflect the schema and hence the structural format of the database. When the database changes, so does the schema and consequently, old programs are no longer usable on the new database. The problem, then, is how to derive from the old and new database descriptions a mechanical means for transforming old application programs to programs on the new database.

In Chapter 8 we consider the automatic program conversion problem in the context of database logic. Our strategy is to treat the "old" database as an external view of the "new" database and build an external-to-conceptual mapping of the old view in the new view. We begin by studying the problem for the relational case in which the DML is the well-known relational SQL. We then show how our method generalizes to the heterogeneous case for generalized SQL, GSQL.

Our methodology involves first compiling the data manipulation language (e.g., relational SQL, GSQL, or other) into equivalent GCALC. We then transform the GCALC on the old database to GCALC on the new database. Next, we try to replace the GCALC programs on the new database view by GCALC programs which are "smaller" but "equivalent." This last step is referred to as logical optimization. Finally, we compile the GCALC on the new database into some data manipulation language (e.g., GSQL or other) on the new database.

External Axiomatization

Given an external view of a conceptual view, the external axiomatization problem is that of finding a description, if one exists at all, of the class of all possible external database instances. Such a description is called an "external axiomatization." In our investigation we use interpretations of external in conceptual views. Hence, the external axiomatization problem reduces to finding a set of constraints, in the external language, that completely capture all induced external databases.

A key concept in our study is that of "onto" interpretations. By Theorem 2.2.2, an interpretation of an external view in a conceptual view maps the class of conceptual models "into" the class of external models. However, the mapping may not be an "onto" mapping. That is, there may be an external model which is not in the "range" of this mapping. If it were onto, the external constraints would completely characterize all the external databases and be an external axiomatization.

In Chapter 9 we study the ontoness problem for both the relational and heterogeneous cases. We first consider the related implied constraint problem. This asks whether or not a wff Q in the external language is true in every instance of an external database induced from a conceptual database. We then show how to demonstrate ontoness two ways. In one we use a sufficient condition, namely, "invertibility." In another, we use a necessary and sufficient condition for finite databases, namely, "faithfulness." We also use the latter characterizations to show non-ontoness.

3.2 DATABASE LANGUAGES AND STRUCTURES

In this section we give the precise definitions of database schema, database language, wff and term of a database language, database structure, and truth in a database structure.

Database Schemas

Definition. A *database schema* S is a finite collection of rules of the form

$$S = \{..., R0 = (R1,...,Rn),... \}.$$

The objects Ri, i = 0,1,...n, are called *names. Higher-order* names appear on the left sides of rules; *zero-order* names appear only on the right sides of rules. The rules of a database schema satisfy the following properties:

1. No two rules can have the same higher-order names on their left sides.
2. Higher-order names and zero-order names are distinct.
3. Names (higher-order and zero-order) on the right side of the same rule are unique.

A rule with the name R0 on its left side is called an R0 *rule.*

We divide the names of a schema into two classes. A name Rj of S is called *external* if Rj appears in S only on the left side of some rule. Otherwise, Rj is called *internal.* Intuitively, a name Rj is external if there can be only one Rj table in any database with schema S. If Rj is internal, there may be many Rj tables or values.

Special classes of schemata are defined by placing restrictions on the set S. We present three such classes.

Definition. A *relational* schema S is a collection of rules

$$S = \{..., R0 = (R1,...,Rn), ...\},$$

where all Rj are zero-order names, j = 1,2,...,n.

The reader can check that S(Rext) of Chapter 1 satisfies the above, hence is a relational schema according to the definition above. Notice that the external names of S(Rext) are the relation names TRANSCRIPT and STUDENT and the internal names are all the zero-order names.

Definition. A *hierarchical* schema S is a collection of rules

$$S = \{..., R0 = (R1,...,Rn), ...\},$$

where

1. For any higher-order name R0 it is not possible for an R0 table to be embedded inside another R0 table.
2. No higher-order name may appear on the right-hand side of two different rules.

Condition 1 ensures that the same record type may not appear above and below itself; condition 2 ensures that every record type has at most one immediate parent. The reader can check that S(Dext) of Chapter 1 obeys the above, hence is a hierarchical schema. Note that the only external name in S(Dext) is TRANSCRIPT; every other name is internal.

Definition. A *network* schema S is a collection of rules

S = {..., R0 = (R1,...,Rn), ...},

where all R0,

R0 = (...,R0,...)

is not in S. That is, the same higher-order name cannot appear on both the left- and right-hand sides of the same rule.

The condition above reflects the often used CODASYL requirement that record types cannot be both owner and member of the same set (cf. [CODASYL]). The reader can easily observe that S(Dcon) of Chapter 2 is a network schema.

Throughout the remainder of this chapter S will denote an arbitrary database schema.

Database Languages and Wffs

By a *typing* T *of the schema* S we mean a set {T1,...,Tk} where for each j = 1,...,k either (1) Tj is a higher-order name of S, or (2) Tj is a set of zero-order names. Further, every higher-order name of S is listed in T and every zero-order name is contained in exactly one set Tj. Each member of the typing T is called a *higher-order type* or *zero-order type* , depending on whether it falls under (1) or (2) above. In particular, if Ri is a zero-order name contained in Tj, then Tj is called the *type for* Ri.

Definition. A *database language* L for a database schema S is comprised of

1. A typing T={T1,...,Tk} of the schema S
2. Nonlogical symbols
   (a) For n and tuple of types (T1,...,Tn) of T, an n-place predicate symbol p called a (T1,...,Tn) *predicate symbol.*
   (b) For n and tuple of types (T1,...,Tn;T0) of T, an n-place function symbol f called a (T1,...,Tn;T0) *function symbol*
   (c) For each type Tj in T, a set of constant symbols {e(Tj):i}, called the set of Tj *constant symbols,* where in the case that Tj represents an external name, there is only one Tj constant
3. Logical symbols
   (a) For each internal name Ri in S, a countably infinite set of variables Ri:1,Ri:2,..., called Ri *variables*
   (b) For each type Tj of T we have the symbol =(Tj)
   (c) E, A, &, V, ~, → ⟷, (,),
   (d) For each higher-order name R0 in S a row predicate R0( )

The formal definitions of terms and wffs of L are given below.

Definition. Let Tj be a type in T. The Tj *terms* of L are defined as follows:

1. The Ri variables, where Ri is of type Tj, are Tj terms.
2. The Tj constant symbols are Tj terms.
3. If ts is a Ts term, s = 1,...,n, and f is a (T1,...,Tn;Tj) function symbol, then

   f(t1,...,tn)

   is a Tj term.

A *term* of L is a Tj-term for some type Tj in T.

Examples of terms of the language L(Dext) of view V(Dext) from Chapter 1 are SMITH ROBERT J., COURSES:1 and TOTCREDITS(COURSES:1) .

Definition. The *well-formed formulas (wffs)* of L are defined as follows.

1. If t1,...,tn are, respectively, T1,...,Tn terms of L and p is a (T1,...,Tn) predicate symbol, then

   p(t1,...,tn)

   is a wff.
2. If t0,t1,...,tn are, respectively, T0,T1,...Tn terms, and if there is a rule R0 = (R1,...,Rn) in S where for s = 0,1,...,n the type of Rs is Ts, then

   t0(t1,...,tn)

   is a wff.
3. If t1 and t2 are both Tj terms, then

   t1 =(Tj) t2

   is a wff.
4. If Q1 and Q2 are wffs of L, then

   Q1 & Q2

   is a wff.
5. If Q1 is a wff of L, then

   ~Q1

   is a wff.
6. If Q1(Ri:m) is a wff, where Ri:m is an Ri variable, then

   (E)Ri:m Q1(Ri:m)

   is a wff.

We define other wffs of L in terms of the above.

7. If Q1 and Q2 are wffs of L, then Q1 V Q2 denotes the wff ~(~Q1 & ~Q2).
8. If Q1(Ri:m) is a wff of L with Ri:m an Ri-variable, then (A)Ri:mQ1(Ri:m) denotes the wff ~(E)Ri:m~Q1(Ri:m).
9. If Q1 and Q2 are wffs of L(S), then Q1 → Q2 denotes the wff ~Q1 V Q2.
10. If Q1 and Q2 are wffs of L(S), then Q1 ⟷ Q2 denotes the wff (Q1 → Q2) & (Q2 → Q1) .

The reader is invited to verify that all the wffs and terms presented in Chapters 1 and 2 conform to the definitions above.

Database Structures and Truth

Definition. By a *database structure* M for L we mean a tuple

$$< U', \{p'\}, \{f'\}, \{e'\} >$$

where

1. The *universe* of M is

$$U' = \underset{Tj \text{ in } T}{\text{UNION}} \; dom(Tj).$$

2. If p is a (T1,...,Tn) predicate symbol of L, then p′ is a mapping of dom(T1) x ... x dom(Tn) into {TRUE,FALSE}.
3. If f is a (T1,...,Tn;T0) function symbol of L, then f′ is a mapping of dom(T1) x ... x dom(Tn) into dom(T0).
4. If e(Tj):i is a Tj-constant symbol, then e′(Tj):i is some element of dom(Tj).

For a predicate symbol p in L, p′ is called the *meaning of* p in M. Similar remarks apply for function and constant symbols.

There is also a fundamental restriction on the tables allowed in the universe. Namely, each table must have a finite depth of nesting (i.e., there cannot be an infinitely decreasing sequence of embedded tables). Clearly, this will be the case if the schema is either relational or hierarchical. If the schema is a network with "recursive" rules [e.g., CATALOGUE in V(Dcon)], this situation is structurally possible. However, even in this case, we prohibit it in any database structure.

The precise definitions of evaluation of terms and truth of wffs in a database structure are given below. Throughout the following let <T> be a sequence of types, <e> a sequence of elements of U′, and <R> a sequence of variables. Also, the j-th element of <e> and the j-th element of <R> are of a type which is the j-th element of <T>.

Definition. Let t be a Tj term. The *evaluation of* t *in a database structure* M *under substitution* <e> *for* <R>, denoted t′<e>, is as follows.

1. e′(Tj):i, if t is the Tj constant symbol e(Tj):i
2. ej, the j-th member of <e>, if t is Rj, the j-th member of <R>
3. f′(t1′<e>,...,tn′<e>), if t is the T0-term f(t1,...,tn) where f is a (T1,...,Tn;T0) function symbol and tj is a Tj term, j = 1,...,n

When term t has no free variables the above simply reduces to the evaluation of t in M, denoted t′.

Definition. Let Q(<R>) be a wff of L. The *truth of* Q(<R>) *in database structure* M *and substitution* <e> *for* <R>, denoted M ⊨ Q(<R>)<e>, is defined as follows.

1. If Q(<R>) is p(t1,...,tn), where p is a (T1,...,Tn) predicate symbol and tj are Tj terms, j = 1,...,n, then

$$M \models Q(<R>)<e> \quad \text{iff} \quad p'(t1<e>,\ldots,tk<e>).$$

2. If Q(<R>) is t0(t1,...,tn) where tj are Tj terms, j = 1,...,n, then

$$M \models Q(<R>)<e> \quad \text{iff} \quad (t1'<e>,\ldots,tn'<e>) \text{ is in } t0'<e>.$$

3. If Q(<R>) is t1 = (Tj) t2, where t1 and t2 are Tj terms, then

$$M \models Q(<R>)<e> \quad \text{iff} \quad t1'<e> = t2'<e>.$$

4. If Q(<R>) is Q1 & Q2 (<R>), then

$$M \models Q(<R>)<e> \quad \text{iff} \quad M \models Q1(<R>)<e> \quad \text{and} \quad M \models Q2(<R>)<e>.$$

5. If Q(<R>)<e> is ~Q1(<R>) then

$$M \models Q(<R>)<e> \quad \text{iff} \quad M \not\models Q1(<R>)<e>.$$

6. If Q(<R>)<e> is (E)Ri:m Q1(<R>,Ri:m), then

$$M \models Q(<R>)<e> \quad \text{iff} \quad \text{for some } e' \text{ in dom(Tj)},$$
$$M \models Q1(<R>,Ri{:}m)(<e>,e')$$

   where the type of Ri is Tj.
7. If Q(<R>) is Q1 ~ Q2 (<R>), then

$$M \models Q(<R>)<e> \quad \text{iff} \quad M \models Q1(<R>)<e> \quad \text{or} \quad M \models Q2(<R>)<e>.$$

8. If Q(<R>)<e> is (A)Ri:m Q1(<R>,Ri:m) then

$$M \models Q(<R>)<e> \quad \text{iff} \quad \text{for all } e' \text{ in dom(Tj)}, M \models Q1(<R>,Ri{:}m)(<e>,e'),$$

   where the type of Ri is Tj.

9. If $Q(<R>)$ is $Q1 \rightarrow Q2\ (<R>)$, then

$$M \models Q(<R>)<e> \quad \text{iff} \quad \text{either } M \models \sim Q1(<R>)<e> \text{ or } M \models Q2(<R>)<e>.$$

10. If $Q(<R>)$ is $Q1 \longleftrightarrow Q2\ (<R>)$, then

$$M \models Q(<R>)<e> \quad \text{iff} \quad (M \models Q1(<R>)<e> \text{ when } M \models Q2(<R>)<e>).$$

When wff Q of L has no free variables (i.e., variables that are not quantified), the above reduces to simply the *truth of* Q *in a database structure* M, denoted $M \models Q$.

The reader is invited to check that according to the definition above, the wffs displayed in Chapters 1 and 2 as integrity constraints are true in the corresponding illustrative database structures.

Exercises

1. Characterize the set of all terms of the language L(Dext) of Chapter 1.
2. Express all the constraints in C(Dext) of Chapter 1 as wffs of L(Dext). Demonstrate that they are indeed wffs using the definition above.
3. Show that the wffs of Exercise 2 are true in the database structure M(Dext) of Figure 1.9 using the definitions above.

Consider the following situation. Suppose that there actually exist two distinct databases, one corresponding to relational view V(Rext) of Figure 1.3 and another corresponding to the database view V(Rcon) of Figure 2.1 . Suppose that the data were divided in such a way that view V(Rext) contains the fall 1979 information while V(Rcon) contains only the spring 1980 information.

4. Specify, in a format similar to that of Figure 1.3, the view V(RUNION) = <S(RUNION), L(RUNION), C(RUNION)> corresponding to the database which is the union of these two views. *Hint:* S(RUNION) is S(Rext) ∪ S(Rcon), etc.
5. Using the data in Figures 1.2 and 2.2, construct the corresponding database structure M(RUNION).

Consider the following situation. Suppose that there actually exist two distinct databases, one corresponding to relational view V(Rcon) of Figure 2.1 and another corresponding to the database view V(Dext) of Figure 1.8 . Suppose that the data were divided such that view V(Rcon) contained the fall 1979 information while V(Dext) contained only the spring 1980 information.

6. Specify, in a format similar to that of Figure 2.9, the view V(DUNION) = <S(DUNION), L(DUNION), C(DUNION)> corresponding to the database which is actually the union of these two views. *Hint:* S(DUNION) is S(Rcon) ∪ S(Dext), etc.
7. Using the data in Figures 2.2 and 1.9, construct the corresponding database structure M(DUNION).

3.3 INTERPRETATIONS

In this section we give precise definitions of the notions of database language interpretation, interpretation of wffs, and induced database structures. We also prove the Flipper Theorem.

Interpretations of Languages

Let V(E) = < S(E),L(E),C(E) > represent an external database view and let V(C) = < S(C),L(C),C(C) > represent a conceptual database view. The components of an interpretation are the "coding section," "defining formula section," and "constant transformation section."

1. Coding section. For each data type Tj, either atomic or higher-order in L(E), we provide a sequence of atomic types < Tj; > of L(C), called the *code* for type Tj.

Convention. If < Oj; > denotes a sequence, then < Oj; > .s will denote the s-th component of the sequence.

2. Defining formula section

2.1. For each (T0,T1,...,Tn) row predicate R0( ) of L(E), we provide a formula

Q(< R0; > , < R1; > ,..., < Rn; >)

of L(C) called the *defining formula of* R0( ). Here < Rs; > denotes some sequence of variables which range over the code for Ts.

2.2. For each nonlogical (T1,...,Tn) predicate symbol p of L(E), we provide a formula

Q(< R1; > ,..., < Rn; >)

of L(C), called the *defining formula of* p.

2.3. For each (T1,...,Tn;T0) function symbol f of L(E), we provide a formula

Q(< R1; > ,..., < Rn; > ; < R0; >)

of L(C), called the *defining formula of* f. In addition, the definition should be "code" definable; that is, there are terms dt1,...,dtk of L(C) such that

dt1(< R1; > ,..., < Rn; >) defines the value of < R0; > .1,
dt2(< R1; > ,..., < Rn; >) defines the value of < R0; > .2,
.
.
.
dtk(< R1; > ,..., < Rn; >) defines the value of < R0; > .k.

The set {dt1, ..., dtk} are called *defining terms for* f.

3. Constant transformation section. For each type Tj of L(E) and code <Tj;> of L(C), we have a procedure CODE(Tj)(-) which inputs a Tj constant e(Tj):i and returns a sequence of constants <e(Tj):i;>, which is its code. Also, for each type Tj of L(E) and code <Tj;> of L(C), we have a procedure DECODE(Tj)(-) which inputs a sequence of constants <e(Tj):i;>, which is a code, and returns the constant e(Tj):i in L(E) coded by the sequence.

Let I = I(E;C) be an interpretation of database language L(E) in L(C). It provides us with a mapping of the language L(E) into the language of L(C).

Definition. Let t be a term of L(E). We define by induction on the height of t a finite sequence <t;> of terms of L(C), called the *code for* t *in* L(C).

1. Let t be a constant symbol e(Tj):i of L(E). Let <e(Tj):i;> be the sequence of constants of L(C) given by the function CODE(Tj)(e(Tj):i). The sequence <e(Tj):i;> is the code for e(Tj):i in L(C).
2. Let t be the variable Ri:m of type Tj. Let <Ri:m;> be a sequence of variables of types <Tj;>, where <Tj;> is the code for Tj. The sequence <Ri:m;> is a code for Ri:m in L(C).
3. Let t be the T0 term f(t1,...,tn) where tj is a Tj term, j = 1,...,n. Hence, f is a (T1,...,Tn;T0) function symbol of L(E). Let <tj;> be a code for tj, j = 1,...,n. Then a code for f(t1,...,tn) in L(C) is

   dt1(<t1;>,...,<tn;>),...,dtk(<t1;>,...,<tn;>);

   where dt1,...,dtk are the defining terms of f in the interpretation I.

For example, recall the variable STUDID:1 of V(Dext). The code for STUDID:1 according to I″ is the sequence ID#:1;. Also, the term

TOTCREDITS(STUDID:1, SEMESTER:1, YEAR:1)

of V(Dext) of is coded via I″ by the sequence

TOTALCREDITS(STUDID:1,SEMESTER:1,YEAR:1);.

Let R0 be a higher-order (table) name and let <t1;> and <t2;> be two codes for the R0 objects t1 and t2. By

(<t1;>) =(R0) (<t2;>)

we mean the wff

DEF(R0)(<t1;>, <R1;>, <R2;>,..., <Rk;>) ⟷
DEF(R0)(<t2;>, <R1;>, <R2;>,..., <Rk;>),

where DEF(R0) is the defining formula for R0 in I. Here the rule R0 = (R1,...,Rk) is in S(E) and <Rs;> are variables for the codes for Rs, s = 1,...,k. The idea is that this wff makes the assertion that the table coded by <t1;> contains the same rows as the table coded by <t2;>.

Let Q be any wff of L(E). With no loss of generality we can assume that Q is in *prenex normal form.* That is, Q has the form

X<R> Q1<R>

where X<R> are all the quantifiers (E's and V's) and Q1(<R>) is quantifier-free with the free variables <R>.

Definition. The formula I(Q) of L(C), called the *interpretation of* Q *in* L(C) *via* I, is defined by induction on the height of Q as follows:

1. Let Q be the atomic wff of L(E)

   p(t1,...,tk),

   where tj have codes <tj;>, j = 1,...,k. Then I(Q) is

   DEF(p)(<t1;>,..., <tk;>),

   where DEF(p) is the defining formula for p in I.
2. Let Q be the atomic wff of L(E),

   t0(t1,...,tk),

   where tj have codes <tj;>, j=0,1,...,k. Then I(Q) is

   DEF(R0)(<t0;>, <t1;>,..., <tk;>),

   where DEF(R0) is the defining formula for the row predicate R0 in I.
3. Let Q be the atomic wff t1 = (Tj) t2 where t1 and t2 are Tj terms of L(E) and <t1;> and <t2;> are their respective codes. Then I(Q) is

   <t1;>.1 = <t2;>.1 & ... & <t1;>.m= <t2;>.m, if Tj is zero-order

   or

   (<t1;> =(Tj)(<t2;>), if Tj is higher-order.

4. Let Q be the wff ~Q1 of L(E). Then I(Q) is the wff ~(Q1).
5. Let Q be the wff (E)Ri:m Q1(Ri:m). Then I(Q) is the wff

   <(E)Ri:m;> I(Q1)<Ri:m;>,

   where <Ri:m;> is a code used throughout I(Q1) for Ri:m and <(E)Ri:m;> denotes existential quantification over all the variables in <Ri:m;>.
6. Let Q be the wff Q1 ~ Q2(t1,...,tk), where tj, j = 1,...,k, are the Tj terms in both wffs Q1 and Q2 (no repetitions). Then I(Q) is the wff

   I(Q1) V I(Q2)(<t1;>,..., <tk;>).

7. Let Q be the wff (A)Ri:m Q1(Ri:m). Then I(Q) is the wff

   <(A)Ri:m;> I(Q1)<Ri:m;>,

where <Ri:m;> is a code used throughout I(Q1) for Ri:m and <(A)Ri:m;> denotes universal quantification over all the variables in <Ri:m;>.

8. Let Q be the wff Q1 → Q2(t1,...,tk), where tj, j = 1,...,k are the Tj terms in both wffs Q1 and Q2 (no repetitions). Then I(Q) is the wff

   I(Q1) → I(Q2)(<t1;>,..., <tk;>) .

9. Let Q be the wff Q1 ⟷ Q2(t1,...,tk), where tj, j = 1,...,k, are the Tj terms in both wffs Q1 and Q2 (no repetitions). Then I(Q) is the wff

   I(Q1) ⟷ I(Q2)(<t1;>,..., <tk;>).

In Section 2.2 we demonstrated how the constraint

```
C(Dext,3)
= TRANSCRIPT-RECORD-COURSES:
      STUDID,SEMESTER,YEAR,DEPT,COURSE#
       → SEC#,TITLE,GRADE,CREDITS
```

of V(Dext) is interpreted via the interpretation I″. The reader can check that the transformation was done according to the definition above.

Induced Database Structures

Definition. Let I be an interpretation of L(E) in L(C) and let M(C) be a database structure for L(C). The database structure

I[M(C)] = <U′, {p′}, {f′}, {e′(Tj):i}>

for L(E) *induced from* M(C) *via* I is defined as follows:

1. *Universe:* For each type Tj of L(E) with code <Tj;> in L(C),

   dom(Tj) = { <ej;>| <ej;>.s is in dom(<Tj;>.s) in M(C) }.

   That is, every member of the set dom(Tj) in I[M(C)] is represented by a sequence whose first component is in dom(<Tj;>.1), second component is in dom(<Tj;>.2),..., n-th component is in dom(<Tj;>.n). The universe of I[M(C)] is defined as

   U′ = UNION dom(Tj)
   Tj in T(E)

   For example, recall the zero-order type SIDTPE in view V(Dext) of Figure 1.8. By the CODING SECTION of I″ of Figure 2.11, the set dom(SIDTPE) [of EBCDIC DEC(9) strings] is coded in any database structure M(Dcon) via dom(IDTPE) [the set of all ASCII DEC(9) strings]. Also, in the induced database structure I″[M(Dcon)] of Figure 2.13, the COURSES table in dom(COURSES) labeled e(COURSES):1 is the one with code 123456789,FALL, 1979;. The COURSES tables which have codes that are not in the picture are all equal to the empty table.

From now on we will identify elements of U′ with sequences of the form $<e;>$.

2. ***Predicates:*** For each nonlogical predicate symbol p of L(E),

$$\begin{aligned} &p'(<e1;>, <e2;>, \ldots, <ek;>) \text{ is true in } I[M(C)] \\ &\text{iff} \quad M(C) \models DEF(p)(<e1;>, <e2;>, \ldots, <ek;>), \end{aligned}$$

where DEF(p) is the defining formula for p in I.

Let Tj be a type in L(E). The definition of equality =(Tj) depends on whether or not Tj is zero- or higher-order.

For the zero-order case,

$$\begin{aligned} &<e1;> \ =(Tj) \ <e2;> \text{ is true in } I[M(C)] \\ &\text{iff} \quad M(C) \models <e1;>.1 = <e2;>.1 \ \&\cdots\& \ <e1;>.m = <e2;>.m. \end{aligned}$$

That is, zero-order elements in I[M(C)] are equal if and only if their codes componentwise equal.

For each higher-order type Tj in T(E),

$$<e1;> \ =(Tj) \ <e2;> \text{ is true in } I[M(C)] \quad \text{iff} \quad M(C) \models (<e1;>) =(Tj) (<e2;>).$$

That is, higher-order tables are equal in I[M(C)]
iff the tables they represent have the same set of rows.

3. ***Functions:*** For each function symbol f of L(E),

$$\begin{aligned} &f'(<e1;>, <e2;>, \ldots, <ek;>) = <e0;> \text{ is true in } I[M(C)] \\ &\text{iff} \quad M(C) \models DEF(f)(<e1;>, <e2;>, \ldots, <ek;>; <e0;>), \end{aligned}$$

where DEF(f) is the defining formula for f in I.

4. ***Constants:*** Suppose that constant symbol e(Tj):i of L(E) is coded by I to the sequence of constant symbols $<e(Tj){:}i;>$ of L(C). Then

$$e'(Tj){:}i = <e(Tj){:}i;>.$$

Flipper Theorem

Theorem. *Let* I *be an interpretation of database language* L(E) *in* L(C). *Then for any closed wff* Q *of* L(E) *and any database structure* M(C) *for* L(C),

$$I[M(C)] \models Q \quad \text{iff} \quad M(C) \models I(Q).$$

Before proving the theorem we prove a lemma.

Lemma. *Let* I *be an interpretation of* L(E) *in* L(C). *Let* t *be a variable-free term of* L(E) *and* $<t;>$ *be the code for* t *in* L(C). *Then for any database structure* M(C) *for* L(C),

$$t' = <t;>.1', <t;>.2', \ldots, <t;>.n';$$

That is, the code for t (in I[M(C)]) is obtained by individually evaluating in M(C) the terms making up the code for term t. We will denote the right-hand side of the above by $< t;' >$.

Proof (of Lemma). Our proof is by an induction on the height of t.

Suppose that t is e(Tj):i, a constant symbol of L(E), and $< e(Tj):i; >$ is its code in L(C). By definition of I[M(C)],

$$e'(Tj):i = < e(Tj):i; > = < e(Tj):i;' >,$$

since we identify atomic constants with their values in all database structures.

Suppose that t is f(t1,...,tk). Then

$$[f(t1,...,tk)]' = f'(t1',...,tk').$$

By the induction hypothesis,

$$= f'(< t1;' >,..., < ts;' >),$$

where $< tj; >$ is the code for tj in L(C), j = 1,...,k. (Observe that tj variable-free implies $< tj; >$ variable-free.) By definition of f′ in I[M(C)] and the induction hypothesis

$$= dt1'(< t1;' >,..., < tk;' >),...,dtn'(< t1;' >,..., < tk;' >);$$
$$= < f(t1,...,tk);' >.$$

Proof (of Theorem). The proof is by induction on the height of a wff Q of L(E) in prenex normal form.

Suppose that Q is p(t1,...,tk). Then

$$I[M(C)] \models p(t1,...,tk) \quad \text{iff} \quad p'(t1',...,tk').$$

Let $< tj; >$ be the code for tj, j = 1,...,k, in L(C). By the Lemma, $tj' = < tj;' >$, hence,

$$\text{iff } p'(< t1;' >,..., < tk;' >).$$

By definition of p′,

$$\text{iff } M(C) \models DEF(p)\ (< t1;' >,..., < tk;' >).$$

By definition of I(p(t1,...,tk)) ,

$$\text{iff } M(C) \models I(p(t1,...,tk)) .$$

Suppose that Q is t0(t1,...,tk). Then

$$I[M(C)] \models t0(t1,...,tk) \quad \text{iff} \quad (t1',...,tk') \text{ is in } t0'.$$

Let $< tj; >$ be the code for tj, j = 0,1,...,k, in L(C). By the Lemma, $tj' = < tj;' >$, hence,

$$\text{iff } (< t1;' >,..., < tk;' >) \text{ is in } < t0;' >.$$

By definition of I[M(C)],

$$\text{iff } M(C) \models DEF(R0(\,))\ (< t1;' >,..., < tk;' >).$$

By definition of $I(t0(t1,...,tk))$,

$$\text{iff } M(C) \models I(t0(t1,...,tk)).$$

Suppose that Q is $t1 = (Tj)\ t2$. Then

$$I[M(C)] \models t1 = (Tj)t2 \quad \text{iff} \quad t1' = t2'.$$

Let $<tj;>$ be codes for tj, $j = 1,2$. By the Lemma $tj' = <tj;'>, j = 1,2$; hence,

$$\text{iff } <t1;'> = <t2;'>.$$

Case 1: The type of t1 and t2 are zero-order. Then by definition of "$=(Tj)$" in $I[M(C)]$,

$$\text{iff } <t1;'>.1 = <t2;'>.1 \quad \text{and} \cdots \text{and} \quad <t1;'>.m = <t2;'>.m.$$

Hence,

$$\text{iff } M(C) \models <t1;'>.1 = <t2;'>.1 \ \& \cdots \& \ <t1;'>.m = <t2;'>.m$$
$$\text{iff } M(C) \models I((t1 = (Tj)\ t2)).$$

Case 2: The type of t1 and t2 is higher-order. Then by definition of "$=(Tj)$" in $I[M(C)]$,

$$\text{iff } M(C) \models (<t1;'> = <t2;'>).$$

By definition of equality in $I[M(C)]$,

$$\begin{aligned} \text{iff } M(C) \models\ & DEF(Tj)\ (<t1;'>, <R1{:}s;>,...,<Rk{:}s;>) \\ & \longleftrightarrow DEF(Tj)\ (<t2;'>, <R1{:}s;>,...,<Rk{:}s;>)) \\ \text{iff } M(C) \models\ & I(t1 = (Tj)\ t2). \end{aligned}$$

[Implicit in the argument above is an induction of the height of tables. One can inductively define the universe U' of $I[M(C)]$ such that every table $<tj;'>$ has a unique height; hence, such an argument is possible.]

Suppose that Q is $\sim Q1$. Then

$$I[M(C)] \models \sim Q1,$$
$$\text{iff } I[M(C)] \not\models Q1.$$

By induction hypothesis,

$$\text{iff } M(C) \not\models I(Q1),$$
$$\text{iff } M(C) \models \sim I(Q1).$$

Suppose that Q is $Q1\ \&\ Q2$. Then

$$I[M(C)] \models Q1\ \&\ Q2 \quad \text{iff} \quad I[M(C)] \models Q1 \text{ and } I[M(C)] \models Q2.$$

By induction hypothesis,

$$\text{iff } M(C) \models I(Q1) \text{ and } M(C) \models I(Q2),$$
$$\text{iff } M(C) \models I(Q1\ \&\ Q2).$$

Similar arguments hold for Q1 V Q2 , Q1 → Q2 and Q1 ⟷ Q2.

Suppose that Q is (E)Ri:m Q1(Ri:m). Then

I[M(C)] $\models$ (E)Ri:m Q1(Ri:m) iff I[M(C)] $\models$ Q1(<e;>), for some <e;> in dom(Tj).

By the induction hypothesis,

iff M(C) $\models$ I(Q1(<e;>)), for some <e;> in dom(Tj).

For <Ri:m;>, the code for Ri:m

iff M(C) $\models$ <(E)Ri:m;> I(Q1(<Ri:m;>)),

where <(E)Ri:m;> denotes quantification over the variables in <Ri:m;>. By definition of the mapping I on wffs of L(E)

iff M(C) $\models$ I((E)Ri:m Q1(Ri:m)).

A similar argument holds for (A)Ri:m Q1(Ri:m).

Exercises

Recall view V(RUNION) from the Exercises of Section 3.2, which represents the union of the two views V(Rext) and V(Rcon). Suppose that an external view is desired over V(RUNION) which is to take on the form V(Rext).

1. Specify, in a format similar to that of Figure 2.3, the interpretation I(Rext;RUNION) of language L(Rext) into language L(RUNION).
2. Let M(UNION) be the database structure for L(RUNION) constructed in Exercise 5 of Section 3.2. Construct the induced database structure I(Rext;RUNION) [M(RUNION)].
3. Is the interpretation of

   TRANSCRIPT:STUDID,SEMESTER,YEAR,DEPT,COURSE#
   → STUDNAME,SEC#,TITLE,GRADE,CREDITS

   under I(Rext;RUNION) [M(RUNION)] a logical consequence of C(RUNION) in L(RUNION)?
4. Is the interpretation of

   TRANSCRIPT:STUDID → STUDNAME

   under I(Rext;RUNION)[M(RUNION)] a logical consequence of C(RUNION) in L(RUNION)?
5. Is the interpretation of

   TRANSCRIPT:DEPT,COURSE# → TITLE

   under I(Rext;RUNION)[M(RUNION)] a logical consequence of C(RUNION) in L(RUNION)?
6. Is the interpretation of

   STUDENT:ID# → NAME,DATEADM

under I(Rext;RUNION)[M(RUNION)] a logical consequence of C(RUNION) in L(RUNION)?

Recall view V(DUNION) from the exercises of Section 3.2, which represents the union of views V(Rcon) and V(Dext). Suppose that an external view is desired over V(DUNION) which is to take on the form V(Dext).

7. Specify, in a format similar to that of Figure 2.12, the interpretation I(Rext;DUNION) of language L(Rext) into language L(DUNION).
8. Let M(UNION) be the database structure for L(DUNION) constructed in Exercise 7 of Section 3.2. Construct the induced database structure I(Dext;DUNION) [M(DUNION)].
9. Is the interpretation of

   TRANSCRIPT:STUDID → STUDNAME,BIRTHDATE,
   DATEADM,RECORD

   under I(Dext;DUNION) [M(DUNION)] a logical consequence of C(DUNION) in L(DUNION)?
10. Is the interpretation of

   TRANSCRIPT-RECORD:
   STUDID,SEMESTER,YEAR → COURSES

   under I(Dext;DUNION)[M(DUNION)] a logical consequence of C(DUNION) in L(DUNION)?
11. Is the interpretation of

   TRANSCRIPT-RECORD-COURSES:
   STUDID,SEMESTER,YEAR,DEPT,COURSE#,
   → SEC#,TITLE,CREDITS,GRADE

   under I(Dext;DUNION)[M(DUNION)] a logical consequence of C(DUNION) in L(DUNION)?

Suppose that we alter view V(Rcon) of Figure 2.1 so that the additional rules are added to S(Rcon):

SYIDINDEX = (STUDID,SEMESTER,YEAR,REGISTRAR),
SYDCSINDEX = (SEMESTER,YEAR,DEPT,COURSE#,
SEC#,REGISTRAR).

Call this new view V(Rcon′). These changes represent two "indexings" of the REGISTRAR record. In the first case, we index by STUDID, SEMESTER, and YEAR. In the second case, we index by SEMESTER, YEAR, DEPT, COURSE#, and SEC#. Observe that view V(Rcon) is longer relational.

12. Using the data in Figures 2.2, construct the corresponding database structure M(Rcon′).
13. Construct an interpretation I(Rext;Rcon′) of language L(Rext) in language L(Dcon′). Notice that now there are two possible choices for the defining formula for the predicate TRANSCRIPT, one that goes through SYININDEX and one that goes through SYDCSINDEX.
14. Use the interpretation of Exercise 13 to translate the query in Example 1.1.1 to V(Rcon′). Determine which of the two choices is better for query execution.
15. Find two queries on V(Rext) in which one translation is better than the other.

3.4 RELATED READING

JACOBS, B.E., "On Database Logic," *Journal of the ACM,* **29,** Apr. 1982, pp. 310–332.

JACOBS, B. E., *On Interpretations in Database Logic and Their Applications,* Department of Computer Science Technical Report TR 815, University of Maryland, College Park, Sept. 1979.

4

VIEW UPDATE I: THE RELATIONAL CASE

In this chapter and the next, we investigate the view update problem. Namely, how does one translate operations (e.g., insert, delete, and update) on an external view into correct simulations on a conceptual view? In this chapter we concentrate on the relational case. In Section 4.1 we use the notion of interpretation of relational views to study four notions of correctness for operation simulators. In Section 4.2 we show how to use our formalism to verify the correctness of a constructed simulator. In Section 4.3 we also show how to build "canonical" simulators for often used external views and provide sufficient conditions that ensure their correctness.

4.1 CORRECTNESS CRITERIA

In this section we study the notion of an operation simulator for external-to-conceptual mappings between relational views and define four criteria for simulator correctness: weak, consistent, independent, and strong.

Example

In Figures 4.1 and 4.2 we define two views. The first view V(FSEA) = <S(FSEA), L(FSEA), C(FSEA)> represents the conceptual view, which contains four relations: FAMILY, SALINFO, EMPLOYEE, and ASSIGNMENT. All the values in this database are stored internally in ASCII. Besides the four relation symbols, there are two typed "less than or equal to" predicate symbols, $\leq$(S), $\leq$(Y), and no function symbols. The constraints definition indicates three functional dependencies, C(FSEA,1),

```
V(FSEA): VIEW DEFINITION
  S(FSEA): SCHEMA DEFINITION
    TABLE FAMILY = (NAME,CHILDNAME)
    TABLE SALINFO = (NAME,SALARY,SALYEAR)
    TABLE EMPLOYEE = (NAME,DEPTMENT,POSITION,SEX)
    TABLE ASSIGNMENT = (DEPTNAME,PROJECT,CLASS)

 L(FSEA): LANGUAGE DEFINITION
   T(FSEA): TYPING DEFINITION
   TYPE NAMTPE = {NAME,CHILDNAME} ASCII CHAR(24)
   TYPE SALTPE = {SALARY} ASCII REAL(8,2)
   TYPE YRTPE = {SALYEAR} ASCII INTEGER (4)
   TYPE DEPTPE = {DEPTNAME} ASCII CHAR(12)
   TYPE POSTPE = {POSITION} ASCII CHAR(10)
   TYPE SEXTPE = {SEX} ASCII CHAR(1)
   TYPE PROTPE = {PROJECT} ASCII CHAR(6)
   TYPE CLATPE = {CLASS} ASCII INTEGER(10)

  NONLOGICAL SYMBOLS DEFINITION
    PREDICATES
      FAMILY:(NAMTPE,NAMTPE) PREDICATE
      SALINFO:(NAMTPE,SALTPE,YRTPE) PREDICATE
      EMPLOYEE:(NAMTPE,DEPTPE,POSTPE,SEXTPE) PREDICATE
      ASSIGNMENT:(DEPTPE,PROTPE,CLATPE) PREDICATE
      ≤(S): (SALTPE,SALTPE) PREDICATE
      ≤(Y): (YRTPE,YRTPE) PREDICATE
    FUNCTIONS
      NONE

  C(FSEA): CONSTRAINTS DEFINITION
    C(FSEA,1):CONSTRAINT SALINFO:NAME,SALYEAR → SALARY
    C(FSEA,2):CONSTRAINT SALINFO:(NAME)
      SALYEAR:1 ≤(Y) SALYEAR:2 → SALARY:1 ≤(S) SALARY:2
    C(FSEA,3):CONSTRAINT EMPLOYEE:NAME → DEPTNAME,POSITION,SEX
    C(FSEA,4):CONSTRAINT ASSIGNMENT:PROJECT → CLASS
```

Figure 4.1 Database logic DDL definition of conceptual view V(FSEA).

C(FSEA,3), and C(FSEA,4), and a constraint C(FSEA,2) which says that salaries do not decrease over the years. The later constraint is expressed in database logic as

$$\begin{aligned}&(\text{SALINFO(NAME:1,SALARY:1,SALYEAR:1)}\\ &\ \&\ \text{SALINFO(NAME:1,SALARY:2,SALYEAR:2)}\\ &\ \&\ \text{SALYEAR:1} \le \text{(Y) SALYEAR:2)}\\ &\ \rightarrow \text{SALARY:1} \le \text{(S) SALARY:2.}\end{aligned}$$

V(FDP) = <S(FDP), L(FDP), C(FDP)> represents an external view that contains three relations, FAMSAL, DEPTINFO, and PROJECTS; two typed "less than or equal to" predicate symbols: ≤(S) and ≤(Y); and no function symbols. The type values in V(FDP) are EBCDIC. V(FDP) has three constraints. It has a functional dependency C(FDP,3) on PROJECTS and a constraint C(FDP,2) on FAMSAL which says that salaries do not decrease over the years.

```
V(FDP): VIEW DEFINITION
  S(FDP): SCHEMA DEFINITION
    TABLE FAMSAL = (EMP,CHILD,SAL,YEAR)
    TABLE DEPTINFO = (EMP,DEPT)
    TABLE PROJECTS = (DEPT,PROJECT,CLASS)

  L(FDP): LANGUAGE DEFINITION
    T(FDP): TYPING DEFINITION
      TYPE NAMTPE = {EMP,CHILD} EBCDIC CHAR(24)
      TYPE SALTPE = {SAL} EBCDIC REAL (8,2)
      TYPE YRTPE = {YEAR} EBCDIC DEC(4)
      TYPE DEPTPE = {DEPT} EBCDIC CHAR(12)
      TYPE TTLTPE = {TITLE} EBCDIC CHAR(25)
      TYPE PROTPE = {PROJECT} EBCDIC CHAR(6)
      TYPE CLATPE = {CLASS} EBCDIC DEC(2)

    NONLOGICAL SYMBOLS DEFINITION
      PREDICATES
        FAMSAL:(NAMTPE,NAMTPE,SALTPE,YRTPE)
                 PREDICATE
        DEPTINFO:(NAMTPE,DEPTPE) PREDICATE
        PROJECTS:(DEPTPE,PROTPE,CLATPE)
                 PREDICATE
        ≤(S): (SALTPE,SALTPE) PREDICATE
        ≤(Y): (YRTPE,YRTPE) PREDICATE
      FUNCTIONS
        NONE
    C(FDP): CONSTRAINTS DEFINITION
     C(FDP,1):CONSTRAINT FAMSAL:EMP →→ CHILD
     C(FDP,2):CONSTRAINT FAMSAL(EMP):
       YEAR:2 ≤(Y) YEAR:1 → SAL:1 ≤(S) SAL:2
     C(FDP,3):CONSTRAINT PROJECTS:PROJECT → CLASS
```

Figure 4.2 Database logic DDL definition of external view V(FDP).

The view also has a "multivalued" dependency

C(FDP,1): CONSTRAINT FAMSAL:EMP →→ CHILD

which says that in the FAMSAL table the set of employees' children are independent of the salaries and years. In database logic, this would be expressed as

(FAMSAL(EMP:1,CHILD:1,SAL:1,YEAR:1)
& FAMSAL(EMP:1,CHILD:2,SAL:2,YEAR:2))
→ FAMSAL(EMP:1,CHILD:2,SAL:1,YEAR:1).

That is, if one row of FAMSAL names an employee's SAL:1, YEAR:1 and another row names an employee's CHILD:2, there will be another row which names them both. The reader can find further details about multivalued dependencies in [Date].

An interpretation I(FDP;FSEA), of L(FDP) in L(FSEA) is given in Figure 4.3 . In it we see that the FAMSAL table is obtained by "joining" the FAMILY and SALINFO tables over the column NAME; the DEPTINFO table is the "projection" of

```
I(FDP;FSEA): INTERPRETATION DEFINITION
  EXTERNAL VIEW IS V(FDP) = <S(FDP),L(FDP),C(FDP)>
  CONCEPTUAL VIEW IS V(FSEA) = <S(FSEA),L(FSEA),C(FSEA)>


  CODING SECTION
    CODE FOR NAMTPE IS NAMTPE;
    CODE FOR SALTPE IS SALTPE;
    CODE FOR YRTPE  IS YRTPE;
    CODE FOR DEPTPE IS DEPTPE;
    CODE FOR PROTPE IS PROTPE;
    CODE FOR CLATPE IS CLATPE;

  DEFINING FORMULA SECTION
    PREDICATE:FAMSAL
    ARGUMENTS ARE: (NAME:1;,CHILDNAME:1;,SALYEAR:1;)
    IS DEFINED BY:
      FAMILY(NAME:1,CHILDNAME:1)
      & SALINFO(NAME:1,SALARY:1,SALYEAR:1)

    PREDICATE: DEPTINFO
    ARGUMENTS ARE: (NAME:1;,DEPTNAME:1;)
    IS DEFINED BY:(E)POSITION:1 (E)SEX:1
      EMPLOYEE(NAME:1,DEPTNAME:1,POSITION:1,SEX:1)

    PREDICATE: PROJECTS
    ARGUMENTS ARE: (DEPTNAME:1;,PROJECT:1;,CLASS:1;)
    IS DEFINED BY:
      ASSIGNMENT(DEPTNAME:1,PROJECT:1,CLASS:1)
      &  ~CLASS:1 = 0
    PREDICATE: ≤(S)
    ARGUMENTS ARE:(SALARY:1;,SALARY:2;)
    IS DEFINED BY: SALARY:1 ≤(S) SALARY:2

    PREDICATE: ≤(Y)
    ARGUMENTS ARE:(SALYEAR:1;,SALYEAR:2;)
    IS DEFINED BY: SALYEAR:1 ≤(Y) SALYEAR:2

    CONSTANT TRANSFORMATION SECTION

    PROC CODE(NAMTPE)(NAMTPE) RETURNS(NAMTPE;);
        .
        .
        .
    END;
  PROC DECODE(NAMTPE)(NAMTPE;) RETURNS(NAMTPE);
        .
        .
        .
     END;

        .
        .
        .
```

Figure 4.3 Interpretation I(FDP;FSEA).

FAMILY	
NAME	CHILDNAME
JOHN SMITH	SUSAN SMITH
JOHN SMITH	JERRY SMITH
KAREN WHITE	ROBERT WHITE
BEVERLY GREEN	STEVEN GREEN
BEVERLY GREEN	JOHN COX

SALINFO		
NAME	SALARY	SALYEAR
CAROL JONES	12635.12	1979
CAROL JONES	19255.24	1980
JOHN SMITH	20568.37	1978
JOHN SMITH	23289.74	1979
JOHN SMITH	26321.66	1980
KAREN WHITE	12150.85	1979
BEVERLY GREEN	25531.54	1979
BEVERLY GREEN	29126.33	1980

EMPLOYEE			
NAME	DEPTNAME	POSITION	SEX
CAROL JONES	PROGRAMMING	PROGRAMMER	F
JOHN SMITH	SYSTEMS	ANALYST	M
KAREN WHITE	SYSTEMS	SECRETARY	F
BEVERLY GREEN	SYSTEMS	MANAGER	F

NOTE: All values are in ASCII.

ASSIGNMENT		
DEPTNAME	PROJECT	CLASS
PROGRAMMING	XY2123	1
PROGRAMMING	ABC568	7
SYSTEMS	LLQ665	5
SYSTEMS	XY2123	1
SYSTEMS	FHQ986	0

Figure 4.4 Part of an instance of M(FSEA).

FAMSAL			
EMP	CHILD	SAL	YEAR
JOHN SMITH	SUSAN SMITH	20568.37	1978
JOHN SMITH	SUSAN SMITH	23289.74	1979
JOHN SMITH	SUSAN SMITH	26321.66	1980
JOHN SMITH	JERRY SMITH	26568.37	1978
JOHN SMITH	JERRY SMITH	23289.74	1979
JOHN SMITH	JERRY SMITH	26321.66	1980
KAREN WHITE	ROBERT WHITE	12150.85	1980
BEVERLY GREEN	STEVEN GREEN	25531.54	1979
BEVERLY GREEN	STEVEN GREEN	28126.33	1980
BEVERLY GREEN	JOHN COX	25531.54	1979
BEVERLY GREEN	JOHN COX	29126.33	1980

(a)

DEPTINFO	
EMP	DEPT
CAROL JONES	PROGRAMMING
JOHN SMITH	SYSTEMS
KAREN WHITE	SYSTEMS
BEVERLY GREEN	SYSTEMS

NOTE: All values are in EBCDIC.

(b)

PROJECTS		
DEPT.	PROJECT	CLASS
PROGRAMMING	XY2123	1
PROGRAMMING	ABC568	7
SYSTEMS	LLQ668	5
SYSTEMS	XY2123	1

(c)

Figure 4.5 Part of an instance of I′[M(FSEA)].

the EMPLOYEE table over the columns NAME and DEPTNAME; and the PROJECTS table is gotten by "selecting" the rows of the ASSIGNMENT table where the CLASS component is nonzero.

The reader can check that all the constraints C(FDP) of V(FDP), when interpreted by I(FDP;FSEA), are logical consequences of the constraints of V(FSEA). Hence, I(FDP;FSEA) is an interpretation of view V(FDP) in view V(FSEA). Throughout this chapter I(FDP,FSEA) will be abbreviated as I′.

Figures 4.4 and 4.5 are instances of relational structures of views V(FSEA) and V(FDP), respectively. The reader can check that the relational structure in Figure 4.5 is also part of the relational structure I′[M(FSEA)] induced from M(FSEA) of Figure 4.4 via I′.

Operations and Simulators

With each table R of a relational schema S we associate three operations: INSERT(R)(W), DELETE(R)(W), and UPDATE(R)(W). In each case W is an array of tuples of appropriate types that are to be, respectively, inserted, deleted, and updated into R. Since these three operations may change the database, we can also regard them as operations on the database which yield a new or, possibly, the same database. Consequently, we write

O(R)(W,M);

for the relational structure obtained by applying O(R) to the input W and relational structure M. For example, the insertion operation on SALINFO of V(FSEA) is denoted as

INSERT(SALINFO)(W,M(FSEA));

We associate with each operation O(R) and array W a set of variable-free formulas of L, called delta(O(R))(W). The idea is that the execution of the operation O(R)(W,M) should make all the formulas in delta(O(R))(W) "true" in the resulting relational structure. The following list provides precise definitions of delta(O(R))(W) for O = INSERT, DELETE and UPDATE, respectively.

1. delta(INSERT(R))(W) = { R(w) | w is in W}.
   For example, if R is the table SALINFO of V(FSEA) and W =

   { <MICHAEL GORDON, 20089.68, 1979>,
   <MICHAEL GORDON, 19375.74, 1980> },

   then delta(INSERT(SALINFO))(W) =

   {SALINFO(MICHAEL GORDON, 20089.68, 1979),
   SALINFO(MICHAEL GORDON, 19375.74, 1980) }.

2. delta(DELETE(R))(W) = { ~ R(w) | w is in W}.
   For example, if R is EMPLOYEE of V(FSEA) and W =

   { <CAROL JONES, PROGRAMMING,PROGRAMMER, F>,
   <JOHN SMITH, SYSTEMS, ANALYST, M>,
   <MICHAEL GORDON, PROGRAMMING, PROGRAMMER, M> },

   then delta(DELETE(EMPLOYEE))(W) =

   { ~EMPLOYEE(CAROL JONES, PROGRAMMING,PROGRAMMER, F),
   ~EMPLOYEE(JOHN SMITH, SYSTEMS, ANALYST, M),
   ~EMPLOYEE(MICHAEL GORDON, PROGRAMMING, PROGRAMMER, M)}.

   For update, we assume that W is an array of pairs W = { <W1(i),W2(i)> }, where W2(i) replaces W1(i) for each i.

3. delta(UPDATE(R))(W) = { ~R(W1(i)) | <W1(i),W2(i)> is in W}
   U {R(W2(i))| <W1(i),W2(i)> is in W}.
   For example, if R is ASSIGNMENT and W =

   { < <PROGRAMMING,XYZ123,1>, <PROGRAMMING,FHQ986,0> > },

   then

   delta(UPDATE(ASSIGNMENT)(W)
   = { ~ASSIGNMENT(PROGRAMMING,XYZ123,1)}
   U {ASSIGNMENT(PROGRAMMING,FHQ986,0) }.

Remark. Strictly speaking, other wffs may be affected besides those given in our definition of delta(O(R))(W). These involve functions, such as TOTCREDITS in V(Rext), whose values are affected by these operations. However, for simplicity of presentation, we shall not consider them.

We place simple restrictions on the three operations. Namely, we assume that some row to be inserted into a database is not already there, some row to be deleted from a database is there, and a combination of these conditions for update. These conditions ensure that an operation will "change" the database if and only if the constraints are not violated.

Let V(E) = <S(E),L(E),C(E)> and V(C) = <S(C),L(C),C(C)> be two relational views, and let I be an interpretation of V(E) in V(C). Let O(R) be an operation on an external database. That is, O(R) has arguments which are an array of tuples W and an induced external relational structure I[M(C)].

Definition. A *simulator for the operation* O(R) *via* I is a program called SIM(O(R)) with inputs an array of codes I[W] and a conceptual relational structure M(C) and outputs a "new" conceptual relational structure. We write

SIM(O(R))[I[W],M(C)]

for the conceptual relational structure that results from applying the simulator.

```
PROC SIM(INSERT(FAMSAL))(CW);

  /* CW is a an array of codes where:

     CW(i).NAME = an NAMTPE code
                = an ASCII CHAR(20) value (NAMTPE;),
     CW(i).CHILDNAME = a NAMTPE code
                = an ASCII CHAR(20) value (NAMTPE;),
     CW(i).SALARY = a SALTPE code
                = an ASCII REAL(8,2) value (SALTPE;),
     CW(i).SALYEAR=a YRTPE code
                = an ASCII INTEGER(4) value (YRTPE;),
i=1,...,length(CW) */

   ESTABLISH CHECKPOINT;

  /* If the simulation should fail [e.g., the resultant conceptual database is not
a model of C(FSEA)], then we can use this checkpoint to reestablish the old data-
base instance.*/
    FOR i = 1 TO LENGTH(CW);

  /* For each row of CW perform the following operations.*/
    INSERT(FAMILY)(CW(i).NAME,CW(i).CHILDNAME);
    INSERT(SALINFO)(CW(i).NAME,CW(i).SALARY,CW(i).SALYEAR);
  /* Insert into FAMILY the name and childname and insert into SALINFO the name,
salary, and salyear for the i-th row of CW.*/
    END i;
   IF M(FSEA) ⊨ C(FSEA) THEN RETURN;

 L1: RESTORE TO LAST CHECKPOINT;

 /* If the current conceptual database instance is a model of C(FSEA) then exit;
otherwise, roll back to the instance of the conceptual database prior to execu-
tion.*/

   END SIM(INSERT(FAMSAL));
```

Figure 4.6 Operation simulator SIM(INSERT(FAMSAL)).

For example, consider the operation INSERT(FAMSAL) on view V(FDP). A simulator corresponding to this operation is SIM(INSERT(FAMSAL)) given in Figure 4.6. To illustrate, consider the operation on I′[M(FSEA)]:

INSERT(FAMSAL)(W,I′[M(FSEA)]);

where W =

{ <MICHAEL GORDON, LINDA GORDON, 20089.68, 1979>,
<MICHAEL GORDON, LINDA GORDON, 21375.74,1980> }.

Figure 4.7(a) illustrates the effect of SIM(INSERT(FAMSAL)) (I′(W),M(FSEA)) on Figure 4.4. Figure 4.7(b) illustrates the effect of the above on the external relational structure.

FAMILY	
NAME	CHILDNAME
JOHN SMITH	SUSAN SMITH
JOHN SMITH	JERRY SMITH
KAREN WHITE	ROBERT WHITE
BEVERLY GREEN	STEVEN GREEN
BEVERLY GREEN	JOHN COX
MICHAEL GORDON	LINDA GORDON

(a)

SALINFO		
NAME	SALARY	SALYEAR
CAROL JONES	12635.12	1979
CAROL JONES	19255.24	1980
JOHN SMITH	20568.37	1978
JOHN SMITH	23289.74	1979
JOHN SMITH	26321.66	1980
KAREN WHITE	12150.85	1980
BEVERLY GREEN	25531.54	1979
BEVERLY GREEN	28126.33	1980
MICHAEL GORDON	20089.68	1979
MICHAEL GORDON	21375.74	1980

FAMSAL			
EMP	CHILD	SAL	YEAR
JOHN SMITH	SUSAN SMITH	20568.37	1978
JOHN SMITH	SUSAN SMITH	23289.74	1979
JOHN SMITH	SUSAN SMITH	26321.66	1980
JOHN SMITH	JERRY SMITH	20568.37	1978
JOHN SMITH	JERRY SMITH	23289.74	1979
JOHN SMITH	JERRY SMITH	26321.66	1980
KAREN WHITE	ROBERT WHITE	12150.85	1980
BEVERLY GREEN	STEVEN GREEN	25531.54	1979
BEVERLY GREEN	STEVEN GREEN	28126.33	1980
BEVERLY GREEN	JOHN COX	25531.54	1979
BEVERLY GREEN	JOHN COX	28126.33	1980
MICHAEL GORDON	LINDA GORDON	20089.69	1979
MICHAEL GORDON	LINDA GORDON	21375.74	1980

(b)

Figure 4.7 Effects of executing SIM(INSERT(FAMSAL)): (a) new FAMILY and SALINFO tables; (b) new FAMSAL table of the induced database.

We will assume throughout that an insertion on an external database is simulated by insertion(s) on the conceptual database, a deletion on the external database is simulated by deletion(s) on the conceptual database, and an update on the external database is simulated by update(s) [deletion(s) and insertion(s)] on the conceptual database. These conditions will greatly simplify our presentation.

Weak Correctness

The delta(O(R)) that corresponds to the operation O(R) represents the "intent" of the operation on the external database. If a change in the conceptual database does take place, one would like a simulator to provide the external user with this intent. Such a simulator is called "weakly" correct.

Definition. We say that SIM(O(R)) is *weakly correct with respect to* I if

$$\text{SIM(O(R))(I(W),M(C))} \neq \text{M(C) implies}$$
$$\text{I[SIM(O(R))(I(W),M(C))]} \models \text{delta(O(R))(W)}$$

for every W and relational structure M(C).

The idea of weak correctness is that if the simulator makes a legal change to the conceptual database M(C) [i.e., SIM(O(R)) (I(W),M(C)) $\neq$ M(C)], then the new induced external database should have the intended changes made to it .

Consider again the operation INSERT(FAMSAL) on V(FDP). We define another simulator SIM1(INSERT(FAMSAL)) which is identical to SIM(INSERT-(FAMSAL)) of Figure 4.6 except that the INSERT(SALINFO) command is removed. That is, the simulator will make insertions only into the FAMILY table of V(FSEA), not into the SALINFO table.

We show that SIM1(INSERT(FAMSAL)) is not weakly correct. Let M(FSEA) be the relational structure given in Figure 4.4 and let W =

{ <MICHAEL GORDON, LINDA GORDON, 20089.68, 1979>,
<MICHAEL GORDON, LINDA GORDON, 21375.74, 1980> }.

It is clear that

$$\text{SIM(INSERT(FAMSAL))(I}'\text{(W),M(FSEA))} \neq \text{M(FSEA)}$$

as the tuple <MICHAEL GORDON, LINDA GORDON> gets inserted into the FAMILY table. However,

$$\text{I}'\text{[SIM(INSERT(FAMSAL))(I}'\text{(W),M(FSEA))]}$$
$$\not\models \text{delta(INSERT(FAMSAL))(W),}$$

since the induced external database contains no FAMSAL tuple with name MICHAEL GORDON. It will be shown in the next section that SIM(FAMSAL), as defined previously, is weakly correct.

Consistent Correctness

Suppose that a user requests a change to the external database that is illegal (i.e., the external constraints are violated). Since the simulation occurs at the conceptual level, one would hope that the mistake would produce a situation in which the conceptual constraints are violated. Consequently, no changes are made at the conceptual level, hence, no changes are made at the external level. A simulator that acts in this way is called "consistently" correct.

```
PROC SIM(DELETE(FAMSAL)(CW);

 /* CW is a an array of codes where:
    CW(i).EMP = a NAMTPE code
                = an ASCII CHAR(20) value (NAMTPE;),
    CW(i).CHILD = a NAMTPE code
                = an ASCII CHAR(20) value (NAMTPE;),
    CW(i).SALARY = a SALTPE code
                = an ASCII REAL(8,2) value (SALTPE;),
    CW(i).SALYEAR = a YRTPE code
                = an ASCII INTEGER(4) value (YRTPE;),

 i = 1,...,length(CW) */

      ESTABLISH CHECKPOINT;

 /* If the simulation should fail [e.g., the resultant conceptual database is not
a model of C(FSEA)], we can use this checkpoint to reestablish the old database in-
stance.*/
     FOR i = 1 TO LENGTH(CW);

 /* For each row of CW perform the following operations.*/

     DELETE(FAMILY)(CW(i).NAME,CW(i).CHILD);

     DELETE(SALINFO)(CW(i).NAME,CW(i).SALARY,CW(i).SALYEAR);

 /* Delete from FAMILY the name and childname and delete from SALINFO the name,
salary, and salyear for the i-th row of CW.*/

     END i;

   IF M(FSEA) |= C(FSEA) THEN RETURN;
 L1: RESTORE TO LAST CHECKPOINT;

 /* If the current conceptual database instance is a model of C(FSEA) then exit;
otherwise, roll back to the instance of the conceptual database prior to execu-
tion.*/

     END SIM(DELETE(FAMSAL)) ;
```

Figure 4.8 Operation simulator SIM(DELETE(FAMSAL)).

Definition. We say that SIM(O(R)) is *consistently correct with respect to* I if

$$\text{SIM(O(R))(I(W),M(C))} \neq \text{M(C)} \quad \text{implies}$$
$$\text{O(R)(W,I[M(C)])} \neq \text{I[M(C)].}$$

for all W and relational structures M(C).

That is, if SIM(O(R)) is consistently correct when the simulator makes a legal update (i.e., changes the conceptual database), then the external user's intended update was legal (i.e., the external database changes).

Consider the deletion operation DELETE(FAMSAL) on external view V(FDP). A simulator SIM(DELETE(FAMSAL)) for it is defined in Figure 4.8. SIM (DELETE(FAMSAL)) deletes rows in "both" the FAMILY and the SALINFO tables in order to simulate a deletion of a row in FAMSAL. We show here that SIM-(DELETE(FAMSAL)) is not consistently correct.

Let M(FSEA) be the relational structure of Figure 4.4 and let W =

$$\{ \langle \text{JOHN SMITH, SUSAN SMITH, 20568.37, 1978} \rangle \}.$$

Now

$$\text{SIM(DELETE(FAMSAL))(I}'\text{(W),M(FSEA))} \neq \text{M(FSEA),}$$

since a tuple is deleted from the FAMILY and SALINFO tables. However,

$$\text{DELETE(FAMSAL)(W,I}'\text{[M(FSEA)])} = \text{I}'\text{[M(FSEA)],}$$

as the deletion of the tuple would falsify the multivalued dependency between CHILD and SALARY, YEAR mandated by constraint C(FDP,1) of Figure 4.2.

Independent Correctness

Suppose that a user requests a change to the external database that is legal as far as the external constraints are concerned. Since the simulation occurs at the conceptual level, one would hope that the simulation also produces a situation in which the conceptual constraints are not violated. A simulator that acts in this way is called "independently" correct.

Definition. We say that SIM(O(R)) is *independently correct with respect to* I if

$$\text{O(R)(W,I[M(C)])} \neq \text{I[M(C)] implies}$$
$$\text{SIM(O(R))(I(W),M(C))} \neq \text{M(C).}$$

for all W and relational structures M(C).

That is, if the external update is legal (i.e., changes the external database), then the simulation at the conceptual level should also be legal (i.e., changes the conceptual database).

For example, consider again SIM(INSERT(FAMSAL)) of Figure 4.6. Suppose that in the external view V(FDP), constraint C(FDP,2) were taken out. That is, as far as the external user is concerned, salaries can decrease over time. With this change occurring, SIM(INSERT(FAMSAL)) would not be independently correct.

Let M(FSEA) be the relational structure of Figure 4.4 and let W =

$$\{<\text{JOHN SMITH, SUSAN SMITH, 20568.37, 1981}>\}.$$

Now

$$\text{INSERT(FAMSAL)(W,I}'[\text{M(FSEA)}]) \neq \text{I}'[\text{M(FSEA)}],$$

as the insertion of the tuple in Figure 4.5 is legal with respect to the new constraints V(FDP). However,

$$\text{SIM(INSERT(FAMSAL))(I}'\text{(W),M(FSEA))} = \text{M(FSEA)},$$

since the inserted tuple in SALINFO of Figure 4.4 would violate the constraint C(FSEA,2). It will be seen in the next section that SIM(INSERT(FAMSAL)) is independently correct with respect to the old constraints.

Strong Correctness

When one performs an operation on the external database I[M(C)], one anticipates a new external database defined by O(R)(W,I[M(C)]). When the simulation occurs the new conceptual database is defined as SIM(O(R))(I(W),M(C)) and the new external database becomes I[SIM(O(R))(I(W),M(C))]. A simulator is called "strongly" correct if what the user anticipates is exactly what the user gets.

Definition. We say that SIM(O(R)) is *strongly correct with respect to* I if

$$\text{I[SIM(O(R))(I(W),M(C))]} = \text{O(R)(W,I[M(C)])}$$

for all W and relational structures M(C).

That is, whenever we start with a conceptual database M(C), we get the same external database structure whether we first obtain the induced external database I[M(C)] and apply the operation O(R) to it, or first apply the simulator to obtain the conceptual database SIM(O(R))(I[W],M(C)) and then take its induced external database. This situation is based on the "commutativity" of the diagram in Figure 4.9.

We can show that SIM(INSERT(FAMSAL)) of Figure 4.6 is not strongly correct with respect to I′. To see this, consider a relational structure M(FSEA) for V(FSEA) which has every table empty except for a single row in FAMILY. Let this row be (JOHN SMITH, SUSAN SMITH). Consequently, the corresponding induced external database I′[M(FSEA)] has all empty tables.

Suppose that an external user wishes to execute

$$\text{INSERT(FAMSAL)(W,I}'[\text{M(FSEA)}]);$$

where W =

$$\{<\text{JOHN SMITH, JERRY SMITH, 29568.37, 1978}>\}.$$

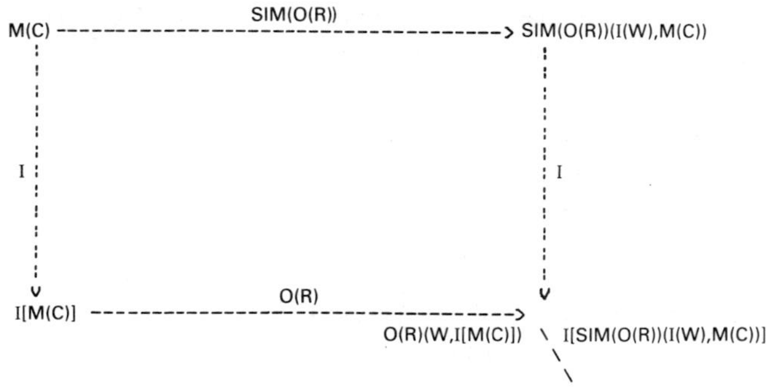

Figure 4.9 Commutative diagram for simulators.

This single row insertion into the empty FAMSAL table does not violate any constraints in C(FDA). Since the external database is empty, the effect of this instruction is to have a single row in FAMSAL.

However, the simulator

SIM(INSERT(FAMSAL))(I′(W),M(FSEA));

places one row in FAMILY and one in SALINFO and causes no violation of the constraints in C(FSEA). Since there is already a row in FAMILY with name JOHN SMITH, the result will be "two" JOHN SMITH rows in the FAMSAL table of the external database. Hence, the equality of external databases in the definition will not hold.

Exercises

Consider a simulator SIM(INSERT(DEPTINFO)) for the operation INSERT(DEPTINFO) on view V(FDA) in which the i-loop has the instruction

INSERT(EMPLOYEE)({ <CW(i).NAME, CW(i).DEPTNAME, NULL, NULL> }); .

This simulator inserts a tuple <CW(i).NAME, CW(i).DEPTNAME, NULL, NULL>, where NULL is a nondefined value, into the EMPLOYEE table if <W(i).NAME, W(i).DEPTNAME> is a tuple to be inserted into the DEPTINFO table.

1. Let M(FSEA) be the relational structure of Figure 4.4. Describe the result of the execution of SIM(INSERT(DEPTINFO)) (W,M(FSEA)) on M(FSEA) and I′[M(FSEA)] when W =

   { <CAROL JONES, SYSTEMS> }.

2. Show that SIM(INSERT(DEPTINFO)) is not independently correct.
3. Show that SIM(INSERT(DEPTINFO)) is not strongly correct.

Consider the simulator SIM(INSERT(PROJECTS)) for the operation INSERT(PROJECTS) on view V(FDA) in which the i-loop contains

```
IF CW(i).CLASS ≠ 0
 THEN
  DO;
  INSERT(ASSIGNMENT)({ <CW(i).DEPTNAME,
     CW(i).PROJECT, CW(i).CLASS)> };
  END;
ELSE
 GO TO L1;
```

The simulator inserts a tuple

<CW(i).DEPTNAME, CW(i).PROJECT, CW(i).CLASS>

into the ASSIGNMENT table if its CLASS component is nonzero. However, if just one of the inserted tuples has a zero CLASS component, a branch is made to L1 which rolls back the conceptual database to its status just prior to execution. In other words, every inserted tuple must have a nonzero class or else nothing is entered.

4. Let M(FSEA) be the relational structure of Figure 4.4. Describe the result of the execution of SIM(INSERT(PROJECTS)) (W,M(FSEA)) on M(FSEA) and I′[M(FSEA)] when W =

{ <PROGRAMMING, FHQ986, 0> }.

5. Show that SIM(INSERT(PROJECTS)) is not independently correct.

6. Show that SIM(INSERT(PROJECTS)) is not strongly correct.

4.2 CHECKING SIMULATOR CORRECTNESS

In this section we demonstrate some sufficient conditions that can be used to verify simulator correctness. These results are also used in Section 4.3 to show when various "canonical" simulators are correct. Proofs of these results are given in Chapter 5.

Some Simulators

1. Recall that in Figure 4.3 the DEPTINFO table from view V(FDP) is defined from the EMPLOYEE table from V(FSEA). The defining formula is

```
PREDICATE: DEPTINFO
ARGUMENTS ARE: (NAME:1;,DEPTNAME:1;)
IS DEFINED BY:(E)POSITION:1 (E)SEX:1
   EMPLOYEE(NAME:1,DEPTNAME:1,POSITION:1,SEX:1).
```

That is, DEPTINFO is obtained from EMPLOYEE by projecting onto the columns NAME and DEPTNAME.

Suppose that the operation INSERT(DEPTINFO) has a simulator that has inside the i-loop the instruction

```
INSERT(EMPLOYEE)({ <CW(i).NAME, CW(i).DEPTNAME,
NULL, NULL> });
```

The simulator inserts a tuple <CW(i).NAME, CW(i).DEPTNAME, NULL, NULL>, where NULL is a nondefined value, into the EMPLOYEE table if <W(i).NAME, W(i).DEPTNAME> is a tuple to be inserted into the DEPTINFO table.

2. Recall that in Figure 4.3 the FAMSAL table from view V(FDP) is defined from the FAMILY and SALINFO tables of V(FSEA). The defining formula is

```
PREDICATE:FAMSAL
ARGUMENTS ARE: (NAME:1;,CHILDNAME:1;,SALARY:1;)
IS DEFINED BY:
  FAMILY(NAME:1,CHILDNAME:1)
& SALINFO(NAME:1,SALARY:1,SALYEAR:1).
```

That is, FAMSAL is obtained from FAMILY and SALINFO by "joining" the two tables over their NAME columns.

Suppose that the operation INSERT(FAMSAL) has a simulator given in Figure 4.6. Notice that inside the i-loop are the instructions

```
INSERT(FAMILY)({ <CW(i).NAME,CW(i).CHILDNAME> });
INSERT(SALINFO)( <CW(i).NAME,CW(i).SALARY,CW(i).YEAR> });
```

The simulator inserts tuples

<CW(i).NAME,CW(i).CHILDNAME> and
<CW(i).NAME,CW(i).SALARY,CW(i).YEAR>

into the FAMILY table and SALINFO table, respectively, for each row

<W(i).NAME,W(i).CHILDNAME,W(i).SALARY,W(i).SALYEAR>

inserted into the FAMSAL table.

3. Recall that in Figure 4.3 the PROJECTS table from view V(FDP) is defined from the ASSIGNMENT table of V(FSEA). The defining formula is

```
PREDICATE: PROJECTS
ARGUMENTS ARE: (DEPTNAME:1;,PROJECT:1;,CLASS:1;)
IS DEFINED BY:
    ASSIGNMENT(DEPTNAME:1,PROJECT:1,CLASS:1)
         & ~ CLASS:1 = 0
```

That is, PROJECTS is obtained from ASSIGNMENT by "selecting" those rows of ASSIGNMENT which have a nonzero CLASS value.

Suppose that operation INSERT (PROJECTS) has a simulator that has inside the i-loop the instructions

```
IF CW(i).CLASS ≠ 0
 THEN
  DO;
  INSERT(ASSIGNMENT)({ <CW(i).DEPTNAME,
     CW(i).PROJECT, CW(i).CLASS)> });
  END;
 ELSE
  GO TO L1;
```

The simulator inserts a tuple

<CW(i).DEPTNAME, CW(i).PROJECT, CW(i).CLASS>

into the ASSIGNMENT table if its CLASS component is nonzero. However, if just one of the inserted tuples has a zero CLASS component, a branch is made to L1 which rolls back the conceptual database to its status just prior to execution. In other words, every inserted tuple must have a nonzero class or else nothing is entered into the ASSIGNMENT table.

Weak Correctness

Throughout these discussions O(R) denotes an operation [e.g., INSERT(R), DELETE(R), UPDATE(R)] in which constraint checking is done and O*(R) denotes the corresponding operation in which constraint checking is not done. Similarly, SIM-(O(R)) denotes an operation simulator in which conceptual constraint checking is done and SIM*(O(R)) denotes a simulator in which constraint checking is not done.

Our first result says that whenever the simulator changes the conceptual database, the "constraint-free" simulator results in a model of I(delta(O(R))(W)), the ordinary simulator is weakly correct.

Theorem 4.2.1 *Suppose that for all* W *and models* M(C) *of* V(C),

SIM(O(R))(I(W),M(C)) $\neq$ M(C) *implies*
SIM*(O(R))(I(W),M(C)) $\models$ I(delta(O(R))(W)).

Then SIM(O(R)) *is weakly correct.*

We can show that SIM(INSERT(DEPTINFO)) is weakly correct using Theorem 4.2.1. For this purpose note that

delta(INSERT(DEPTINFO))(W)
 = { DEPTINFO (W(i).EMP, W(i).DEPT) | i = 1,...,LENGTH(W) },

so

I′(delta(INSERT(DEPTINFO))(W))
= {(E)POSITION:1 (E)SEX:1
EMPLOYEE(I′(W(i).NAME),I′(W(i).DEPTNAME),
POSITION:1,SEX:1)| i = 1,...,LENGTH(W)}.

From the definition of SIM*(INSERT(DEPTINFO)) it is clear that for all W and M(FSEA),

SIM*(INSERT(DEPTINFO))(I‘(W),M(C))
$\models$ I‘(delta(INSERT(DEPTINFO))(W)).

One can also prove that SIM(INSERT(FAMSAL)) and SIM(INSERT(PROJECTS)) are both weakly correct using a similar argument.

Consistent Correctness

Our next result says that whenever the constraint-free simulator changes the conceptual database, if the corresponding induced external database satisfies the external constraints implies that the external operation also satisfies them, the simulator is consistently correct.

Theorem 4.2.2. *Suppose that for all arrays* W *and models* M(C) *of* V(C), *either*

SIM*(O(R))(I(W),M(C)) = M(C)

or else

I[SIM*(O(R))(I(W),M(C))] $\models$ C(E) *implies*
O*(R)(W,I[M(C)]) $\models$ C(E) .

Then SIM(O(R)) is consistently correct.

We prove that SIM(INSERT(DEPTINFO)) is consistently correct using Theorem 4.2.2. For this purpose we show that for all W and M(FSEA)

I′[SIM*(INSERT(DEPTINFO))(I′(W),M(FSEA))]
= INSERT*(DEPTINFO)(W,I′[M(FSEA)])

Clearly, this condition satifies the hypothesis of Theorem 4.2.2.

Fix W and M(FSEA).

I′[SIM*(INSERT(DEPTINFO))(I′(W),M(FSEA))]

and

INSERT*(DEPTINFO)(W,I′[M(FSEA)])

agree on all predicates except possibly DEPTINFO. This is because SIM(INSERT-(DEPTINFO)) inserts only into the EMPLOYEE table and in the definition of I′ of

Figure 4.3, the EMPLOYEE predicate appears only on the right-hand side of the defining formula for DEPTINFO.

However, they also agree on the DEPTINFO predicate.

INSERT*(DEPTINFO)(W,I′[M(FSEA)])

has a new DEPTINFO table which contains the additional tuples of W.

SIM*(INSERT(DEPTINFO))(I′(W),M(FSEA))

has a new EMPLOYEE table which contains the additional tuples of I′(W) (with padded NULL values). So its projection in

I′[SIM*(INSERT(DEPTINFO))(I′(W),M(FSEA))]

must be the same as in

INSERT*(DEPTINFO)(W,I′[M(FSEA)]).

SIM(INSERT(FAMSAL)) is not consistently correct. We show this by an example where M(FSEA) is the database of Figure 4.4 and I′[M(FSEA)] is the database of Figure 4.5. Let W =

{ <BEVERLY GREEN, MICHAEL GREEN, 25531.54, 1979> }.

Now

INSERT(FAMSAL)(W,I′[M(FSEA)]) = I′[M(FSEA)]

because INSERT*(FAMSAL)(W,I′[M(FSEA)]) violates the constraint C(FDP,1). However,

SIM(INSERT(FAMSAL))(I′(W),M(FSEA)) $\neq$ M(FSEA)

as the insertion of <BEVERLY GREEN, MICHAEL GREEN> into the FAMILY table and <BEVERLY GREEN, 25531.54, 1979> into the SALINFO table of M(FSEA) causes no problems.

One can show that SIM(INSERT(PROJECTS)) is consistently correct in the same way that we verified the consistent correctness of SIM(INSERT(DEPTINFO)).

Independent Correctness

Our next result gives a sufficient condition for independent correctness which is a dual to the one for consistent correctness.

Let C and C′ be sets of wffs in language L and STR a subclass of relational structures of L.

Definition. We say that C *logically implies* C′ *over* STR if for all M in STR,

$$M \models C \quad \text{implies} \quad M \models C' .$$

We denote this by $C \models C'$ over STR.

If STR is the set of all relational structures for language L, then logical implication over STR is the same as the usual notion of logical implication in first-order logic.

Let SIM*(O(R)) be a constraint-free simulator for O(R). Let STR(SIM*(O(R))) be the image of SIM*(O(R)); that is,

$$\begin{aligned}&\mathrm{STR(SIM^*(O(R)))}\\ &\quad = \{\mathrm{M(C)} \mid \text{for some array W and model } \mathrm{M'(C)} \text{ of } \mathrm{V(C)},\\ &\qquad \mathrm{M(C)} = \mathrm{SIM^*(I(W),M'(C))}\}.\end{aligned}$$

Theorem 4.2.3. *Suppose that* I(C(E)) ⊨ C(C) *over* STR(SIM*(O(R))) *and suppose that for all* W *and models* M(C) *of* V(C), *either*

$$\mathrm{SIM^*(O(R))(I(W),M(C))} = \mathrm{M(C)}$$

or else

$$\begin{aligned}\mathrm{O^*(R)(W,I[M(C)])} &\models \mathrm{C(E)} \quad \textit{implies}\\ \mathrm{I[SIM^*(O(R))(I(W),M(C))]} &\models \mathrm{C(E)}.\end{aligned}$$

Then SIM(O(R)) *is independently correct.*

We first show that INSERT(DEPTINFO) is not independently correct. Recall database M(FSEA) of Figure 4.4 and I′[M(FSEA)] of Figure 4.5. Let W = { <CAROL JONES, SYSTEMS> }. Then

$$\mathrm{INSERT(DEPTINFO)(W,I'[M(FSEA)])} \neq \mathrm{I'[M(FSEA)]}$$

since a tuple is inserted. However,

$$\mathrm{SIM(INSERT(DEPTINFO))(I'(W),M(FSEA))} = \mathrm{M(FSEA)}$$

since the addition of the tuple <CAROL JONES, SYSTEMS, NULL, NULL> to EMPLOYEE of M(FSEA) violates constraint C(FSEA,3).

Suppose that we expand C(FDP) to

$$\mathrm{C(FDP')} = \mathrm{C(FDP)} \cup \{\mathrm{DEPTINFO{:}EMP} \rightarrow \mathrm{DEPT}\}.$$

Note that now the insertion of <CAROL JONES, SYSTEMS> above violates the new constraint. We can show that with C(FDP′) replacing C(FDP), SIM(INSERT-(DEPTINFO)) is now independently correct. (In fact, with this change, it is also strongly correct.)

By the discussion above concerning the consistent correctness of SIM(INSERT-(DEPTINFO)), we know that the second half of the hypothesis of Theorem 4.2.3 holds. All that remains to be verified is the first half.

To do this we show that for any model M(FSEA) of C(FSEA)

$$\begin{aligned}\mathrm{SIM^*(INSERT(DEPTINFO))(I'(W),M(FSEA))} &\models \mathrm{I'[C(FDP)]} \quad \text{implies}\\ \mathrm{SIM^*(INSERT(DEPTINFO))(I'(W),M(FSEA))} &\models \mathrm{C(FSEA)}.\end{aligned}$$

So suppose that M(FSEA) $\models$ C(FSEA) and

$$\text{SIM*(INSERT(DEPTINFO))(I}'\text{(W),M(FSEA))} \not\models \text{C(FSEA)}.$$

Then an insertion into the EMPLOYEE table must have occurred which resulted in two different DEPTs for the same NAME. But then

$$\begin{aligned}&\text{I}'\text{[SIM*(INSERT(DEPTINFO))(I}'\text{(W),M(FSEA))]}\\ &\not\models \text{C(FDP).}\end{aligned}$$

since there would be a row in DEPTINFO with two different DEPTs for the same NAME. By the Flipper Theorem,

$$\begin{aligned}&\text{SIM*(INSERT(DEPTINFO))(I}'\text{(W),M(FSEA))}\\ &\not\models \text{I}'\text{[C(FDP)].}\end{aligned}$$

SIM(INSERT(FAMSAL)) is not independently correct. To see this, let M(FSEA) and I′[M(FSEA)] be the databases of Figures 4.4 and 4.5 and let W =

{ <JOHN SMITH, SUSAN SMITH, 24248.76, 1979>,
<JOHN SMITH, JERRY SMITH, 24248.76, 1979> }.

Now

$$\text{INSERT(FAMSAL)(W,I}'\text{[M(FSEA)])} \neq \text{I}'\text{[M(FSEA)]}$$

since the two tuples can be inserted into the FAMSAL table without violating C(FDP). However, the addition of the tuple <JOHN SMITH, 24248.76, 1979> to the SALINFO table violates constraint C(FSEA,1), so

$$\text{SIM(INSERT(FAMSAL))(I}'\text{(W),M(FSEA))} = \text{M(FSEA).}$$

SIM(INSERT(PROJECTS)) is not independent, either. To see this, consider the databases M(FSEA) and I′[M(FSEA)] of Figures 4.4 and 4.5, and let W =

{ <PROGRAMMING,FHQ986,0> }.

Then

$$\text{INSERT(PROJECTS)(W,I}'\text{[M(FSEA)])} \neq \text{I}'\text{[M(FSEA)],}$$

which is obtained from I′[M(FSEA)] by the addition of the tuple in W to the PROJECTS table. However, since for this tuple CLASS is 0,

$$\text{SIM*(INSERT(PROJECTS))(I}'\text{(W),M(FSEA))} = \text{M(FSEA),}$$

so,

$$\text{SIM(INSERT(PROJECTS))(I}'\text{(W),M(FSEA))} = \text{M(FSEA).}$$

Strong Correctness

Let Q be a wff of L(C), W an array, and M(C) a model of V(C).

Definition. Q is called *incrementally independent of* SIM*(O(R))(I(W),M(C)) if

$$M(C) \models Q \quad \text{iff} \quad SIM^*(O(R))(I(W),M(C)) \models Q.$$

That is, a wff Q is incrementally independent of SIM*(O(R))(I(W),M(C)) if its truth is not effected by the constraint-free simulation operation.

Theorem 4.2.4. *Let* SIM(O(R)) *be a weakly correct simulator for* O(R) *with respect to* I. *Suppose that*

1. SIM(O(R)) *is consistently and independently correct.*
2. *For any array* W *and model* M(C) *of* V(C) *and any variable-free atom* Q *of* L(E) *not used in* delta(O(R))(W), I(Q) *is incrementally independent of* SIM*(O(R)) (I(W),M(C)).

Then SIM(O(R)) *is strongly correct.*

Two results relating strong correctness with others are given below. We leave their proofs as exercises.

Theorem 4.2.5. *If* SIM(O(R)) *is strongly correct, then it is independently correct.*

Theorem 4.2.6. *If* SIM(O(R) *is both strongly and consistently correct, then it is weakly correct.*

Theorem 4.2.5 is particularly useful in its contrapositive form to show that a simulator is not strongly correct. Recall that the three simulators above were shown not to be independently correct. Consequently, none of the three are strongly correct.

However, recall that when we added the constraint DEPTINFO: EMP → DEPT to C(FDP), SIM(INSERT(DEPTINFO)) became independently correct. It was also shown above that SIM(INSERT(DEPTINFO)) was weakly and consistently correct, even without the addition of the constraint. We can use Theorem 4.2.4 to show strong correctness; we just have to verify that condition (2) holds.

Let W be an array and M(FSEA) be any relational structure which is a model of V(FSEA). Let Q be any variable-free atom in L(FDP) not used in delta(INSERT-(DEPTINFO))(W). We have to show that

$$\begin{aligned}&M(FSEA) \models I'(Q) \quad \text{iff}\\ &SIM^*(INSERT(DEPTINFO))(I'(W),M(FSEA)) \models I'(Q).\end{aligned}$$

1. If Q is of the form FAMSAL(-) or PROJECTS(-), then I′(Q) is not affected by the execution of the constraint-free simulator. This is because I′(Q) does not use the predicate EMPLOYEE, which is changed by the simulator.

2. If Q has the form DEPTINFO(-) and is not in delta(INSERT(DEPTINFO))(W), then insertions into EMPLOYEE also cannot affect the truth of I′(Q).

Hence, all the criteria of Theorem 4.2.4 are satisfied.

Another useful condition for strong correctness is given by the following result. Its proof is also left as an exercise.

Theorem 4.2.7. *Suppose that for all* W *and models* M(C) *of* V(C),

1. SIM*(O(R))(I(W),M(C)) $\neq$ M(C) *implies* I[SIM*(O(R))(W),M(C))] = O(R)*(W,I[M(C)]).
2. I(C(E)) $\models$ C(C) over STR(SIM*(O(R))).
3. SIM*(O(R))(I,M(C)M(C)) = M(C) *implies* O(R)*(W,I[W]) $\not\models$ C(E). *Then* SIM(O(R)) *is strongly correct.*

Corollary 4.2.8. *Suppose that hypotheses* 1, 2, *and* 3 *of Theorem 4.2.7 hold. Then* SIM(O(R)) *is independently correct.*

Exercises

1. Verify that SIM(INSERT(FAMSAL)) and SIM(INSERT(PROJECTS)) are weakly correct.
2. Verify that SIM(INSERT(PROJECTS)) is consistently correct.
3. Prove Theorem 4.2.5.
4. Prove Theorem 4.2.6.
5. Prove Theorem 4.2.7.
6. Let SIM(DELETE(DEPTINFO)) be a simulator for (DELETE(DEPTINFO)) in which the instructions in the i-loop are

```
GET W (POSITION:1,SEX:1)
  EMPLOYEE(CW(i).NAME,CW(i).DEPT,POSITION:1,SEX:1);
FOR j = 1 TO LENGTH(W);
  DO;
    DELETE(EMPLOYEE)({ <CW(i).NAME,CW(i).DEPTNAME,
       W(j).POSITION,W(j).SEX)> };
END;
```

   Show that SIM(DELETE(DEPTINFO)) is weakly, consistently, independently, and strongly correct.
7. Let SIM(DELETE(PROJECTS)) be a simulator for (DELETE(PROJECTS)) in which the instructions in the i-loop are

```
IF CW(i).CLASS = 0 THEN GO TO L1;
DELETE(ASSIGNMENT)({ <CW(i).DEPT,CW(i).PROJECT, CW(i).CLASS)> };
```

   Here the instruction L1 causes a rollback to the status of the database prior to execution of the simulation.

Show that SIM(DELETE(PROJECTS)) is weakly, consistently, independently, and strongly correct.

4.3 CANONICAL SIMULATORS

In this section we consider the most commonly used methods for defining relational external views: projection, join, and selection, and construct "canonical" simulators for insertions on the external database. We also prove the correctness properties of these simulators and show that under other conditions, further correctness properties hold. Corresponding results for deletion and update are left as exercises.

Results for insertion are summarized in the chart in Figure 4.10. The conditions in the boxes are sufficient for the correctness properties to hold. A "yes" indicates that the canonical simulator has the correctness property without any additional conditions, whereas a "no" is used to indicate that no nice sufficient conditions are known. Results for deletion and update are summarized in Figures 4.11 and 4.12.

Insertion and Deletion Properties

Let V = <S,L,C> be a relational view with table names R1,...,Rn.

Definition. We say that C has the *insertion property for* R1, ..., Rn if whenever M $\models$ C and M′ is obtained from M by inserting one or more rows into R1, ..., Rn tables of M, then M′ $\models$ C. Similarly, we say that C has the *deletion property for* R1, ..., Rn if whenever M $\models$ C and M′ is obtained from M by deleting one or more rows from R1, ..., Rn tables of M, then M′ $\models$ C.

Observe that the empty set of constraints has both insertion and deletion properties for any set of tables. A set of functional dependencies has the deletion property for any set of relations. This follows since the deletion of rows cannot violate the fact that certain columns determine other columns.

Let V(E) and V(C) again be two relational views and I be an interpretation of V(E) in V(C). Let R be some table in external view V(E). Consider operation INSERT(R) and its simulator SIM(INSERT(R)). If C(E) has the insertion property for R, then for all W and relational structures M(C)

$$\text{INSERT(R)(W,I[M(C)])} \models \text{C(E)}.$$

Hence, any simulator is consistently correct. If C(C) has the insertion property for the tables used in the program for SIM(INSERT(R)), and since insertions are simulated by insertions, then for all W and relational structures M(C)

$$\text{SIM(INSERT(R))(I(W),M(C))} \models \text{C(C)}.$$

Hence, the simulator is independently correct.

Similarly, for deletion, if C(E) has the deletion property for R, then SIM(DE-

	Weak Correctness	Consistent Correctness	Independent Correctness	Strong Correctness
General	No	C(E) has the insertion property for R	C(E) has the insertion property for the RC used in the simulator	No
Projection	Yes	Yes	I(C(E)) ⊨ C(C) over STR(SIM*(INSERT(R)))	I(C(E)) ⊨ C(C) over STR(SIM*(INSERT(R))
Join	Yes	C(E) has the insertion property for R	C(E) has the deletion property for R and I(C(E)) ⊨ C(C) over STR(SIM*(INSERT(R)))	No
Selection	Yes	Yes	I(C(E)) ⊨ C(C) over STR(SIM*(INSERT(R) and Q1 in C(E)	I(C(E)) ⊨ C(C) over STR(SIM*(INSERT(R)) and Q1 in C(E)

Q1 = RE(X:1,Y:1,Z:1) → Q(X:1,Y:1,Z:1).

Figure 4.10 Correctness properties for the canonical insertion simulators.

	Weak Correctness	Consistent Correctness	Independent Correctness	Strong Correctness
General	No	C(E) has the deletion property for R	C(E) has the deletion property for the RC used in the simulator	No
Projection	Yes	Yes	I(C(E)) ⊨ C(C) over STR(SIM*(DELETE(R)))	I(C(E)) ⊨ C(C) over STR(SIM*(DELETE(R))
Join	Yes	C(E) has the insertion property for R	C(E) has the deletion property for R and I(C(E)) ⊨ C(C) over STR(SIM*(DELETE(R)))	No
Selection	Yes	Yes	I(C(E)) ⊨ C(C) over STR(SIM*(DELETE(R)))	I(C(E)) ⊨ C(C) over STR(SIM*(DELETE(R))

Figure 4.11 Correctness properties for the canonical deletion simulators.

	Weak Correctness	Consistent Correctness	Independent Correctness	Strong Correctness
General	No	C(E) is empty	C(E) has the insertion and deletion properties for the RC used in the simulator	No
Projection	Yes	Yes	I(C(E)) ⊨ C(C) over STR(SIM*(UPDATE(R)))	I(C(E)) ⊨ C(C) over STR(SIM*(UPDATE(R))
Join	Yes	C(E) is empty	C(E) is empty and I(C(E)) ⊨ C(C) over STR(SIM*(UPDATE(R)))	No
Selection	Yes	Yes	I(C(E)) ⊨ C(C) over STR(SIM*(UPDATE(R))) and Q1 in C(E)	I(C(E)) ⊨ C(C) over STR(SIM*(UPDATE(R)) and Q1 in C(E)

Figure 4.12 Correctness properties for the canonical update simulators.

LETE(R)) is consistently correct and if C(C) has the deletion property for the tables used in the program for SIM(DELETE(R)), then the simulator is independently correct. Finally, for update we can combine these conditions. Thus, if C(E) has both the insertion and deletion properties for R, then SIM(UPDATE(R)) is consistently correct. Also, if C(C) has both the insertion and deletion properties for the tables used in the program for SIM(UPDATE(R)), then SIM(UPDATE(R)) is independently correct.

We provide other results which involve insertion simulators and the insertion and deletion properties. The proofs are left as exercises for the reader.

Theorem 4.3.1. *If* C(E) *has the deletion property for* R, *then* SIM (INSERT(R)) *is consistently correct.*

Theorem 4.3.2. *If* C(E) *has the insertion property for* R *and*

$$\mathrm{I(C(E))} \models \mathrm{C(C)} \text{ over } \mathrm{STR(SIM^{*}(INSERT(R)))},$$

then SIM(INSERT(R)) *is independently correct.*

We now begin our study of the correctness properties for canonical simulators.

Insertions on a Projection

Our first view is a projection in which the conceptual schema contains (only) a relation RC(X,Y,Z,V) and the external database contains (only) a relation R(X,Y). The defining formula is

```
PREDICATE R
ARGUMENTS ARE (X:1;,Y:1;)
IS DEFINED BY (E)Z:1(E)V:1 RC(X:1,Y:1,Z:1,V:1).
```

That is, R is obtained from RC by projecting onto the attributes X and Y.

The operation INSERT(R) has a "canonical" simulator SIM(INSERT(R)) which has inside its i-loop the instruction

```
INSERT(RC)({ <CW(i).X, CW(i).Y, NULL, NULL> });
```

This simulator inserts a tuple <CW(i).X, CW(i).Y, NULL, NULL>, where NULL is a nondefined value, into the RC table if <W(i).X, W(i).Y> is a tuple to be inserted into the R table.

The simulator SIM(INSERT(R)) is always weakly correct. This can be shown using Theorem 4.2.1 in the same way in which we showed that SIM(INSERT(DEPTINFO)) was weakly correct in Section 4.2. It can also be shown that SIM(INSERT(R)) is always consistently correct in the same way in which it was shown that SIM(INSERT(DEPTINFO)) was consistently correct in Section 4.2. As seen in the case of SIM(INSERT(DEPTINFO)), independent correctness need not hold. By Theorem 4.2.5, we need not have strong correctness, either.

Observe the three hypotheses of Theorem 4.2.7. The reader can easily check that the canonical simulator always obeys conditions 1 and 3. Hence, it follows that condition 2,

$$I(C(E)) \models C(C) \text{ over } STR(SIM^*(O(R))),$$

is a sufficient condition for strong correctness in the simulation of insertion on a projection. By Theorem 4.2.5 it is also a sufficient condition for independent correctness.

Recall that in Section 4.2 we added a new constraint,

$$DEPTINFO\colon EMP \rightarrow DEPT.$$

What we actually did was to force condition 2. Consequently, we ensured the strong and independent correctness of SIM(INSERT(DEPTINFO)).

Insertions on a Join

We use the setup in which the conceptual database contains (only) the relations RC1(X,Y) and RC2(X,Z,V), while the external database contains (only) a relation R(X,Y,Z,V). The defining formula is

```
PREDICATE:R
ARGUMENTS ARE:(X:1;,Y:1;,Z:1;,V:1;)
IS DEFINED BY:
  RC1(X:1,Y:1) & RC2(X:1,Z:1,V:1).
```

That is, R is obtained from RC1 and RC2 by joining the two relations over the common attribute X. The operation INSERT(R) has a canonical simulator SIM(INSERT(R)) which has inside its i-loop the instructions

```
INSERT(RC1)({ <CW(i).X,CW(i).Y> });
INSERT(RC2)( <CW(i).X,CW(i).Z,CW(i).V> });
```

The simulator inserts a tuple <CW(i).X, CW(i).Y> into the RC1 table and <CW(i).X, CW(i).Z, CW(i).V> into the RC2 table if <W(i).X, W(i).Y,W(i).Z, W(i).V> is a tuple to be inserted in the R table.

The simulator SIM(INSERT(R)) is always weakly correct. This can be shown using Theorem 4.2.1 in the same way in which one shows that SIM(INSERT(FAMSAL)) is weakly correct in Section 4.2. SIM(INSERT(R)) need not be consistently or independently correct, as seen in the case of SIM(INSERT(FAMSAL)) of Section 4.2. By Theorem 4.2.5, SIM(INSERT(R)) need not be strongly correct.

Recall the definitions of the insertion and/or deletion properties. We already know that, in general, if C(E) has the insertion property for R, then SIM(INSERT(R)) is consistently correct. It follows from Theorem 4.3.1 that if C(E) has the deletion property for R, then SIM(INSERT(R)) is consistently correct.

We also know that if C(C) has the insertion property for RC1, RC2, then SIM (INSERT(R)) is independently correct. It follows from Theorem 4.3.2, that if C(E) has the the insertion property for R and

$$I(C(E)) \models C(C) \text{ over } STR(SIM^*(INSERT(R))),$$

then SIM(INSERT(R)) is independently correct.

At this time no nice sufficient conditions are known for strong correctness.

Insertions on a Selection

For selection we use the following situation. The conceptual database contains (only) a relation RC(X,Y,Z) and the external database has (only) the relation R(X,Y,Z). The defining formula is

```
PREDICATE:R
ARGUMENTS ARE:(X:1;,Y:1;,Z:1;)
IS DEFINED BY:
   RC(X:1,Y:1,Z:1) & I(Q)(X:1,Y:1,Z:1).
```

That is, R is obtained from RC by selecting only those rows which satisfy the predicate I(Q). The predicate Q is in the external language L(E), while its interpretation I(Q) is in the conceptual language. We assume that for any row w [in L(E)] and any M(C),

$$\text{either} \quad M(C) \models I(Q(w)) \quad \text{or } M(C) \models \sim I(Q(w)),$$

that is, I(Q(w)) is always true or always false.

The operation INSERT(R) has a canonical simulator SIM(INSERT(R)) which has inside its i-loop the instructions

```
IF I(Q)(CW(i).X,CW(i).Y,CW(i).Z)
 THEN
  DO;
    INSERT(RC)({ <CW(i).X,CW(i).Y,CW(i).Z)> };
  END;
 ELSE GO TO L1;
```

The simulator inserts a tuple

<(CW(i).X,CW(i).Y,CW(i).Z)>

into the RC table if I(Q)(CW(i)) is true. However, if just one of the inserted rows fails to satisfy I(Q), then a branch is made to L1 which rolls back the conceptual database to its status just prior to execution. In other words, every inserted tuple must have I(Q) or else nothing is entered.

The simulator SIM(INSERT(R)) is always weakly correct. This can be seen using Theorem 4.2.1 in the same way in which it is shown that SIM(INSERT(PROJECTS)) is weakly correct in Section 4.2. Consistent correctness for SIM(INSERT(R)) always holds. This follows from Theorem 4.2.2 in the same way in which it is shown that SIM(INSERT(PROJECTS)) is consistently correct. SIM(INSERT(R)) need not be independently correct, as seen in the case of SIM(INSERT(PROJECTS)). By Theorem 4.2.5, SIM(INSERT(R)) need not be strongly correct.

We can use Corollary 4.2.8 to get a sufficient condition for independent correctness. Let Q1 be the wff of L(C),

$$R(X{:}1,Y{:}1,Z{:}1) \rightarrow Q(X{:}1,Y{:}1,Z{:}1).$$

We show that the two conditions

1. I(C(E)) $\models$ C(C) over STR(SIM*(INSERT(R))), and
2. Q1 in C(E).

together imply independent correctness.

First, suppose that

$$SIM^*(INSERT(R))(I(W),M(C)) \neq M(C).$$

Then the insertion takes place so that

$$I[SIM^*(INSERT(R))(I(W),M(C))] = INSERT^*(R)(W,I[M(C)]).$$

Second, suppose that

$$SIM^*(INSERT(R))(I(W),M(C)) = M(C).$$

Then the insertion does not take place, hence, for some w in **W**, Q(w) is false. Whereas, from Q1,

$$M(C) \not\models I(Q(w)) \text{ and } I[M(C)] \not\models Q(w),$$

thus,

$$INSERT^*(R)(W,I[M(C)]) \not\models C(E).$$

Since SIM(INSERT(R)) need not be independently correct, by Theorem 4.2.5, it need not be strongly correct. Using Theorem 4.2.7, if

1. I(C(E)) $\not\models$ C(C) over STR(SIM*(INSERT(R))), and
2. Q1 in C(E).

then SIM(INSERT(R)) is also strongly correct. The proof of this is identical to the foregoing argument for independent correctness.

Recall that in Section 4.2, SIM(INSERT(PROJECTS)) was neither independently nor strongly correct. Suppose that we modify V(FDP) to V(FDP′), where

$$C(FDP') = C(FDP) \cup \{PROJECTS(DEPT{:}1,PROJECT{:}1,CLASS{:}1) \rightarrow \sim CLASS{:}1 = 0\}.$$

The reader can check that the modification made to V(FDP) is such that the two conditions above are satisfied. Hence, simulator SIM(INSERT(PROJECTS)) becomes independently and strongly correct.

Deletions and Updates

As mentioned earlier, the charts in Figures 4.11 and 4.12 summarize the situations for deletions and updates. The validation of these charts are left as exercises.

More Complex Simulations

Until now we have considered simulations when the external view is obtained from the conceptual view by projection, join, or selection. We now consider the situation in which the external view is obtained by a combination of these operations. The definition of the simulators given above can be combined to obtain simulators for such views.

Suppose that the external view is obtained by means of a projection and a selection and suppose that the operation is insertion. We use the setup where the conceptual schema contains (only) a relation RC(X,Y,Z,V) and the external schema contains (only) a relation R(X,Y). The defining formula is

```
PREDICATE IS: R
ARGUMENTS ARE: (X:1;,Y:1;)
IS DEFINED BY (E)Z:1 (E)V:1
  RC(X:1,Y:1,Z:1,V:1) & I(Q)(X:1,Y:1).
```

The operation INSERT(R) has canonical simulator SIM(INSERT), which has the instructions inside its i-loop:

```
IF M(C) ⊨ I(Q)(CW(i).X,CW(i).Y)
   THEN INSERT(RC)({ <CW(i).X,CW(i).Y,NULL,NULL> });
   ELSE GO TO L1;
```

It can be shown that SIM(INSERT(R)) is weakly and consistently correct. Weak correctness follows from Theorem 4.2.1 and consistent correctness from Theorem 4.2.2. Strong correctness (and hence independent correctness) follows if

$$I(C(E)) \models C(C) \text{ over } STR(SIM^*(INSERT(R)))$$

holds and Q1 is in C(E) (see Figure 4.10) by Theorem 4.2.7. We leave the verification of these facts as exercises.

As a second illustration, we consider an external view obtained by means of a projection, a join and a selection and suppose that the operation to be simulated is deletion. We use the setup where the conceptual schema contains (only) the relations RC1(X,Y) and RC2(X,Z,V) and the external schema contains (only) R(X,Y,Z). The defining formula is

```
PREDICATE IS: R
ARGUMENTS ARE: (X:1;,Y:1;,Z:1;)
IS DEFINED BY: RC1(X:1,Y:1)
   & (E)V:1 RC2(X:1,Z:1,V:1) & I(Q)(X:1,Y:1,Z:1).
```

The operation DELETE(R) has a canonical simulator SIM(DELETE(R)) which has instructions inside its i-loop:

```
IF M(C) |= I(Q)(CW(i).X,CW(i).Y,CW(i).Z )
 THEN
  DO;
    DELETE(RC1)({ <CW(i).X,CW(i).Y> });
    GET W1(V:1) : RC2(CW(i).X,CW(i).Z,V:1);
    FOR j = 1 TO LENGTH(W1);
    DO;
    DELETE(RC2)({ <CW(i).X,CW(i).Z,W1.V(j)> });
  END;
 END;
ELSE GO TO L1;
```

The weak correctness of this simulator follows from Theorem 4.2.1 . The other correctness properties need not hold. However, if C(E) has the deletion property for R, then the simulator is consistently correct. If, in addition,

$$I(C(E)) \models C(C) \text{ over } STR(SIM(DELETE(R))),$$

then the simulator is independently correct. These last remarks are left as exercises.

Exercises

1. Prove Theorem 4.3.1.
2. Prove Theorem 4.3.2 .
3. Consider the setup of the projection R of RC above (in the subsection Insertions on a Projection). A canonical simulator SIM(DELETE(R)) for DELETE(R) has the following instructions in its i-loop:

   ```
   GET W1 (Z:1,V:1) : RC(CW(i).X,CW(i).Y,Z:1,V:1) ;
   FOR j = 1 TO LENGTH(W1);
    DO;
      DELETE(RC)({ <CW(i).X,C-
      W(i).Y,W1(j).Z,W1(j).V> });
   END;.
   ```

   Show that SIM(DELETE(R)) has the properties displayed in Figure 4.11.
4. Show that SIM(DELETE(EMPLOYEE)) possesses all four correctness properties.
5. Consider the setup of the join R of RC1 and RC2 above (in the subsection Insertions on a Join). A canonical simulator SIM(DELETE(R)) for DELETE(R) has the following instructions in its i-loop:

   ```
   DELETE(RC1)({ <CW(i).X,CW(i).Y)> });
   DELETE(RC2)({ <CW(i).X,CW(i).Z,CW(i).V> });
   ```

   Show that SIM(DELETE(R)) has the properties displayed in Figure 4.11.
6. Show that SIM(DELETE(FAMSAL)) is weakly and independently correct, but not consistently and strongly correct.

7. Consider the setup of the selection R of RC via Q above (in the subsection Insertions on a Selection). A canonical simulator SIM(DELETE(R)) for DELETE(R) has the following instructions in its i-loop:

```
IF M(C) ⊨ I(Q)(CW(i).X,CW(i).Y,CW(i).Z)
THEN DELETE(RC)({ <CW(i).X,CW(i).Y,CW(i).Z> });
```

Show that SIM(DELETE(R)) has all the properties displayed in Figure 4.11.

8. Show that SIM(DELETE(PROJECTS)) possesses all four correctness properties.

9. Consider the setup of the projection R of RC above (in the subsection Insertions on a Projection). A canonical simulator SIM(UPDATE(R)) for UPDATE(R) has the following instructions in its i-loop:

```
GET W (Z:1,V:1): RC(CW1(i).X,CW1(i).Y,Z:1,V:1);
FOR j = 1 TO LENGTH(W1);
 DO;
   DELETE(RC)({ <CW1(i).X,CW1(i).Y,W1(j).Z,W(j).V);
   INSERT(RC)({ <CW2(i).X,CW2(i).Y,W(j).Z,W(j).V);
END;
```

Show that SIM(UPDATE(R)) has all the properties displayed in Figure 4.12.

10. Show that if the constraint DEPTINFO:EMP → DEPT is added to C(FDP), then SIM (UPDATE(DEPTINFO)) possesses all four correctness properties.

11. Consider the setup of the join R of RC1 and RC2 above (in the subsection Insertions on a Join). A canonical simulator SIM(UPDATE(R)) for UPDATE(R) has the following instructions in its i-loop:

```
DELETE(RC1)({ <CW1(i).X,CW1(i).Y> };
INSERT(RC1)({ <CW2(i).X,CW2(i).Y> };
DELETE(RC2)({ <CW1(i).X,CW1(i).Z,CW1(i).V> };
INSERT(RC2)({ <CW2(i).X,CW2(i).Z,CW2(i).V> };
```

Show that SIM(UPDATE(R)) has all the properties displayed in Figure 4.12.

12. Find the correctness properties of SIM(UPDATE(FAMSAL)).

13. Consider the setup of the selection R of RC via Q above (in the subsection Insertions on a Selection). A canonical simulator SIM(UPDATE(R)) for UPDATE(R) has the following instructions in its i-loop:

```
IF M(C) ⊨ I(Q)(CW2(i).X,CW2(i).Y,CW2(i).Z)
 THEN
 DO;
   DELETE(RC)({ <CW1(i).X,CW1(i).Y,CW1(i).Z> });
   INSERT(RC)({ <CW2(i).X,CW2(i).Y,CW2(i).Z> });
 END;
ELSE GO TO L1;
```

Show that SIM(UPDATE(R)) has all the properties displayed in Figure 4.12.

14. Show that SIM(UPDATE(PROJECTS)) is weakly and consistently correct, but does not have the other correctness properties.

15. Verify the claims made at the end of Section 4.3 about the insertion simulator for the combination projection and selection.

16. Verify the claims made at the end of Section 4.3 about the deletion simulator for the combination projection, join and selection.

4.4 RELATED READING

BANCILHON, F. AND SPYRATOS, N., "Update Semantics of Relational Views," *ACM Transactions on Database Systems,* **6** Dec. 1981, pp. 557-575.

CHAMBERLIN, D. D., GRAY, J. N., AND TRAIGER, I. L., "Views, Authorization and Locking in a Relational Data Base System," *Proceedings National Computer Conference,* Vol. **44,** AFIPS Press, Arlington, Va., May 1975.

DAYAL, U. AND BERNSTEIN, P.A., "On the Correct Translation of Update Operations on Relational Views," *ACM Transactions on Database Systems,* **7,** Dec. 1982, pp. 381-416.

FAGIN, R., ULLMAN, J. D., AND VARDI, M.Y., "On the Semantics of Updates in Databases," *Proceedings Second ACM SIGACT-SIGMOD Symposium on Principles of Database Systems,* Atlanta, 1983, pp. 352-365.

FURTADO, A.L., SEVCIK, K.C. AND DOS SANTOS, C.S., "Permitting Updates Through Views of Data Bases," *Information Systems,* **4,** 1979, pp. 269-283.

GRANT, J. AND JACOBS, B. E., *On the Simulation of View Updates For Relational Databases,* Department of Computer Science Technical Report, University of Maryland, College Park, 1980.

KELLER, A. M., "Updates to Relational Databases Through Views Using Joins," in *Improving Database Usability and Responsiveness* (ed. P. Scheurmann) Academic Press, New York, 1982, pp. 363-384.

KLUG, A. C., *Theory of Database Mappings,* Department of Computer Science Technical Report TR CSRG-98, University of Toronto, 1978.

OSMAN, I. M., "Updating Defined Relations," *Proceedings National Computer Conference,* Vol. 48, AFIPS Press, Arlington, Va., 1979, pp. 733-740.

TODD, S., "Automatic Constraint Maintenance and Updating Defined Relations," *Information Processing 77,* North-Holland, Amsterdam, 1977, pp. 145-148.

5

VIEW UPDATE II— THE HETEROGENEOUS CASE

In Chapter 5 we investigate the view update problem for heterogeneous databases. In Section 5.1 we use the notion of interpretation of database views to study the four notions of simulator correctness. In Section 5.2 we also show how to use the formalism to verify the correctness of simulators in the heterogeneous case. In Section 5.3 we prove necessary and sufficient characterizations for the four correctness criteria.

5.1 CORRECTNESS CRITERIA

To illustrate the ideas of this chapter, we once again use the views V(Dext) = < S(Dext), L(Dext), C(Dext) > and V(Dcon) = < S(Dcon), L(Dcon), C(Dcon) > considered in Chapters 1 and 2. We repeat in Figure 5.1 the interpretation I″ = I(Dext;Dcon) of V(Dext) in V(Dcon). We also repeat in Figure 5.2 the operation simulator SIM(INSERT(COURSES)).

Operations and Simulators

Recall that with each table name of a database schema S we associate the operations

INSERT(R)(W), DELETE(R)(W), and UPDATE(R)(W).

In each case W is an array of constants of appropriate types. For each row, the first component names a table in which the remaining components are to be, respectively, inserted, deleted, and updated.

```
DEFINING FORMULA SECTION

  PREDICATE: COURSES
  ARGUMENTS ARE:(STUDID:1,SEMESTER:1,YEAR:1;,DEPT:1;,
    COURSE#:1;,SEC#:1;,TITLE:1;,GRADE:1;,CREDITS:1;)
    IS DEFINED BY:(E)STUDNAME:1(E)BIRTHDATE:1,
    (E)DATEADM:1(E)COURSE:1(E)SECTION:1
    (E)INSTRUCT:1(E)LOCAT:1(E)TIMES:1(E)STUDENT:1
    (E)LINK:1(E)DESCR:1
      SYSTEM-REGISTRAR-COURSE-SECTION-STUDENT
      (SEMESTER:1,YEAR:1,COURSE:1,DEPT:1,COURSE#:1,SECTION:1,
      SEC#:1,INSTRUCT:1,LOCAT:1,TIMES:1,STUDENT:1,STUDID:1,
      STUDNAME:1,GRADE:1)
      & SYSTEM-CATALOGUE
      (DEPT:1,COURSE#:1,TITLE:1,CREDITS:1,DESCR:1,LINK:1)
      & SYSTEM-STUDINFO
      (STUDID:1,STUDNAME:1,BIRTHDATE:1,DATEADM:1)

  PREDICATE:RECORD
  ARGUMENTS ARE:(STUDID:1;,SEMESTER:1,YEAR:1;,
    STUDID:1,SEMESTER:1,YEAR:1;)
  IS DEFINED BY:
    (E)COURSE:1 (E)STUDNAME:1(E)BIRTHDATE:1
    (E)DATEADM:1
      SYSTEM-REGISTRAR(SEMESTER:1,YEAR:1,COURSE:1)
      & SYSTEM-STUDINFO
      (STUDID:1,STUDNAME:1,BIRTHDATE:1,DATEADM:1)

  PREDICATE:TRANSCRIPT
  ARGUMENTS ARE: (STUDID:1;,STUDNAME:1;,BIRTHDATE:1,
    DATEADM:1;,STUDID:1;)
  IS DEFINED BY:
    SYSTEM-STUDINFO
    (STUDID:1,STUDNAME:1,BIRTHDATE:1,DATEADM:1)
```

Figure 5.1 Interpretation I″ = I(Dext;Dcon).

As before, these operations can be regarded as operations on the database which yield a new (or possibly, the same) database. Consequently,

O(R)(W,M);

denotes the database structure obtained by applying operation O(R) with input W to the database structure M. For example, an insertion operation on COURSES of V(Dext) is denoted

INSERT(COURSES)(W,M(Dext));

We also associate with each operation O(R) and array W a set of variable-free formulas of L, called delta(O(R))(W). Again, the formulas in delta(O(R))(W) are to be made "true" as a result of executing the operation. Thus, they represent the "intent"

```
    PROC SIM(INSERT(COURSES))(CW);

      /* CW is a an array of codes where:

         CW(i).COURSES.STUDID
                      = an ASCII DEC(9) value (IDTPE),
         CW(i).COURSES.SEMESTER
                      = AN ASCII CHAR(8) value (SEMTPE)
         CW(i).COURSES.YEAR
                      = an ASCII DEC(4) value (YRTPE)
         CW(i).COURSES = a COURSES code

         CW(i).DEPT = a  DEPTPE code
                       = an ASCII CHAR(10) value (DEPTPE;),
         CW(i).COURSE# = a CS#TPE code
                       = an ASCII CHAR(3) value (CS#TPE;),
         CW(i).SEC#    = a SEC# code
                       = an ASCII DEC(3) value (SEC#;),
         CW(i).TITLE = a TTLTPE code
                       = an ASCII CHAR(25) value (TTLTPE;),
         CW(i).GRADE   = a GRDTPE code
                       = an ASCII CHAR(1) value (GRDTPE;),
         CW(i).CREDITS = a CRDSTPE code
                       = an ASCII DEC(2) value (CRDSTPE;),

i = 1,...,length(CW) */

      ESTABLISH CHECKPOINT;

   /* If the simulation should fail [e.g., the resultant conceptual database is
not a model of C(Dcon)], we can use this checkpoint to reestablish the old database
instance.*/

     FOR i = 1 TO LENGTH(CW);

    /* For each row of CW perform the following operations.*/

    GET W(STUDENT:1,STUDNAME:1):
              (E)BIRTHDATE:1(E)DATEADM:1(E)COURSE:1
             (E)SECTION:1(E)INSTRUCT:1(E)LOCAT:1
             (E)TIMES:1(E)LINK:1(E)DESCR:1
           SYSTEM-REGISTRAR-COURSE-SECTION
             CW(i).COURSES.SEMESTER,CW(i).COURSES.YEAR,COURSE:1,
             CW(i).DEPT,CW(i).COURSE#,SECTION:1,
             CW(i).SEC#,INSTRUCT:1,LOCAT:1,TIMES:1,STUDENT:1)
          & SYSTEM-CATALOGUE
             (CW(i).DEPT:1,CW(i).COURSE#,CW(i).TITLE,
              CW(i).CREDITS,DESCR:1,LINK:1)
           & SYSTEM-STUDINFO
              (CW(i).COURSES.STUDID,STUDNAME:1,BIRTHDATE:1,DATEADM:1)
```

Figure 5.2 (*cont. next page*)

(continued)

```
/* We look for a STUDENT table corresponding to the class in which the student is
enrolled. We also find the name of the student. */

  IF LENGTH(W) = 0 THEN GO TO L1;

  INSERT(STUDENT)(<(W(1).STUDENT,CW(i).COURSES.STUDID,
          W(1).STUDNAME,CW(i).GRADE);

/* If no such STUDENT table of NAME value is found, we go to L1 and restore the
old database instance. Otherwise, we insert a row into that STUDENT table.*/

      END i;

    IF M(Dcon) |= C(Dcon) THEN RETURN;

L1: RESTORE TO LAST CHECKPOINT;

/* If the current conceptual database instance is a model of C(Dcon), then exit;
otherwise, roll back to the instance of the conceptual database prior to execu-
tion.*/

   END SIM(INSERT(COURSES));
```

Figure 5.2 Operation simulator SIM(INSERT(COURSES)).

of the operation. The following list provides precise definitions of delta(O(R))(W) for O = INSERT, DELETE, and UPDATE.

Let R = (R1,...,Rn) be the rule in S defining table R.

1. delta(INSERT(R))(W)

$$= \{ \text{W(i).R(W(i).R1,...,W(i).Rn)} \mid \text{i} = 1,..., \text{LENGTH(W)} \}.$$

   For example, if R is the table name COURSES of V(Dext) and W =

$$\{ <\text{e(COURSES):1,BIO,103,101,INTRO,B,3}> \},$$

   then delta(INSERT(COURSES))(W) =

$$\{\text{e(COURSES):1(BIO,103,101,INTRO,B,3)}\}.$$

2. delta(DELETE(R))(W)

$$= \{ \sim \text{W(i).R(W(i).R1,...,W(i).Rn)} \mid \text{i} = 1,...,\text{LENGTH(W)} \}.$$

   For example, if R is RECORD of V(Dext) and W =

$$\{ <\text{e(RECORD):1,FALL,1979,e(COURSES):1}>, <\text{e(RECORD):1,SPRING,1980,e(COURSES):2}> \},$$

   then delta(DELETE(RECORD))(W) =

$$\{ \sim\text{e(RECORD):1(FALL,1979,e(COURSES):1)}, \sim\text{e(RECORD):1(SPRING,1980,e(COURSES):2)} \}.$$

For each update, we assume that W is an array of triples W = { <w1(i),w2(i),w3(i)> }, where w1(i) names an R table in which w3(i) replaces w2(i) for each i.

3. delta(UPDATE(R))(W)

 = { ~w1(i).R(w2(i).R1,...,w2(i).Rn) | <w1(i),w2(i),w3(i)> is in W}
 U {w1(i).R(w3(i).R1,...,w3(i).Rn) | <w1(i),w2(i),w3(i)> is in W}.

 For example, if R is TRANSCRIPT and W =

 { <TRANSCRIPT,
 <123456789,SMITH ROBERT J.,APR 13 1961,SEPT 1 1979,e(RECORD):1>,
 <123456789,SMITH ROBERT J.,MAY 22 1961,SEPT 1 1979,e(RECORD):1> },

 then

 delta(UPDATE(TRANSCRIPT))(W)
 = { ~TRANSCRIPT(123456789,SMITH ROBERT J.,
 APR 13 1961,SEPT 1 1979,e(RECORD):1),
 TRANSCRIPT(123456789,SMITH ROBERT J.,
 MAY 22 1961,SEPT 1 1979,e(RECORD):1)}.

Remark. Strictly speaking, other wffs may be effected besides those given in our definition of delta(O(R))(W). These involve functions, such as TOTCREDITS, and table equality predicates. However, for simplicity of presentation, we will not consider them here.

We place similar restrictions on the various operations. Namely, we assume that some row to be inserted into a database is not already there, some row to be deleted from a database is there, and a combination of these conditions for update. These conditions ensure that an operation will "change" the database if and only if the constraints are not violated.

Let V(E) = <S(E),L(E),C(E)> and V(C) = <S(C),L(C),C(C)> be two database views and let I be an interpretation of V(E) in V(C).

Definition. A *simulator for the operation* O(R) *via* I is a program called SIM(O(R)) with inputs an array of codes I[W] and a conceptual database structure M(C) and outputs a "new" conceptual database structure. We write

SIM(O(R))(I[W],M(C))

for the conceptual database structure that results from applying the simulator.

For example, consider the operation INSERT(COURSES) on view V(Dext). A simulator corresponding to this operation is SIM(INSERT(COURSES)) given in Figure 5.2. An illustration of the effects of SIM(INSERT(COURSES)) was given in Figure 2.15. As in Chapter 4, we will assume that insertions are simulated by insertions, deletions by deletions, and updates by updates.

Again, O(R) denotes an operation [e.g., INSERT(R), DELETE(R), UPDATE(R)] in which constraint checking is done and O*(R) denotes the corresponding operation in which constraint checking is not done. Similarly, SIM(O(R)) represents an operation simulator in which conceptual constraint checking is done and SIM*(O(R)) denotes a simulator in which conceptual constraint checking is not done.

The four correctness criteria of Chapter 4 generalize to the heterogeneous case. They are the same except that "relational" is replaced by "database." Theorems 4.2.1 to 4.2.4 also generalize to the heterogeneous case in a like manner.

Weak Correctness

Definition. We say that SIM(O(R)) is *weakly correct with respect to* I if

$$\text{SIM(O(R))(I(W),M(C))} \neq \text{M(C)} \quad \text{implies}$$
$$\text{I[SIM(O(R))(I(W),M(C))]} \models \text{delta(O(R))(W)}$$

for every W and database structure M(C).

Theorem 5.1.1. *Suppose that for all* W *and models* M(C) *of* V(C),

$$\text{SIM(O(R))(I(W),M(C))} \neq \text{M(C)} \quad \textit{implies}$$
$$\text{SIM*(O(R))(I(W),M(C))} \models \text{I(delta(O(R))(W))}.$$

Then SIM(O(R)) *is weakly correct.*

Consistent Correctness

Definition. We say that SIM(O(R)) is *consistently correct with respect to* I if

$$\text{SIM(O(R))(I(W),M(C))} \neq \text{M(C)} \quad \text{implies}$$
$$\text{O(R)(W,I[M(C)])} \neq \text{I[M(C)]}$$

for every W and database structure M(C).

Theorem 5.1.2. *Suppose that for all arrays* W *and models* M(C) *of* V(C), *either*

$$\text{SIM*(O(R))(I(W),M(C))} = \text{M(C)}$$

or else

$$\text{I[SIM*(O(R))(I(W),M(C))]} \models \text{C(E)} \quad \textit{implies}$$
$$\text{O*(R)(W,I[M(C)])} \models \text{C(E)}.$$

Then SIM(O(R)) *is consistently correct.*

Independent Correctness

Definition. We say that SIM(O(R)) is *independently correct with respect to* I if

$$\text{O(R)(W,I[M(C)])} \neq \text{I[M(C)]} \quad \text{implies}$$
$$\text{SIM(O(R))(I(W),M(C))} \neq \text{M(C)}$$

for every W and database structure M(C).

Let C and C′ be sets of wffs in language L and STR a subclass of database structures of L.

Definition. We say that C *logically implies* C′ *over* STR if for all M in STR,

$$\text{M} \models \text{C} \quad \text{implies} \quad \text{M} \models \text{C}' .$$

We denote this by C $\models$ C′ over STR.

If STR is the set of all database structures for language L, then logically implies over STR is the same as the usual notion of logically implies in database logic.

Let SIM*(OP(R)) be a constraint-free simulator for OP(R). Let STR(SIM*(OP(R))) be the image of SIM*(OP(R)); that is,

$$\begin{aligned} &\text{STR(SIM*(OP(R)))} \\ &\quad = \{\text{M(C)} \mid \text{for some array W and model M}'\text{(C) of V(C),} \\ &\qquad\qquad \text{M(C)}=\text{SIM*(I(W),M}'\text{(C))}\}. \end{aligned}$$

Theorem 5.1.3. *Suppose that* I(C(E)) $\models$ C(C) *over* STR(SIM*(O(R))) *and that for all* W *and models* M(C) *of* V(C), *either*

$$\text{SIM*(O(R))(I(W),M(C))} = \text{M(C)}$$

or else

$$\text{O*(R)(W,I[M(C))])} \models \text{C(E)} \quad \textit{implies}$$
$$\text{I[SIM*(OP(R))(I(W),M(C))]} \models \text{C(E)}.$$

Then SIM(O(R)) *is independently correct.*

Strong Correctness

Definition. We say that SIM(O(R)) is *strongly correct* with respect to I if

$$\text{I[SIM(O(R))(I(W),M(C))]} = \text{O(R)(W,I[M(C)])}$$

for every W and database structure M(C).

Let Q be a wff of L(C), W an array, and M(C) a model of V(C).

Definition. Q is called *incrementally independent of* SIM*(O(R))(I(W),M(C)) if

$$M(C) \models Q \quad \text{iff} \quad SIM^*(O(R))(I(W),M(C)) \models Q.$$

That is, a wff Q is incrementally independent of SIM*(O(R))(I(W),M(C)) if its truth is not effected by the constraint-free simulation operation.

Theorem 5.1.4. *Let* SIM(O(R)) *be a weakly correct simulator for* O(R) *with respect to* I. *Suppose that*

1. SIM(O(R)) *is consistently and independently correct.*
2. *For any array* W *and model* M(C) *of* V(C) *and any variable-free atom* Q *of* L(E) *not used in* delta(O(R))(W), I(Q) *is incrementally independent of* SIM*(O(R)) (I(W),M(C)).

Then SIM(O(R)) *is strongly correct.*

Exercises

1. State and prove an analogue of Theorem 4.2.5 for the heterogeneous case.
2. State and prove an analogue of Theorem 4.2.6 for the heterogeneous case.
3. State and prove analogues of Theorem 4.2.7 and Corollary 4.2.8 for the heterogeneous case.
4. State and prove an analogue of Theorem 4.3.1 for the heterogeneous case.
5. State and prove an analogue of Theorem 4.3.2 for the heterogeneous case.

5.2 CHECKING SIMULATOR CORRECTNESS

In this section we show how Theorems 5.1.1 to 5.1.4 can be used to verify simulator correctness in the heterogeneous case. It will be seen in Section 5.3 that these are half of the necessary and sufficient conditions which characterize the four correctness criteria.

Weak Correctness

We can use Theorem 5.1.1 to show that INSERT(COURSES) is weakly correct. First, observe that

delta(INSERT(COURSES))(W)
  = {W(i).COURSES (W(i).DEPT,W(i).COURSE#,W(i).SEC#,
      W(i).TITLE,W(i).GRADE,W(i).CREDITS) |
       i = 1,...,LENGTH(W)}.

Letting CW(i) represent the coding of the row W(i), we have from the definition of I″ in Figure 5.1,

I″(delta(INSERT(COURSES))(W))
= {(E)STUDNAME:1(E)BIRTHDATE:1...(E)DESCR:1
SYSTEM-REGISTRAR-COURSE-SECTION-STUDENT
(CW(i).COURSES.SEMESTER,CW(i).COURSES.YEAR,COURSE:1,
CW(i).DEPT,CW(i).COURSE#,SECTION:1,CW(i).SEC#,
INSTRUCT:1,LOCAT:1,TIMES:1,STUDENT:1,
CW(i).COURSES.STUDID,STUDNAME:1,CW(i).GRADE)
& SYSTEM-CATALOGUE
(CW(i).DEPT,CW(i).COURSE#,CW(i).TITLE,
CW(i).CREDITS,DESCR:1,LINK:1)
& SYSTEM-STUDINFO
(CW(i).COURSES.STUDID,STUDNAME:1,BIRTHDATE:1,
DATEADM:1) |
i = 1,...,LENGTH(W)}.

Inside the i-loop of SIM(INSERT(COURSES)) of Figure 5.2, the GET instruction checks to see that the formula above, without the atom,

STUDENT:1(CW(i).STUDID,STUDNAME:1,CW(i).GRADE),

is true in M(Dcon). If it is not, then a branch is made to L1, and the whole simulation is canceled. If it is, then the appropriate row is inserted into the STUDENT table found. Consequently, if

SIM(INSERT(COURSES))(I″(W),M(Dcon)) ≠ M(Dcon),

then

SIM*(INSERT(COURSES))(I″(W),M(Dcon))
⊨ I″(delta(INSERT(COURSES))(W)).

Consistent Correctness

We can use Theorem 5.1.2 to show that SIM(INSERT(COURSES)) is consistently correct. To do this we show that for all W and M(Dcon),

I″[SIM*(INSERT(COURSES)(I″(W),M(Dcon))]
= INSERT*(COURSES)(W,I″[M(Dcon)]) .

Clearly, this condition satisfies the hypothesis of the theorem.

Fix W and M(Dcon).

I″[SIM*(INSERT(COURSES)(I″(W),M(Dcon))] and
INSERT*(COURSES)(W,I″[M(Dcon)])

agree on all predicates of the form TRANSCRIPT(-) and RECORD(-). This is because SIM*(INSERT(COURSES)) inserts only into STUDENT tables and in the definition of I″ of Figure 5.1, the STUDENT predicate only appears on the right-hand side of the defining formula for COURSES.

However, they also agree on all COURSES predicates. The i-th row of W in

INSERT*(COURSES)(W,I″[M(Dcon)])

results in the insertion of

<W(i).DEPT,W(i).COURSE#,W(i).SEC#,W(i).TITLE,
W(i).GRADE,W(i).CREDITS>

into the table named by

W(i).COURSES.

The corresponding i-th row of

SIM*(INSERT(COURSES)(I″(W),M(Dcon))

results in the insertion of the row

<CW(i).COURSES.STUDID,e(NAMTPE):j,CW(i).GRADE>

into the STUDENT table for the section CW(i).SEC# of course CW(i).DEPT, CW(i).COURSE#, in the semester, year CW(i).COURSES.SEMESTER, CW(i).COURSES.YEAR. Consequently, the changes in the induced external database

I″[SIM*(INSERT(COURSES)(I″(W),M(Dcon))]

are the same as in

INSERT*(COURSES)(W,I″[M(Dcon)]) .

Independent Correctness

We use Theorem 5.1.3 to show that SIM(INSERT(COURSES)) is independently correct. From the above we know that

INSERT*(COURSES)(W,I″[M(Dcon))])
= I″[SIM*(INSERT(COURSES)(I″(W),M(Dcon))].

Hence, the latter condition holds. To see the former, suppose that for some W and model M(Dcon) of V(Dcon),

SIM*(INSERT(COURSES))(I″(W),M(Dcon)) ≠ C(Dcon).

We have to show that

SIM*(INSERT(COURSES))(I″(W),M(Dcon)) ≠ I″(C(Dext)).

By the Flipper Theorem, we have to show that

I″[SIM*(INSERT(COURSES))(I″(W),M(Dcon))] ≠ C(Dext).

Since SIM(INSERT(COURSES)) only adds to STUDENT tables, constraints C(Dcon,1)-C(Dcon,3), C(Dcon,5)-C(Dcon,6) cannot be violated either.

If C(Dcon,4) were violated, there would be two rows in a single STUDENT table, for a given SEMESTER, YEAR, DEPT, COURSE#, and SEC#, with the same STUDID and different NAMEs or GRADEs.

1. The NAMEs could not be different, since then there would have to be two rows in STUDINFO in M(Dcon) with the same ID# and different STUDNAMEs. But this would violate constraint C(Dcon,5), which is impossible since M(Dcon) $\models$ C(Dcon).
2. The GRADEs are different. In this case, the resulting external database would have two rows in the same COURSES table with the same DEPT and COURSE# but different GRADEs. But this means that

   $$I''[SIM^*(INSERT(COURSES))(I''(W),M(Dcon))] \not\models C(Dext)$$

   since it violates constraint C(Dext,3) of Figure 1.8.

A similar argument holds if C(Dcon,7) of Figure 2.9 were violated. In this case, external constraint C(Dext,3) would be also be violated. Since all possibilities are exhausted, we are done.

Strong Correctness

We demonstrate that SIM(INSERT(COURSES)) is strongly correct using Theorem 5.1.4 . By the previous discussion we have shown that it is weakly, consistently, and independently correct. All that remains is to show that (2) also holds.

For this purpose let W and M(Dcon) be given and consider any variable-free atom Q in L(Dext) not used in delta(INSERT(COURSES))(W). We have to show that

$$M(Dcon) \models I''(Q) \quad \text{iff}$$
$$SIM^*(INSERT(COURSES))(I''(W),M(Dcon)) \models I''(Q) .$$

1. Suppose that Q is of the form TRANSCRIPT(-) or e(RECORD):i(-). Then I″(Q) is not affected by the execution of the simulator. This is because I″(Q) does not use the predicate STUDENT, which is changed by the simulator.
2. Suppose that Q is of the form e(COURSES):i(-) and is not in delta(INSERT-(COURSES))(W). Then insertions into the STUDENT tables, as prescribed by the simulator, also cannot affect the truth of I″(Q). This is because the only wffs of the form I″(e(COURSES):j(-)) that are made true are those where e(COURSES)(-):j is in W.

Hence, all the criteria of Theorem 5.1.4 are satisfied.

```
  PROC SIM(DELETE(COURSES))(CW);

    /* CW is a an array of codes where:

       CW(i).COURSES.STUDID
                     = an ASCII DEC(9) value (IDTPE),
       CW(i).COURSES.SEMESTER
                     = an ASCII CHAR(8) value (SEMTPE)
       CW(i).COURSES.YEAR
                     = an ASCII DEC(4) value (YRTPE)
       CW(i).COURSES = a COURSES code

       CW(i).DEPT = a  DEPTPE code
                     = an ASCII CHAR(10) value (DEPTPE;),
       CW(i).COURSE# = a CS#TPE code
                     = an ASCII CHAR(3) value (CS#TPE;),
       CW(i).SEC#    = a SEC# code
                     = an ASCII DEC(3) value (SEC#;),
       CW(i).TITLE = a TTLTPE code
                     = an ASCII CHAR(25) value (TTLTPE;),
       CW(i).GRADE   = a GRDTPE code
                     = an ASCII CHAR(1) value (GRDTPE;),
       CW(i).CREDITS= a CRDSTPE code
                     = an ASCII DEC(2) value (CRDSTPE;),

i = 1,...,length(CW) */

      ESTABLISH CHECKPOINT;

  /* If the simulation should fail [e.g., the resultant conceptual database is
not a model of C(Dcon)], we can use this checkpoint to reestablish the old database
instance.*/

      FOR i = 1 TO LENGTH(CW);

  /* For each row of CW perform the following operations.*/

i = 1,...,length(CW) */

      ESTABLISH CHECKPOINT;

  /* If the simulation should fail (i.e., the resultant conceptual database is
not a model of C(Dcon), then we can use this checkpoint to reestablish the old da-
tabase instance.*/

     FOR i = 1 TO LENGTH(CW);

  /* For each row of CW perform the following operations.*/

  GET W (STUDENT:1,STUDNAME:1):
             (E)BIRTHDATE:1(E)DATEADM:1(E)COURSE:1
            (E)SECTION:1(E)INSTRUCT:1(E)LOCAT:1
            (E)TIMES:1(E)LINK:1(E)DESCR:1
```

Figure 5.3 (*cont. next page*)

(continued)

```
          SYSTEM-REGISTRAR-COURSE-SECTION-STUDENT
           (CW(i).COURSES.SEMESTER,CW(i).COURSES.YEAR,COURSE:1,
            CW(i).DEPT,CW(i).COURSE#,SECTION:1,
            CW(i).SEC#,INSTRUCT:1,LOCAT:1,TIMES:1,STUDENT:1,
            CW(i).COURSES.STUDID,STUDNAME:1,CW(i).GRADE);
        & SYSTEM-CATALOGUE
           (CW(i).DEPT:1,CW(i).COURSE#,CW(i).TITLE,
            CW(i).CREDITS,DESCR:1,LINK:1)
        & SYSTEM-STUDINFO
           (CW(i).COURSES.STUDID,STUDNAME:1,BIRTHDATE:1,DATEADM:1)

/* We look for a STUDENT-table corresponding to the class that the student is en-
rolled in. We also find the name of the student. */

    IF LENGTH(W) = 0 THEN GO TO L2;

  /* If no such STUDENT table of NAME value is found, we
      go to L2 and delete another row.*/

     FOR j = 1 TO LENGTH(W);
      DO;
       DELETE(STUDENT)(<(W(j).STUDENT,CW(i).COURSES.STUDID,
               W(j).STUDNAME,CW(i).GRADE);
      END j;

L2: END i;

     IF M(Dcon) |= C(Dcon) THEN RETURN;

 L1: RESTORE TO LAST CHECKPOINT;

 /* If the current conceptual database instance is a model of C(Dcon), then exit;
otherwise roll back to the instance of the conceptual database prior to execu-
tion.*/

    END SIM(DELETE(COURSES));
```

Figure 5.3 Operation simulator SIM(DELETE(COURSES)).

Exercises

1. Determine if the deletion simulator SIM(DELETE(COURSES)) of Figure 5.3 is weakly, consistently, independently, and strongly correct.
2. Let SIM(INSERT(TRANSCRIPT)) be a simulator for INSERT(TRANSCRIPT) in which the instructions in the i-loop are

   INSERT(STUDINFO)({ <CW(i).STUDID,CW(i).STUDNAME,
   CW(i).BIRTHDATE,CW(i).DATEADM);

Determine if SIM(INSERT(TRANSCRIPT)) is weakly, consistently, independently, and strongly correct.

3. Let SIM(INSERT(RECORD)) be a simulator for INSERT(RECORD) in which the instructions in the i-loop are

```
GET W1 (COURSE:1):
  (E)COURSE:1(E)STUDNAME:1(E)BIRTHDATE:1(E)DATEADM:1
     SYSTEM-REGISTRAR(CW(i).SEMESTER,CW(i).YEAR,COURSE:1)
& ~SYSTEM-STUDINFO(CW(i).STUDID,STUDNAME:1,BIRTHDATE:1,
     DATEADM:1);
IF LENGTH(W1) = 0 THEN GO TO L1;
INSERT(STUDINFO)({ <CW(i).STUDID,NULL,NULL,NULL> });
```

Determine if SIM(INSERT(RECORD)) is weakly, consistently, independently, and strongly correct.

4. Let SIM(DELETE(TRANSCRIPT)) be a simulator for DELETE(TRANSCRIPT) in which the instructions in the i-loop are

```
GET W1: (CW(i).STUDID):
  SYSTEM-STUDINFO(CW(i).STUDID,CW(i).STUDNAME,
            CW(i).BIRTHDATE,CW(i).DATEADM)
IF LENGTH(W1) = 0 GO TO L1;
DELETE(STUDINFO)({ <CW(i).STUDID,CW(i).STUDNAME,
    CW(i).BIRTHDATE,CW(i).DATEADM> });
```

Determine if SIM(DELETE(TRANSCRIPT)) is weakly, consistently, independently, and strongly correct.

5. Let SIM(DELETE(RECORD)) be a simulator for DELETE(RECORD) in which the instructions in the i-loop are

```
GET W1(STUDNAME:1,BIRTHDATE:1,DATEADM:1):
   (E)COURSE:1
   SYSTEM-REGISTRAR(CW(i).SEMESTER,CW(i).YEAR,COURSE:1)
& SYSTEM-STUDINFO(CW(i).STUDID,STUDNAME:1,BIRTHDATE:1,
           DATEADM:1);
IF LENGTH(W1) = 0 THEN GO TO L1;
DELETE(STUDINFO)({ <CW(i).STUDID,W1(1).STUDNAME,
           W1(1).BIRTHDATE,W(1).DATEADM> });
```

Determine if SIM(DELETE(RECORD)) is weakly, consistently, independently, and strongly correct.

5.3 CHARACTERIZATIONS OF CORRECTNESS CRITERIA

In this section, we prove necessary and sufficient conditions for the various correctness criteria used in this and the preceding chapter.

Weak Correctness

Theorem 5.1.1. *Suppose that for all* W *and models* M(C) *of* V(C),

$$\text{SIM(O(R))(I(W),M(C))} \neq \text{M(C)} \quad \textit{implies}$$
$$\text{SIM*(O(R))(I(W),M(C))} \models \text{I(delta(O(R))(W))}.$$

Then SIM(O(R)) *is weakly correct.*

Proof. Let W be an array and M(C) a model of V(C) and suppose that

$$\text{SIM(O(R))(I(W),M(C))} \neq \text{M(C)}.$$

We have to show that

$$\text{I[SIM(O(R))(I(W),M(C))]} \models \text{delta(O(R))(W)}.$$

Since SIM(O(R))(I(W),M(C)) $\neq$ M(C), it must be that

$$\text{SIM((O(R))(I(W),M(C))} = \text{SIM*((O(R))(I(W),M(C))}$$

and both are not M(C). By this and the hypothesis,

$$\text{SIM(O(R))(I(W),M(C))} \models \text{I(delta(O(R))(W))}.$$

By the Flipper Theorem,

$$\text{I[SIM(O(R))(I(W),M(C))]} \models \text{delta(O(R))(W)}.$$

Theorem 5.3.1. *Suppose that* SIM(O(R)) *is weakly correct. Then for all* W *and models* M(C) *of* V(C),

$$\text{SIM(O(R))(I(W),M(C))} \neq \text{M(C)} \quad \textit{implies}$$
$$\text{SIM*(O(R))(I(W),M(C))} \models \text{I(delta(O(R))(W))}.$$

Proof. Suppose that for some W and M(C),

$$\text{SIM(O(R))(I(W),M(C))} \neq \text{M(C)}$$

but

$$\text{SIM*(O(R))(I(W),M(C))} \not\models \text{I(delta(O(R))(W))}.$$

Then again,

$$\text{SIM(O(R))(I(W),M(C))} = \text{SIM*(O(R))(I(W),M(C))}$$

and both are not M(C). Thus,

$$\text{SIM(O(R))(I(W),M(C))} \neq \text{M(C)}$$

and

$$\text{I[SIM(O(R))(I(W),M(C))]} \not\models \text{delta(O(R))(W)}.$$

Hence, SIM(O(R)) cannot be weakly correct.

Consistent Correctness

Theorem 5.1.2. *Suppose that for all arrays* W *and models* M(C) *of* V(C), either

$$\mathrm{SIM}^*(\mathrm{O(R)})(\mathrm{I(W)},\mathrm{M(C)}) = \mathrm{M(C)}$$

or else

$$\mathrm{I}[\mathrm{SIM}^*(\mathrm{O(R)})(\mathrm{I(W)},\mathrm{M(C)})] \models \mathrm{C(E)} \quad \textit{implies} \quad \mathrm{O}^*(\mathrm{R})(\mathrm{W},\mathrm{I}[\mathrm{M(C)}]) \models \mathrm{C(E)}.$$

Then SIM(O(R)) *is consistently correct.*

Proof. Suppose that for some W and M(C)

$$\mathrm{SIM}(\mathrm{O(R)})(\mathrm{I(W)},\mathrm{M(C)}) \neq \mathrm{M(C)}.$$

We have to show that

$$\mathrm{O(R)}(\mathrm{W},\mathrm{I}[\mathrm{M(C)}]) \neq \mathrm{I}[\mathrm{M(C)}].$$

Then it must be that

$$\mathrm{SIM}^*(\mathrm{O(R)})(\mathrm{I(W)},\mathrm{M(C)}) \neq \mathrm{M(C)}$$

and that

$$\mathrm{SIM}^*(\mathrm{O(R)})(\mathrm{I(W)},\mathrm{M(C)}) \models \mathrm{C(C)}.$$

By the definition of interpretation I of V(E) in V(C), C(C) $\models$ I(C(E)); hence,

$$\mathrm{SIM}^*(\mathrm{O(R)})(\mathrm{I(W)},\mathrm{M(C)}) \models \mathrm{I(C(E))}.$$

By the Flipper Theorem,

$$\mathrm{I}[\mathrm{SIM}^*(\mathrm{O(R)})(\mathrm{I(W)},\mathrm{M(C)})] \models \mathrm{C(E)}.$$

By the hypothesis,

$$\mathrm{O}^*(\mathrm{R})(\mathrm{W},\mathrm{I}[\mathrm{M(C)}]) \models \mathrm{C(E)};$$

hence,

$$\mathrm{O(R)}(\mathrm{W},\mathrm{I}[\mathrm{M(C)}]) \neq \mathrm{I}[\mathrm{M(C)}].$$

Theorem 5.3.2. *Suppose that* I(C(E)) $\models$ C(C) *over* STR(SIM*(O(R)). *Then if* SIM(O(R)) *is consistently correct, then for all arrays* W *and models* M(C) *of* V(C), *either*

$$\mathrm{SIM}^*(\mathrm{O(R)})(\mathrm{I(W)},\mathrm{M(C)}) = \mathrm{M(C)}$$

or else

$$\mathrm{I}[\mathrm{SIM}^*(\mathrm{O(R)})(\mathrm{I(W)},\mathrm{M(C)})] \models \mathrm{C(E)} \quad \textit{implies} \quad \mathrm{O}^*(\mathrm{R})(\mathrm{W},\mathrm{I}[\mathrm{M(C)}]) \models \mathrm{C(E)}.$$

Proof. Suppose that for some array W and M(C),

$$\mathrm{SIM}^*(\mathrm{O(R)})(\mathrm{I(W)},\mathrm{M(C)}) \neq \mathrm{M(C)}$$

and

$$\mathrm{I}[\mathrm{SIM}^*(\mathrm{O(R)})(\mathrm{I(W)},\mathrm{M(C)})] \models \mathrm{C(E)}.$$

We must show that

$$\mathrm{O}^*(\mathrm{R})(\mathrm{W},\mathrm{I}[\mathrm{M(C)}]) \models \mathrm{C(E)}\ .$$

By the Flipper Theorem,

$$\mathrm{SIM}^*(\mathrm{O(R)})(\mathrm{I(W)},\mathrm{M(C)}) \models \mathrm{I(C(E))}.$$

Since I(C(E)) |= C(C) over STR(SIM*(O(R)),

$$\mathrm{SIM}^*(\mathrm{O(R)})(\mathrm{I(W)},\mathrm{M(C)}) \models \mathrm{C(C)}\ ;$$

hence,

$$\mathrm{SIM}(\mathrm{O(R)})(\mathrm{I(W)},\mathrm{M(C)}) \neq \mathrm{M(C)}.$$

Since SIM(O(R)) is consistently correct,

$$\mathrm{O(R)}(\mathrm{W},\mathrm{I}[\mathrm{M(C)}]) \neq \mathrm{I}[\mathrm{M(C)}]\ ;$$

hence,

$$\mathrm{O}^*(\mathrm{R})(\mathrm{W},\mathrm{I}[\mathrm{M(C)}]) \models \mathrm{C(E)}.$$

Independent Correctness

Theorem 5.1.3. *Suppose that* I(C(E)) ⊨ C(C) *over* STR(SIM*(O(R))) *and that for all* W *and models* M(C) *of* V(C), *either*

$$\mathrm{SIM}^*(\mathrm{O(R)})\ (\mathrm{I(W)},\mathrm{M(C)}) = \mathrm{M(C)}$$

or else

$$\mathrm{O}^*(\mathrm{R})(\mathrm{W},\mathrm{I}[\mathrm{M(C)})]) \models \mathrm{C(E)} \quad \textit{implies} \quad \mathrm{I}[\mathrm{SIM}^*(\mathrm{O(R)})(\mathrm{I(W)},\mathrm{M(C)})] \models \mathrm{C(E)}.$$

Then SIM(O(R)) *is independently correct.*

Proof. Suppose that

$$\mathrm{O(R)}(\mathrm{W},\mathrm{I}[\mathrm{M(C)})]) \neq \mathrm{I}[\mathrm{M(C)}].$$

We have to show that

$$\mathrm{SIM}(\mathrm{O(R)})(\mathrm{I(W)},\mathrm{M(C)}) \neq \mathrm{M(C)}).$$

It must be that

$$\mathrm{O}^*(\mathrm{R})(\mathrm{W},\mathrm{I}[\mathrm{M(C)})]) \models \mathrm{C(E)}.$$

By hypothesis,

$$I[SIM^*(O(R))(I(W),M(C))] \models C(E).$$

By the Flipper Theorem,

$$SIM^*(O(R))(I(W),M(C)) \models I(C(E)).$$

Since, $I(C(E)) \models C(C)$ over STR(SIM*(O(R))),

$$SIM^*(O(R))(I(W),M(C)) \models C(C).$$

Thus,

$$SIM(O(R))(I(W),M(C)) \neq M(C).$$

Theorem 5.3.3. *Let* SIM(O(R)) *be independently correct. Then for all* W and M(C) *for* V(C), *either*

$$SIM^*(O(R))\ (I(W),M(C)) = M(C)$$

or else

$$O^*(R)(W,I[M(C))]) \models C(E) \quad \textit{implies} \quad I[SIM^*(O(R))(I(W),M(C))] \models C(E).$$

Proof. Suppose that for some W and M(C)

$$SIM^*(O(R))(I(W),M(C)) \neq M(C)$$

and

$$(*)\ O^*(R)(W,I[M(C)]) \models C(E)$$

but

$$I[SIM^*(O(R))(I(W),M(C))] \not\models C(E).$$

By the Flipper Theorem,

$$SIM^*(O(R))(I(W),M(C)) \not\models I(C(E)).$$

Since $C(C) \models I(C(E))$,

$$SIM^*(O(R))(I(W),M(C)) \not\models C(C);$$

hence,

$$SIM(O(R))(I(W),M(C)) = M(C).$$

But by (*),

$$O(R)(W,I[M(C))]) \neq I[M(C)];$$

hence, SIM(O(R)) is not an independently correct simulator of O(R).

Strong Correctness

Theorem 5.1.4. *Let* SIM(O(R)) *be a weakly correct simulator for* O(R) *with respect to* I. *Suppose that*

1. SIM(O(R)) *is consistently and independently correct.*
2. *For any array* W *and* M(C) *of* V(C) *and any variable-free atom* Q *of* L(E) *not used in* delta(O(R))(W), I(Q) *is incrementally independent of* SIM* (O(R)) (I(W),M(C)).

Then SIM(O(R)) *is strongly correct.*

Proof. Let W be any array and M(C) a model of V(C). We show that

$$I[SIM(O(R))(I(W),M(C))] = O(R)(W,I[M(C)]).$$

Case 1: SIM(O(R))(I(W),M(C)) = M(C) .
Since SIM(O(R)) is independently correct,

$$O(R)(W,I[M(C)]) = I[M(C)],$$

and the result follows.

Case 2: SIM(O(R))(I(W),M(C)) $\neq$ M(C).
Then the new conceptual database is

$$(*)\ SIM(O(R))(I(W),M(C)) = SIM^*(O(R))(I(W),M(C)) .$$

We show that for all variable-free atomic wffs Q of L(E),

$$O(R)(W,I[M(C)]) \models Q \text{ iff}$$
$$SIM(O(R))(I(W),M(C)) \models I(Q).$$

(a) Suppose that Q is not used in delta(O(R))(W). Then by (2) and (*),

$$M(C) \models I(Q) \text{ iff}$$
$$SIM(O(R))(I(W),M(C)) \models I(Q).$$

By the Flipper Theorem,

$$I[M(C)] \models Q \text{ iff}$$
$$I[SIM(O(R))(I(W),M(C))] \models Q.$$

Since Q is not used in delta(O(R))(W),

$$O(R)(W,I[M(C)]) \models Q \quad \text{iff}$$
$$I[SIM(O(R))(I(W),M(C))] \models Q.$$

(b) Suppose that Q is in delta(O(R))(W). Since SIM(O(R)) is consistently correct,

$$O(R)(W,I[M(C)]) \neq I[M(C)];$$

hence,

$$O(R)(W,I[M(C)]) \models Q.$$

Since SIM(O(R)) is weakly correct [and Q is in delta(O(R))(W)],

$$I[SIM(O(R))(I(W),M(C))] \models Q.$$

A similar argument holds if ~Q is in delta.

Since O(R)(W,I[M(C)]) and I[SIM(O(R))(I(W),M(C))] agree on all variable-free atomic wffs, they are equal.

Corollary 5.3.4. *Let* SIM(O(R)) *be a weakly correct simulator for* O(R) *with respect to* I. *Suppose that*

1. SIM(O(R)) *is consistently and independently correct.*
2. *The defining formula in I for all atoms of* L(E) *other than* R *have no atomic symbols in common with the defining formula a* R.
3. *For all arrays* W, *every variable-free atomic wff* Q *of the form* R(-) *not used in* delta(O(R))(W) *and any model* M(C) *of* V(C), I(Q) *is incrementally independent of* SIM*(O(R))(I(W),M(C)).

Then SIM(O(R)) *is strongly correct.*

Proof. From conditions 2 and 3 it follows, for any array W, that any variable-free atomic Q of L(E) not used in delta(O(R))(W) is incrementally independent of SIM*(O(R))(I(W)),M(C)). Hence, the hypothesis of Theorem 5.1.4 holds.

Theorem 5.3.5. *Suppose that* SIM(O(R)) *is weakly correct. Then if* SIM(O(R)) *is strongly correct, conditions* 1 *and* 2 *of Theorem 5.1.4 both hold.*

Proof. (1) Assume that consistent correctness fails; that is, there is a W and an M(C) where

$$(*)\ \mathrm{SIM(O(R))(I(W),M(C))} \neq \mathrm{M(C)}$$

but

$$(**)\ \mathrm{O(R)(W,I[M(C)])} = \mathrm{I[M(C)]}.$$

Since SIM(O(R)) is weakly correct, by (*),

$$\mathrm{I[SIM(O(R))(I(W),M(C))]} \models \mathrm{delta(O(R))(W)}.$$

By (**),

$$\mathrm{O(R)(W,I[M(C)))} \not\models \mathrm{delta(O(R))(W)};$$

hence,

$$\mathrm{I[SIM(O(R))(I(W),M(C))]} \neq \mathrm{O(R)(W,I[M(C)])}$$

and SIM(O(R)) is not strongly correct. A similar argument holds for independent correctness.

(2) Suppose that for some W variable-free atom Q not used in delta(O(R))(W), and M(C), I(Q) is not incrementally independent of SIM*(O(R))(I(W),M(C)). Assume that

$$\mathrm{M(C)} \models \mathrm{I(Q)}$$

and

$$SIM^*(O(R))(I(W),M(C)) \not\models I(Q).$$

By the Flipper Theorem,

$$(*)\ I[M(C)] \models Q$$

and

$$(+)\ I[SIM^*(O(R))(I(W),M(C))] \not\models Q.$$

Claim. 5.3.6. SIM(O(R))(I(W),M(C))] = SIM*(O(R))(I(W),M(C))].

From the Claim and (+),

$$(++)\ I[SIM(O(R))(I(W),M(C))] \not\models Q.$$

Since Q is not used in delta(O(R))(W), by (*)

$$O(R)(W,I[M(C)]) \models Q.$$

From this and (++), SIM(O(R)) cannot be strongly correct.

Proof (of Claim). By (*) and (+) it cannot be that

$$SIM^*(O(R))(I(W),M(C)) = M(C).$$

It also cannot be that

$$SIM(O(R))(I(W),M(C)) = M(C).$$

for then SIM(O(R)) cannot be strongly correct Hence,

$$SIM(O(R))(I(W),M(C)) = SIM^*(O(R))(I(W),M(C)).$$

A similar argument holds if

$$M(C) \not\models I(Q)$$

and

$$SIM(O(R))(I(W),M(C)) \models I(Q)\ .$$

Exercises

1. Prove that if for all W and models M(C) of V(C),

$$SIM(O(R))(I(W),M(C)) \neq M(C) \quad \textit{implies}$$
$$I[SIM(O(R))(I(W),M(C))] = O(R)(W,I[M(C)]),$$

then SIM(O(R)) is consistently correct.

2. Prove that if

1. SIM(O(R))(I(W),M(C)) $\neq$ M(C) *implies*
   I[SIM(O(R))(I(W),M(C))] = O(R)(W,I[M(C)]),

2. I[SIM(O(R))(I(W),M(C))] $\models$ C(E) *implies*
   SIM(O(R))(I(W),M(C)) $\models$ C(C), and

3. SIM(O(R))(I(W),M(C)) = M(C) *implies*
   O(R)(W,I[M(C)]) $\not\models$ C(E),

then SIM(O(R)) is strongly correct.

We say that simulator SIM(O(R)) is *relatively correct* if

O(R)(W,I[M(C)]) $\neq$ I[M(C)] implies
SIM(O(R))(I(W),M(C)) = O(R)(W,I[M(C)]).

Relative correctness is like strong correctness except that the commutative diagram of Figure 4.9 holds only when the external operation is legal.

3. Prove that if SIM(O(R)) is relatively correct, then it is independently correct.

4. Prove that if SIM(O(R)) is relatively and consistently correct, then it is weakly correct.

5. Show that relative and strong correctness are different.

5.4 RELATED READINGS

DAYAL, U., AND BERNSTEIN, P.A., "On the Updatability of Network Views— Extending Relational Views Theory to the Network Model," *Information Systems,* **7,** (1), 1982, pp. 29-46.

JACOBS, B. E., *Applications of Database Logic to the View Update Problem,* Department of Computer Science Technical Report TR-960, University of Maryland, College Park, 1980.

6

VIEW INTEGRATION

In Chapter 6 we study the view integration problem, namely, given a collection of databases, how one can construct a single database that can simultaneously support each of these as external views. In Section 6.1 we illustrate the methodology in the case where all of the views are relational. In Section 6.2 we describe the methodology in the general case and illustrate it with a heterogeneous example. In Section 6.3 we consider the problem of inconsistent views and the notion of composition of interpretations.

6.1 A RELATIONAL EXAMPLE

In this section we illustrate our methodology for the case in which all views are relational. The process inputs a sequence of relational views in order of importance; that is, the most important are first, the least important are last. The output of the process is a relational conceptual view together with a set of external-to-conceptual mappings.

Candidate Views

We illustrate our ideas using three relational views. These are V(R1), V(R2), and V(R3), whose definitions are given in Figure 6.1 (a)–(c). These are three typical external views for a university. Pictures for their tables are given in Figure 6.2 (a)–(c). We assume that the views are ordered in decreasing order of importance [i.e., V(R1) is the most important; V(R3) is the least important].

V(R1) represents a registrar's view: STUDENT contains student information and REGISTRAR table has enrollment and grade information. V(R2) represents a

```
V(R1): VIEW DEFINITION
  S(R1): SCHEMA DEFINITION
    TABLE STUDENT = (ID#,NAME,BIRTHDATE,DATEADM,MAJOR)
    TABLE REGISTRAR = (SEMESTER,YEAR,DEPT,COURSE#,
      TITLE,CREDITS,SEC#,INSTRUCT,LOCAT,TIMES,STUDID,GRADE)

  L(R1): LANGUAGE DEFINITION
    T(R1): TYPING DEFINITION
      TYPE SIDTPE = {ID#,STUDID} ASCII CHAR(9)
      TYPE NAMTPE = {NAME,INSTRUCT} ASCII CHAR(20)
      TYPE DATPE = {BIRTHDATE,DATEADM} ASCII CHAR(15)
      TYPE DEPTPE = {DEPT,MAJOR} ASCII CHAR(10)
      TYPE SEMTPE = {SEMESTER} ASCII CHAR(8)
      TYPE YRTPE = {YEAR} ASCII DEC(4)
      TYPE CS#TPE = {COURSE#} ASCII DEC(3)
      TYPE TTLTPE = {TITLE} ASCII CHAR(25)
      TYPE CRDSTPE = {CREDITS} ASCII DEC(2)
      TYPE SEC#TPE = {SEC#} ASCII CHAR(3)
      TYPE LOCTPE = {LOCAT} ASCII CHAR(30)
      TYPE TIMTPE = {TIMES} ASCII CHAR(20)
      TYPE GRDTPE = {GRADE} ASCII CHAR(1)

      NONLOGICAL SYMBOLS DEFINITION
        PREDICATES
          STUDENT: (IDTPE,NAMTPE,DATPE,
            DATPE,DEPTPE) PREDICATE
            REGISTRAR: (SEMTPE,YRTPE,DEPTPE,
            CS#TPE,TTLTPE,CRDSTPE,SEC#TPE,NAMTPE,
            LOCTPE,TIMTPE,SIDTPE,GRDTPE) PREDICATE
        FUNCTIONS
        NONE
  C(R1): CONSTRAINTS DEFINITION
    C(R1,1):CONSTRAINT STUDENT: ID#
    → NAME,BIRTHDATE,DATEADM,MAJOR
    C(R1,2):CONSTRAINT REGISTRAR:SEMESTER,YEAR,DEPT,
      COURSE#,SEC# → INSTRUCT,LOCAT,TIMES
    C(R1,3):CONSTRAINT REGISTRAR:SEMESTER,YEAR,DEPT,
      COURSE#,SEC#,STUDID → GRADE
```

(a)

```
V(R2): VIEW DEFINITION
  S(R2): SCHEMA DEFINITION
    TABLE TRANSCRIPT = (STUDID,STUDNAME,SEMESTER,YEAR,DEPT,
      COURSE#,SEC#,TITLE,GRADE,CREDITS)
    TABLE STUDENT = (ID#,NAME,DATEADM)

  L(R2): LANGUAGE DEFINITION
    T(R2): TYPING DEFINITION
      TYPE SIDTPE = {ID#,STUDID} EBCDIC CHAR(9)
      TYPE NAMTPE = {NAME,STUDNAME} EBCDIC CHAR(20)
      TYPE DATPE = {DATEADM} EBCDIC CHAR(15)
      TYPE SEMTPE = {SEMESTER} EBCDIC CHAR(8)
      TYPE YRTPE = {YEAR} EBCDIC DEC(4)
      TYPE DEPTPE = {DEPT} EBCDIC CHAR(10)
      TYPE CS#TPE = {COURSE#} EBCDIC DEC(3)
      TYPE SEC#TPE = {SEC#} EBCDIC CHAR(3)
      TYPE TTLTPE = {TITLE} EBCDIC CHAR(25)
```

Figure 6.1 *(cont. next page)*

(continued)

```
        TYPE GRDTPE = {GRADE} EBCDIC CHAR(1)
        TYPE CRDSTPE = {CREDITS} EBCDIC DEC(2)

        NONLOGICAL SYMBOLS DEFINITION
          PREDICATES
            TRANSCRIPT:(SIDTPE,NAMTPE,SEMTPE,
            YRTPE,DEPTPE,CS#TPE,SEC#TPE,TTLTPE,GRDTPE,
            CRDSTPE) PREDICATE
        STUDENT: (SIDTPE,NAMTPE,DATPE)
                  PREDICATE
       FUNCTIONS
         NONE

    C(R2): CONSTRAINTS DEFINITION
      C(R2,1):CONSTRAINT STUDENT:ID# → NAME,DATEADM
      C(R2,2):CONSTRAINT TRANSCRIPT:STUDID → STUDNAME
      C(R2,3):CONSTRAINT TRANSCRIPT:DEPT,COURSE#
        → TITLE,CREDITS
      C(R2,4):CONSTRAINT TRANSCRIPT:
        STUDID,SEMESTER,YEAR,DEPT,COURSE#
      → STUDNAME,SEC#,TITLE,GRADE,CREDITS
```

(b)

```
V(R3): VIEW DEFINITION
  S(R3): SCHEMA DEFINITION
    TABLE MAJORS = (MAJOR,ID#,NAME,CLASS)
    TABLE CATALOGUE = (DEPT,COURSE#,TITLE,CREDITS,
      DESCR,PREDEPT,PRECOURSE#)

  L(R3): LANGUAGE DEFINITION
    T(R3): TYPING DEFINITION
      TYPE DEPTPE = {MAJOR,DEPT,PREDEPT} ASCII CHAR(10)
      TYPE ID#TPE = {ID#} ASCII CHAR(9)
      TYPE NAMTPE = {NAME} ASCII CHAR(20)
      TYPE CLTPE = {CLASS} ASCII CHAR(10)
      TYPE CS#TPE = {COURSE#,PRECOURSE#} ASCII DEC(3)
      TYPE CRDSTPE = {CREDITS} ASCII DEC(2)
      TYPE TTLTPE = {TITLE} ASCII CHAR(25)
      TYPE DESCTPE = {DESCR} ASCII CHAR(50)

      NONLOGICAL SYMBOLS DEFINITION
        PREDICATES
          MAJORS: (DEPTPE,ID#TPE,NAMTPE,
            CLTPE) PREDICATE
        CATALOGUE: (DEPTPE,CS#TPE,TTLTPE,CRDSTPE
           DESCTPE,DEPTPE,CS#TPE) PREDICATE
           ≤: (CS#TPE,CS#TPE) PREDICATE
         FUNCTIONS
           NONE

  C(R3): CONSTRAINTS DEFINITION
    C(R3,1):CONSTRAINT MAJORS:ID# → NAME,CLASS
    C(R3,2):CONSTRAINT CATALOGUE:DEPT,COURSE#
    → TITLE,CREDITS,DESCR
```

(c)

Figure 6.1 Candidate relational views: (a) V(R1); (b) V(R2); (c) V(R3).

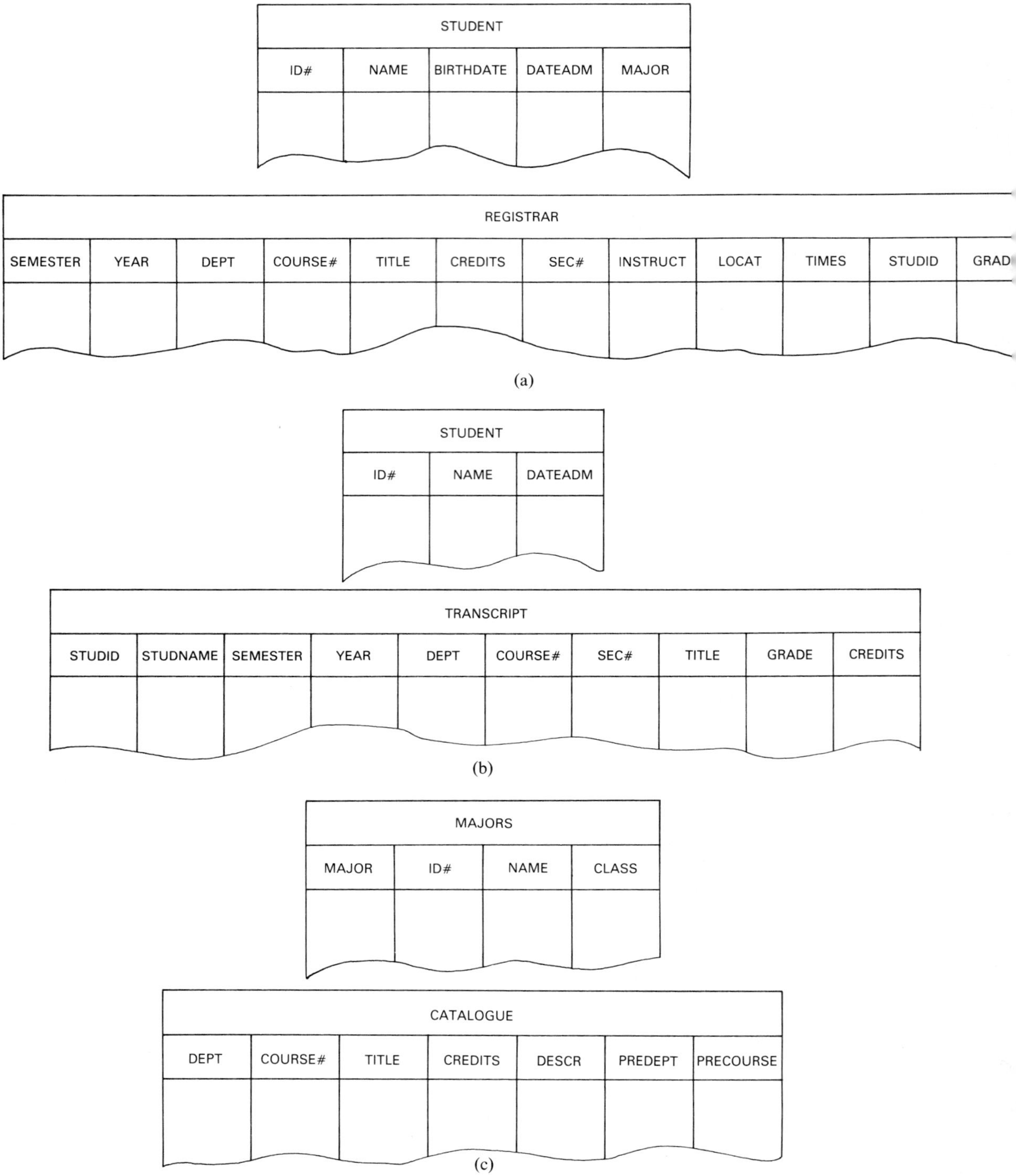

Figure 6.2 Relational structures for the candidate views: (a) V(R1); (b) V(R2); (c) V(R3).

student's view: STUDENT contains student information and TRANSCRIPT contains student course information. V(R3) is a departmental view: MAJORS contains the departmental majors and CATALOGUE contains course and prerequisite information. Also, V(R3) has a (CS#TPE, CS#TPE) predicate symbol ≤, representing the usual "less than or equal to" relation on CS#TPE.

Integration Methodology

Our integration methodology is comprised of two parts: a main part and a second part. The main part inputs the candidate views V(Ei), i = 1,...,k, and outputs a conceptual view V(C) together with corresponding interpretations I(Ei;C) of the external views V(Ei) into the conceptual view V(C). The second part deals with the construction of operation simulators. We will concentrate mostly on the former since the latter is dealt with in Chapters 4 and 5.

The main part of the methodology is a loop that iterates from i = 1 to the number of external views. At each iteration step i, the result is (see Figure 6.3):

1. A temporary conceptual view V(Ci)
2. An interpretation I(Ei;Ci) of the external view V(Ei) in V(Ci)
3. An interpretation I(Ci-1;Ci) of the previous conceptual view V(Ci-1) in V(Ci)

By induction, the previous views V(Ej), j < i, have been interpreted in view V(Ci-1) via interpretations I(Ej;Ci-1), j < i. We "compose" interpretation I(Ci-1,Ci) with the {I(Ej;Ci-1) | j < i } to get interpretations {I(Ej;Ci) | j < i } of views { V(Ej) | j

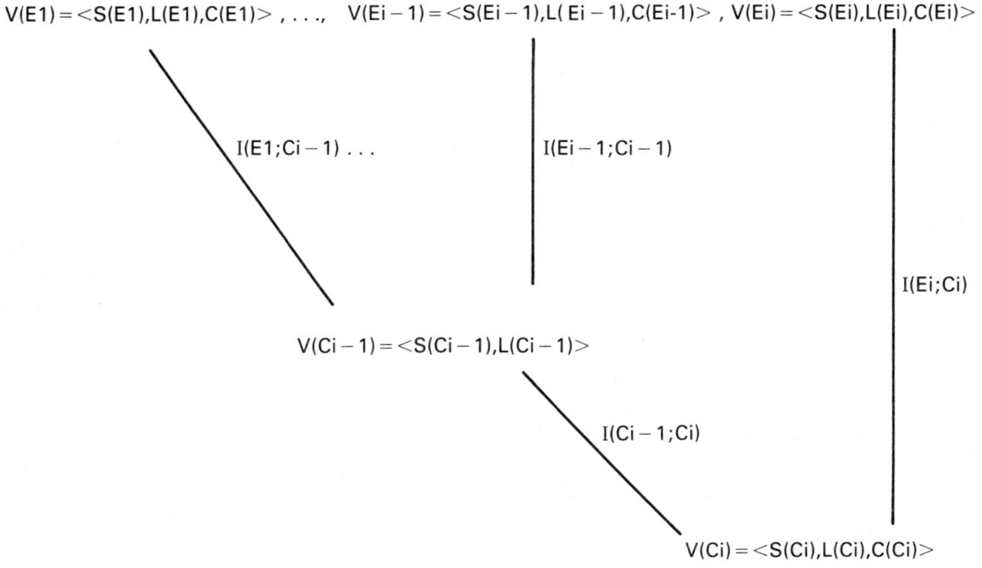

Figure 6.3 i-th iteration of the main part of the construction.

$< i \}$ in V(Ci). When $i = k$, we set V(C), the final conceptual view, to V(Ck) and the interpretations $\{ \text{I(Ei;C)} \mid i \leq k \}$ to $\{ \text{I(Ei;Ck)} \mid i \leq k \}$.

The remainder of this section details the integration process for the relational example above.

Integrating V(R1)

We begin with the first external view,

$$V(R1) = <S(R1),L(R1),C(R1)>,$$

given in Figure 6.1 (a). The first temporary conceptual view,

$$V(C1) = <S(C1),L(C1),C(C1)>,$$

is given in Figure 6.4 (a). Notice that S(C1) equals S(R1), L(C1) equals L(R1), and C(C1) equals C(R1). That is, the first temporary conceptual view is identical to the first external view V(R1).

The interpretation I(R1;C1) of view V(R1) in V(C1) is given in Figure 6.4(b). Notice that since V(R1) equals V(C1), then I(R1;C1) is the "identity." This follows what will be our general policy, namely, the more important the external view, the closer it will be to the final conceptual view. Consequently, less "overhead" will result from the final external-to-conceptual mapping.

Integrating V(R2)

Next, we consider the second external view,

$$V(R2) = <S(R2),L(R2),C(R2)>,$$

given in Figure 6.1(b). In this step we will construct a new temporary conceptual view V(C2) and two interpretations I(R2;C2) of view V(R2) in V(C2) and I(C1;C2) of temporary conceptual view V(C1) in temporary conceptual view V(C2). The interpretation I(R1;C2) will be obtained by "composing" I(R1;C1) and I(C1;C2).

The first thing that has to be determined is how to merge schema S(R2) into S(C1). In merging the two schemata we have to choose between two extremes. On the one hand, we can simply add all the rules in S(R2) (with appropriate renaming to avoid conflicts) to the set of rules S(C1). The other extreme is to identify within S(C1) as much as possible of S(R2) and add to S(C1) names and rules of S(R2) that do not exist in S(C1). The degree to which this is done is determined by how much overhead one is willing to allow during the conversion of operations from S(R2) to S(C1).

In our example, we are able to capture S(R2) completely within S(C1). Figure 6.4(a) contains the schema S(C2), which is identical to schema S(C1). Hence, we choose the second of the two extremes. Since language L(R2) contains no new types, predicate, or function symbols outside L(C1), we make L(C2) the same as L(C1). This is also seen in Figure 6.4(a).

Figure 6.4(c) contains the interpretation I(R2;C2) of external language L(R2) into conceptual language L(C2). I(R2;C2) essentially tells us how to obtain, from a

```
V(C1): VIEW DEFINITION
  S(C1): SCHEMA DEFINITION
    TABLE STUDENT = (ID#,NAME,BIRTHDATE,DATEADM,MAJOR)
    TABLE REGISTRAR = (SEMESTER,YEAR,DEPT,COURSE#,
    TITLE,CREDITS,SEC#,INSTRUCT,LOCAT,TIMES,STUDID,GRADE)

  L(C1): LANGUAGE DEFINITION
    T(C1): TYPING DEFINITION
      TYPE SIDTPE = {ID#,STUDID} ASCII CHAR(9)
      TYPE NAMTPE = {NAME,INSTRUCT} ASCII CHAR(20)
      TYPE DATPE = {BIRTHDATE,DATEADM} ASCII CHAR(15)
      TYPE DEPTPE = {DEPT,MAJOR} ASCII CHAR(10)
      TYPE SEMTPE = {SEMESTER} ASCII CHAR(8)
      TYPE YRTPE = {YEAR} ASCII DEC(4)
      TYPE CS#TPE = {COURSE#} ASCII DEC(3)
      TYPE TTLTPE = {TITLE} ASCII CHAR(25)
      TYPE CRDSTPE = {CREDITS} ASCII DEC(2)
      TYPE SEC#TPE = {SEC#} ASCII CHAR(3)
      TYPE LOCTPE = {LOCAT} ASCII CHAR(30)
      TYPE TIMTPE = {TIMES} ASCII CHAR(20)
      TYPE GRDTPE = {GRADE} ASCII CHAR(1)

      NONLOGICAL SYMBOLS DEFINITION
        PREDICATES
          STUDENT: (IDTPE,NAMTPE,DATPE,
            DEPTPE,DATPE) PREDICATE
            REGISTRAR: (SEMTPE,YRTPE,DEPTPE,
            CS#TPE,TTLTPE,CRDSTPE,SEC#TPE,NAMTPE,
            LOCTPE,TIMTPE,SIDTPE,GRDTPE) PREDICATE
          FUNCTIONS
            NONE

  C(C1): CONSTRAINTS DEFINITION
    C(C1,1):CONSTRAINT STUDENT: ID#
    → NAME,BIRTHDATE,DATEADM,MAJOR
    C(C1,2):CONSTRAINT REGISTRAR:SEMESTER,YEAR,DEPT,
      COURSE#,SEC# → INSTRUCT,LOCAT,TIMES
    C(C1,3):CONSTRAINT REGISTRAR:SEMESTER,YEAR,DEPT,
      COURSE#,SEC#,STUDID → GRADE
```

To obtain the definition of V(C2), change all occurrences of C1 to C2 and add the constraints

```
    C(C2,4) CONSTRAINT REGISTRAR:DEPT,COURSE# → TITLE,CREDITS
```

and

```
    C(C2,5) CONSTRAINT REGISTRAR:STUDID,SEMESTER,YEAR,DEPT,
      COURSE# → SEC#
```

(a)

Figure 6.4 (*cont. next page*)

(continued)

```
I(R1;C1): INTERPRETATION DEFINITION

  EXTERNAL VIEW IS V(R1) = <S(R1),L(R1),C(R1)>
  CONCEPTUAL VIEW IS V(C1) = <S(C1),L(C1),C(C1)>

  CODING SECTION

   CODE FOR SIDTPE IS SIDTPE;
    .
    .
    .
   CODE FOR GRDTPE IS GRDTPE;

 DEFINING FORMULA SECTION

   PREDICATE: STUDENT
   ARGUMENTS ARE: (ID#:1;,NAME:1;,BIRTHDATE:1;,
     DATEADM:1;,MAJOR:1;)
   IS DEFINED BY:
     STUDENT(ID#:1,NAME:1,BIRTHDATE:1,
     DATEADM:1,MAJOR:1)

   PREDICATE: REGISTRAR
   ARGUMENTS ARE: (SEMESTER:1;,YEAR:1;,DEPT:1;,
     COURSE#:1;,TITLE:1;,CREDITS:1;,SEC#:1;,
     INSTRUCT:1;,LOCAT:1;,TIMES:1;,STUDID:1;,
     GRADE:1;)
   IS DEFINED BY:
     REGISTRAR(SEMESTER:1;,YEAR:1;,DEPT:1;,
      COURSE#:1;,TITLE:1;,CREDITS:1;,SEC#:1;,
      INSTRUCT:1;,LOCAT:1;,TIMES:1;,STUDID:1;,
      GRADE:1;)

 CONSTANT TRANSFORMATION SECTION
       .
       .
       .

To obtain I(C1;C2), replace I(R1;C1) with I(C1;C2), V(R1) =
<S(R1),L(R1),C(R1)> with
V(C1) = <S(C1),L(C1),C(C1)> and V(C1) = <S(C1),L(C1),C(C1)> with
V(C2) = <S(C2),L(C2),C(C2)> .

To obtain I(R1;C2), replace I(R1;C1) with I(R1;C2) and V(C1) =
<S(C1),L(C1),C(C1)> with
V(C2) = <S(C2),L(C2),C(C2)>.
```

(b)

```
I(R2;C2): INTERPRETATION DEFINITION
  EXTERNAL VIEW IS V(R2) = <S(R2),L(R2),C(R2)>
  CONCEPTUAL VIEW IS V(C2) = <S(C2),L(C2),C(C2)>
```

Figure 6.4 *(cont. next page)*

(continued)

```
CODING SECTION
  CODE FOR SIDTPE IS SIDTPE;
    .
    .
    .
  CODE FOR GRDTPE IS GRDTPE;
DEFINING FORMULA SECTION

  PREDICATE: STUDENT
  ARGUMENTS ARE: (ID#:1;,NAME:1;,DATEADM:1;)
  IS DEFINED BY:
    (E)BIRTHDATE:1(E)MAJOR:1
    STUDENT(ID#:1,NAME:1,BIRTHDATE:1,
    DATEADM:1,MAJOR:1)

  PREDICATE: TRANSCRIPT
  ARGUMENT ARE: (STUDID:1;,NAME:1;,SEMESTER:1;,
    YEAR:1;,DEPT:1;,COURSE#:1;,SEC#:1;,
    TITLE:1;,GRADE:1;,CREDITS:1;)
  IS DEFINED BY:
    (E)BIRTHDATE:1(E)DATEADM:1(E)MAJOR:1
    (E)INSTRUCT:1(E)LOCAT:1(E)TIMES:1
    STUDENT(STUDID:1,NAME:1,BIRTHDATE:1,
      DATEADM:1,MAJOR:1)
    & REGISTRAR(SEMESTER:1;,YEAR:1;,DEPT:1;,
      COURSE#:1;,TITLE:1;,CREDITS:1;,SEC#:1;,
      INSTRUCT:1;,LOCAT:1;,TIMES:1;,STUDID:1;,
      GRADE:1;)

CONSTANT TRANSFORMATION SECTION
      .
      .
      .
```

To obtain I(R2;C3), replace I(R2;C2) with I(R2;C3), V(C2) = <S(C2),L(C2),C(C2)> with V(C3) = <S(C3),L(C3),C(C3)> and in the defining formulas for STUDENT and TRANSCRIPT

replace

```
STUDENT(STUDID:1,NAME:1,BIRTHDATE:1,
  DATEADM:1,MAJOR:1)
```

by

```
(E)CLASS:1 STUDENT(STUDID:1,NAME:1,BIRTHDATE:1,
  DATEADM:1,MAJOR:1,CLASS:1).
```

(c)

Figure 6.4 *(cont. next page)*

(continued)

```
I(C1;C2)(C(C1)) (= C(C1)) =
{C(C1,1) = STUDENT:ID# → NAME,BIRTHDATE,DATEADM,MAJOR,
 C(C1,2) = REGISTRAR:SEMESTER,YEAR,DEPT,COURSE#,SEC#
 → INSTRUCT,LOCAT,TIMES,

 C(C1,3) = REGISTRAR:SEMESTER,YEAR,DEPT,COURSE#,SEC#,
   STUDID → GRADE}

I(R2;C2)(C(R2)) =
{I(R2;C2)(C(R2,1)) = I(R2;C2)(STUDENT:ID# → NAME,DATEADM)
  = ((E)BIRTHDATE:1(E)MAJOR:1
      STUDENT(STUDID:1,NAME:1,BIRTHDATE:1,DATEADM:1,MAJOR:1))
   & ((E)BIRTHDATE:2(E)MAJOR:2
      STUDENT(STUDID:1,NAME:2,BIRTHDATE:2,DATEADM:2,MAJOR:2))
  → (NAME:1 = NAME:2 & DATEADM:1 = DATEADM:2),

I(R2;C2)(C(R2,2)) = I(R2;C2)(TRANSCRIPT:STUDID → STUDNAME)
  = ((E)BIRTHDATE:1 ... (E)TIMES:1
  STUDENT(STUDID:1,NAME:1,BIRTHDATE:1,DATEADM:1,MAJOR:1)
  & REGISTRAR(SEMESTER:1,YEAR:1,DEPT:1,COURSE#:1,TITLE:1,
      CREDITS:1,SEC#:1,INSTRUCT:1,LOCAT:1,TIMES:1,STUDID:1,GRADE:1) )
  & ((E)BIRTHDATE:2 ... (E)TIMES:2
      STUDENT(STUDID:1,NAME:2,BIRTHDATE:2,DATEADM:2,MAJOR:2)
  & REGISTRAR(SEMESTER:2,YEAR:2,DEPT:2,COURSE#:2,TITLE:2,
      CREDITS:2,SEC#:2,INSTRUCT:2,LOCAT:2,TIMES:2,STUDID:1,
      GRADE:2) )
      → STUDNAME:1 = STUDNAME:2,

I(R2;C2)(C(R2,3)) = I(R2;C2)(TRANSCRIPT:DEPT,COURSE#
  → TITLE:1,CREDITS:1)
  = ((E)BIRTHDATE:1 ... (E)TIMES:1
    STUDENT(STUDID:1,NAME:1,BIRTHDATE:1,DATEADM:1,MAJOR:1)
  & REGISTRAR(SEMESTER:1,YEAR:1,DEPT:1,COURSE#:1,TITLE:1,
      CREDITS:1,SEC#:1,INSTRUCT:1,LOCAT:1,TIMES:1,STUDID:1,
      GRADE:1) )
  & ((E)BIRTHDATE:2 ... (E)TIMES:2
     STUDENT(STUDID:2,NAME:2,BIRTHDATE:2,DATEADM:2,MAJOR:2)
 & REGISTRAR(SEMESTER:2,YEAR:2,DEPT:1,COURSE#:1,TITLE:2,
     CREDITS:2,SEC#:2,INSTRUCT:2,LOCAT:2,TIMES:2,STUDID:2,
     GRADE:2))
     → (TITLE:1 = TITLE:2 & CREDITS:1 = CREDITS:2),

I(R2;C2)(C(R2,4)) = I(R2;C2)(TRANSCRIPT:STUDID,SEMESTER,
  YEAR,DEPT,COURSE# → STUDNAME,SEC#,TITLE,GRADE,CREDITS)
  = ((E)BIRTHDATE:1(E)DATEADM:1(E)MAJOR:1(E)INSTRUCT:1
     (E)LOCAT:1(E)TIMES:1
      STUDENT(STUDID:1,NAME:1,BIRTHDATE:1,DATEADM:1,MAJOR:1)
    & REGISTRAR(SEMESTER:1,YEAR:1,DEPT:1,COURSE#:1,TITLE:1,
      CREDITS:1,SEC#:1,INSTRUCT:1,LOCAT:1,TIME:1,STUDID:1,
      GRADE:1))
```

Figure 6.4 (*cont. next page*)

(continued)

```
& ((E)BIRTHDATE:2(E)DATEADM:2(E)MAJOR:2(E)INSTRUCT:2
   (E)LOCAT:2(E)TIMES:2
    STUDENT(STUDID:1,NAME:2,BIRTHDATE:2,DATEADM:2,MAJOR:2)
& REGISTRAR(SEMESTER:1,YEAR:1,DEPT:1,COURSE#:1,TITLE:2,
  CREDITS:2,SEC#:2,INSTRUCT:2,LOCAT:2,TIMES:2,STUDID:1,
  GRADE:2))
  →(NAME:1 = NAME:2 & SEC#:1 = SEC#:2 & TITLE:1 = TITLE:2
  & GRADE:1 = GRADE:2)  }
```

(d)

```
V(C3): VIEW DEFINITION
  S(C3): SCHEMA DEFINITION
    TABLE STUDENT = (ID#,NAME,BIRTHDATE,DATEADM,MAJOR,CLASS)
    TABLE REGISTRAR = (SEMESTER,YEAR,DEPT,COURSE#,
      TITLE,SEC#,INSTRUCT,LOCAT,TIMES,STUDID,GRADE)
    TABLE CATALOGUE = (DEPT,COURSE#,TITLE,CREDITS,
      DESCR,PREDEPT,PRECOURSE#)

L(C3): LANGUAGE DEFINITION
  T(C3): TYPING DEFINITION
    TYPE SIDTPE = {ID#,STUDID} ASCII CHAR(9)
    TYPE NAMTPE = {NAME,INSTRUCT} ASCII CHAR(20)
              .
              .
              .
    TYPE DEPTPE = {DEPT,MAJOR,PREDEPT} ASCII CHAR(10)
    TYPE CS#TPE = {COURSE#,PRECOURSE#} ASCII DEC(3)
    TYPE SEC#TPE = {SEC#} ASCII CHAR(3)
              .
              .
              .
    TYPE GRDTPE = {GRADE} ASCII CHAR(1)
    TYPE DESCTPE = {DESCR} ASCII CHAR(50)
    TYPE CLTPE = {CLASS} ASCII CHAR(10)

    NONLOGICAL SYMBOLS DEFINITION
       PREDICATES
         STUDENT: (IDTPE,NAMTPE,DATPE,
           DEPTPE,DATPE,CLTPE) PREDICATE
           REGISTRAR: (SEMTPE,YRTPE,DEPTPE,
           CS#TPE,TTLTPE,CRDSTPE,SEC#TPE,
           NAMTPE,LOCTPE,TIMTPE,SIDTPE,
           GRDTPE) PREDICATE
           CATALOGUE:(DEPTPE,CS#TPE,TTLTPE,
           CRDSTPE,DESCTPE,DEPTPE,
           CS#TPE) PREDICATE
           ≤: (CS#TPE,CS#TPE)-PREDICATE
        FUNCTIONS
          NONE
```

Figure 6.4 *(cont. next page)*

(continued)

```
C(C3): CONSTRAINTS DEFINITION
  C(C3,1):CONSTRAINT STUDENT: ID#
  → NAME,BIRTHDATE,DATEADM,MAJOR,CLASS
  C(C3,2):CONSTRAINT REGISTRAR:SEMESTER,YEAR,DEPT,
    COURSE#,SEC# → INSTRUCT,LOCAT,TIMES
  C(C3,3):CONSTRAINT REGISTRAR:SEMESTER,YEAR,DEPT,
    COURSE#,SEC#,STUDID → GRADE
  C(C3,4):CONSTRAINT REGISTRAR:DEPT,COURSE#
    → TITLE,CREDITS
  C(C3,5):CONSTRAINT REGISTRAR:STUDID,SEMESTER,YEAR,
    DEPT,COURSE# → SEC#
  C(C3,6):CONSTRAINT CATALOGUE;DEPT,COURSE# → TITLE,
    CREDITS,DESCR
```

(e)

```
I(R3;C3): INTERPRETATION DEFINITION
  EXTERNAL VIEW IS V(R3) = <S(R3),L(R3),C(R3)>
  CONCEPTUAL VIEW IS V(C3) = <S(C3),L(C3),C(C3)>

  CODING SECTION

   CODE FOR DEPTPE IS DEPTPE;
   CODE FOR ID#TPE IS ID#TPE;
   CODE FOR NAMETPE IS NAMTPE;
   CODE FOR CLTPE IS CLTPE;
   CODE FOR CS#TPE IS CS#TPE;
   CODE FOR TTLTPE IS TTLTPE;
   CODE FOR CRDSTPE IS CRDSTPE;
   CODE FOR DESCTPE IS DESCTPE;

 DEFINING FORMULA SECTION

   PREDICATE: MAJORS
   ARGUMENTS ARE: (MAJOR:1;,ID#:1;,
     NAME:1;,CLASS:1;)
   IS DEFINED BY:
     (E)BIRTHDATE:1(E)DATEADM:1
     STUDENT(ID#:1,NAME:1,BIRTHDATE:1,
     DATEADM:1,MAJOR:1,CLASS:1)

   PREDICATE: CATALOGUE
   ARGUMENT ARE: (DEPT:1;,COURSE#:1;TITLE:1;,
     CREDITS:1;,DESRC:1;,PREDEPT:1;,PRECOURSE#:1;)
   IS DEFINED BY:
     CATALOGUE(DEPT:1,COURSE#:1,TITLE:1,
     CREDITS:1,DESRC:1,PREDEPT:1,PRECOURSE#:1)

   PREDICATE:≤
   ARGUMENTS ARE (COURSE#:1;,COURSE#:2;)
   IS DEFINED BY:
     ≤(COURSE#:1,COURSE#:2)
```

Figure 6.4 (*cont. next page*)

(continued)

```
        CONSTANT TRANSFORMATION SECTION
          .
          .
          .
```

(f)

```
    I(C2;C3): INTERPRETATION DEFINITION
      EXTERNAL VIEW IS V(C2) = <S(C2),L(C2),C(C2)>
      CONCEPTUAL VIEW IS V(C3) = <S(C3),L(C3),C(C3)>

      CODING SECTION

        CODE FOR SIDTPE IS SIDTPE;
          .
          .
          .
        CODE FOR GRDTPE IS GRDTPE;

      DEFINING FORMULA SECTION

        PREDICATE: STUDENT
        ARGUMENTS ARE: (ID#:1;,NAME:1;,BIRTHDATE:1;,
          DATEADM:1;,MAJOR:1;)
        IS DEFINED BY:
          (E)CLASS:1
          STUDENT(ID#:1,NAME:1,BIRTHDATE:1,
          DATEADM:1,MAJOR:1,CLASS:1)

        PREDICATE: REGISTRAR
        ARGUMENTS ARE: (SEMESTER:1;,YEAR:1;,DEPT:1;,
          COURSE#:1;,TITLE:1;,CREDITS:1;,SEC#:1;,
          INSTRUCT:1;,LOCAT:1;,TIMES:1;,STUDID:1;,
          GRADE:1;)
        IS DEFINED BY:
          REGISTRAR(SEMESTER:1,YEAR:1,DEPT:1,
          COURSE#:1,TITLE:1,CREDITS:1,SEC#:1,
          INSTRUCT:1,LOCAT:1,TIMES:1,STUDID:1,
            GRADE:1;)

      CONSTANT TRANSFORMATION SECTION
            .
            .
            .
    To obtain I(R1;C3) replace I(C2;C3) with I(R1;C3) and
  V(C2) = <S(C2),L(C2),C(C2)> with V(R1) = <S(R1),L(R1),C(R1)>.
```

(g)

Figure 6.4 Integration of views V(R1), V(R2) and V(R3): (a) temporary conceptual views V(C1) and V(C2); (b) interpretations I(R1;C1), I(C1;C2), and I(R1;C2); (c) interpretations I(R2;C2) and I(R2;C3); (d) C′(C2) = I(C1;C2)(C(C1)) ∪ I(R2;C2)(C(R2)); (e) temporary conceptual views V(C3) and V(C); (f) interpretation I(R3;C3); (g) interpretations I(C2;C3) and I(R1;C3).

relational structure M(C2) for L(C2), an external relational structure I(R2;C2)[M(C2)] for L(R2). Also, Figure 6.4(b) contains the interpretation I(C1;C2) of temporary conceptual view V(C1) in temporary conceptual view V(C2). Since L(C2) is identical to L(C1), the interpretation I(C1;C2) is the "identity" interpretation.

We next see if the two views V(R2) and V(C1) do not "contradict" one another. To do this we first obtain the interpretation of the constraints in C(C1) under I(C1;C2) [i.e., I(C1;C2)(C(C1))] and the interpretation of the constraints C(R2) under I(R2;C2) [i.e., I(R2;C2)(C(R2))]. We then check to see if the wffs

$$C'(C2) = I(C1;C2)(C(C1)) \cup I(R2;C2)(C(R2))$$

are "logically consistent" in L(C2). This is done by finding a relational structure for L(C2) which is a model of C′(C2), that is, in which all the wffs in C′(C2) are true.

The interpretation of the constraints C(C1) under I(C1;C2) is given in Figure 6.4(d). Notice that since I(C1;C2) is the identity interpretation, I(C1;C2)(C(C1)) is identical to C(C1). The interpretation of the constraints C(R2) under I(R2;C2) is also given in Figure 6.4(d). The reader can check that a relational structure with no rows is a trivial model for C′(C2). Consequently, the set of wffs C(C2) are logically consistent.

Remark. The task of finding a model for a set of wffs (i.e., discovering consistency), is generally a difficult one. However, we show in Section 6.3 that in many real database applications, the set of resulting wffs is "always" consistent. Hence, this step can be omitted.

By the above, C′(C2) is consistent in L(C2) and trivially implies

$$I(C1;C2)(C(C1)) \cup I(R2;C2)(C(R2)).$$

Hence, we can choose C′(C2) to be the constraints for the temporary conceptual view V(C2). However, by examining the set of wffs in C′(C2), we can find a "smaller" set C(C2) which logically implies C′(C2). Such a set C(C2) is found in Figure 6.4(a).

At this point we have constructed view

$$V(C2) = \langle S(C2),L(C2),C(C2) \rangle,$$

the second temporary conceptual view. By the above we also have the interpretation I(R2;C2) of view V(R2) in V(C2). We conclude this part by constructing the interpretation I(R1;C2) of view V(R1) in V(C2). To do this we "compose" the interpretations I(R1;C1) and I(C1;C2).

Definition. Let I(S1;S2) be an interpretation of L(S1) in L(S2) and I(S2;S3) be an interpretation of L(S2) in L(S3). Then

$$I(S1;S3) = I(S1;S2) \circ I(S2;S3),$$

the *composition of* I(S1;S2) *with* I(S2;S3), has

1. A coding section made up from the coding section of I(S2;S3) by replacing the types of L(S2) in the codes by their codes [in L(S1)] from I(S1;S2)

2. A defining formula section made up from the defining formula section of I(S2;S3) by replacing the atoms of L(S2) by their defining formulas according to I(S1;S2)
3. A constant transformation section made up by composing the translation functions [CODE( ) and DECODE( )] of I(S1;S2)

Examples of compositions of interpretations will be given throughout this chapter.

Since I(R1;C1) and I(C1;C2) are identity interpretations on language L(C2) [= L(R1) = L(C1)], it turns out that their composition, I(R1;C1) o I(C1;C2), is also the identity on L(C2). Figure 6.4(b) also contains I(R1;C2).

Integrating V(R3)

Next, we consider the third external view

V(R3) = <S(R3),L(R3),C(R3)>

given in Figure 6.1(c). In this part we will construct a new temporary conceptual view V(C3) and two interpretations I(R3;C3) of view V(R3) in V(C3) and I(C2;C3) of temporary conceptual view V(C2) in temporary conceptual view V(C3). The interpretations I(R1;C3) and I(R2;C3) will be obtained by "composing" I(R1;C2) and I(R2;C2) with I(C2;C3), respectively.

Schema S(C2) is not sufficient to represent all the data in schema S(R3). Thus, we merge S(R3) into S(C2) by adding the field name, CLASS, to the STUDENT rule and adding a new rule

CATALOGUE = (DEPT,COURSE#,TITLE,CREDITS,DESCR,
PREDEPT,PRECOURSE#).

The new temporary conceptual schema S(C3) is given in Figure 6.4(e).

Language L(C2) also has to be enhanced to incorporate language L(R3). This includes adding the new types DESTPE = {DESCR}, CLTPE = {CLASS}, the names PREDEPT, PRECOURSE# within the old types DEPTPE and CS#TPE, respectively, and the (CS#TPE, CS#TPE) predicate symbol $\leq$. The conceptual language L(C3) is also given in Figure 6.4(e).

Figure 6.4(f) contains the interpretation I(R3;C3) of external language L(R3) in temporary conceptual language L(C3). Notice that not only are the L(R3) predicates MAJORS and CATALOGUE defined in terms of language L(C3), but so is the L(R3) predicate symbol $\leq$.

Figure 6.4(g) contains the interpretation I(C2;C3) of temporary conceptual language L(C2) in temporary conceptual language L(C3). Interpretation I(C2;C3) is very much like the identity on L(C2) except for the defining formula for the predicate STUDENT. The addition of the field CLASS to the STUDENT rule produces the extra existential quantifier in the formula.

The interpretations of the constraints in C(C2) under I(C2;C3) [i.e.,

I(C2;C3)(C(C2))] and the interpretations of the constraints C(R3) under I(R3;C3) [i.e., I(R3;C3)(C(R3))] are left as exercises.The reader can check that

$$C'(C3) = I(C2;C3)(C(C2)) \cup I(R3;C3)(C(R3))$$

has the empty relational structure for a model; hence is consistent for L(C3). The reader can also check that the set of wffs C(C3) given in Figure 6.4(e) logically implies C'(C3).

At this point we have constructed

$$V(C3) = \langle S(C3), L(C3), C(C3) \rangle,$$

the third temporary conceptual view. The interpretations

$$I(R1;C3) = I(R1;C2) \circ I(C2;C3) \text{ and } I(R2;C3) = I(R2;C2) \circ I(C2;C3)$$

of languages L(R1) and L(R2) in L(C3), respectively, are given in Figure 6.4(g) and (c), respectively. It will be shown in Section 6.3 that these are also interpretations of views V(R1) and V(R2) in V(C3), respectively.

Since $k = 3$, we can set V(C), the final conceptual view to V(C3). We can also set interpretations I(R1;C), I(R2;C), and I(R3;C) to I(R1;C3), I(R2;C3), and I(R3;C3), respectively. Notice that interpretation I(R1;C) [Figure 6.4(g)] is very close to the identity interpretation on L(R1). Consequently, I(R1;C) will provide little overhead in supporting V(R1), the most important external view.

Exercises

1. Show that the relational structure for L(C2) which has no rows is a model for C'(C2).
2. Show that the set of wffs C(C2) in Figure 6.4(a) logically implies in L(C2) the set of wffs C'(C2).
3. Evaluate the set C'(C3) and show that the relational structure for L(C3) with no rows is a model for it.
4. Show that the set of wffs C(C3) given in Figure 6.4(e) logically implies the set C'(C3).
5. Show that the interpretations I(R1;C3) and I(R2;C3) are, respectively, interpretations of views V(R1) and V(R2) in V(C3).
6. Suppose that the order of importance of the views was V(R2), V(R1), and V(R3). Integrate the views according to this new ordering.
7. Suppose that the order of importance of the views was V(R3), V(R1), and V(R2). Integrate the views according to this new ordering.

6.2 THE VIEW INTEGRATION METHODOLOGY

In this section we present our methodology for view integration in the most general terms. We also illustrate the methodology using a heterogeneous example.

Integration Methodology

Let

$$\{V(Ei) = <S(Ei),L(Ei),C(Ei)> \mid i = 1,...,k\}$$

be an ordered sequence of database views such that the lower the index, the more important the view. The determination of the ordering of these views can be made by various factors, including frequency of use of the view, cost of operations on the view, and so on. Further details are outside the scope of this presentation.

The methodology of view integration is comprised of two parts. The main part inputs the views

$$\{V(Ei) = <S(Ei),L(Ei),C(Ei)> \mid i = 1,...,k\}$$

and outputs an integrated conceptual view

$$V(C) = <S(C),L(C),C(C)>$$

and a set of interpretations

$$\{I(Ei;C) \mid i = 1,...,k\}$$

of the external views V(Ei) in V(C). The second part builds the operation simulators for the external operations.

Main Part

```
FOR i = 1 to k;
```

Beginning with the most important view V(E1), we proceed to sequentially merge all the views.

```
L1: IF i = 1
    THEN
    DO;
      SET S(C1) ← S(E1);
      SET L(C1) ← L(E1);
      SET C(C1) ← C(E1);
      SET I(E1;C1) ← the identity interpretation on L(E1);
      GO TO L4;
    END;
```

If i equals 1, then we make the first temporary conceptual view $V(C1) = <S(C1), L(C1), C(C1)>$ identical to the most important external view $V(E1) = <S(E1), L(E1), C(E1)>$. We also make interpretation I(E1;C1) of V(E1) in V(C1) the identity interpretation [on language L(E1)]. This concurs with our objective of producing as little overhead as possible in the external-to-conceptual mapping on the most important view V(E1). When done we go to L4 to increase i.

SET S(Ci) ← merge S(Ei) into S(Ci-1);
SET L(Ci) ← merge L(Ei) into L(Ci-1);

At this point we have to incorporate view V(Ei), which is not the first view. We merge schema S(Ei) with schema S(Ci-1). By this we mean that we add on to S(Ci-1) (if necessary) enough names and rules so that S(Ei) can be extracted from the new schema. Our general philosophy is to make as few structural changes to Ci-1 since it represents the incorporation of more important views than V(Ei). Similarly, we merge the language L(Ei) into the language L(Ci-1).

L2: SET I(Ei;Ci) ← an interpretation of L(Ei) in L(Ci);

From the previous steps, we have constructed a temporary conceptual schema S(Ci) and a temporary conceptual language L(Ci). We construct an interpretation I(Ei;Ci) of the external language L(Ei) into the language L(Ci). This tells us how to extract the i-th external database from the i-th temporary conceptual database.

SET I(Ci-1;Ci) ← an interpretation of L(Ci-1) in L(Ci);

Similarly, we construct an interpretation I(Ci-1;Ci) of the (i − 1)st temporary conceptual language into the i-th temporary conceptual language. This tells us how to extract the (i−1)st temporary conceptual database from the i-th temporary conceptual database. This will be used below to construct interpretations of external view V(Ej), j < i , in the i-th temporary conceptual view V(Ci).

L3: SET C′(Ci) ← I(Ci-1;Ci)(C(Ci-1)) ∪ I(Ei;Ci)(C(Ei));

We place into C′(Ci) the interpretations of the (i − 1)st conceptual constraints under I(Ci-1;Ci) and the interpretations of the i-th external constraints under I(Ei;Ci). C′(Ci) is used below to check consistency of view V(Ei) (under I(Ei;Ci)) with the previously incorporated external views [in V(Ci-1)]. C′(Ci) is also used to obtain C(Ci), the i-th conceptual constraints.

IF C′(Ci) is inconsistent in L(Ci-1)
THEN EITHER

We can check to see if C′(Ci) is consistent or not by trying to construct a database structure for L(Ci) in which all of C′(Ci) is true. If such a model is found, then C′(Ci) is consistent in L(Ci). If a model does not exist, then attempts at finding one will often isolate those formulas in C′(Ci) that conflict.

These conflicting formulas can be used to try to resolve the situation as follows.

1. CHANGE C(Ei);
GO TO L3;

Find the wff(s) in C(Ei) whose interpretation [under I(Ei;Ci)] conflicts with those in I(Ci-1;Ci)(C(Ci)). We can then ask the class of users of view V(Ei) to alter their constraints so that conflict is eliminated. Since view V(Ei) has the lowest priority (thus far), it is appropriate that we first try to change V(Ei), rather than any previously incorporated view [in V(Ci-1)]. If such a change is made, we go back to L3.

```
2. CHANGE S(Ci);
   GO TO L2;
```

The i-th temporary conceptual schema is changed. For example, suppose that two constraints conflict with each other over the same data. Then the schema S(Ci) could be changed so that the data are duplicated, hence, allowing each constraint to be maintained independently of one another. When this is done we return to L2.

```
3. CHANGE C(Ej), SOME j < i ;
   SET i ← j ;
   GO TO L1;
```

We alter the constraints of a previously incorporated external view V(Ej), j < i, even though it has a higher priority. In this case the construction falls back to the j-th iterative step and repeats.

```
4. EJECT VIEW V(Ei);
   FOR j = i TO k - 1;
     SET V(Ej) ← V(Ej+1);
     END;
     GO TO L1;
```

This is the most drastic of the solutions. Namely, we eliminate view V(Ei) from the community of shared views. We set V(Ej) to V(Ej+1), j ≤ i and proceed to L1 to add on view V(Ei).

In Section 6.3 we will provide an illustration of such a conflict and show how these four steps can be used to resolve the situation. We also present in Section 6.3 a sufficient condition that will ensure that such conflicts never occur. It turns out that most real databases fall into this situation.

```
SET C(Ci) ← C*(Ci)
where   C*(Ci) is consistent and C*(Ci) ⊨ C′(Ci) in L(Ci);
```

Once we have established that C′(Ci) is consistent in L(Ci), we then try to find a consistent set of constraints C*(Ci) which logically imply C′(Ci). Such a set can always be found, namely, C′(Ci). By properties of interpretations, if the conceptual database satisfies these constraints, then all the supported databases automatically satisfy their respective constraints.

```
SET V(Ci) ← <S(Ci),L(Ci), C(Ci)>;
```

We have completed the i-th temporary conceptual view.

```
FOR j = 1 TO i - 1;
  SET I(Ej;Ci) ← I(Ej;Ci-1) ∘ I(Ci-1;Ci);
END;
```

For each of the previously incorporated views, V(Ej), j < i, we form the interpretation of L(Ej) in L(Ci). This is obtained by composing (o) the interpretation I(Ej;Ci-1) with the interpretation I(Ci-1;Ci). The proof that I(Ej;Ci) is an interpretation of view V(Ej) in V(Ci) is given in Section 6.3.

```
L4: END;
```

We increment i and proceed to incorporate the i + 1st external view.

```
SET V(C) ← V(Ck);
FOR i = 1 TO k;
  SET I(Ei;C) ← I(Ei;Ck);
END;
```

At this point we have incorporated all the external views V(Ei), i ≤ k, into the k-th temporary conceptual view V(Ck). We set V(C), the final conceptual view, to V(Ck), and the interpretations {I(Ei;C)} to {I(Ei;Ck)}. This concludes the main part of the construction.

Second Part

The purpose of this part is to construct the set of operation simulators for the external operations of the views V(Ei), i = 1,...,k. Since operation simulator construction and checking are studied in Chapters 4 and 5, we do not consider this aspect of view integration in great detail.

```
FOR i = 1 TO k;
  FOR HIGHER-ORDER R in S(Ei);
    SET SIMi ← EMPTY;
      FOR O IN {INSERT(R),DELETE(R),UPDATE(R)}
      SET SIMi ← SIMi U {SIM(O(R))};
      END;
    END;
END;
```

For each external view V(Ei) and each higher-order name R in Ei, we construct the operation simulators SIM(INSERT(R)), SIM(DELETE(R)) and SIM(UPDATE(R)) for external operators.

```
  SET PHI(Ei) ← <I(Ei;C), SIMi>;
END;
```

For each i, i = 1,...,k, the external-to-conceptual mapping, PHI(Ei), is comprised of the interpretation I(Ei;C) and the set of operation simulators.

The reason that we postponed the building of the simulators is that throughout the construction, the interpretations were always changing. Consequently, if we had built the simulators along with the interpretations, then they, too, would have undergone changes.

Adding and Reordering Views

Although the methodology concerns the problem of view integration, our construction can also be used to add on additional external views to an already existing set of supported external views. Suppose that views $\{V(Ei) \mid i = 1,\ldots k\}$ are incorporated in conceptual view V(Ck). The task of adding on a new view V(Ek+1), with lowest priority, is that of doing one more iteration to the main part of the construction followed by a complete pass through the second part.

However, we should point out that if, by adding V(Ek+1), the conceptual view V(Ck+1) differs from the old conceptual view V(Ck), some problems may arise. First, some previously constructed external-to-conceptual mappings [of views V(Ej) in V(Ck)] may have to be changed. Second, the physical storage for the conceptual database may have to be altered; hence, the whole database may have to be reloaded. Third, all the application programs on the external views V(Ej), $j \leq k$, may have to be retranslated to the new conceptual view and subsequently to the new "internally" stored database. If, however, there is no difference between V(Ck) and V(Ck+1), then none of this must be done.

In practice, the sequence of external views changes. For example, when the integrated database was first designed, external view V(E1) was the most important view. Since that time view V(E1) may become less and less important; in fact, V(E1) may no longer be used. We can use our construction on a revised sequence to obtain a new conceptual view and a new set of external-to-conceptual mappings (and also a new "internally" stored database). A key point is that application programs reflecting the external views still supported do not have to be rewritten.

Heterogeneous Example

We illustrate the methodology using three heterogeneous database views. These are $V(D1) = <S(D1), L(D1), C(D1)>$, $V(D2) = <S(D2), L(D2), C(D2)>$, and $V(D3) = <S(D3), L(D3), C(D3)>$, whose definitions are given in Figure 6.5 (a)–(c). Pictures for these views are given in Figure 6.6 (a)–(c). These views are three typical external views for a university and are the heterogeneous analogues to those used in Section 6.1. We assume that the views V(D1), V(D2), and V(D3) are ordered in decreasing order of importance.

i = 1. The first temporary conceptual view $V(C1) = <S(C1), L(C1), C(C1)>$ is given in Figure 6.7(a). According to the construction, view V(C1) is identical to the first external view V(D1). The identity interpretation I(D1;C1) on L(C1) [= L(D1)] is given in Figure 6.7(b).

i = 2. In this example, we can also capture schema S(D2) within S(C1). Figure 6.7(a) contains schema S(C2), which is identical to schema S(C1). Since language L(D2) contains no new types, predicates or function symbols outside of L(C1), we make L(C2) the same as L(C1). This is also seen in Figure 6.7(a).

Figure 6.7(c) contains the interpretation I(D2;C2) of language L(D2) in tempo-

```
V(D1): VIEW DEFINITION
  S(D1): SCHEMA DEFINITION
    TABLE REGISTRAR = (SEMESTER,YEAR,COURSE)
    TABLE COURSE = (DEPT,COURSE#,TITLE,CREDITS,SECTION)
    TABLE SECTION = (SEC#,INSTRUCT,LOCAT,TIMES,STUDENT)
    TABLE STUDENT = (STUDID,STUDNAME,GRADE)
    TABLE STUDINFO = (ID#,STUDNAME,BIRTHDATE,DATEADM,MAJOR)

L(D1): LANGUAGE DEFINITION
  T(D1): TYPING DEFINITION
    TYPE SEMTPE = {SEMESTER} ASCII CHAR(8)
    TYPE YRTPE = {YEAR} ASCII DEC(4)
    TYPE DEPTPE = {DEPT,MAJOR} ASCII CHAR(10)
    TYPE CS#TPE = {COURSE#} ASCII DEC(3)
    TYPE TTLTPE = {TITLE} ASCII CHAR(25)
    TYPE CRDSTPE = {CREDITS} ASCII DEC(2)
    TYPE SEC#TPE = {SEC#} ASCII DEC(3)
    TYPE NAMTPE = {INSTRUCT,STUDNAME} ASCII CHAR(20)
    TYPE LOCTPE = {LOCAT} ASCII CHAR(30)
    TYPE TIMTPE = {TIMES} ASCII CHAR(20)
    TYPE SIDTPE = {STUDID,ID#} ASCII CHAR(9)
    TYPE GRDTPE = {GRADE} ASCII CHAR(1)
    TYPE DATPE = {BIRTHDATE,DATEADM} ASCII CHAR(15)

    NONLOGICAL SYMBOLS DEFINITION
      PREDICATES
        REGISTRAR-COURSE-SECTION-STUDENT:
          (SEMTPE,YRTPE,COURSE,DEPTPE,CS#TPE,TTLTPE,
          CRDSTPE,SECTION,SEC#TPE,NAMTPE,LOCTPE,
          TIMTPE,STUDENT,IDTPE,NAMTPE,GRDTPE)
          FULL CLUSTER PREDICATE
        STUDINFO:
          (IDTPE,NAMTPE,DATPE,DATPE) PREDICATE
     FUNCTIONS
       NONE

C(D1): CONSTRAINTS DEFINITION
  C(D1,1):CONSTRAINT REGISTRAR:SEMESTER,
    YEAR → COURSE
  C(D1,2):CONSTRAINT REGISTRAR-COURSE:
    SEMESTER,YEAR,DEPT,COURSE#
    → TITLE,CREDITS,SECTION
  C(D1,3):CONSTRAINT REGISTRAR-COURSE-SECTION:
    SEMESTER,YEAR,DEPT,COURSE#,SEC#
      → INSTRUCT,LOCAT,TIMES,STUDENT
  C(D1,4):CONSTRAINT
    REGISTRAR-COURSE- SECTION-STUDENT:
    SEMESTER,YEAR,DEPT,COURSE#,SEC#,STUDID
    → STUDNAME,GRADE
  C(D1,5):CONSTRAINT STUDINFO:ID# → STUDNAME,
    BIRTHDATE,DATEADM,MAJOR
```

(a)

Figure 6.5 (*cont. next page*)

(continued)

```
V(D2): VIEW DEFINITION
  S(D2): SCHEMA DEFINITION
    TABLE TRANSCRIPT = (STUDID,STUDNAME,BIRTHDATE,DATEADM,RECORD)
    TABLE RECORD = (SEMESTER,YEAR,COURSES)
    TABLE COURSES = (DEPT,COURSE#,SEC#,TITLE,GRADE,CREDITS)

L(D2): LANGUAGE DEFINITION
  T(D2): TYPING DEFINITION
    TYPE SIDTPE = {STUDID} EBCDIC CHAR(9)
    TYPE NAMTPE = {STUDNAME} EBCDIC CHAR(20)
    TYPE DATPE = {BIRTHDATE,DATEADM} EBCDIC CHAR(15)
    TYPE SEMTPE = {SEMESTER} EBCDIC CHAR(6)
    TYPE YRTPE = {YEAR} EBCDIC DEC(4)
    TYPE DEPTPE = {DEPT} EBCDIC CHAR(8)
    TYPE CS#TPE = {COURSE#} EBCDIC DEC(3)
    TYPE SEC#TPE = {SEC#} EBCDIC CHAR(10)
    TYPE TTLTPE = {TITLE} EBCDIC CHAR(25)
    TYPE GRDTPE = {GRADE} EBCDIC CHAR(1)
    TYPE CRDSTPE = {CREDITS} EBCDIC DEC(2)

    NONLOGICAL SYMBOLS DEFINITION
      PREDICATES
        TRANSCRIPT-RECORD-COURSES:
          (SIDTPE,NAMTPE,DATPE,DATPE,RECORD,SEMTPE,
          YRTPE,COURSES,DEPTPE,CS#TPE,SEC#TPE,TTLTPE,
          GRDTPE,CRDSTPE) FULL CLUSTER PREDICATE

      FUNCTIONS
        NONE

C(D2): CONSTRAINTS DEFINITION
  C(D2,1) CONSTRAINT TRANSCRIPT:
    STUDID → STUDNAME,BIRTHDATE,DATEADM,RECORD
  C(D2,2):CONSTRAINT TRANSCRIPT-RECORD:
    STUDID,SEMESTER,YEAR → COURSES
  C(D2,3):CONSTRAINT TRANSCRIPT-RECORD-COURSES:
    STUDID,SEMESTER,YEAR,DEPT,COURSE#
    → SEC#,TITLE,CREDITS,GRADE
```

(b)

```
V(D3): VIEW DEFINITION
  S(D3): SCHEMA DEFINITION
    TABLE CATALOGUE = (DEPT,COURSE#,TITLE,CREDITS,DESCR,
                                 LINK)
    TABLE LINK = (CATALOGUE)
    TABLE MAJORS = (MAJOR,DEPTMAJ)
    TABLE DEPTMAJ = (ID#,NAME,CLASS)
  L(D3): LANGUAGE DEFINITION
    T(D3): TYPING DEFINITION
```

Figure 6.5 *(cont. next page)*

(continued)

```
TYPE DEPTPE  = {DEPT,MAJOR} ASCII CHAR(10)
TYPE CS#TPE  = {COURSE#} ASCII DEC(3)
TYPE TTLTPE  = {TITLE} ASCII CHAR(25)
TYPE CRDTPE  = {CREDITS} ASCII DEC(2)
TYPE DESTPE  = {DESCR} ASCII CHAR(50)
TYPE ID#TPE  = {STUDID,ID#} ASCII CHAR(9)
TYPE NAMTPE  = {NAME} ASCII CHAR(20)
TYPE CLATPE  = {CLASS} ASCII CHAR(10)

NONLOGICAL SYMBOLS DEFINITION
  PREDICATES
    CATALOGUE-LINK-CATALOGUE:
     (DEPTPE,CS#TPE,TTLTPE,CRDTPE,DESTPE,LINK,
     CATALOGUE,DEPTPE,CS#TPE,TTLTPE,CRDTPE,DESTPE,
     LINK,) FULL CLUSTER PREDICATE
 MAJORS-DEPTMAJ:
   (DEPTPE,DEPTMAJ,ID#TPE,NAMTPE,CLATPE)
   PREDICATE
   ≤: (CS#TPE,CS#TPE)-PREDICATE
 FUNCTIONS
   NONE

C(D3): CONSTRAINTS DEFINITION
  C(D3,1):CONSTRAINT CATALOGUE:DEPT,COURSE#
  → TITLE,CREDITS,DESCR,LINK
  C(D3,2):CONSTRAINT MAJORS:MAJOR → DEPTMAJ
  C(D3,3) CONSTRAINT MAJORS-DEPTMAJ:
    MAJOR,ID# → NAME,CLASS
```

(c)

Figure 6.5 Candidate heterogeneous views: (a) V(D1); (b) V(D2); (c) V(D3).

rary conceptual language L(C2). Since L(C1) and L(C2) are identical, the interpretation I(C1;C2) of L(C1) in L(C2) is the identity interpretation given in Figure 6.7(b).

We leave it as an exercise to check that

$$C'(C2) = I(C1;C2)(C(C1))) \cup I(D2;C2)(C(D2))$$

is consistent in L(C2). This can also be seen using a database structure that has no rows in its tables. We also leave it to the reader to check that the wffs C(C2) of L(C2) of Figure 6.7(a) logically imply the set C′(C2). Since I(D1;C1) and I(C1;C2) are both identity interpretations on L(C2) [=L(D1) = L(C1)], their composition

$$I(D1;C2) = I(D1;C1) \circ I(C1;C2)$$

is also the identity interpretation on L(C2) [see Figure 6.7(b)].

i = 3. Schema S(C3) of Figure 6.7(d) represents the merging of S(D3) in S(C2).

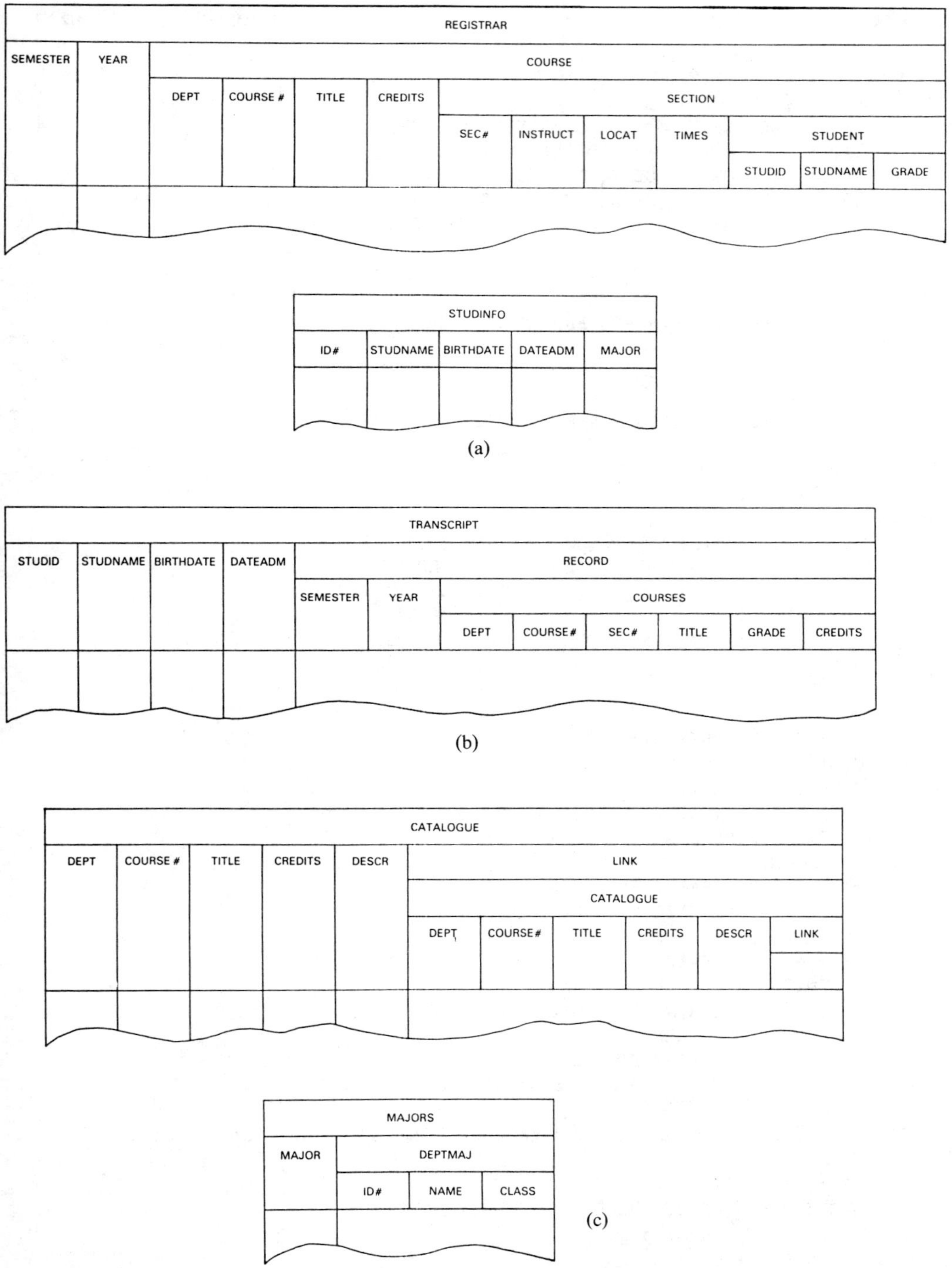

Figure 6.6 Database structures for the candidate views: (a) V(D1); (b) V(VD2); (c) V(D3).

```
V(C1): VIEW DEFINITION
  S(C1): SCHEMA DEFINITION
    TABLE REGISTRAR = (SEMESTER,YEAR,COURSE)
    TABLE COURSE = (DEPT,COURSE#,TITLE,CREDITS,SECTION)
    TABLE SECTION = (SEC#,INSTRUCT,LOCAT,TIMES,STUDENT)
    TABLE STUDENT = (STUDID,STUDNAME,GRADE)
    TABLE STUDINFO = (ID#,STUDNAME,BIRTHDATE,DATEADM,MAJOR)

  L(C1): LANGUAGE DEFINITION
    T(C1): TYPING DEFINITION
      TYPE SEMTPE = {SEMESTER} ASCII CHAR(8)
              .
              .
              .
      TYPE DATPE = {BIRTHDATE,DATEADM} ASCII CHAR(15)

    NONLOGICAL SYMBOLS DEFINITION
      PREDICATES

           CRDSTPE,SECTION,SEC#TPE,NAMTPE,LOCTPE,
           TIMTPE,STUDENT,IDTPE,NAMTPE,GRDTPE) FULL
                                 CLUSTER PREDICATE
        STUDINFO:
          (IDTPE,NAMTPE,DATPE,DATPE) PREDICATE
    FUNCTIONS
      NONE

  C(C1): CONSTRAINTS DEFINITION
    C(C1,1):CONSTRAINT REGISTRAR:SEMESTER,
      YEAR → COURSE
    C(C1,2):CONSTRAINT REGISTRAR-COURSE:
      SEMESTER,YEAR,DEPT,COURSE#
      → TITLE,CREDITS,SECTION
    C(C1,3):CONSTRAINT REGISTRAR-COURSE-
      SECTION:SEMESTER,YEAR,DEPT,COURSE#,SEC#
      → INSTRUCT,LOCAT,TIMES,STUDENT
    C(C1,4):CONSTRAINT
      REGISTRAR-COURSE-SECTION-STUDENT:
      SEMESTER,YEAR,DEPT,COURSE#,SEC#,STUDID
      → STUDNAME,GRADE
    C(C1,5):CONSTRAINT STUDINFO:
      ID# → STUDNAME,BIRTHDATE,DATEADM,MAJOR
```

To obtain V(C2), replace all occurrences of C1 by C2 and add the constraints

```
C(C2,6): CONSTRAINT REGISTRAR-COURSE:
  SEMESTER,YEAR,DEPT,COURSE# → TITLE,CREDITS
```

and

```
C(C2,7):CONSTRAINT
  REGISTRAR-COURSE-SECTION-STUDENT:
  SEMESTER,YEAR,DEPT,COURSE#,STUDID → SEC#.
```

(a)

Figure 6.7 *(cont. next page)*

(continued)

```
I(D1;C1): INTERPRETATION DEFINITION
  EXTERNAL VIEW IS V(D1) = <S(D1),L(D1),C(D1)>
  CONCEPTUAL VIEW IS V(C1) = <S(C1),L(C1),C(C1)>

  CODING SECTION
    CODE FOR SEMTPE IS SIDTPE;
      .
      .
      .
    CODE FOR DATPE IS GRDTPE;
    CODE FOR COURSE IS SEMESTER,YEAR;
    CODE FOR SECTION IS SEMESTER,YEAR,DEPT,COURSE#
    CODE FOR STUDENT IS SEMESTER,YEAR,DEPT,COURSE#,SEC#;

  DEFINING FORMULA SECTION
    PREDICATE: REGISTRAR-COURSE-SECTION-STUDENT
    ARGUMENTS ARE:
    (SEMESTER:1;,YEAR:1;,SEMESTER:1,YEAR;,DEPT:1;,COURSE#:1;,
      TITLE:1;,CREDITS:1;,SEMESTER:1,YEAR:1,DEPT:1,COURSE#:1;,
      SEC#:1;,INSTRUCT:1;,LOCAT:1;,TIMES:1;,
      SEMESTER:1,YEAR:1,DEPT:1,COURSE#:1,SEC#:1;,STUDID:1;,
      STUDNAME:1;,GRADE:1;)
     IS DEFINED BY: (E)COURSE:1(E)SECTION:1(E)STUDENT:1
      REGISTRAR(SEMESTER:1,YEAR:1,COURSE:1)
      & COURSE:1(DEPT:1,COURSE#:1,TITLE:1,CREDITS:1,SECTION:1)
      & SECTION:1(SEC#:1,INSTRUCT:1,LOCAT:1,TIMES:1,STUDENT:1)
      & STUDENT:1(STUDID:1,STUDNAME:1,GRADE:1)

      PREDICATE: STUDINFO
      ARGUMENTS ARE: (ID#:1;,STUDNAME:1;,BIRTHDATE:1;,DATEADM:1;,
        MAJOR:1;)
      IS DEFINED BY:
        STUDINFO(ID#:1,STUDNAME:1,BIRTHDATE:1,DATEADM:1,MAJOR:1)

      CONSTANT TRANSFORMATION SECTION
            .
            .
            .
```

To obtain I(C1;C2), replace I(D1;C1) with I(C1;C2), V(D1) = <S(D1),L(D1),C(D1)> with V(C1) = <S(C1),L(C1),C(C1)> and V(C1) = <S(C1),L(C1),C(C1)> with V(C2) = <S(C2),L(C2),C(C2)> .

To obtain I(D1;C2), replace I(D1;C1) with I(D1;C2) and V(C1) = <S(C1),L(C1),C(C1)> with V(C2) = <S(C2),L(C2),C(C2)>.

(b)

```
I(D2;C2): INTERPRETATION DEFINITION
  EXTERNAL VIEW IS V(D2) = <S(D2),L(D2),C(D2)>
  CONCEPTUAL VIEW IS V(C2) = <S(C2),L(C2),C(C2)>
```

Figure 6.7 (*cont. next page*)

(continued)

```
    CODING SECTION
      CODE FOR SIDTPE IS IDTPE;
                  .
                  .
                  .
      CODE FOR CRDSTPE IS CRDSTPE;
      CODE FOR RECORD IS IDTPE;
      CODE FOR COURSES IS IDTPE,SEMTPE,YRTPE;

    DEFINING FORMULA SECTION
      PREDICATE:TRANSCRIPT-RECORD-COURSES
      ARGUMENTS ARE: (STUDID:l;,STUDNAME:l;,BIRTHDATE:l,
        DATEADM:l;,STUDID:l;,SEMESTER:l,YEAR:l;,
        STUDID:l,SEMESTER:l,YEAR:l;,DEPT:l;,
        COURSE#:l;,SEC#:l;,TITLE:l;,GRADE:l;,
        CREDITS:l;)
      IS DEFINED BY:(E)COURSE:l(E)SECTION:l
        (E)INSTRUCT:l(E)LOCAT:l(E)TIMES:l(E)STUDENT:l
        REGISTRAR-COURSE-SECTION-STUDENT
        (SEMESTER:l,YEAR:l,COURSE:l,DEPT:l,COURSE#:l,TITLE:l,
        CREDITS:l, SECTION:l,
        SEC#:l,INSTRUCT:l,LOCAT:l,TIMES:l,STUDENT:l,STUDID:l,
        STUDNAME:l,GRADE:l)
        & STUDINFO
          (STUDID:l,STUDNAME:l,BIRTHDATE:l,DATEADM:l)

    PREDICATE:TRANSCRIPT
    ARGUMENTS ARE: (STUDID:l;,STUDNAME:l;,BIRTHDATE:l,
      DATEADM:l;,STUDID:l;)
    IS DEFINED BY:
      STUDINFO(STUDID:l,STUDNAME:l,BIRTHDATE:l,DATEADM:l)

  CONSTANT TRANSFORMATION SECTION
              .
              .
              .
```

Interpretation I(D2;C3) is obtained from the above by replacing I(D2;C2) by I(D2;C3), V(C2) = <S(C2),L(C2),C(C2)> by V(C3) = <S(C3),L(C3),C(C3)> and in the defining formula for TRANSCRIPT-RECORD-COURSES replace

```
  STUDINFO(STUDID:l,STUDNAME:l,BIRTHDATE:l,DATEADM:l)
```

by

```
(E)MAJOR:l(E)CLASS:l
   STUDINFO(STUDID:l,STUDNAME:l,BIRTHDATE:l,DATEADM:l,
   MAJOR:l,CLASS:l).
```

(c)

Figure 6.7 *(cont. next page)*

(continued)

```
V(C3): VIEW DEFINITION
  S(C3): SCHEMA DEFINITION
    TABLE REGISTRAR = (SEMESTER,YEAR,COURSE)
    TABLE COURSE = (DEPT,COURSE#,TITLE,CREDITS,SECTION)
    TABLE SECTION = (SEC#,INSTRUCT,LOCAT,TIMES,STUDENT)
    TABLE STUDENT = (STUDID,STUDNAME,GRADE)
    TABLE STUDINFO = (ID#,STUDNAME,BIRTHDATE,DATEADM,MAJOR,CLASS)
    TABLE CATALOGUE = (DEPT,COURSE#,TITLE,CREDITS,DESCR,LINK)
    TABLE LINK = (CATALOGUE)

  L(C3): LANGUAGE DEFINITION
  T(C3): TYPING DEFINITION
    TYPE SEMTPE = {SEMESTER} ASCII CHAR(8)
              .
              .
              .
    TYPE DATPE = {BIRTHDATE,DATEADM} ASCII CHAR(15)
    TYPE DESTPE = {DESCR} ASCII CHAR(50)
    TYPE CLASTPE = {CLASS} ASCII CHAR(10)

    NONLOGICAL SYMBOLS DEFINITION
      PREDICATES
        REGISTRAR-COURSE-SECTION-STUDENT:
          (SEMTPE,YRTPE,COURSE,DEPTPE,CS#TPE,TTLTPE,
           CRDSTPE,SECTION,SEC#TPE,NAMTPE,LOCTPE,
           TIMTPE,STUDENT,IDTPE,NAMTPE,GRDTPE)
                     FULL CLUSTER PREDICATE
        STUDINFO
          (IDTPE,NAMTPE,DATPE,DATPE,DEPTPE,CLTPE) PREDICATE
        CATALOGUE-LINK-CATALOGUE:
          (DEPTPE,CS#TPE,TTLTPE,CRDTPE,DESTPE,LINK,
          CATALOGUE,DEPTPE,CS#TPE,TTLTPE,CRDTPE,DESTPE,
          LINK,)-FULL CLUSTER PREDICATE
          ≤: (CS#TPE,CS#TPE) PREDICATE
  FUNCTIONS
  NONE

  C(C3): CONSTRAINTS DEFINITION
    C(C3,1):CONSTRAINT REGISTRAR:SEMESTER,
      YEAR → COURSE
  C(C3,2):CONSTRAINT REGISTRAR-COURSE:
    SEMESTER,YEAR,DEPT,COURSE#
    → TITLE,CREDITS,SECTION
  C(C3,3):CONSTRAINT REGISTRAR-COURSE-
    SECTION:SEMESTER,YEAR,DEPT,COURSE#,SEC#
    → INSTRUCT,LOCAT,TIMES,STUDENT
  C(C3,4):CONSTRAINT REGISTRAR-COURSE-
    SECTION-STUDENT:SEMESTER,YEAR,DEPT,COURSE#,
    SEC#,STUDID → STUDNAME,GRADE
  C(C3,5):CONSTRAINT STUDINFO:ID#
    → STUDNAME,BIRTHDATE,DATEADM,MAJOR,CLASS
```

Figure 6.7 *(cont. next page)*

(continued)

```
C(C3,6): CONSTRAINT REGISTRAR-COURSE:
  SEMESTER,YEAR,DEPT,COURSE# → TITLE,CREDITS
C(C3,7):CONSTRAINT
  REGISTRAR-COURSE-SECTION-STUDENT:
  SEMESTER,YEAR,DEPT,COURSE#,STUDID → SEC#
```

(d)

```
I(D3;C3): INTERPRETATION DEFINITION
  EXTERNAL VIEW IS V(D3) = <S(D3),L(D3),C(D3)>
  CONCEPTUAL VIEW IS V(C3) = <S(C3),L(C3),C(C3)>

  CODING SECTION
    CODE FOR DEPTTPE IS DEPTPE;
    CODE FOR CS#TPE IS CS#TPE;
    CODE FOR TTLTPE IS TTLTPE;
    CODE FOR CRDSTPE IS CRDSTPE;
    CODE FOR DESCTPE IS DESCTPE;
    CODE FOR ID#TPE IS ID#TPE;
    CODE FOR NAMTPE IS NAMTPE;
    CODE FOR CLASTPE IS CLASTPE;
    CODE FOR CATALOGUE IS DEPTPE,CS#TPE;
    CODE FOR LINK IS DEPTPE,CS#TPE;
    CODE FOR DEPTMAJ IS DEPTPE;

    DEFINING FORMULA SECTION
     PREDICATE:CATALOGUE-LINK-CATALOGUE
     ARGUMENTS ARE:(DEPT:1;,COURSE#:1;,TITLE:1;,CREDITS:1;,
      DESCR:1;,DEPT:1,COURSE#:1;,DEPT:1,COURSE#:1;
      DEPT:2;,COURSE#:2;,TITLE:2;,CREDITS:2;,
      DESCR:2;,DEPT:2,COURSE#:2;)
     IS DEFINED BY:(E)LINK:1(E)CATALOGUE:1(E)LINK:2
      CATALOGUE(DEPT:1,COURSE#:1,TITLE:1,CREDITS:1,
      DESCR:1,LINK:1)
      & LINK:1(CATALOGUE:1)
      & CATALOGUE:1(DEPT:2,COURSE#:2,TITLE:2,CREDITS:2,
      DESCR:2,LINK:2)

    PREDICATE: MAJORS-DEPTMAJ
    ARGUMENTS ARE:(MAJOR:1;,MAJOR:1;,ID#:1;,
     STUDNAME:1;,CLASS:1;)
    IS DEFINED BY:(E)BIRTHDATE:1(E)DATEADM:1
      STUDINFO(ID#:1,STUDNAME:1,BIRTHDATE:1,
      DATEADM:1,MAJOR:1,CLASS:1)

     PREDICATE:  ≤
     ARGUMENT ARE:(COURSE#:1;,COURSE#:2;)
     IS DEFINED BY:COURSE#:1 ≤ COURSE#:2
CONSTANT TRANSFORMATION SECTION
          .
          .
          .
```

(e)

Figure 6.7 (*cont. next page*)

(continued)

```
I(C2;C3): INTERPRETATION DEFINITION
  EXTERNAL VIEW IS V(C2) = <S(C2),L(C2),C(C2)>
  CONCEPTUAL VIEW IS V(C3) = <S(C3),L(C3),C(C3)>

  CODING SECTION

    CODE FOR SEMTPE IS SIDTPE;
       .
       .
       .
    CODE FOR DATTPE IS GRDTPE;
    CODE FOR COURSE IS SEMESTER,YEAR;
    CODE FOR SECTION IS SEMTPE,YRTPE,DEPTPE,CS#TPE#;
    CODE FOR STUDENT IS SEMTPE,YRTPE,DEPTPE,CS#TPE#,SEC#TPE;

  DEFINING FORMULA SECTION

    PREDICATE: REGISTRAR-COURSE-SECTION-STUDENT
    ARGUMENTS ARE: (SEMESTER:1;,YEAR:1;,SEMESTER:1,YEAR;,
      DEPT:1;,COURSE#:1;,
      TITLE:1;,CREDITS:1;,SEMESTER:1,YEAR:1,DEPT:1,COURSE#:1;,
      SEC#:1;,INSTRUCT:1;,LOCAT:1;,TIMES:1;,
      SEMESTER:1,YEAR:1,DEPT:1,COURSE#:1,SEC#:1;,STUDID:1;,
      STUDNAME:1;,GRADE:1;)
    IS DEFINED BY: (E)COURSE:1(E)SECTION:1(E)STUDENT:1
      REGISTRAR(SEMESTER:1,YEAR:1,COURSE:1)
      & COURSE:1(DEPT:1,COURSE#:1,TITLE:1,CREDITS:1,SECTION:1)
      & SECTION:1(SEC#:1,INSTRUCT:1,LOCAT:1,TIMES:1,STUDENT:1)
      & STUDENT:1(STUDID:1,STUDNAME:1,GRADE:1)

    PREDICATE: STUDINFO
    ARGUMENTS ARE: (ID#:1;,STUDNAME:1;,BIRTHDATE:1;,DATEADM:1;,
      MAJOR:1;)
    IS DEFINED BY: (E)CLASS:1
      STUDINFO(ID#:1,STUDNAME:1,BIRTHDATE:1,DATEADM:1,
      MAJOR:1,CLASS:1);

  CONSTANT TRANSFORMATION SECTION
         .
         .
         .
  To obtain I(D1;C3), replace I(C2;C3) with
I(D1;C3), V(C2) = <S(C2),L(C2),C(C2)> with
  V(D1) = <S(D1),L(D1),C(D1)> .
```

(f)

Figure 6.7 Integration of views V(D1), V(D2), and V(D3): (a) temporary conceptual views V(C1) and V(C2); (b) interpretations I(D1;C1), I(C1;C2), and I(D1;C2); (c) interpretations I(D2;C2) and I(D2;C3); (d) temporary conceptual views V(C3) and V(C); (e) interpretation I(D3;C3); (f) interpretations I(C2;C3).

Language L(C3) of Figure 6.7(d) represents the merging of L(D3) in L(C3). Figure 6.7(e) contains the interpretation I(D3;C3) of L(D3) in L(C3). Figure 6.7(f) contains the interpretation I(C2;C3) of L(C2) in L(C3).

We leave it as an exercise to check that the set

$$C'(C3) = I(C2;C3)(C(C2)) \cup I(D3;C3)(C(D3))$$

is consistent in L(C3). Figure 6.7(d) contains a set of wffs C(C3) which logically imply the set C′(C3) in L(C3). We also leave this last fact as an exercise for the reader. The interpretations

$$I(D1;C3) = I(D1;C2) \circ I(C2;C3) \quad \text{and} \quad I(D2;C3) = I(D2;C2) \circ I(C2;C3)$$

are given in Figure 6.7(f) and (c), respectively. As will be seen in Section 6.3, these are also interpretations of views V(D1) and V(D2) in view V(C3).

Since $k = 3$, we set V(C), the final conceptual view, to be V(C3) and I(D1;C), I(D2;C), and I(D3;C) to be, respectively, I(D1;C3), I(D2;C3), and I(D3;C3).

Exercises

1. Show that the set of wffs

$$C'(C2) = I(C1;C2)(C(C1)) \cup I(D2;C2)(C(D2))$$

is consistent in L(C2).

2. Show that the wffs C(C2) of L(C2) of Figure 6.7(a) logically imply the set C′(C2) of Exercise 1.
3. Show that the set of wffs

$$C'(C3) = I(C2;C3)(C(C2))) \cup I(D3;C3)(C(D3))$$

is consistent in L(C3).

4. Show that the wffs C(C3) of L(C3) of Figure 6.7(d) logically imply the set C′(C3) of Exercise 3.
5. Show that the interpretations I(D1;C3) and I(D2;C3) are, respectively, interpretations of views V(D1) and V(D2) in V(C3).
6. Perform the integration methodology in the situation where the order of importance is V(D2), V(D1), V(D3).
7. Perform the integration methodology in the situation where the order of importance is V(D3), V(D2), V(D1).

6.3 CONSISTENCY AND COMPOSITION OF INTERPRETATIONS

In this section we examine a situation in which inconsistencies arise in the view integration process and illustrate how the four steps in the methodology can be used to alleviate the problem. We also examine a sufficient condition on candidate databases which implies that inconsistencies never arise. Finally, we discuss composition of interpretations and prove that our methodology builds view interpretations.

An Example of Inconsistency

Recall the example from Section 6.1 in which we integrated relational views V(R1), V(R2), and V(R3). Suppose that in addition to its two constraints, external view V(R3) had a third constraint:

C(R3,3) = (E)MAJOR:1(E)MAJOR:2(E)ID#:1
(E)NAME:1(E)CLASS:1
MAJORS(MAJOR:1,ID#:1,NAME:1,CLASS:1)
& MAJORS(MAJOR:2,ID#:1,NAME:1,CLASS:1)
& ~MAJOR:1 = MAJOR:2.

That is, there is a student who has a joint major between two departments. A model M(R3) can easily be constructed for the new set of constraints

C′(R3) = C(R3) ∪ {C(R3,3) };

hence, C′(R3) is consistent in L(R3).

In executing the third iteration of our methodology, we discover now that the set of wffs

C′(C3) = I(C2;C3)(C(C2)) ∪ I(R3;C3)(C′(R3))

is inconsistent in L(C3). This is due to the fact that [see Figure 6.4 (f)]

I(R3;C3)(C(R3,3))
= (E)MAJOR:1(E)MAJOR:2(E)ID#:1(E)NAME:1(E)CLASS:1
((E)BIRTHDATE:1(E)DATEADM:1
STUDENT(ID#:1,NAME:1,BIRTHDATE:1,DATEADM:1,MAJOR:1,CLASS:1))
& ((E)BIRTHDATE:2(E)DATEADM:2
STUDENT(ID#:1,NAME:1,BIRTHDATE:2,DATEADM:2,MAJOR:2,CLASS:1))
& ~MAJOR:1 = MAJOR:2

and [see Figure 6.4(g)]

I(C2;C3)(C(C2,1))
= ((E)CLASS:1
STUDENT(ID#:1,NAME:1,BIRTHDATE:1,DATEADM:1,MAJOR:1,CLASS:1))
& ((E)CLASS:2
STUDENT(ID#:1,NAME:2,BIRTHDATE:2,DATEADM:2,MAJOR:2,CLASS:2))
→ (NAME:1 = NAME:2 & BIRTHDATE:1 = BIRTHDATE:2 &
DATEADM:1 = DATEADM:2 & MAJOR:1 = MAJOR:2)

are contradictory. Our methodology in Section 6.2 suggests four alternative solutions.

First, we could ask the users of the external view V(R3) to retract the constraint C(R3,3). If this were done, we would have exactly the external view V(R3) used in the illustration in Section 6.1. Hence, our integration methodology would proceed to a successful conclusion.

Second, we could change the third temporary conceptual schema to

S(C3′)
= {STUDENT = (ID#,NAME,BIRTHDATE,DATEADM,MAJOR,CLASS),
STUDENTA = (ID#,NAME,CLASS,MAJOR),
REGISTRAR = (SEMESTER,YEAR,...,GRADE),
CATALOGUE = (DEPT,COURSE#,...,PRECOURSE#)}.

We resolve our conflict by creating two copies of student majors. The interpretation I(C2;C3) of L(C2) in L(C3) will be exactly as before. The MAJORS table in V(R3) will be obtained using only STUDENTA. The defining formula for MAJORS will now be

PREDICATE MAJORS
ARGUMENTS ARE: (MAJOR:1;,ID#:1;,NAME:1;,CLASS:1;)
IS DEFINED BY
(E)BIRTHDATE:1(E)DATEADM:1(E)MAJOR:2
STUDENT(ID#:1,NAME:1,BIRTHDATE:1,DATEADM:1,MAJOR:2,CLASS:1)
& STUDENTA(ID#:1,MAJOR:1).

The reader can check that under this new interpretation I′(R3;C3),

I′(R3;C3)(C(R3,3))
= (E)MAJOR:1(E)MAJOR:2(E)ID#:1(E)NAME:1(E)CLASS:1
STUDENTA(ID#:1,NAME:1,CLASS:1,MAJOR:1)
& STUDENTA(ID#:1,NAME:1,CLASS:1,MAJOR:2)
& ~ MAJOR:1 = MAJOR:2.

Thus,

I′(C2;C3)(C(C2,1)) [= I(C2;C3)(C(C2,1))] and I′(R3;C3)(C(R3,3))

are both consistent in L(C3).

Third, we could find out which of the previously incorporated external views was responsible for the part of the constraint C(C2,1) whose interpretation under I(C2;C3) conflicted with I(R3;C3)(C(R3,3)). In our example, it was view V(R1); in particular, the constraint

C(R1,1) = STUDENT:ID# → NAME,BIRTHDATE,DATEADM,MAJOR.

Suppose the users of view V(R1) agreed to change this constraint to, say

C(R1,1) = STUDENT:ID# → NAME,BIRTHDATE,DATEADM.

Then this would make

I(C2;C3)(C(C2,1))
= ((E)CLASS:1 (E)MAJOR:1
STUDENT(ID#:1,NAME:1,BIRTHDATE:1,DATEADM:1,MAJOR:1,CLASS:1))

& ((E)CLASS:2(E)MAJOR:2
STUDENT(ID#:1,NAME:2,BIRTHDATE:2,DATEADM:2,MAJOR:2,CLASS:2))
→ (NAME:1 = NAME:2 & BIRTHDATE:1 = BIRTHDATE:2
& DATEADM:1 = DATEADM:2)

and we would have no conflicts.

Fourth, we could take the most drastic action and reject view V(R3) from our community of views.

Sufficient Condition for Consistency

In many situations it is not necessary to test for

C′(Ci) = I(Ci-1;Ci)(C(i-1)) U I(Ei;Ci)(C(Ei))

for consistency. This is explained below.

Definition. A wff Q of L is called a *positive Horn formula* if it is logically equivalent to a wff of the form

(Q1(<R>) & ··· & Qk(<R>)) → Qk+1(<R>)

where Qi(<R>) are all positive (i.e., not negated) atomic formula with free variables <R> and for i = 1,...k, Qi(<R>) are nonequality symbols.

For example, it is easy to check that all the dependency constraints listed in all of the views in Figures 6.1 (a)–(c) and 6.5 (a)–(c) are expressible (in their appropriate languages) as sets of positive Horn formulas. Also, as seen in [Grant and Jacobs] most of the usually studied relational constraints are positive Horn.

Theorem 6.3.1. *Let* C *be any set of positive Horn formulas in database language* L. *Then* C *is consistent in* L.

Proof. Consider the database structure M of L in which every row predicate of the form R( ), where R is a table name, is false. That is, M has no rows in any of its tables. Then M is trivially a model for C since every wff in C must be true. Hence, C is consistent in L.

Definition. We call an interpretation I of L(E) in L(C) *positive Horn preserving,* abbreviated pHp, if all its defining formulas are of the form

PREDICATE p
ARGUMENTS ARE: (<R1;>,...<Rn;>)
IS DEFINED BY (E)<R>p1 & p2 & ... & pk(<R;>,<R1;>,...<Rn;>).

That is, the defining formula for pHp interpretations are existentially quantified conjunctions (&). It is easily seen that most of the interpretations used in this book are pHp interpretations.

Theorem 6.3.2. *Let* C(Ci-1) *and* C(Ei) *be sets of positive Horn formulas in their respective languages. Let* I(Ci-1,Ci) *and* I(Ei;Ci) *be* pHp *interpretations. Then*

$$C'(Ci) = I(Ci\text{-}1;Ci)(C(Ci-1)) \cup I(Ei;Ci)(C(Ei))$$

is always consistent in L(Ci).

The main idea of the proof of Theorem 6.3.2 is that when positive Horn constraints are interpreted by pHp interpretations, the resulting wffs always have the empty database as model. The details are left as an exercise for the reader. An example of a situation in which a formula in C(Ei) is not positive Horn was given in the first part of this section.

Composing Interpretations

In the i-th iteration of the integration methodology, we constructed I(Rj;Ci) $j < i$ by "composing" I(Rj;Ci-1) with I(Ci-1;Ci). In this subsection we show that the interpretation I(Rj;Ci) of language L(Rj) in language L(Ci) is, in fact, an interpretation of view V(Rj) in view V(Ci), $j < i$.

Theorem 6.3.3. *For each* $i \leq k$ *and each* $j \leq i$, I(Ej;Ci) *is an interpretation of view* V(Ej) *in* V(Ci).

Proof. We have to show that

$$C(Ci) \models I(Ej;Ci)(C(Ej))$$

in L(Ci). Suppose that

$$M(Ci) \models C(Ci),$$

where M(Ci) is a database structure for L(Ci). We show that

$$M(Ci) \models I(Ej;Ci)\ (C(Ej)).$$

Since I(Ci-1;Ci) is an interpretation of V(Ci-1) in V(Ci),

$$C(Ci) \models I(Ci\text{-}1;Ci)(C(Ci\text{-}1))$$

in L(Ci); hence,

$$M(Ci) \models I(Ci\text{-}1;Ci)(C(Ci\text{-}1)) .$$

By the Flipper Theorem,

$$I(Ci\text{-}1;Ci)[M(Ci)] \models C(Ci\text{-}1) .$$

By the induction hypothesis, I(Ej;Ci-1) is an interpretation of V(Ej) in V(Ci-1). Hence,

$$C(Ci\text{-}1) \models I(Ej;Ci\text{-}1)(C(Ej))$$

in L(Ci-1); thus,

$$I(Ci\text{-}1;Ci)[M(Ci)] \models I(Ej;Ci\text{-}1)(C(Ej)).$$

By the Flipper Theorem again,

$$M(Ci) \models I(Ej;Ci\text{-}1)\ (\ I(Ci\text{-}1;Ci)\ (C(Ej))\ )$$
$$\text{or}\quad M(Ci) \models I(Ej;Ci\text{-}1) \circ I(Ci\text{-}1;Ci)\ (C(Ej)).$$

By the definition of I(Ej;Ci),

$$M(Ci) \models I(Ej;Ci)\ (C(Ej)).$$

Exercises

Recall from Section 6.2 in which we integrated heterogeneous views V(D1), V(D2), and V(D3). Suppose that in addition to its three constraints, external view V(D3) had another constraint:

```
C(D3,4)
= (E)MAJOR:1(E)MAJOR:2(E)DEPTMAJ:1
  (E)DEPTMAJ:2(E)ID#:1(E)NAME:1(E)CLASS:1
   MAJORS-DEPTMAJ(MAJOR:1,DEPTMAJ:1,ID#:1,NAME:1,CLASS:1)
& MAJORS-DEPTMAJ(MAJOR:2,DEPTMAJ:2,ID#:1,NAME:1,CLASS:1)
& ~MAJOR:1 = MAJOR:2
```

Let C′(D3) = C(D3) ∪ {C(D3,4)}.

1. Show that I(C2;C3)(C(C2)) ∪ I(D3;C3)(C′(D3)) is inconsistent in L(C3).
2. Alleviate the inconsistency of Exercise 1 by the first solution.
3. Alleviate the inconsistency of Exercise 1 by the second solution.
4. Alleviate the inconsistency of Exercise 1 by the third solution.
5. Prove Theorem 6.3.2.

6.4 RELATED READING

BERNSTEIN, P. A., "Sythesizing Third Normal Form Relations from Functional Dependencies," *ACM Transactions on Database Systems,* **1,** (4), Dec. 1976, pp. 277–298.

BISKUP, J., DAYAL, U. AND BERNSTEIN, P.A., "Synthesizing Independent Database Schemas," *ACM SIGMOD International Symposium on Management of Data,* 1979, pp. 143–152.

DAHL, V., "On Database Systems Development Through Logic," *ACM Transactions on Database Systems,* **7,** (1) pp. 102–123.

DYBA, J., *Principles of Data Element Identification,* Auerbach Data Base Management Services, Portfolio 23-01–03, 1977.

EL MASRI, R. AND WEIDERHOLD, G., "Data Model Integration Using the Structural Model," *ACM SIGMOD International Symposium on Management of Data,* 1979, pp. 191–202.

GRANT, J. AND JACOBS, B.E., "On the Family of Generalized Dependency Constraints," *Journal of the ACM,* **29,** (4), October 1982, pp. 986–997.

JACOBS, B. E., *Applications of Database Logic to the View Integration Problem,* Department of Computer Science Technical Report TR-904, University of Maryland, College Park, Dec. 1980.

MITOMA, M.F., AND IRANI, K.B., "Automatic Data Base Schema Design and Optimization," *Proceeding's First Conference on Very Large Databases, Sept. 1975.*

NAVATHE, S.B., AND SCHKOLNICK, M. "View Representation in Logical Database Design," *Proceedings ACM/SIGMOD International Conference on Management of Data,* Austin, Tex., May 1978, pp. 144–156.

RAVER, N. AND HUBBARD, G. U., "Automatic Logical Database Design: Concepts and Applications," *IBM Systems Journal,* **16,** (3), 1977.

WANG, D.P., AND WEDEKIND. H.H., "Segment Synthesis in Logical Database Design," *IBM Journal of Research and Development,* Jan. 1975.

YAO, S.B., WADDLE, V., AND HOUSEL, B.C., "View Modeling and Integration Using the Functional Data Model," *NYU Symposium on Database Design,* New York University Press, New York, 1978.

ZANIOLO, C., AND MELKANOFF, M. A., "A Formal Approach to the Definition and the Design of Conceptual Schemata for Database Systems," *ACM Transactions on Database Systems,* **7,** (1) ,1982, pp. 24–59.

ZANIOLO, C., AND MELKANOFF, M. A., "On the Design of Relational Database Schemata," *ACM Transactions on Database Systems,* **6,** (1), 1981, pp. 1–47.

7

DATABASE CONVERSION AND QUERY PROCESSING

In Chapter 7 we investigate the database conversion problem, namely, how one can construct from an already existing database a brand new database with possible data transformations. The idea is to express the transformation by an interpretation of the new database view in the old database view. In Section 7.1 we consider the simplest case in which all the databases concerned are relational. In fact, this is equivalent to the problem of relational query processing over relational databases. In Section 7.2 the methodology is extended to the heterogeneous case. In Section 7.3 we study the interpretation decomposition problem, which is a generalization of the query decomposition problem. The entire topic of database conversion and query processing is the subject of the book **Applied Database Logic II: Heterogeneous Distributed Query Processing.**

7.1 RELATIONAL DATABASE CONVERSION

In this section we introduce our methodology by first illustrating a conversion of one relational database to another. We also show that relational query processing is a special case of database conversion.

We will use V(Rcon) in Figure 7.1 as our old database view and V(Rext) of Figure 7.2 as our new database view. An instance of the old database is given in Figure 7.3. In Figure 7.4 there is an interpretation I(Rext;Rcon) of view V(Rext) in V(Rcon). Notice that we build V(Rext) by constructing a TRANSCRIPT table that contains student enrollment information for the fall 1979 semester from the STUDENT, REG-

```
V(Rcon): VIEW DEFINITION
  S(Rcon): SCHEMA DEFINITION
    TABLE STUDENT = (ID#,STUDNAME,BIRTHDATE,DATEADM)
    TABLE REGISTRAR = (SEMESTER,YEAR,DEPT,COURSE#,
      SEC#,INSTRUCT,LOCAT,TIMES,STUDID,GRADE)
    TABLE CATALOGUE = (DEPT,COURSE#,TITLE,CREDITS,
      DESCR,PREDEPT,PRECOURSE#)


L(Rcon): LANGUAGE DEFINITION
  T(Rcon): TYPING DEFINITION
    TYPE IDTPE = {ID#,STUDID} ASCII CHAR(9)
    TYPE NAMTPE = {STUDNAME,INSTRUCT} ASCII CHAR(20)
    TYPE DATPE = {BIRTHDATE,DATEADM} ASCII CHAR(15)
    TYPE SEMTPE = {SEMESTER} ASCII CHAR(8)
    TYPE YRTPE = {YEAR} ASCII DEC(4)
    TYPE DEPTPE = {DEPT,PREDEPT} ASCII CHAR(10)
    TYPE CS#TPE = {COURSE#,PRECOURSE#} ASCII DEC(3)
    TYPE SEC#TPE = {SEC#} ASCII CHAR(3)
    TYPE LOCTPE = {LOCAT} ASCII CHAR(30)
    TYPE TIMTPE = {TIMES} ASCII CHAR(20)
    TYPE GRDTPE = {GRADE} ASCII CHAR(1)
    TYPE TTLTPE = {TITLE} ASCII CHAR(25)
    TYPE CRDSTPE = {CREDITS} ASCII DEC(2)
    TYPE DESCR = {DESCR} ASCII CHAR(50)

    NONLOGICAL SYMBOLS DEFINITION
      PREDICATES
        STUDENT: (IDTPE,NAMTPE,DATPE,DATPE)
                         PREDICATE
        REGISTRAR: (SEMTPE,YRTPE,DEPTPE,CS#TPE,
          SEC#TPE,NAMTPE,LOCTPE,TIMTPE,IDTPE,
          GRDTPE) PREDICATE
        CATALOGUE: (DEPTPE,CS#TPE,TTLTPE,CRDSTPE,
          DESCTPE,DEPTPE,CS#TPE) PREDICATE
        ≤: (YRTPE,YRTPE) PREDICATE
      FUNCTIONS
        TOTALCREDITS:(IDTPE,SEMTPE,YRTPE;
          CRDSTPE) FUNCTION

C(Rcon): CONSTRAINTS DEFINITION
  C(Rcon,1):CONSTRAINT STUDENT: ID# → STUDNAME,
    BIRTHDATE,DATEADM
  C(Rcon,2):CONSTRAINT REGISTRAR:SEMESTER,YEAR,DEPT,
    COURSE#,SEC# → INSTRUCT,LOCAT,TIMES
  C(Rcon,3):CONSTRAINT REGISTRAR:SEMESTER,YEAR,DEPT,
    COURSE#,SEC#,STUDID → GRADE
  C(Rcon,4):CONSTRAINT REGISTRAR :
    SEMESTER,YEAR,DEPT,COURSE#,STUDID → SEC#
  C(Rcon,5):CONSTRAINT CATALOGUE:DEPT,COURSE#
    → TITLE,CREDITS,DESCR
```

Figure 7.1 Database logic DDL for view V(Rcon).

```
V(Rext): VIEW DEFINITION
  S(Rext): SCHEMA DEFINITION
    TABLE TRANSCRIPT = (STUDID,STUDNAME,SEMESTER,YEAR,DEPT,
      COURSE#,SEC#,TITLE,GRADE,CREDITS)
    TABLE STUDENT = (ID#,NAME,DATEADM)

  L(Rext): LANGUAGE DEFINITION
    T(Rext): TYPING DEFINITION
      TYPE SIDTPE = {ID#,STUDID} EBCDIC CHAR(9)
      TYPE NAMTPE = {NAME,STUDNAME} EBCDIC CHAR(20)
      TYPE DATPE = {DATEADM} EBCDIC CHAR(15)
      TYPE SEMTPE = {SEMESTER} EBCDIC CHAR(8)
      TYPE YRTPE = {YEAR} EBCDIC DEC(4)
      TYPE DEPTPE = {DEPT} EBCDIC CHAR(8)
      TYPE CS#TPE = {COURSE#} EBCDIC DEC(4)
      TYPE SEC#TPE = {SEC#} EBCDIC CHAR(10)
      TYPE TTLTPE = {TITLE} EBCDIC CHAR(25)
      TYPE GRDTPE = {GRADE} EBCDIC CHAR(1)
      TYPE CRDSTPE = {CREDITS} EBCDIC DEC(2)

      NONLOGICAL SYMBOLS DEFINITION
        PREDICATES
          TRANSCRIPT:(SIDTPE,NAMTPE,SEMTPE,YRTPE,
            DEPTPE,CS#TPE,SEC#TPE,TTLTPE,GRDTPE,
              CRDSTPE) PREDICATE
          STUDENT: (SIDTPE,NAMTPE,DATPE) PREDICATE
          ≤ :(YRTPE,YRTPE) PREDICATE
        FUNCTIONS
          TOTCREDITS:(SIDTPE,SEMTPE,YRTPE;
            CRDSTPE) FUNCTION

C(Rext): CONSTRAINTS DEFINITION
  C(Rext,1):CONSTRAINT TRANSCRIPT:STUDID,
    SEMESTER,YEAR,DEPT,COURSE#,SEC#
    → STUDNAME,TITLE,GRADE,CREDITS
  C(Rext,2):CONSTRAINT TRANSCRIPT:STUDID → STUDNAME
  C(Rext,3):CONSTRAINT TRANSCRIPT:DEPT,COURSE#
    → TITLE,CREDITS
  C(Rext,4):CONSTRAINT STUDENT:ID# → NAME,DATEADM
```

Figure 7.2 Database logic DDL for view V(Rext).

ISTRAR, and CATALOGUE tables of V(Rcon). We also build a STUDENT table from the STUDENT predicate of V(Rcon).

Conversion Methodology

Our methodology for converting one database to another is comprised of six steps (see Figure 7.5). First, we construct an interpretation of the new view in the existing old view. Second, we perform an external-to-conceptual translation of the interpretation if

REGISTRAR

SEMESTER	YEAR	DEPT	COURSE#	SEC#	INSTRUCT	LOCAT	TIMES	STUDID	GRADE
FALL	1979	ART	103	001	BLUE	2100 ART BLDG	2-3 MWF	123456789	B
FALL	1979	COMP SCI	103	001	GREEN	2301 COMP CENTER	12-1 MWF	123456789	B
FALL	1979	HIST	101	001	YELLOW	3600 SOC SCI	8-9 MWF	123456789	B
FALL	1979	MATH	103	001	WHITE	4303 SCI	9-1 MWF	123456789	B
FALL	1979	BIO	103	001	PINK	4102 SCI	9-12 MWF	—	—
SPRING	1980	COMP SCI	220	001	GREEN	4612 COMP CENTER	8-9 MWF	123456789	B
SPRING	1980	MATH	104	001	WHITE	4201 SCI	10-11 MWF	123456789	B
SPRING	1980	ECO	101	001	RED	3200 SOC SCI	1-3 MWF	123456789	C
SPRING	1980	ENG	105	001	PINK	4200 HUMANITIES	3-4 MWF	123456789	A
SPRING	1980	MATH	104	001	WHITE	4201 SCI	10-11 MWF	361258823	A
SPRING	1980	ECON	101	001	RED	3200 SOC SCI	1-3 MWF	361258823	C
SPRING	1980	PHYSICS	102	001	WHITE	3600 SCI	8-9 MWF	361258823	D
SPRING	1980	ENG	105	001	PINK	4200 HUMANITIES	3-4 MWF	361258823	I

CATALOGUE

DEPT	COURSE #	TITLE	CREDITS	DESCR	PREDEPT	PRECOURSE#
COMP SCI	412	DATABASE SYSTEMS	3	---	COMP SCI	220
COMP SCI	412	DATABASE SYSTEMS	3	---	COMP SCI	250
COMP SCI	220	DISCRETE STRUCTURE	3	---	COMP SCI	103
COMP SCI	250	INTRO	3	---	---	---
COMP SCI	103	LOGIC	3	---	---	---
MATH	416	CALC	3	---	MATH	103
MATH	103	INTRO	3	---	---	---
MATH	103	INTRO	3	---	---	---

STUDENT

ID#	STUDNAME	BIRTHDATE	DATEADM
123456789	SMITH ROBERT J.	APRIL 13 1961	SEPTEMBE 1 1979
361258823	JONES MARY T.	AUGUST 25 1960	FEBRUARY 1 1980

Figure 7.3 Instance of the database M(Rcon).

```
I(Rext;Rcon): INTERPRETATION DEFINITION
  EXTERNAL VIEW IS V(Rext) = <S(Rext),L(Rext),C(Rext)>
  CONCEPTUAL VIEW IS V(Rcon) = <S(Rcon),L(Rcon),C(Rcon)>

  CODING SECTION
    CODE FOR SIDTPE IS IDTPE;
    CODE FOR NAMTPE IS NAMTPE;
    CODE FOR DATPE  IS DATPE;
    CODE FOR SEMTPE IS SEMTPE;
    CODE FOR YRTPE  IS YRTPE;
    CODE FOR DEPTPE IS DEPTPE;
    CODE FOR CS#TPE IS CS#TPE;
    CODE FOR SEC#TPE IS SEC#TPE;
    CODE FOR TTLTPE IS TTLTPE;
    CODE FOR GRDTPE IS GRDTPE;
    CODE FOR CRDSTPE IS CRDSTPE;

DEFINING FORMULA SECTION
  PREDICATE: TRANSCRIPT
  ARGUMENTS ARE: (STUDID:1;,STUDNAME:1;,
    SEMESTER:1;,YEAR:1;,DEPT:1;,COURSE#:1;,SEC#:1;,
    TITLE:1;,GRADE:1;,CREDITS:1;)
  IS DEFINED BY:(E)BIRTHDATE:1(E)DATEADM:1
    (E)INSTRUCT:1(E)LOCAT:1(E)TIMES:1(E)DESCR:1
    (E)PREDEPT:1(E)PRECOURSE#:1
      STUDENT(STUDID:1,STUDNAME:1,BIRTHDATE:1,DATEADM:1)
    & REGISTRAR(SEMESTER:1,YEAR:1,DEPT:1,COURSE#:1,
      SEC#:1,INSTRUCT:1,LOCAT:1,TIMES:1,STUDID:1,GRADE:1)
    & CATALOGUE(DEPT:1,COURSE#:1,TITLE:1,CREDITS:1,DESCR:1,
      PREDEPT:1,PRECOURSE#:1)
    & SEMESTER:1 = FALL
    & YEAR:1 = 1979

  PREDICATE: STUDENT
  ARGUMENTS ARE: (ID#:1,STUDNAME:1,DATEADM:1)
  IS DEFINED BY:(E) BIRTHDATE:1
    STUDENT(ID#:1,STUDNAME:1,BIRTHDATE:1,DATEADM:1)

  PREDICATE: ≤
  ARGUMENTS ARE:(YEAR:1;,YEAR:2;)
  IS DEFINED BY: ≤ YEAR:2

  FUNCTION: TOTCREDITS
  ARGUMENTS ARE: (ID#:1;,SEMESTER:1;,YEAR:1;,CREDITS:1;)
  IS DEFINED BY: TOTALCREDITS(ID#:1,SEMESTER:1,YEAR:1)= CREDITS:1

CONSTANT TRANSFORMATION SECTION
      .
      .
      .
```

Figure 7.4 Interpretation I(Rext;Rcon).

```
Step 1. Interpreting the New Database View
                 ↓
Step 2. External-to-Conceptual Translation
                 ↓
Step 3. Decomposition
                 ↓
Step 4. Execution
                 ↓
Step 5. Assembly
                 ↓
Step 6. Loading
```

Figure 7.5 Database conversion methodology.

the old view is actually an external view of another view. Following this step we can assume that the old database exists rather than is external.

In the next four steps we treat the interpretation as a set of "queries" and perform "query evaluation." In step 3 we decompose the defining formulas of the interpretation to determine an order of execution. In step 4 we execute the "tree" produced from step 3. This results in sets of records and mappings that tell how these records will combine. In step 5 we assemble the records that are related to one another. In step 6 we project out those values that are to be stored in the new database and load the new database into storage.

Interpreting the New Database

We specify the new database in terms of the old one using an interpretation of the new view in the old view. In our example, this is given by I(Rext;Rcon) of Figure 7.4. The new database becomes a realization of the external database induced from the old database via the interpretation. This is why database conversion can also be referred to as **actual external view construction** as opposed to **virtual external view construction.**

For example, suppose that Figure 7.3 represents an instance of the old database M(Rcon). Then the new database would be a manifestation of I(Rext;Rcon)[M(Rcon)]. This is illustrated in Figure 7.6. We will see at the end of this section how our database conversion methodology is related to relational query processing.

External-to-Conceptual Translation

Sometimes, the old database view is itself an external view of an underlying conceptual view. In this case we have to modify the conversion interpretation. We do this by composing the external-to-conceptual interpretation with the conversion interpretation. As a result, we obtain an interpretation of the new database view in an underlying conceptual database view.

In addition, it may be necessary to perform some optimization on the interpretation obtained from the composition. The method that will be introduced in Section 8.3 is called *logical optimization* and can be used to shrink the resultant defining formulas. In our example, the old view V(Rcon) is not an external view; hence, composition and logical optimization are not necessary. Examples of this sort are given in exercises.

TRANSCRIPT									
STUDID	STUDNAME	SEMESTER	YEAR	DEPT	COURSE#	SEC#	TITLE	GRADE	CREDIT
123456789	SMITH ROBERT J.	FALL	1979	COMP SCI	103	001	INTRO	B	3
123456789	SMITH ROBERT J.	FALL	1979	MATH	103	001	CALC	B	3
123456789	SMITH ROBERT J.	FALL	1979	ART	101	001	INTRO	B	3
123456789	SMITH ROBERT J.	FALL	1979	HIST	102	001	AM HIST	C	3

(a)

STUDENT		
ID#	NAME	DATEADM
1234[6789	SMITH ROBERT J.	SEPT 2 1979
3612[8823	JONES MARY T.	FEB 1 1980

(b)

Figure 7.6 Instance of the new database M(Rext).

Decomposition

Each defining formula is now treated as a query. In this step we break the query down or "decompose" it to determine the execution steps. The input to this process is a query graph which is a pictorial representation of the query. The output is an execution tree which indicates the order of operations. The decomposition process is described in Section 7.3.

For example, recall the defining formula for TRANSCRIPT given in I(Rext;R-con) of Figure 7.4. The corresponding query graph is in Figure 7.7(a). Each large node represents a relation, namely, STUDENT, REGISTRAR, and CATALOGUE. Arcs between the nodes denote relationships between rows of the tables as specified by the query. For example, one of the arcs between the REGISTRAR and CATALOGUE circles is labled "DEPT = DEPT" to indicate that the rows of the two tables should have the same DEPT values. Also, there are nodes representing selections. These are indicated by double circles attached to the relation nodes.

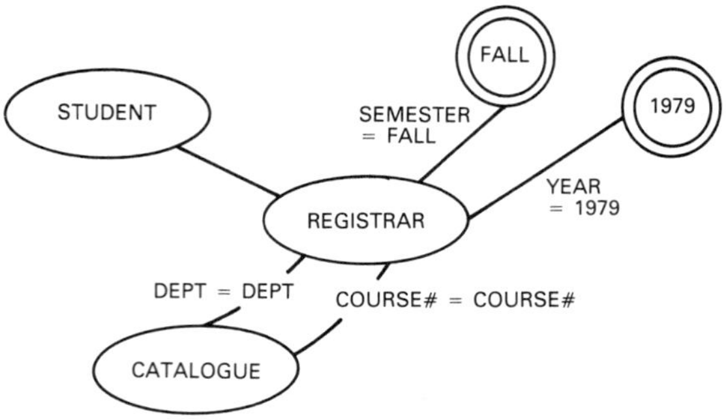

(a)

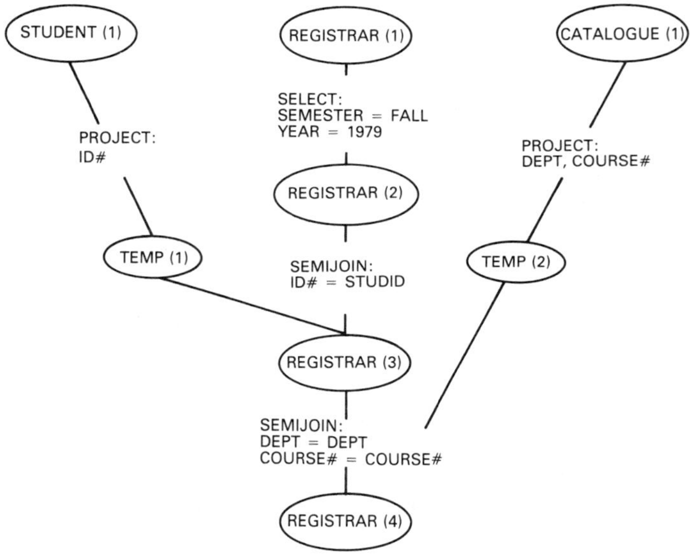

(b)

Figure 7.7 (a) Query graph; (b) execution tree.

The execution tree in Figure 7.7(b) corresponds to the query graph of Figure 7.7(a). The first operations are selections for the rows in REGISTRAR [= REGISTRAR(1)] that have SEMESTER, YEAR values FALL, 1979, respectively. The selected rows are placed in REGISTRAR(2). Next the ID# values of the rows of STUDENT [= STUDENT(1)] are projected out and "semijoined" with the rows of REGISTRAR(2). This means that for every row of projected values, a search is made through REGISTRAR(2) for all rows that match. If a row of REGISTRAR(2) matches that row is placed into REGISTRAR(3). Finally, the DEPT and COURSE# values of CATALOGUE [= CATALOGUE(1)] are projected out and semijoined with the rows of REGISTRAR(3). The rows of REGISTRAR(3) that matched are placed into REGISTRAR(4).

Execution

Figure 7.8 illustrates an execution of the execution tree of Figure 7.7(b) on M(Rcon) of Figure 7.3. Notice we associate with each row of REGISTRAR(1) an integer j corresponding either to a pointer, address, or some other integer identifier. Similarly, we identify STUDENT(1) and CATALOGUE(1) rows with integers i and k, respectively.

First, a selection is performed on the REGISTRAR table for rows with SEMESTER, YEAR values FALL, 1979, respectively. The results of these operations are placed into the new table REGISTRAR(2). The rows of REGISTRAR(2) are physically closer together so that their access will require fewer "page" fetches.

Next, the i and ID# values from each of the rows of STUDENT(1) are projected out into a table called TEMP1(1). TEMP1(1) will be used for matching up values with those rows in REGISTRAR(2). The i values will be used to keep track of which rows of TEMP1(1) [hence, STUDENT(1)] which matched rows of REGISTRAR(2).

The rows in TEMP1(1) are "semijoined" with the rows in REGISTRAR(2) using the values of ID# and STUDID. This means that for every ID# in a row in TEMP1(1), all the rows in REGISTRAR(2) are found which have the same values of STUDID. For each such match, the i value of the row of TEMP1(1) and the j value for the row of REGISTRAR(2) are recorded in a table MAP1(1). Hence, MAP1(1) keeps track of all the matches that were made. The rows in REGISTRAR(2) that were matched are placed in REGISTRAR(3).

Next, the k and DEPT, COURSE# values from each of the rows of CATALOGUE are projected out into a table called TEMP2(1). Then the rows of TEMP2(1) are semijoined with the rows of REGISTRAR(3) using the values DEPT and COURSE#. For each such match, the j value of the row in REGISTRAR(3) and the k value of the row in TEMP2(1) are recorded in table MAP2(1). Hence, MAP2(1) keeps track of all the matches that were made. The rows of REGISTRAR(3) that were matched are placed into REGISTRAR(4).

When MAP2(1) and REGISTRAR(4) have been constructed, execution is complete. The tables STUDENT(1), REGISTRAR(4), CATALOGUE(1), MAP1(1), and MAP2(1) are sent over for assembly and loading.

Remark. Variations on this execution procedure are also possible. For example, if a selection is followed by a projection, both can be done during the same pass. Also, new tables such as REGISTRAR(2), REGISTRAR(3), and REGISTRAR(4) do not have to be constructed. They can exist "virtually" in the form of pointers in the original table REGISTRAR. Also, intermediary tables can be "compressed." That is, if rows in a table (with different pointers) are duplicated, the table can be compressed into a smaller table in which duplicates are removed. The correspondence between the

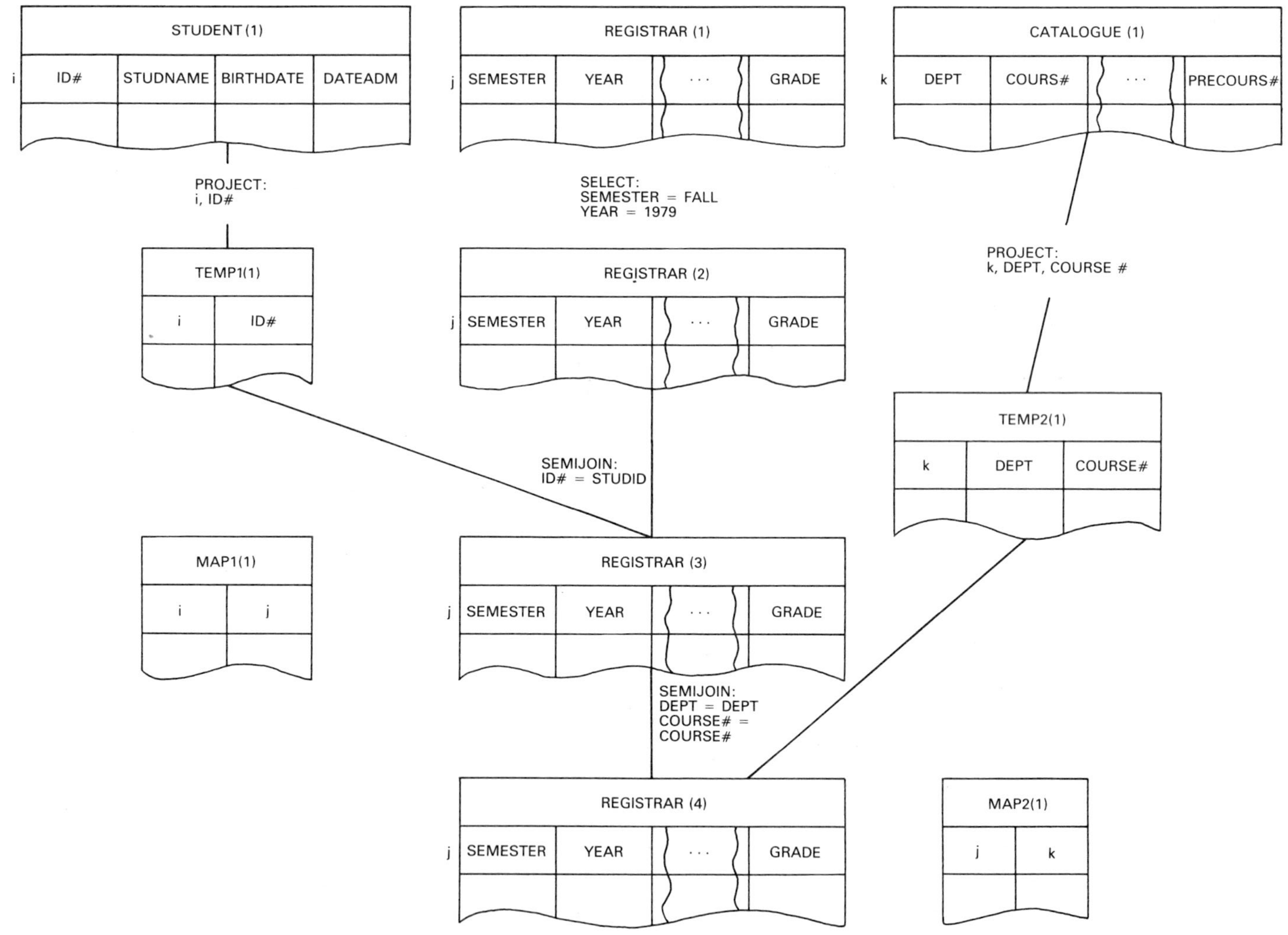

Figure 7.8 Execution.

compressed and the decompressed tables are given by some mapping. The choice of which combination of these alternatives to take is based on performance issues.

Assembly and Loading

In the assembly process, the records that are related to each other are brought together. This is illustrated for our example in Figure 7.9(a). For each i and j appearing as an entry in MAP1(1) and matching j and k in MAP2(1), the i-th row of STUDENT(1), the j-th row of REGISTRAR(4), and the k-th row of CATALOGUE(1) are retrieved. In the loading process, the values that are needed are projected from the assembled records, and the resultant database is stored. In our example, the values of the STUDID, STUDNAME, ..., CREDITS fields are extracted, converted to EBCDIC, and inserted into a TRANSCRIPT record in a buffer. The set of all these TRANSCRIPT records are then stored as a new database.

There are two strategies for storing the new database [see Figure 7.9(b).]. One is to store each record as it is assembled. This might be done if the order that the records are being assembled is the same as the order in which they are being physically stored. This would also be done if the records are located via some hashing scheme from its arguments. A second approach is to collect all the records in temporary storage and sort them in the order they are to be stored and then store them. This would be done if the physical ordering is different from the order of assembly.

Relational Query Processing and Database Conversion

Relational query processing is a special case of our methodology of program conversion. This is because any relational query can be transformed into a corresponding interpretation on views. To see this, consider the following query on V(Rcon).

> Find the id#s, names, and dates of admission of all students who took an instructor named Green during the fall 1979 semester. Store the results as EBCDIC values.

The GSQL solution for this query on V(Rcon) is as follows:

```
SELECT C(STUDID),C(STUDNAME),C(DATEADM)
FROM REGISTRAR,STUDENT
WHERE SEMESTER = FALL
  AND YEAR = 1979
  AND INSTRUCT = GREEN
  AND STUDID = ID#;
```

Here the function C(-) converts from ASCII to EBCDIC.

This query can be regarded as a database conversion from our point of view.

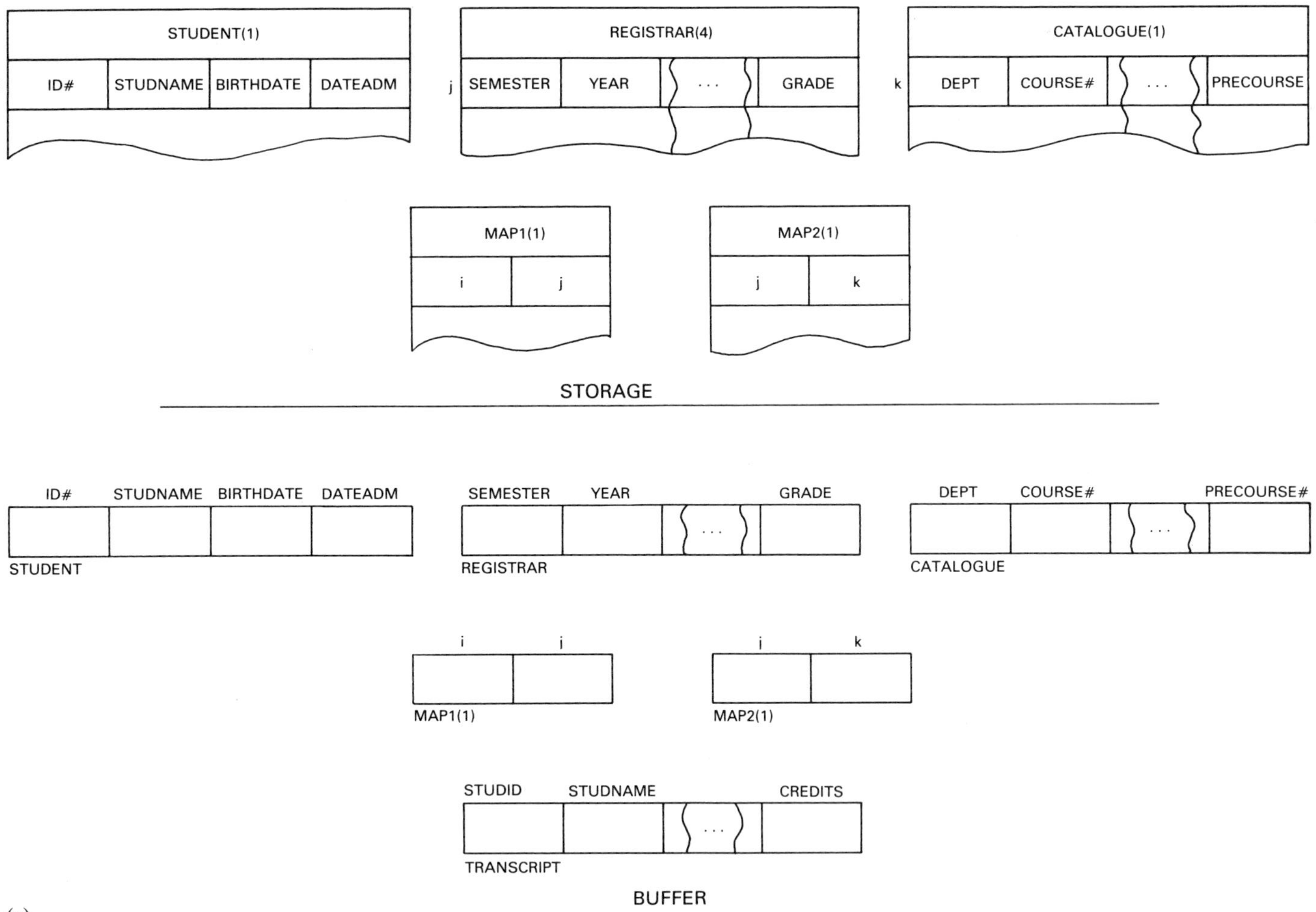

(a)

Figure 7.9 *(cont. next page)*

(continued)

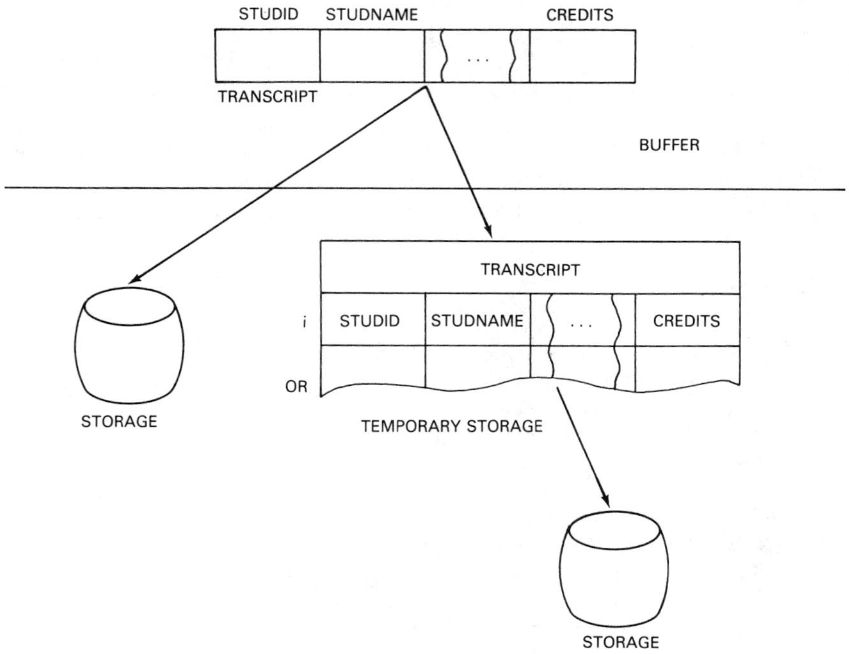

(b)

Figure 7.9 (a) Assembly; (b) loading.

First, the view corresponding to the old database is V(Rcon), the view on which the query is based. Second, V(Rquery), the view corresponding to the new database, has a schema

$$\{\text{RESULT} = (\text{STUDID,STUDNAME,DATEADM})\}.$$

The language L(Rquery) has types that are the outputs to the query, namely, EBCDIC values and a nonlogical predicate symbol RESULT. There are no explicit constraints on the new database view.

The interpretation of the new view in the old view has coding section in which the ASCII types code the EBCDIC types in the result. The defining formula for RESULT is

PREDICATE: RESULT
ARGUMENTS ARE:(STUDID:1;,STUDNAME:1;,DATEADM:1;)

```
IS DEFINED BY:
   (E)DEPT:1...(E)BIRTHDATE:1
   REGISTRAR(FALL1979,DEPT:1,COURSE#:1,
      SEC#:1, GREEN, LOCAT:1,TIMES:1,STUDID:1,GRADE:1)
& STUDENT(STUDID:1,STUDNAME:1,BIRTHDATE:1,DATEADM:1)
```

which is the GCALC definition of the query. Finally, the constant transformation functions translate between ASCII and EBCDIC. Notice that since the new view does not have constraints, this interpretation is automatically a view interpretation.

Exercises

1. Perform the six conversion steps on M(Rcon) (Figure 7.3) for the construction of the STUDENT table in view V(Rext).

   Suppose that V(Rcon) was an external view in which REGISTRAR had the following definition:

```
PREDICATE: REGISTRAR
ARGUMENTS ARE:(SEMESTER:1;,YEAR:1;,DEPT:1;,COURSE#:1;,SEC#:1;,
INSTRUCT:1;,LOCAT:1;,TIMES:1;,STUDID:1;,GRADE:1;)
IS DEFINED BY:
   REGISTRAR(SEMESTER:1,YEAR:1,DEPT:1,COURSE#:1,
      SEC#:1,INSTRUCT:1,LOCAT:1,TIMES:1,STUDID:1,GRADE:1;)

UNION
PREDICATE: REGISTRAR
ARGUMENTS ARE:(SEMESTER:1;,YEAR:1;,DEPT:1;,COURSE#:1;,SEC#:1;,
INSTRUCT:1;,LOCAT:1;,TIMES:1;,STUDID:1;,GRADE:1;)
IS DEFINED BY:
   (E)STUDNAME:1(E)TITLE:1(E)CREDITS:1
   TRANSCRIPT((STUDID:1,STUDNAME:1,SEMESTER:1,YEAR:1,DEPT:1,
      COURSE#:1,SEC#:1,TITLE:1,GRADE:1,CREDITS:1)
& SCHEDULE(SEMESTER:1,YEAR:1,DEPT:1,COURSE#:1,SEC#:1,
      INSTRUCT:1,LOCAT:1,TIMES:1)
```

   That is, REGISTRAR is made up from the union of another REGISTRAR table and the TRANSCRIPT and SCHEDULE tables. Here SCHEDULE is a table that contains the added information that TRANSCRIPT need to form REGISTRAR.

2. What would be the interpretation representing composition of the conversion interpretation and the external-to-conceptual interpretation?
3. Construct query graphs corresponding to the defining formula for TRANSCRIPT under the interpretation of Exercise 2.
4. Construct execution trees corresponding to the two query graphs of Exercise 3.

5. Consider the following relational query on V(Rcon) in relational SQL:

```
SELECT STUDID
FROM REGISTRAR
WHERE SEMESTER = FALL
    AND YEAR = 1979
    AND DEPT = MATH
    AND COURSE# = 103
    AND GRADE = B;
```

Describe the interpretation and views corresponding to the query.

6. Suppose that V(Rcon) was an external view as considered above. Describe the interpretation and views corresponding to the query of Exercise 5.

7.2 HETEROGENEOUS DATABASE CONVERSION

In this section we extend our methodology to the heterogeneous case. We will use V(Dcon) in Figure 7.10 as our old database view and V(Dext) of Figure 7.11 as our new database view. An instance of the old database M(Dcon) is given in Figure 7.12. Figure 7.13 contains an interpretation I(Dext;Dcon) of view V(Dext) in V(Dcon).

In the relational case, a "row of a table" is the same as the record in the table. In the heterogeneous case, a "row of a cluster" is one occurrence of each of the records partaking in the cluster plus the names of the nonunique (i.e., internal, see Chapter 3) tables in which these rows belong. For example, a row of the cluster instance in Figure 7.12 would be

(FALL,1979,e(COURSE):1,COMPSCI,103,e(SECTION):2,001,GREEN,
2301 COMP CENTER, 12-1 MWF,e(STUDENT):2,123456789, SMITH ROBERT J.).

Clearly, a relational row is a special case of cluster row. It is this extension that enables us to generalize relational query processing to the heterogeneous case in database logic.

Interpreting the New Database

Our methodology for the heterogeneous case is identical to the relational case discussed in Section 7.1 (see Figure 7.5). The first step also involves establishing an interpretation of the new view in the old view. In our example, this is demonstrated by I(Dext;Dcon) in Figure 7.13. The new database is also a manifestation of the induced external database. For example, if Figure 7.12 represents an instance of the old database M(Dcon), then the new database would be I(Dext;Dcon) [M(Dcon)] of Figure 7.14.

```
V(Dcon): VIEW DEFINITION
  S(Dcon): SCHEMA DEFINITION
    TABLE SYSTEM = (REGISTRAR,STUDINFO,CATALOGUE)
    TABLE REGISTRAR = (SEMESTER,YEAR,COURSE)
    TABLE COURSE = (DEPT,COURSE#,SECTION)
    TABLE SECTION = (SEC#,INSTRUCT,LOCAT,TIMES,STUDENT)
    TABLE STUDENT = (STUDID,STUDNAME,GRADE)
    TABLE STUDINFO = (ID#,STUDNAME,BIRTHDATE,DATEADM)
    TABLE CATALOGUE = (DEPT,COURSE#,TITLE,CREDITS,DESCR,
                       LINK)
    TABLE LINK = (CATALOGUE)

L(Dcon): LANGUAGE DEFINITION
  T(Dcon): TYPING DEFINITION
    TYPE SEMTPE = {SEMESTER} ASCII CHAR(8)
    TYPE YRTPE = {YEAR} ASCII DEC(4)
    TYPE DEPTPE = {DEPT} ASCII CHAR(10)
    TYPE CS#TPE = {COURSE#} ASCII DEC(3)
    TYPE TTLTPE = {TITLE} ASCII CHAR(25)
    TYPE CRDSTPE = {CREDITS} ASCII DEC(2)
    TYPE SEC##TPE = {SEC##} ASCII CHAR(10)
    TYPE NAMTPE = {STUDNAME} ASCII CHAR(20)
    TYPE LOCTPE = {LOCAT} ASCII CHAR(30)
    TYPE TIMTPE = {TIMES} ASCII CHAR(20)
    TYPE IDTPE = {STUDID,ID#} ASCII CHAR(9)
    TYPE GRDTPE = {GRADE} ASCII CHAR(1)
    TYPE DATPE = {BIRTHDATE,DATEADM} ASCII CHAR(15)
    TYPE DESCTPE = {DESCR} ASCII CHAR(50)

    NONLOGICAL SYMBOLS DEFINITION
      PREDICATES
        SYSTEM-REGISTRAR-COURSE-SECTION-STUDENT:
          (SEMTPE,YRTPE,COURSE,DEPTPE,CS#TPE,SECTION,
          SEC#TPE,NAMTPE,LOCTPE,TIMTPE,STUDENT,IDTPE,
          NAMTPE,GRDTPE) FULL CLUSTER PREDICATE
        SYSTEM-STUDINFO:
          (IDTPE,NAMTPE,DATPE,DATPE) PREDICATE
        SYSTEM-CATALOGUE-LINK-CATALOGUE:
          (DEPTPE,CS#TPE,TTLTPE,CRDSTPE,DESCTPE,LINK,
          CATALOGUE,DEPTPE,CS#TPE,TTLTPE,CRDSTPE,DESCTPE,
          LINK,) FULL CLUSTER PREDICATE
    ≤: (YRTPE,YRTPE) PREDICATE
      FUNCTIONS
      TOTALCREDITS:(IDTPE,SEMTPE,YRTPE;
        CRDSTPE) FUNCTION

C(Dcon): CONSTRAINTS DEFINITION
  C(Dcon,1):CONSTRAINT SYSTEM-REGISTRAR:SEMESTER,
    YEAR → COURSE
  C(Dcon,2):CONSTRAINT SYSTEM-REGISTRAR-COURSE:
    SEMESTER,YEAR,DEPT,COURSE# → SECTION
  C(Dcon,3):CONSTRAINT SYSTEM-REGISTRAR-COURSE-
    SECTION:SEMESTER,YEAR,DEPT,COURSE#,SEC#
      → INSTRUCT,LOCAT,TIMES,STUDENT
```

Figure 7.10 (*cont. next page*)

(continued)

```
C(Dcon,4):CONSTRAINT SYSTEM-REGISTRAR-COURSE-
  SECTION-STUDENT:
  SEMESTER,YEAR,DEPT,COURSE#,SEC#,STUDID
  → STUDNAME,GRADE
C(Dcon,5):CONSTRAINT SYSTEM-STUDINFO:
  ID# → STUDNAME,BIRTHDATE,DATEADM
C(Dcon,6):CONSTRAINT SYSTEM-CATALOGUE:
  DEPT,COURSE# → TITLE,CREDITS,DESCR,LINK
  C(Dcon,7) = CONSTRAINT SYSTEM-REGISTRAR-
  COURSE-SECTION-STUDENT:
  SEMESTER,YEAR,DEPT,COURSE#,STUDID → SEC#
```

Figure 7.10 Database logic DDL for view V(Dcon).

```
V(Dext): VIEW DEFINITION
  S(Dext): SCHEMA DEFINITION
    TABLE TRANSCRIPT = (STUDID,STUDNAME,BIRTHDATE,DATEADM,RECORD)
    TABLE RECORD = (SEMESTER,YEAR,COURSES)
    TABLE COURSES = (DEPT,COURSE#,SEC#,TITLE,GRADE,CREDITS)

  L(Dext): LANGUAGE DEFINITION
  T(Dext): TYPING DEFINITION
    TYPE SIDTPE = {STUDID} EBCDIC CHAR(9)
    TYPE NAMTPE = {STUDNAME} EBCDIC CHAR(20)
    TYPE DATPE = {BIRTHDATE,DATEADM} EBCDIC CHAR(15)
    TYPE SEMTPE = {SEMESTER} EBCDIC CHAR(6)
    TYPE YRTPE = {YEAR} EBCDIC DEC(4)
    TYPE DEPTPE = {DEPT} EBCDIC CHAR(8)
    TYPE CS#TPE = {COURSE#} EBCDIC DEC(3)
    TYPE SEC#TPE = {SEC#} EBCDIC CHAR(10)
    TYPE TTLTPE = {TITLE} EBCDIC CHAR(25)
    TYPE GRDTPE = {GRADE} EBCDIC CHAR(1)
    TYPE CRDSTPE = {CREDITS} EBCDIC DEC(2)

    NONLOGICAL SYMBOLS DEFINITION
      PREDICATES
        TRANSCRIPT-RECORD-COURSES:
          (SIDTPE,NAMTPE,DATPE,DATPE,RECORD,SEMTPE,
          YRTPE,COURSES,DEPTPE,CS#TPE,SEC#TPE,TTLTPE,
          GRDTPE,CRDSTPE) FULL CLUSTER PREDICATE
        ≤: (YRTPE,YRTPE) PREDICATE
      FUNCTIONS
        TOTCREDITS:(SIDTPE,SEMTPE,YRTPE;
          CRDSTPE) FUNCTION

C(Dext): CONSTRAINTS DEFINITION
  C(Dext,1) CONSTRAINT TRANSCRIPT:
    STUDID → STUDNAME,BIRTHDATE,DATEADM,RECORD
  C(Dext,2):CONSTRAINT TRANSCRIPT-RECORD:
    STUDID,SEMESTER,YEAR → COURSES
  C(Dext,3):CONSTRAINT TRANSCRIPT-RECORD-COURSES:
    STUDID,SEMESTER,YEAR,DEPT,COURSE#,
    → SEC#,TITLE,CREDITS,GRADE
```

Figure 7.11 Database logic DDL for view V(Dext).

SYSTEM		
REGISTRAR	STUDINFO	CATALOGUE

STUDINFO			
ID#	STUDNAME	BIRTHDATE	DATEADM
123456789	SMITH ROBERT J.	APRIL 13 1961	SEPTEMBER 1 1979
361258823	JONES MARY T.	AUGUST 25 1961	FEBRUARY 1 1980

Figure 7.12 Instance of the database M(Dcon).

```
I(Dext;Dcon): INTERPRETATION DEFINITION
  EXTERNAL VIEW IS V(Dext) = <S(Dext),L(Dext),C(Dext)>
  CONCEPTUAL VIEW IS V(Dcon) = <S(Dcon),L(Dcon),C(Dcon)>

  CODING SECTION
    CODE FOR SIDTPE IS IDTPE;
    CODE FOR NAMTPE IS NAMTPE;
    CODE FOR DATPE  IS DATPE;
    CODE FOR SEMTPE IS SEMTPE;
    CODE FOR YRTPE  IS YRTPE;
    CODE FOR DEPTPE IS DEPTPE;
    CODE FOR CS#TPE IS CS#TPE;
    CODE FOR SEC#TPE IS SEC#TPE;
    CODE FOR TTLTPE IS TTLTPE;
    CODE FOR GRDTPE IS GRDTPE;
    CODE FOR CRDSTPE IS CRDSTPE;
    CODE FOR RECORD IS IDTPE;
    CODE FOR COURSES IS IDTPE,SEMTPE,YRTPE;

  DEFINING FORMULA SECTION
    PREDICATE:TRANSCRIPT-RECORD-COURSES
    ARGUMENTS ARE: (STUDID:1;,STUDNAME:1;,BIRTHDATE:1,
      DATEADM:1;,STUDID:1;,SEMESTER:1,YEAR:1;,
      STUDID:1,SEMESTER:1,YEAR:1;,DEPT:1;,
      COURSE#:1;,SEC#:1;,TITLE:1;,GRADE:1;,
      CREDITS:1;)
    IS DEFINED BY:(E)COURSE:1(E)SECTION:1
      (E)INSTRUCT:1(E)LOCAT:1(E)TIMES:1(E)STUDENT:1
```

(continued)

```
(E)LINK:1(E)DESCR:1
  SYSTEM-REGISTRAR-COURSE-SECTION-STUDENT
    (SEMESTER:1,YEAR:1,COURSE:1,DEPT:1,COURSE#:1,SECTION:1,
    SEC#:1,INSTRUCT:1,LOCAT:1,TIMES:1,STUDENT:1,STUDID:1,
  STUDNAME:1,GRADE:1)
& SYSTEM-CATALOGUE
    (DEPT:1,COURSE#:1,TITLE:1,CREDITS:1,DESCR:1,LINK:1)
& SYSTEM-STUDINFO
    (STUDID:1,STUDNAME:1,BIRTHDATE:1,DATEADM:1)
& SEMESTER'= FALL
& YEAR = 1979

PREDICATE:TRANSCRIPT
ARGUMENTS ARE: (STUDID:1;,STUDNAME:1;,BIRTHDATE:1,
  DATEADM:1;,STUDID:1;)
  IS DEFINED BY:
SYSTEM-STUDINFO
(STUDID:1,STUDNAME:1,BIRTHDATE:1,DATEADM:1)

PREDICATE: ≤
ARGUMENTS ARE:(YEAR:1;,YEAR:2;)
IS DEFINED BY: YEAR:1 ≤ YEAR:2

PREDICATE: TOTCREDITS
ARGUMENTS ARE: (ID#:1,SEMESTER:1,YEAR:1;,CREDITS:1;)
  IS DEFINED BY:
  TOTALCREDITS(ID#:1,SEMESTER:1,YEAR:1) = CREDITS:1

CONSTANT TRANSFORMATION SECTION
        •
        •
        •
```

Figure 7.13 Interpretation I(Dext;Dcon).

TRANSCRIPT											
STUDID	STUDNAME	BIRTHDATE	DATEADM	RECORD							
				SEMESTER	YEAR	COURSES					
						DEPT	COURSE#	SEC#	TITLE	GRADE	CREDITS
				RECORD (e(RECORD):1)							
						COURSES (e(COURSE):1)					
123456789	SMITH ROBERT J.	APRIL 13 1961	SEPT 1 1979	FALL	1979	COMP SCI	103	001	INTRO	B	3
						MATH	103	001	CALC	B	3
						ART	101	001	INTRO	B	3
						HIST	102	001	AM HIST	C	3

Figure 7.14 Instance of the new database M(Dext).

External-to-Conceptual Translation

Again, the old database view may be an external view of an underlying conceptual view. In this case we have to transform the interpretation by composing the external-to-conceptual interpretation with the conversion interpretation. In addition, it may be necessary to perform some logical optimization on the interpretation obtained from the composition. In our example, the old view V(Dcon) is not an external view; hence, composition and logical optimization of this kind are not needed. Illustrations where these are needed will be given in the exercises.

For the remaining steps, as in the preceding section, we regard each of the defining formulas in the interpretation as queries and process them.

Decomposition

We next decompose each query representing a defining formula. The input to this process is a query graph. The output is an execution tree that indicates the order of execution. The decomposition process is described for the heterogeneous case in Section 7.3. The relational situation is a special case of this process.

For example, recall the defining formula for the TRANSCRIPT-RECORD-COURSES cluster given in I(Dext;Dcon) of Figure 7.13. The corresponding query graph is in Figure 7.15(a) . Each large node represents a cluster, namely, SYSTEM-REGISTRAR-COURSE-SECTION-STUDENT, SYSTEM-CATALOGUE, and SYSTEM-STUDINFO. Arcs between the nodes denote relationships between cluster rows as specified by the query. For example, one of the arcs between the two nodes is labeled "DEPT = DEPT" to indicate that the two cluster rows should have the same DEPT values. Also, there are nodes representing selections. These are indicated by double circles attached to the cluster nodes.

The tree in Figure 7.15(b) is the output of the decomposition process and indicates the operations that are to be done to evaluate the query. The execution parallels the execution for the relational example in Section 7.1. First, a selection is performed on the cluster SYSTEM-REGISTRAR-COURSE-RECORD-STUDENT(1) for cluster rows with SEMESTER, YEAR values FALL, 1979. The selected clusters are placed into SYSTEM-REGISTRAR-COURSE-RECORD-STUDENT(2).

Next, the ID# values of SYSTEM-STUDINFO(1) are projected out into TEMP(1) and "semijoined" with the rows of SYSTEM-REGISTRAR-COURSE-RECORD-STUDENT(2). That is, for every row of projected values, a search is made through SYSTEM-REGISTRAR-COURSE-RECORD-STUDENT(2) for all rows that match. If a cluster row matches, it is placed into SYSTEM-REGISTRAR-COURSE-RECORD-STUDENT(3). Finally, the DEPT and COURSE# values of SYSTEM-CATALOGUE(1) are projected out into TEMP(2) and semijoined with the rows of SYSTEM-REGISTRAR-COURSE-RECORD-STUDENT(3). The cluster rows that match are placed in SYSTEM-REGISTRAR-COURSE-RECORD-STUDENT(4).

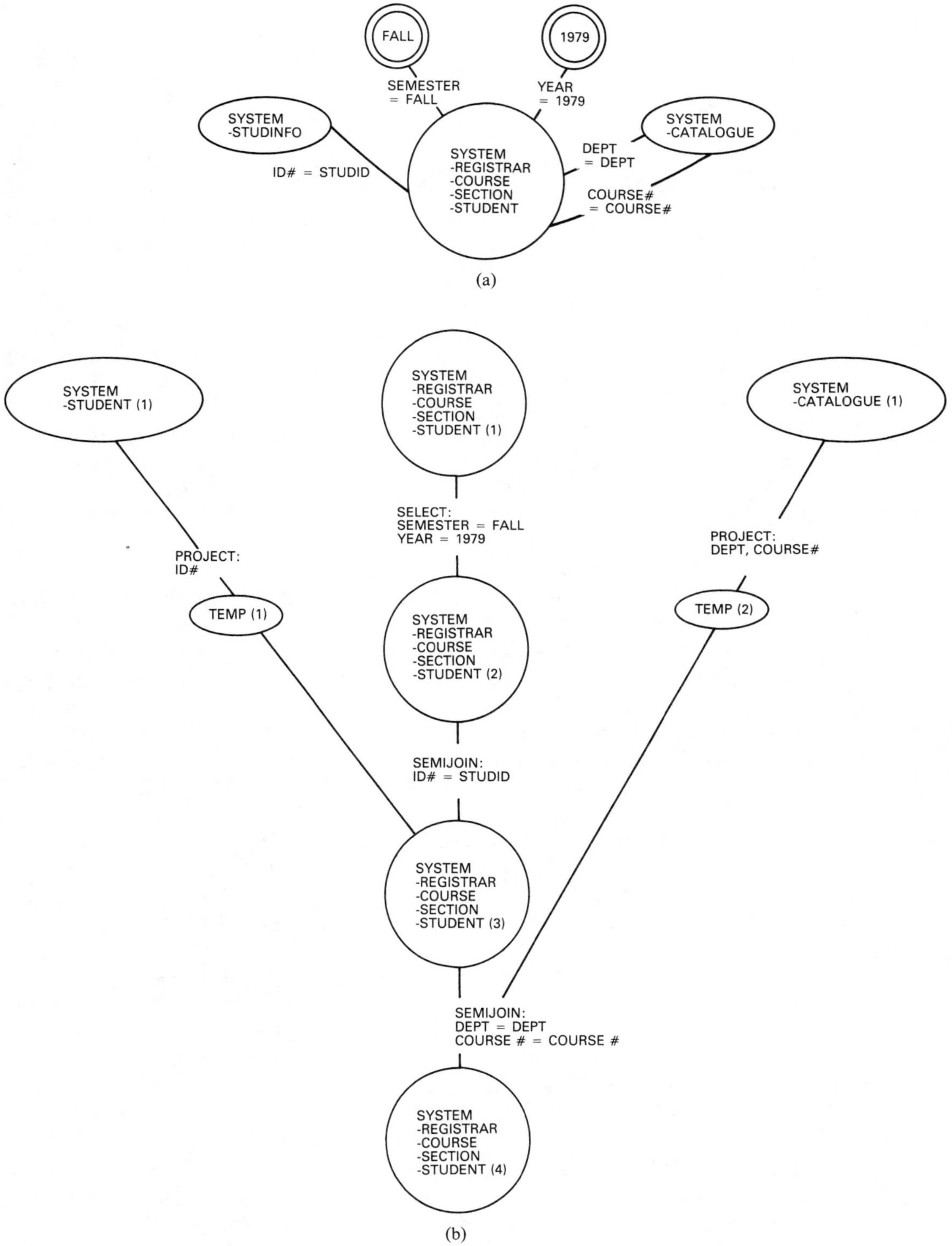

Figure 7.15 (a) Query graph; (b) execution tree.

Execution

Figure 7.16 illustrates an execution of the tree of Figure 7.15(b) on M(Dcon) of Figure 7.12. Notice that SYSTEM-REGISTRAR-COURSE-SECTION-STUDENT(1) is regarded as tables with a mapping table (MAPRCRS) indicating linkages. Also, notice each cluster row is represented by an integer o. The latter is analogous to the integer identifier associated with each record in the relational case.

First, selections are performed on SYSTEM-REGISTRAR-COURSE-SECTION-STUDENT(1) for cluster rows with SEMESTER, YEAR values equal to FALL, 1979. The results of these operations are placed into new tables representing SYSTEM-REGISTRAR-COURSE-SECTION-STUDENT(2). Again, we choose to do this to eliminate unnecessary page fetching later.

Next, the m and ID# values from each of the rows of SYSTEM-STUDINFO are projected into table TEMP1(1). TEMP1(1) will be used for matching values with those cluster rows in SYSTEM-REGISTRAR-COURSE-SECTION-STUDENT(2). The m values will be used to keep track of which rows of TEMP1(1) [hence, SYSTEM-STUDINFO(1)] matched with which rows of SYSTEM-REGISTRAR-COURSE-SECTION-STUDENT(2).

The rows in TEMP1(1) are "semijoined" with the cluster rows in SYSTEM-REGISTRAR-COURSE-SECTION-STUDENT(2) using the values of ID# and STUDID. What this means is that for every row in TEMP1(1), all the cluster rows are found which have the same values of ID# and STUDID. For each such match, the k value of the row of TEMP1(1) and the o value for the cluster row of SYSTEM-REGISTRAR-COURSE-SECTION-STUDENT(2) are recorded in a table MAP1(1). Hence, MAP1(1) keeps track of all the matches that were made. The cluster rows that were matched are placed in SYSTEM-REGISTRAR-COURSE-SECTION-STUDENT(3).

Next, the n and DEPT, COURSE# values from the rows of SYSTEM-CATALOGUE are projected into TEMP2(1) and semijoined with SYSTEM-REGISTRAR-COURSE-SECTION-STUDENT(3). The file MAP2(1) keeps track of the matching and the matched clusters are placed into SYSTEM-REGISTRAR-COURSE-SECTION-STUDENT(4).

When MAP2(1) has been constructed execution is complete. The tables representing

SYSTEM-REGISTRAR-COURSE-SECTION-STUDENT(4),
SYSTEM-STUDINFO(1),
SYSTEM-CATALOGUE(1)

and the tables MAP1(1) and MAP2(1) are sent over for assembly and loading. As mentioned in the relational case, variations on the execution such as merging operations, having "virtual" cluster tables and compression, can also be done here.

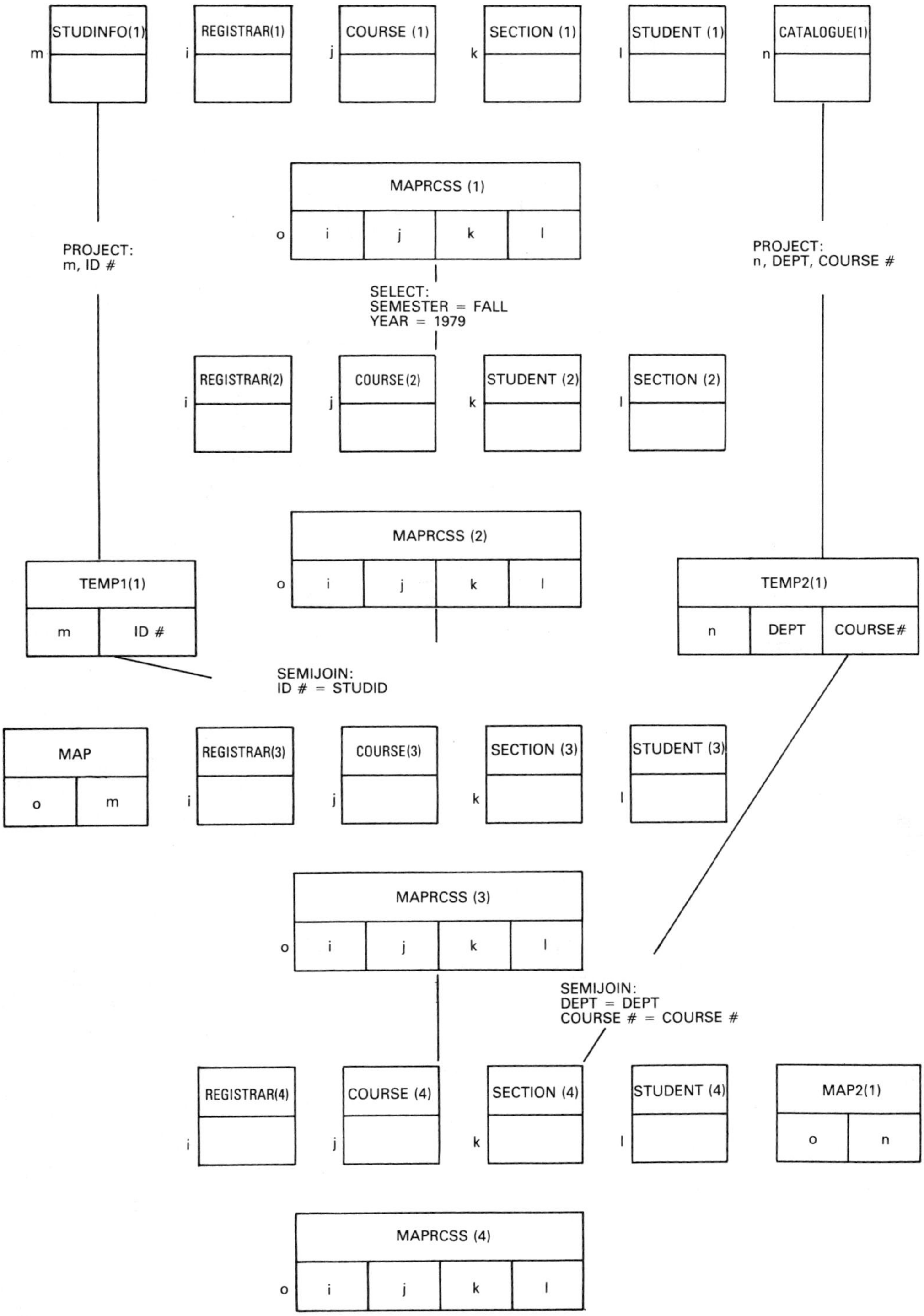

Figure 7.16 Execution.

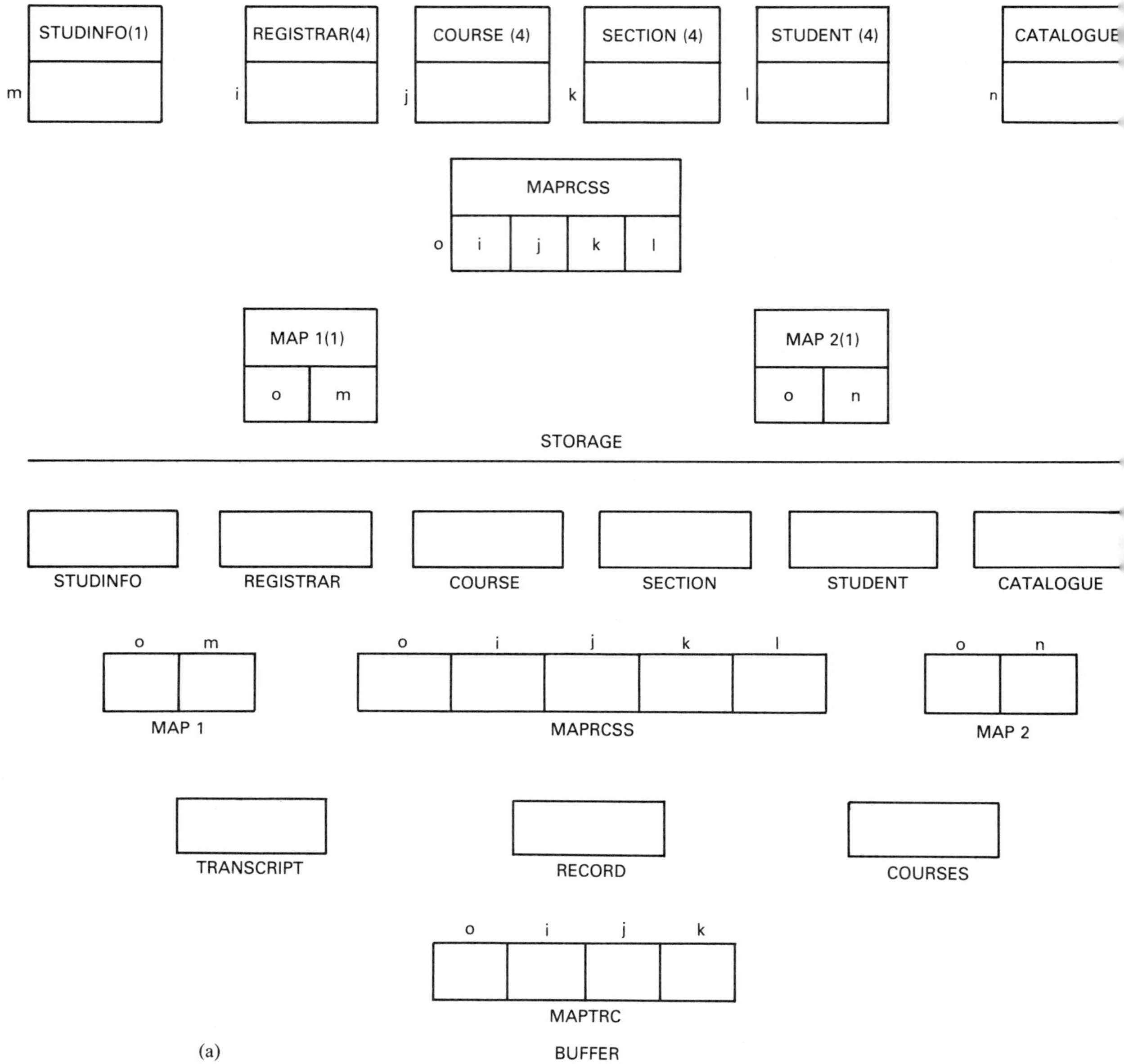

Figure 7.17 (*cont. next page*)

(continued)

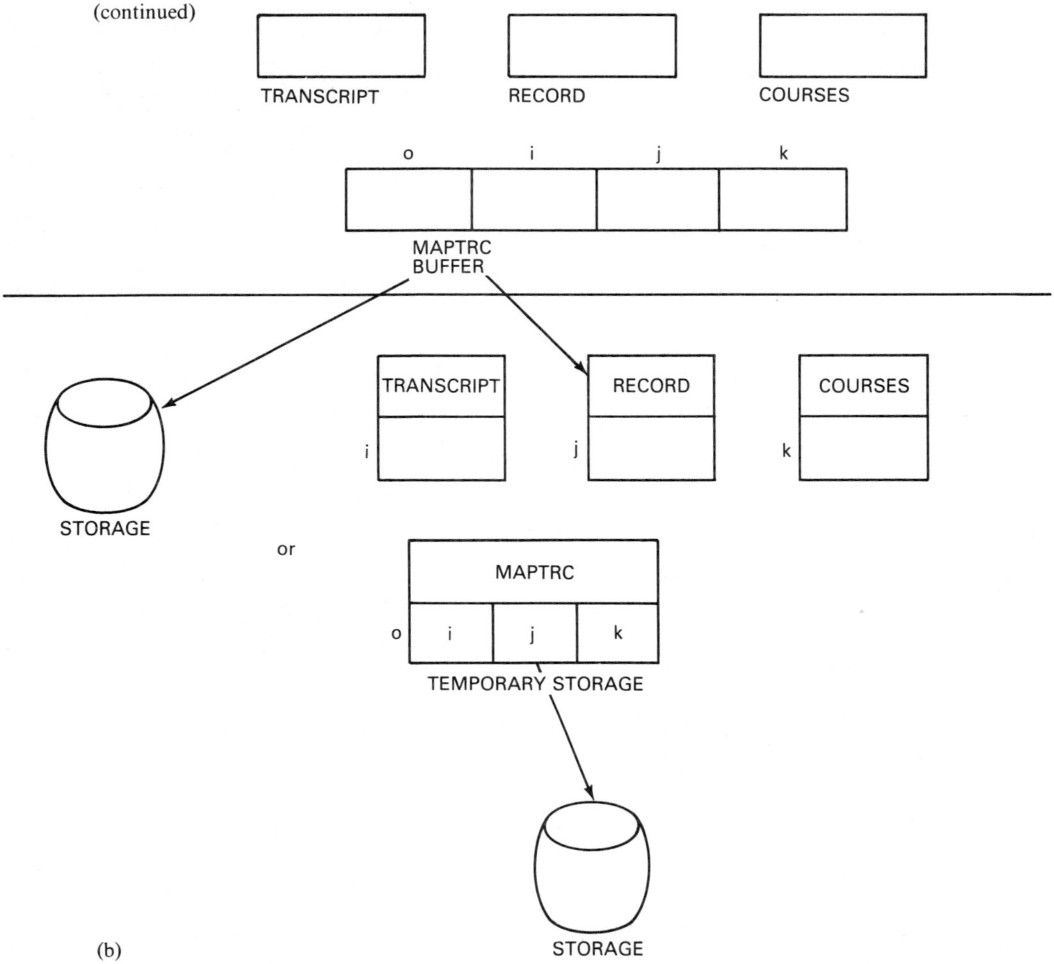

(b)

Figure 7.17 (a) Assembly; (b) loading.

Assembly and Loading

In the assembly process, the records that are related to each other are brought together. This is illustrated for our example in Figure 7.17(a). For each o and m appearing in MAP1(1) and o and n appearing in MAP2(1), the o-th cluster of SYSTEM-REGISTRAR-COURSE-SECTION-STUDENT, the m-th row of STUDINFO, and the n-th row of CATALOGUE are retrieved. In the loading process, the values that are needed are projected from the assembled records and the resultant database is stored. In our example, all the field values are extracted, converted to EBCDIC, and then placed into a TRANSCRIPT-RECORD-COURSES cluster in a buffer. The set of all constructed TRANSCRIPT-RECORD-COURSES rows are then stored as a new database.

As in the relational case, there are two strategies for loading the new database [See Figure 7.17(b)]. One is to store each new cluster row as it is assembled. This might be done if the order in which the records are being assembled is the same as the order in which they are being physically stored. This would also be done if the records are located via some hashing scheme from its arguments. A second approach is to collect all of the cluster row in temporary storage and sort the records in the order they are to be stored and then store them. This would be done if the physical ordering of the records is different from the order of assembly.

Exercises

Suppose that V(Dcon) was an external view in which SYSTEM-REGISTRAR-COURSE-SECTION-STUDENT had the following definition.

```
PREDICATE: SYSTEM-REGISTRAR-COURSE-SECTION-STUDENT:
ARGUMENTS ARE:(SEMESTER:1;,YEAR:1;,COURSE:1;,
  DEPT:1;,COURSE#:1;,SECTION:1;,SEC#:1;,INSTRUCT:1;,
  LOCAT:1;,TIMES:1;,STUDENT:1;,STUDID:1;,STUDNAME:1;,GRADE:1;)
IS DEFINED BY:
   SYSTEM-REGISTRAR-COURSE-SECTION-STUDENT
      (SEMESTER:1,YEAR:1,COURSE:1,DEPT:1,COURSE#:1,SECTION:1,
      SEC#:1,INSTRUCT:1,LOCAT:1,TIMES:1,STUDENT:1,STUDID:1,
      STUDNAME:1,GRADE:1)

PREDICATE: SYSTEM-REGISTRAR-COURSE-SECTION-STUDENT:
ARGUMENTS ARE:(SEMESTER:1;,YEAR:1;,COURSE:1;,
  DEPT:1;,COURSE#:1;,SECTION:1;,SEC#:1;,INSTRUCT:1;,
  LOCAT:1;,TIMES:1;,STUDENT:1;,STUDID:1;,STUDNAME:1;,GRADE:1;)
IS DEFINED BY:
   ((E)RECORD:1,(E)COURSES:1(E)TITLE:1(E)CREDITS:1
     TRANSCRIPT-RECORD-COURSES(STUDID:1,
STUDNAME:1,BIRTHDATE:1,DATEADM:1,RECORD:1,SEMESTER:1,YEAR:1,
   COURSES:1,DEPT:1,COURSE#:1,SEC#:1,TITLE:1,GRADE:1,CREDITS:1)
& (E)DEPTSCHED:1(E)CLASSCHED:1(E)INSTRUCT:1
   SCHEDULE-DEPTSCHED-CLASSCHED
      (SEMESTER:1,YEAR:1,DEPTSCHED:1,DEPT:1,COURSE#:1,
       CLASSCHED:1,SEC#:1,INSTRUCT:1,LOCAT:1,TITLE:1,TIME:1))
```

That is, SYSTEM-REGISTRAR-COURSE-SECTION-STUDENT is made up from the union of another SYSTEM-REGISTRAR-COURSE-SECTION-STUDENT cluster and TRANSCRIPT-RECORD-COURSES and SCHEDULE-DEPTSCHED-CLASSCHED clusters. Here the SCHEDULE-DEPTSCHED-CLASSCHED contains information that TRANSCRIPT-RECORD-COURSES does not have to form SYSTEM-REGISTRAR-COURSE-SECTION-STUDENT.

1. What would be the interpretation representing composition of the conversion interpretation and the external-to-conceptual interpretation?
2. Construct query graphs corresponding to the defining formula for TRANSCRIPT-RECORD-COURSES under the interpretation of Exercise 1.

3. Construct execution trees corresponding to the two query graphs of Exercise 2.
4. Consider the following query on V(Dcon) in GSQL.

```
SELECT STUDID,STUDNAME
FROM PREDICATE: SYSTEM-REGISTRAR-COURSE-SECTION-STUDENT:
WHERE SEMESTER = FALL
   AND YEAR = 1979
   AND DEPT = MATH
   AND COURSE# =103
   AND GRADE = B;
```

   Describe the interpretation and views corresponding to the query.
5. Suppose that V(Dcon) was an external view as considered above. Describe the interpretation and views corresponding to the query of Exercise 4.

7.3 DECOMPOSITION

In this section we investigate the decomposition stage in more detail. We illustrate the method for the relational case and then for the heterogeneous case. We conclude by discussing the problem of predicting subquery sizes.

Decomposition Methodology

The methodology begins with an initial query graph and an initial execution tree which has one node for each cluster in the query graph. The first thing that is done is to remove all the nodes that represent selections. For each one we insert the appropriate commands into the partial execution tree. The result of the execution of these selections are subsets of the original cluster instances. Selections are done first, because they can eliminate significant amounts of the data for subsequent operations.

Now we have a graph having only nodes with cluster names. We next pick out a cluster node from which we will project values for semijoins. The choice of which node to pick out can be decided by several factors which will be discussed at the end of the section. In any event, we remove the node from the graph and add to the partial execution tree instructions for projection and semijoin. The result of the execution of these operations will be the files for the projected values, subsets of the cluster instances, and mapping tables that indicate the results of the semijoins.

When all the connected nodes have been eliminated from the query graph, the decompostion is completed. As mentioned earlier, optimizations such as combining operations, maintaining "virtual" cluster instances, and compressing subresults can enhance the execution tree. In the next two subsections we illustrate the decomposition methodology for the relational and heterogenous cases, respectively.

A Relational Decomposition

Recall the defining formula for TRANSCRIPT given in I(Rext;Rcon) of Figure 7.4. The query graph and the initial execution tree corresponding to this are given in Figure 7.18(a).

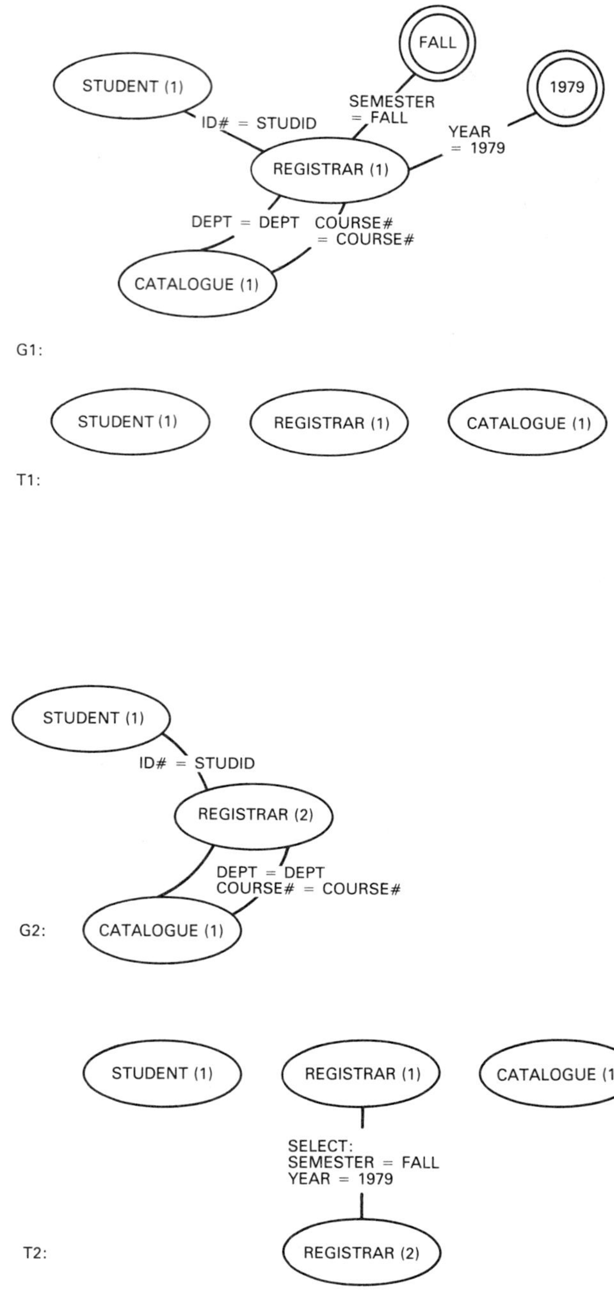

(a)

(b)

Figure 7.18 (*cont. next page*)

(continued)

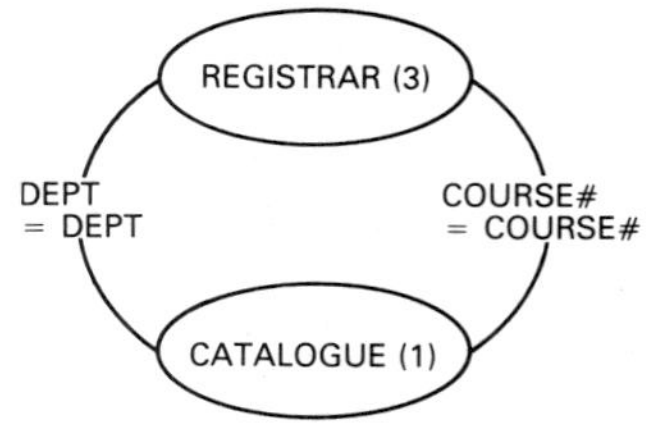

G3:

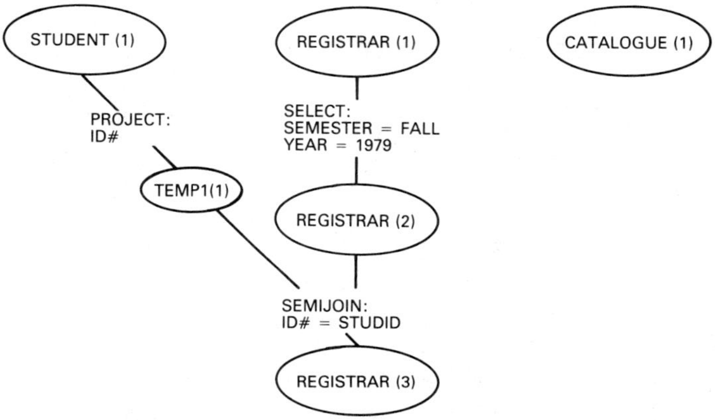

(c) T3:

G4:

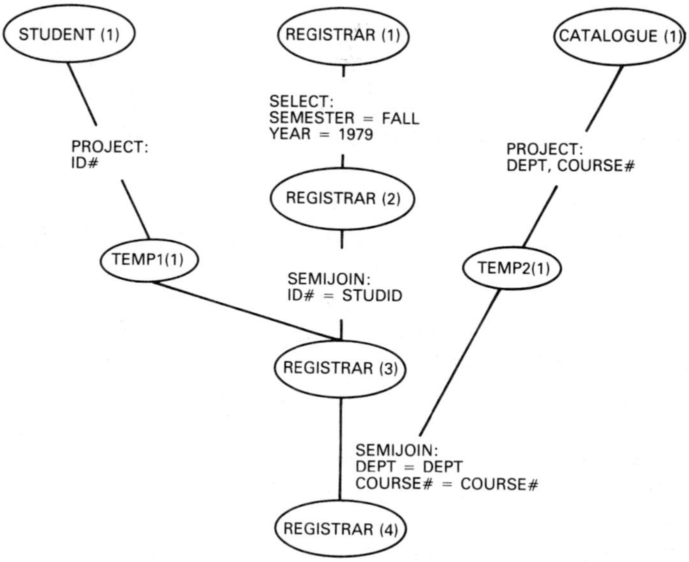

(d) T4:

Figure 7.18 Relational query decomposition: (a) query graph G1 and partial tree T1; (b) query graph G2 and partial tree T2; (c) query graph G3 and partial tree T3; (d) query graph G4 and partial tree T4.

The first thing we do is to remove from the query graph all the selection nodes. In this case, they are the SEMESTER = FALL and YEAR = 1979 nodes coming out of the REGISTRAR(1) node. As mentioned above, this serves to eliminate many of the rows from REGISTRAR(1). The new query graph and the corresponding partial execution tree are given in Figure 7.18(b). Notice that there is a REGISTRAR(2) node representing a reduction in the original table.

We now have to decompose the query graph in Figure 7.18(b). This represents a matching of the DEPT, COURSE# values of the rows from REGISTRAR(2) and CATALOGUE(1) and the STUDID and ID# values from REGISTRAR(2) and STUDENT(1). One possibility is to project STUDENT(1) and semijoin on REGISTRAR(2). A second is to project on REGISTRAR(2) and semijoin on STUDENT(1). Strategies for choosing one node over another will be discussed at the end of this section. For now let us assume that our choice is to project STUDENT(1) and semijoin on REGISTRAR(2).

We remove the STUDENT(1) node from the query graph together with the arc eminating out of it. The result is shown in Figure 7.18(c). We add to the partial tree a projection operation out of STUDENT(1) and a semijoin operation between the projection and REGISTRAR(2). We add on a resulting node labeled REGISTRAR(3). The resulting tree in also given in Figure 7.18(c).

Once again, we have to make a choice—either we project on REGISTRAR(3) or we project on CATALOGUE(1). Suppose that we choose the latter. Then we delete the CATALOGUE(1) node from the graph and its labeled arc. We also add to the partial tree a projection operation coming out of CATALOGUE(1) and a semijoin operation on REGISTRAR(3). The result of these operations is the node labled REGISTRAR(4).

Both the new query graph and the partial tree are in Figure 7.18(d). Since the query graph has no more connected nodes, we are done.

A Heterogeneous Decomposition

Recall the defining formula for TRANSCRIPT-RECORD-COURSES in I(Dext;Dcon) of Figure 7.13. The query graph corresponding to this is given in Figure 7.19(a). The initial tree is also given in Figure 7.19(a).

The first thing we have to do is to remove from the query all the selection nodes. In this case they are the SEMESTER = FALL and YEAR = 1979 nodes coming out of the SYSTEM-REGISTRAR-COURSE-SECTION-STUDENT(1) node. The new query graph and the corresponding partial execution tree are given in Figure 7.19(b). Notice that there is a SYSTEM-REGISTRAR-COURSE-SECTION-STUDENT(2) node representing a reduction in the original cluster.

We now have to decompose the query graph in Figure 7.19(b). One possibility is to project DEPT, COURSE# from SYSTEM-REGISTRAR-COURSE-SECTION-STUDENT(2) and semijoin on SYSTEM-CATALOGUE(1). The other is to do the projection on the latter and semijoin. Also, we could project ID# from SYSTEM-STUDINFO(1) and semijoin on SYSTEM-REGISTRAR-COURSE-SECTION-STU-

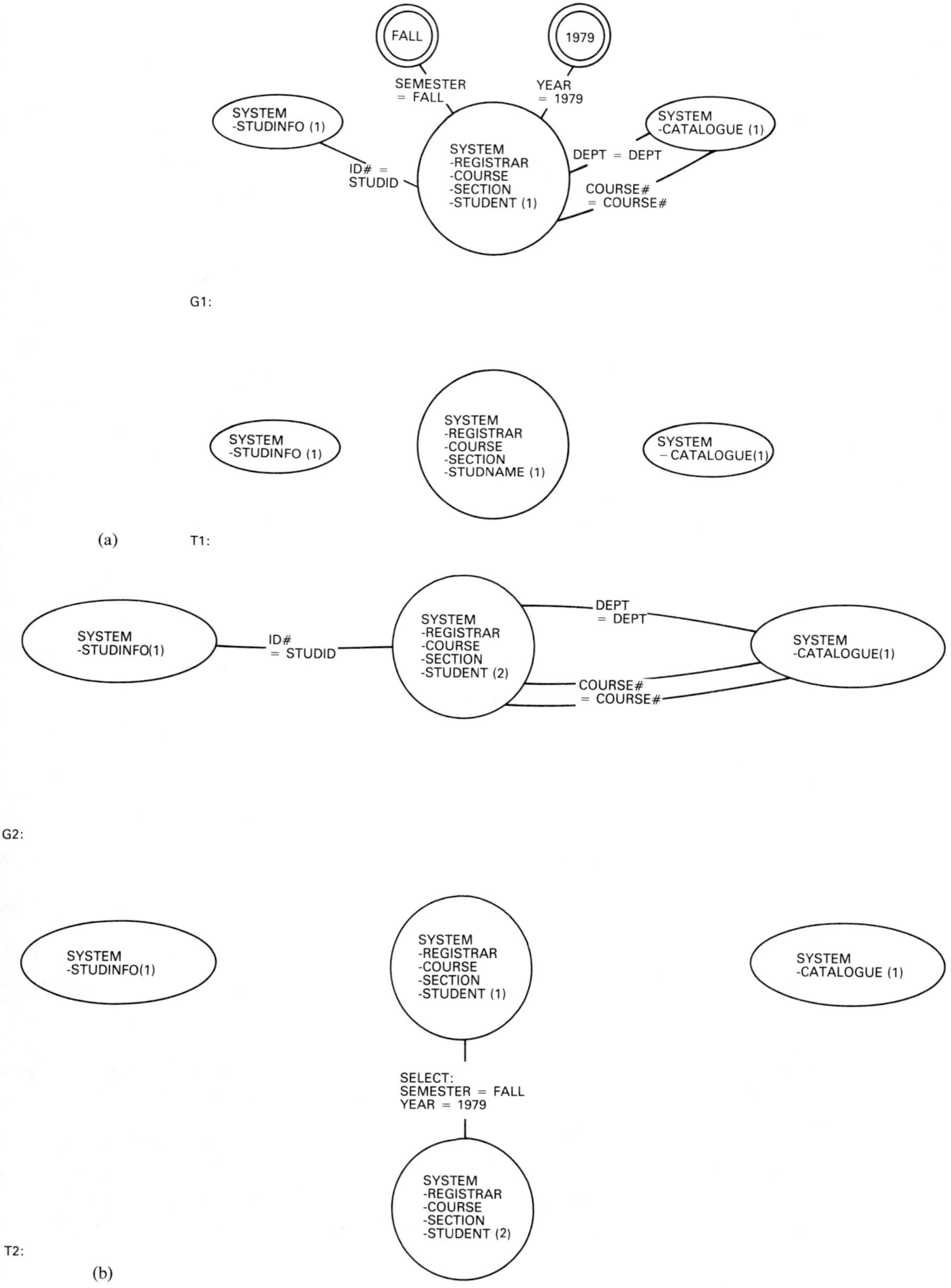

Figure 7.19 (*cont. next page*)

(continued)

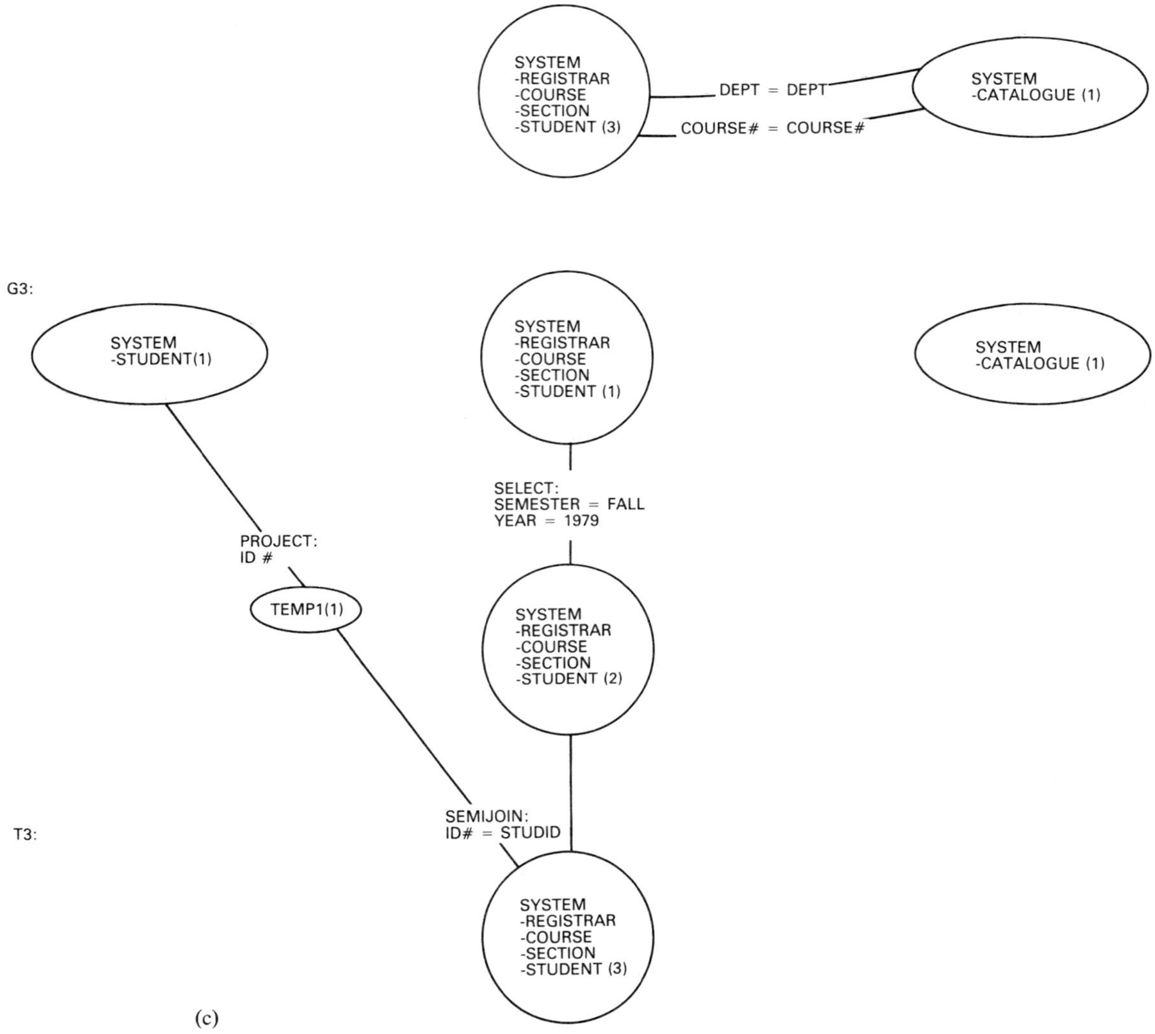

Figure 7.19 (*cont. next page*)

DENT(2) , or vice versa. Again, strategies for choosing one node over another will be discussed at the end of this section. For now let us assume that our choice is the third one.

We remove the SYSTEM-STUDINFO(1) node from the query graph together with the arc eminating out of it. The result is shown in Figure 7.19(c). We add to the partial tree a projection operation out of SYSTEM-STUDENT(1) and a semijoin operation between the projection and SYSTEM-REGISTRAR-COURSE-SECTION-

(continued)

G4:

T4:

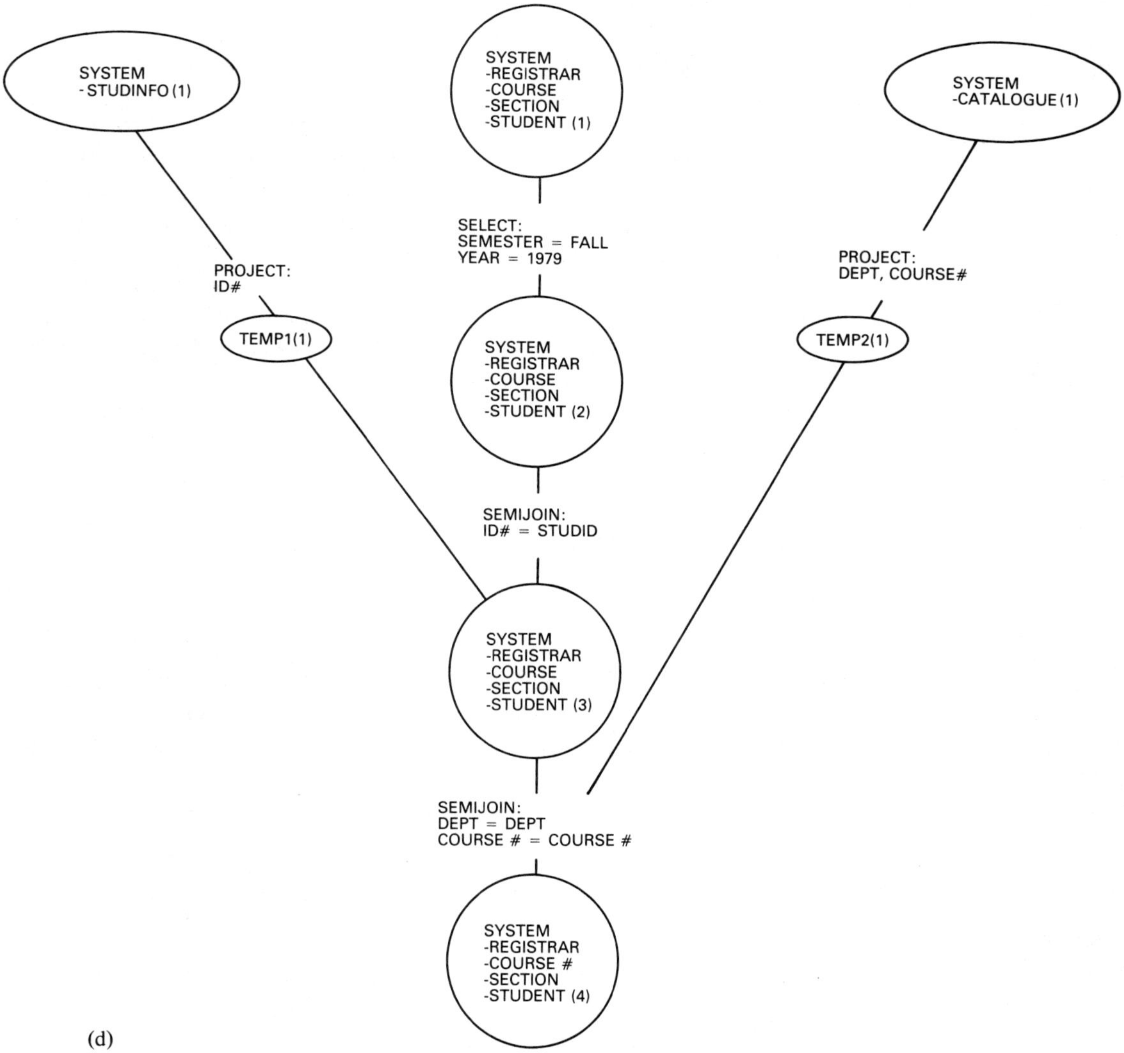

(d)

Figure 7.19 Heterogeneous query decomposition: (a) query graph G1 and partial tree T1; (b) query graph G2 and partial tree T2; (c) query graph G3 and partial tree T3; (d) query graph G4 and partial tree T4.

STUDENT(2). We add on a resulting node labeled SYSTEM-REGISTRAR-COURSE-SECTION-STUDENT(2). The resulting tree in also given in Figure 7.19(c).

Finally, we decompose the query graph of Figure 7.19(c) by removing the SYSTEM-CATALOGUE node. The resultant query graph and execution tree are given in Figure 7.19(d). Since the query graph of Figure 7.19(d) has no connected nodes, we are done.

Predicting Subquery Sizes

Given an execution tree, it is important to be able to predict the sizes of the subresults indicated by the nodes. In the decomposition process, a query graph can generate a number of alternative execution trees. Hence, we should choose the tree that produces an execution with the least "cost." This cost may be measured in terms of the local computation, input/output (e.g., page fetching) or communication in the case where the database is physically distributed over a net. In any event, knowledge of the sizes of the subresults can be used to predict these costs (see [Jacobs]).

Every node in an execution tree, obtained from a selection, projection, or semijoin, can be characterized by a defining formula. For example, Figure 7.20 contains the defining formulas for the nodes of the execution tree in Figure 7.18(d). Also, Figure 7.21 contains the defining formulas for the nodes in the tree in Figure 7.19(d). Consequently, the problem of predicting sizes of subresults reduces to predicting sizes of evaluations of defining formulas.

Let

PREDICATE: <cluster id>
ARGUMENTS ARE:(<R;>)
IS DEFINED BY:
(E)<R′>C1(<R>,<R′>,<c>) &···& Cn(<R>,<R′>,<c>);

be an arbitrary defining formula. The part in the **IS DEFINED BY** part is called the *wff.* The quantifier part of the wff is called the *prefix.* The remainder of the wff is called the *matrix.* Our procedure to predict the size of the query execution has three parts.

1. We compute the cardinality of the Cartesian product of the clusters making up the matrix. This is

$$c(\mathrm{CART}) = c(\mathrm{C1}) \times \cdots \times c(\mathrm{Cn}),$$

where c(Ci) is the number of rows of cluster Ci.

2. We compute a reduction factor rf(WFF) for the wff. The reduction factor tells how the wff reduces the cardinality of the Cartesian product. This is the major part and is described in more detail below.

```
PREDICATE: REGISTRAR(2)
ARGUMENTS ARE:(FALL;,1979;,DEPT:1;,...,GRADE:1;)
IS DEFINED BY:
  REGISTRAR(FALL,1979,DEPT:1,COURSE#:1,
    SEC#:1,INSTRUCT:1,LOCAT:1,TIMES:1,STUDID:1,GRADE:1);

PREDICATE: TEMP(1)
ARGUMENTS ARE: (ID#:1;)
IS DEFINED BY:(E)STUDNAME:1(E)BIRTHDATE:1(E)DATEADM:1
  STUDENT(ID#:1,STUDNAME:1,BIRTHDATE:1,DATEADM:1);

PREDICATE: REGISTRAR(3):
ARGUMENTS ARE: (FALL;,1979;,DEPT:1;,...,GRADE:1;)
IS DEFINED BY:
  (E)STUDNAME:1(E)BIRTHDATE:1(E)DATEADM:1
  REGISTRAR(FALL,1979,DEPT:1,COURSE#:1,
    SEC#:1,INSTRUCT:1,LOCAT:1,TIMES:1,STUDID:1,GRADE:1);
  & STUDENT(STUDID:1,STUDNAME:1,BIRTHDATE:1,DATEADM:1);

PREDICATE: TEMP(2)
ARGUMENTS ARE: (DEPT:1;,COURSE#:1;)
IS DEFINED BY:
  (E)TITLE:1(E)CREDITS:1(E)DESCR:1(E)PREDEPT:1(E)PRECOURSE#:1
  CATALOGUE(DEPT:1,COURSE#:1,TITLE:1,CREDITS:1,DESCR:1,
    PREDEPT:1,PRECOURSE#:1);

PREDICATE: REGISTRAR(4)
ARGUMENTS ARE: (FALL;,1979;,DEPT:1;,...,GRADE:1;)
IS DEFINED BY:
  (E)BIRTHDATE:1 ... (E)PRECOURSE#:1
  STUDENT(STUDID:1,STUDNAME:1,BIRTHDATE:1,DATEADM:1)
  & REGISTRAR(FALL,1979,DEPT:1,COURSE#:1,
      SEC#:1,INSTRUCT:1,LOCAT:1,TIMES:1,STUDID:1,GRADE:1)
  & CATALOGUE(DEPT:1,COURSE#:1,TITLE:1,CREDITS:1,DESCR:1,
      PREDEPT:1,PRECOURSE#:1);
```

Figure 7.20 Defining formulas for execution tree Figure 7.18 (d).

3. We calculate the predicted size of the evaluation as

   $$\text{size(SUBRESULT)} = \text{rf(WFF)} \times \text{c(CART)} \times \text{length(ROW)}$$

   where length(ROW) is the "expected length" of a single row of the result. Length(ROW) is not always the sum of the lengths of the fields in <R>. This is because the result of a query may be stored as different records that are linked up to one another (e.g., a hierarchy).

Figure 7.22 indicates the strategy used to compute rf(WFF). The first thing we do is to check if rf(WFF) is stored in the *Directory of Previous Results,* DOPR. If not, we have to compute it. The tree tells us that rf(WFF) equals the reduction factor of

```
PREDICATE: SYSTEM-REGISTRAR-COURSE-SECTION-STUDENT(2)
ARGUMENTS ARE: (FALL;, 1979;,...,GRADE:1;)
IS DEFINED BY:
  SYSTEM-REGISTRAR-COURSE-SECTION-STUDENT
       (FALL,1979,COURSE:1,DEPT:1,COURSE#:1,SECTION:1,
       SEC#:1,INSTRUCT:1,LOCAT:1,TIMES:1,STUDENT:1,STUDID:1,
       STUDNAME:1,GRADE:1);

PREDICATE: TEMP(1)
ARGUMENTS ARE: (ID#:1;)
IS DEFINED BY:
  (E)STUDNAME:1(E)BIRTHDATE:1(E)DATEADM:1
  SYSTEM-STUDINFO(ID#:1,STUDNAME:1,BIRTHDATE:1,DATEADM:1);

PREDICATE: SYSTEM-REGISTRAR-COURSE-SECTION-STUDENT(3)
ARGUMENTS ARE: (FALL;, 1979;,...,GRADE:1;)
IS DEFINED BY:
  (E)STUDNAME:1(E)BIRTHDATE:1(E)DATEADM:1
  SYSTEM-REGISTRAR-COURSE-SECTION-STUDENT(
     FALL,1979,COURSE:1,DEPT:1,COURSE#:1,SECTION:1,
     SEC#:1,INSTRUCT:1,LOCAT:1,TIMES:1,STUDENT:1,STUDID:1,
     STUDNAME:1,GRADE:1);
  & SYSTEM-STUDINFO(STUDID:1,STUDNAME:1,BIRTHDATE:1,DATEADM:1);

PREDICATE: TEMP(2)
ARGUMENTS ARE: (DEPT:1;,COURSE#:1;)
IS DEFINED BY:
  (E)TITLE:1(E)CREDITS:1(E)DESCR:1(E)LINK:1
  SYSTEM-CATALOGUE(DEPT:1,COURSE#:1,TITLE:1,
       CREDITS:1,DESCR:1,LINK:1);

PREDICATE: SYSTEM-REGISTRAR-COURSE-SECTION-STUDENT(4)
ARGUMENTS ARE: (FALL;,1979;,...,GRADE:1;)
IS DEFINED BY:
  (E)COURSE:1 ...
  (E)DESCR:1
  SYSTEM-REGISTRAR-COURSE-SECTION-STUDENT
       (FALL,1979,COURSE:1,DEPT:1,COURSE#:1,SECTION:1,
       SEC#:1,INSTRUCT:1,LOCAT:1,TIMES:1,STUDENT:1,STUDID:1,
       STUDNAME:1,GRADE:1)
& SYSTEM-CATALOGUE
  (DEPT:1,COURSE#:1,TITLE:1,CREDITS:1,DESCR:1,LINK:1)
& SYSTEM-STUDINFO
  (STUDID:1,STUDNAME:1,BIRTHDATE:1,DATEADM:1)
```

Figure 7.21 Defining formulas for execution tree Figure 7.19 (d).

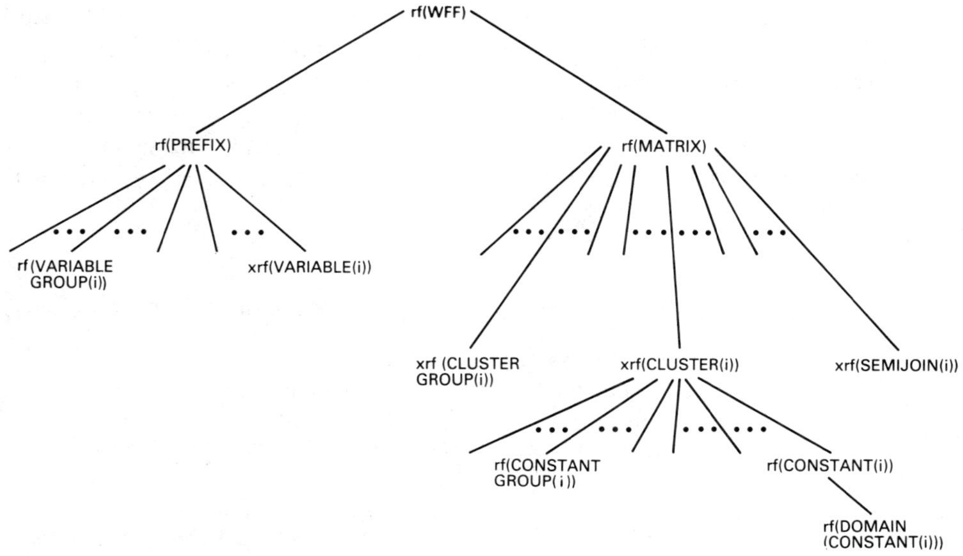

Figure 7.22 Computing rf(WFF).

the prefix (rf(PREFIX)) times the reduction factor of the matrix (rf(MATRIX)). If both of these are in DOPR, we are done; otherwise, they must be computed.

rf(MATRIX) is obtained by first trying to arrange the clusters into groups. Then rf(MATRIX) is computed by multiplying the reduction factors for each group with the reduction factors for the semijoin operations between the groups. In the best case, a cluster group is in DOPR and its reduction factor is available. In the worst case, a group contains a single cluster CLUSTER(i) and its reduction factor, rf(CLUSTER(i), has to be computed.

rf(CLUSTER(i)) is calculated by first trying to arrange its constants into groups. Then rf(CLUSTER(i)) is obtained by multiplying the reduction factors for each group. In the best case, a constant group is in DOPR. In the worst case, each group contains a single constant CONSTANT(i) and its reduction factor, rf(CONSTANT(i)), has to be computed. In the latter, either we look up the constant in DOPR, or if it is not there, we look up the reduction factor attributed to its domain in DOPR.

In the case where the results of the query are not compressed, rf(PREFIX) is 1. This follows since each row of the answer corresponds to a unique row of the reduced Cartesian product. However, if compression is performed, then rf(PREFIX) is not necessarily 1. Its value is obtained by first trying to arrange its variables into groups and multiplying the reduction factors for each group. In the best case, a variable group is in DOPR and its reduction factor is available. In the worst case, a variable group contains a single variable which should also be in DOPR.

Notice that in the strategy above, we try to use as much accumulated knowlege in DOPR as possible to compute the reduction factors. Also, note that there is a least amount of information needed for calculating a reduction factor for any defining formula. These are the reduction factors for (1) individual variables used in quantifications, (2) individual domains used in selections, and (3) linkages used in semijoins. More information than this base set (in DOPR) would probably provide better predictions.

A Relational Prediction

Consider the defining formula in Figure 7.20 associated with REGISTRAR(4).

```
    PREDICATE: REGISTRAR(4)
    ARGUMENTS ARE: (FALL;,1979;,DEPT:1;,...,GRADE:1;)
    IS DEFINED BY:
     (E)BIRTHDATE:1(E)DATEADM:1(E)INSTRUCT:1
     (E)LOCAT:1(E)TIMES:1(E)DESCR:1
     (E)PREDEPT:1(E)PRECOURSE#:1
   STUDENT(STUDID:1,STUDNAME:1,BIRTHDATE:1,DATEADM:1)
 & REGISTRAR(FALL,1979,DEPT:1,COURSE#:1,
      SEC#:1,INSTRUCT:1,LOCAT:1,TIMES:1,
      STUDID:1,GRADE:1)
 & CATALOGUE(DEPT:1,COURSE#:1,TITLE:1,CREDITS:1,DESCR:1,
      PREDEPT:1,PRECOURSE#:1);
```

We first compute the size of the Cartesian product of the tables in the matrix. Suppose that in the database c(STUDENT) $= 1 \times 10^4$, c(REGISTRAR) $= 4 \times 10^5$ and c(CATALOGUE) $= 4 \times 10^2$. Then

$$\begin{aligned} c(CART) &= c(STUDENT) \times c(REGISTRAR) \times c(CATALOGUE) \\ &= 1 \times 10^4 \times 4 \times 10^5 \times 4 \times 10^2 \\ &= 1.6 \times 10^{12} \end{aligned}$$

Assuming that rf(WFF) is not in DOPR, Figure 7.23(a) shows a possible calculation. Notice that rf(MATRIX) is the product of the rfs of the clusters times the rfs of the two semijoins. rf(STUDENT) and rf(CATALOGUE) are both 1 since no selections are made. rf(REGISTRAR) is rf(FALL,1979) which is 5×10^{-2} (i.e., a 1/20 reduction). This is because the database has 10 years of records with two semesters per year.

The rf for the CATALOGUE, REGISTRAR semijoin is 1. This is because every semester, roughly all courses are offered. Hence, no reduction results from the semijoin. The rf for the STUDENT, REGISTRAR semijoin is 3.4×10^{-1}. Each student stays in college roughly 4 years. Thus, in one semester of the 10 years of the database, 34/100 of all the students will be enrolled.

The rf(PREFIX) is the product of the rfs of the clusters STUDENT and CATALOGUE. Since we are projecting out DEPT, COURSE#, which is a key of CATALOGUE, no reduction results from the CATALOGUE quantification. Similarly, since STUDID is being projected and it is the key of STUDENT, no collapse occurs due to the STUDENT quantification.

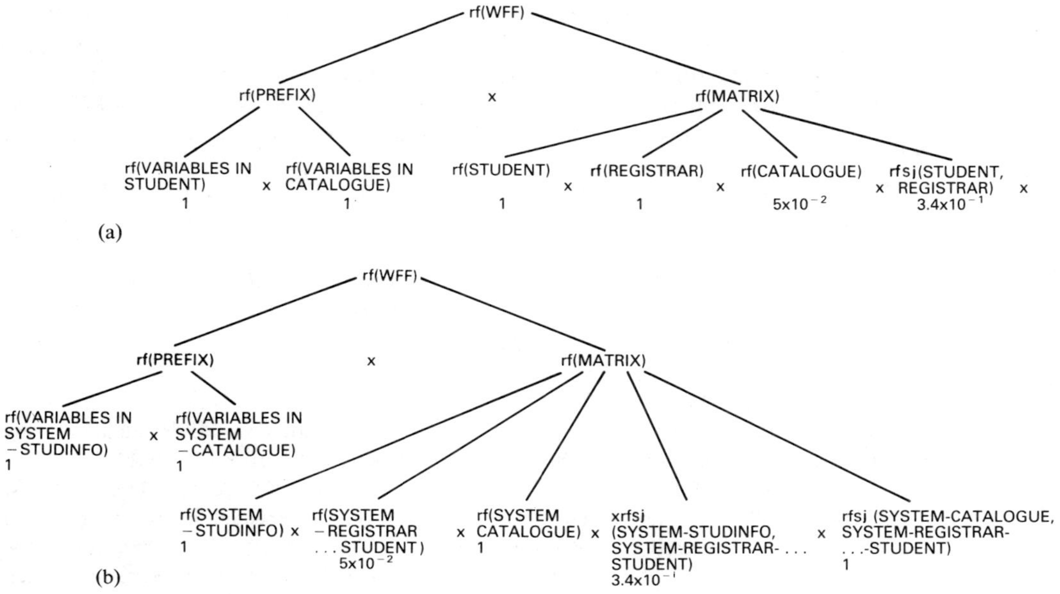

Figure 7.23 Example of rf(WFF) computations: (a) Example 7.3.1; (b) Example 7.3.2.

By multiplying the data on the tree in Figure 7.22, we get that rf(WFF) is (1.7 x 10^{-2}). The expected length of each row of the answer is 108 bytes, the length of a REGISTRAR record. Thus, the projected size of the result of the query is

size(REGISTRAR(4)) = rf(WFF) $\times$ c(CART) $\times$ length(ROW)
$= (1.7 \times 10^{-2}) \times (1.6 \times 10^{12}) \times (1.08 \times 10^{2}$ bytes)
$= 1.836 \times 10^{11}$ bytes.

A Heterogeneous Prediction

Consider the defining formula in Figure 7.21 associated with SYSTEM-REGISTRAR-COURSE-SECTION-STUDENT(4):

PREDICATE: SYSTEM-REGISTRAR-COURSE-SECTION-
STUDENT(4)
ARGUMENTS ARE: (FALL,1979,DEPT:1,...,GRADE:1)
IS DEFINED BY:
(E)COURSE:1 ... (E)DESCR:1
SYSTEM-REGISTRAR-COURSE-SECTION-STUDENT
(FALL,1979,COURSE:1,DEPT:1,COURSE#:1,SECTION:1,
SEC#:1,INSTRUCT:1,LOCAT:1,TIMES:1,STUDENT:1,
STUDID:1,STUDNAME:1,GRADE:1)
& SYSTEM-CATALOGUE
(DEPT:1,COURSE#:1,TITLE:1,CREDITS:1,DESCR:1,LINK:1)
& SYSTEM-STUDINFO
(STUDID:1,STUDNAME:1,BIRTHDATE:1,DATEADM:1);

Suppose that the number of REGISTRAR, COURSE, SECTION and STUDENT records in the database are 2×10^1, 8×10^3, 1.6×10^4 and 4×10^5, respectively. Suppose also that the number of CATALOGUE records is 4×10^2 and that the number of STUDINFO-records is 1×10^4. Then c(SYSTEM-REGISTRAR-COURSE-SECTION-STUDENT), the number of cluster rows, is equal to the number of STUDENT records, 4×10^5.

We first compute the size of the Cartesian product of the clusters in the matrix. That is,

$$\begin{aligned}\text{c(CART)} &= \text{c(SYSTEM-REGISTRAR-COURSE-SECTION-STUDENT)}\\ &\quad \times \text{c(SYSTEM-CATALOGUE)} \times \text{c(SYSTEM-STUDINFO)}\\ &= 4 \times 10^5 \times 4 \times 10^2 \times 1 \times 10^4\\ &= 1.6 \times 10^{12}\end{aligned}$$

Assuming that rf(WFF) is not in DOPR, Figure 7.23(b) shows a possible calculation. By multiplying the data on the tree in Figure 7.23(b), we get that rf(WFF) $= 1.7 \times 10^{-2}$.

The result of the query will be stored as four sets of records REGISTRAR, COURSE, SECTION, and STUDENT. Consequently, the expected length of a row of a SYSTEM-REGISTRAR-COURSE-SECTION-STUDENT cluster is not the sum of the lengths of the records. Rather, the expected length will be sum of the lengths of each record times the probabilities that the record physically exists. Thus,

$$\begin{aligned}&\text{length(row)}\\ &= \text{length(REGISTRAR)} \times 5 \times 10^{-5}\\ &+ \text{length(COURSE)} \times 2 \times 10^{-2}\\ &+ \text{length(SECTION)} \times 4 \times 10^{-2}\\ &+ \text{length(STUDENT)} \times 1\\ &= (12 \text{ bytes} \times 5 \times 10^{-5})\\ &+ (13 \text{ bytes} \times 2 \times 10^{-2})\\ &+ (73 \text{ bytes} \times 4 \times 10^{-2})\\ &+ (39 \text{ bytes} \times 1) = 42.18 \text{ bytes.}\end{aligned}$$

The decimal weight indicates the fraction of the number of record occurrences to the number of cluster rows.

Thus, the expected size of the evaluation is

$$\begin{aligned}&\text{size(REGISTRAR-COURSE-SECTION-STUDENT(4))}\\ &\quad = \text{rf(WFF)} \times \text{c(CART)} \times \text{length(ROW)}\\ &\quad = (1.7 \times 10^{-2}) \times (1.6 \times 10^{12}) \times (4.218 \times 10^1 \text{ bytes})\\ &\quad = 1.1473 \times 10^{11} \text{ bytes.}\end{aligned}$$

Remark. The expected sizes of the cluster rows above are for the entire database. A more accurate way of getting the expected sizes is to get the expected size with respect to the query. The disadvantage of calculating this is that it would require more computation effort to find the expected size in this manner.

```
V(Rext'): VIEW DEFINITION
  S(Rext'): SCHEMA DEFINITION
    TABLE TRANSCRIPT = (STUDID,STUDNAME,SEMESTER,YEAR,DEPT,
      COURSE#,SEC#,TITLE,GRADE,CREDITS)
    TABLE STUDENT = (ID#,NAME,DATEADM)
    TABLE BIRTH = (ID#,BIRTHDATE)
    TABLE CATALOGUE = (DEPT,COURSE#,TITLE,CREDITS,DESCR,
      PREDEPT,PRECOURSE#)
    TABLE SCHEDULE(SEMESTER,YEAR,DEPT,COURSE#,SEC#,INSTRUCT,
      LOCAT,TIMES)
  L(Rext'): LANGUAGE DEFINITION
    T(Rext'): TYPING DEFINITION
      TYPE SIDTPE = {ID#,STUDID} EBCDIC CHAR(9)
      TYPE NAMTPE = {NAME,STUDNAME,INSTRUCT} EBCDIC CHAR(20)
      TYPE DATPE = {DATEADM,BIRTHDATE} EBCDIC CHAR(15)
      TYPE SEMTPE = {SEMESTER} EBCDIC CHAR(8)
      TYPE YRTPE = {YEAR} EBCDIC DEC(4)
      TYPE DEPTPE = {DEPT,PREDEPT} EBCDIC CHAR(8)
      TYPE CS#TPE = {COURSE#,PRECOURSE#} EBCDIC DEC(4)
      TYPE SEC#TPE = {SEC#} EBCDIC CHAR(10)
      TYPE TTLTPE = {TITLE} EBCDIC CHAR(25)
      TYPE GRDTPE = {GRADE} EBCDIC CHAR(1)
      TYPE CRDSTPE = {CREDITS} EBCDIC DEC(2)
      TYPE DESTPE = {DESCR} EBCDIC CHAR(50)
      TYPE LOCTPE = {LOCAT} EBCDIC CHAR(30)
      TYPE TIMTPE = {TIMES} EBCDIC CHAR(20)

      NONLOGICAL SYMBOLS DEFINITION
        PREDICATES
          TRANSCRIPT:(SIDTPE,NAMTPE,SEMTPE,YRTPE,
            DEPTPE,CS#TPE,SEC#TPE,TTLTPE,GRDTPE,
            CRDSTPE) PREDICATE
          STUDENT: (SIDTPE,NAMTPE,DATPE)
                         PREDICATE
          BIRTH:(SIDTPE,DATPE) PREDICATE
          CATALOGUE:(DEPTPE,CS#TPE,TTLTPE,CRDTPE,
            DESTPE,DEPTPE,CS#TPE) PREDICATE
          SCHEDULE:(SEMTPE,YRTPE,DEPTPE,CS#TPE,
            SEC#TPE,NAMTPE,LOCTPE,TIMTPE) PREDICATE
          ≤: (YRTPE,YRTPE) PREDICATE
        FUNCTIONS
          TOTCREDITS:(SIDTPE,SEMTPE,YRTPE;
          CRDSTPE) FUNCTION

  C(Rext'): CONSTRAINTS DEFINITION
    C(Rext',1):CONSTRAINT TRANSCRIPT:STUDID,
      SEMESTER,YEAR,DEPT,COURSE#
     → STUDNAME,SEC#,TITLE,GRADE,CREDITS
    C(Rext',2):CONSTRAINT TRANSCRIPT:STUDID → STUDNAME
    C(Rext',3):CONSTRAINT TRANSCRIPT:DEPT,COURSE#
     → TITLE,CREDITS
    C(Rext',4):CONSTRAINT STUDENT:ID# → NAME,DATEADM
    C(Rext',5):CONSTRAINT BIRTH:ID# → BIRTHDATE
    C(Rext',6):CONSTRAINT CATALOGUE:DEPT,COURSE#
      → TITLE,CREDITS,DESCR
    C(Rext',7):CONSTRAINT SEMESTER,YEAR,DEPT,COURSE#,SEC#
      → INSTRUCT,LOCAT,TIMES
```

Figure 7.24 Database logic view V(Rext').

```
I(Rcon;Rext'): INTERPRETATION DEFINITION
  EXTERNAL VIEW IS V(Rcon) = <S(Rcon),L(Rcon),C(Rcon)>
  CONCEPTUAL VIEW IS V(Rext') = <S(Rext'),L(Rext'),C(Rext')>

  CODING SECTION
    CODE FOR IDTPE IS SIDTPE;
    CODE FOR NAMTPE IS NAMTPE;
    CODE FOR DATPE  IS DATPE;
    CODE FOR SEMTPE IS SEMTPE;
    CODE FOR YRTPE  IS YRTPE;
    CODE FOR DEPTPE IS DEPTPE;
    CODE FOR CS#TPE IS CS#TPE;
    CODE FOR SEC#TPE IS SEC#TPE;
    CODE FOR LOCTPE IS LOCTPE;
    CODE FOR TIMTPE IS TIMTPE;
    CODE FOR GRDTPE IS GRDTPE;
    CODE FOR TTLTPE IS TTLTPE;
    CODE FOR CRDSTPE IS CRDSTPE;
    CODE FOR DESTPE IS DESTPE;

  DEFINING FORMULA SECTION
    PREDICATE: REGISTRAR
    ARGUMENTS ARE:(SEMESTER:1;,YEAR:1;,DEPT:1;,COURSE##:1;,
      SEC##:1;,INSTRUCT:1;,LOCAT:1;,TIMES:1;,STUDID:1;,GRADE:1;)
    IS DEFINED BY:
      (E)STUDNAME:1(E)TITLE:1(E)CREDITS:1
        TRANSCRIPT((STUDID:1,STUDNAME:1,SEMESTER:1,YEAR:1,DEPT:1,
           COURSE#:1,SEC#:1,TITLE:1,GRADE:1,CREDITS:1)
      & SCHEDULE(SEMESTER:1,YEAR:1,DEPT:1,COURSE#:1,SEC#:1,INSTRUCT:1,
           LOCAT:1,TIMES:1)
      & SEMESTER:1 = FALL & YEAR:1 = 1979

    PREDICATE: STUDENT
    ARGUMENTS ARE:(STUDID:1;,STUDNAME:1;,BIRTHDATE:1;,DATEADM:1;)
    IS DEFINED BY:
      STUDENT(STUDID:1,STUDNAME:1,DATEADM:1)
      & BIRTH(STUDID:1,BIRTHDATE:1)

    PREDICATE: CATALOGUE
    ARGUMENT ARE:(DEPT:1;,COURSE##:1;,TITLE:1;,
      CREDITS:1;,DESCR:1;,PREDEPT:1;,PRECOURSE##:1;)
    IS DEFINED BY: CATALOGUE(DEPT:1,COURSE##:1,
    TITLE:1,CREDITS:1,DESCR:1,PREDEPT:1,PRECOURSE##:1)

    PREDICATE: ≤
    ARGUMENTS ARE:(YEAR:1;,YEAR:2;)
    IS DEFINED BY: YEAR:1 ≤ YEAR:2

    FUNCTION: TOTCREDITS
    ARGUMENTS ARE: (ID#:1;,SEMESTER:1;,YEAR:1;,CREDITS:1;)
    IS DEFINED BY: TOTALCREDITS(ID#:1,SEMESTER:1,YEAR:1) = CREDITS:1

    CONSTANT TRANSFORMATION SECTION
            .
            .
            .
```

Figure 7.25 Interpretation I(Rcon;Rext').

Exercises

Consider V(Rext′) of Figure 7.24 and I(Rcon;Rext′) of Figure 7.25.

1. Decompose the query corresponding to the defining formula for REGISTRAR in I(Rcon; Rext′).
2. Decompose the query corresponding to the defining formula for STUDENT in I(Rcon; Rext′).
3. Decompose the query corresponding to the defining formula for CATALOGUE in I(Rcon; Rext′).
4. Using the data in Example 7.3.1, try to predict the sizes of the other defining formulas in Figure 7.20.
5. Using the data in Example 7.3.2, try to predict the sizes of the other defining formulas in Figure 7.21.

7.4 RELATED READING

BERNSTEIN, P. A., GOODMAN, N. A., WONG, E., REEVE, C. L., AND ROTHNIE, J. B., "Query Processing in a System for Distributed Databases," *ACM Transactions on Database Systems,* **6** (4), Dec. 1981, pp. 602–625.

BIRSS, E. W., AND FRY, J.P, "Generalized Software for Translating Data," *Proceedings National Computer Conference, Vol.* **15,** AFIPS Press, Arlington, Va., 1976, pp. 889–899.

FRY, J. P., et al, "An Assessment of the Technology for Data and Program-Related Conversion" *Proceedings National Computer Conference,* Vol. **47,** AFIPS Press, Arlington, Va, 1978, pp. 887–907.

FRY, J.P., AND JERIS, D., "Towards a Formulation of Data Reorganization," *Proceedings SIGMOD Workshop on Data Description, Access and Control,* (ed. R. Rustin) ACM, New York, 1974, pp. 77–107.

HALL, P. A. V., "Optimization of Single Expressons in a Relational Database System" *IBM Journal of Systems and Development,* May 1976, pp. 244–257.

HEVNER, A. R., AND YAO, S. B., "Query Processing in Distributed Database Systems," *IEEE Transactions on Software Engineering,* **SE-5,** (3), May 1979, pp. 177–187.

HOUSEL, B. C., "Pipelining: A Technique for Implementing Data Restructurers," *ACM Transactions on Database Systems,* **4** (4), Dec. 1979, pp. 470–492.

JACOBS, B. E., *Applied Database Logic II: Heterogeneous Distributed Query Processing,* Prentice-Hall, Englewood Cliffs, N. J., in preparation.

KIM, W., *On Optimizing an SQL-like Nested Query,* RJ 3063(37958), IBM Research Laboratory, San Jose, Calif., 1981.

LUM, V. Y., SHU, N.C., AND HOUSEL, B.C., "A General Method for Data Conversion and Restructuring, " *IBM Journal of Research and Development,* **20** (5), 1976, pp. 483–497.

MEHL, J.W., AND WANG, C.P., "A Study of Order Transformation of Hierarchical Structures in IMS Data Bases," *Proceedings ACM SIGFIDET Workshop on Data Description, Access and Control,* pp. 191–205.

NAVATHE, S. B., "Schema Analysis for Databases Restructuring," *ACM Transactions on Database Systems,* **5** (2), June 1980, pp. 157–184.

NAVATHE, S. B., AND FRY, J.P., "Restructuring for Large Data Bases: Three Levels of Abstraction," *ACM Transactions on Database Systems,* **1** (2), June 1976, pp. 138–158.

SELINGER, P.G., ASTRAHAN, M.M., CHAMBERLIN, D.D., LORIE, R.A., AND PRICE, T.G., "Access Path Selection in a Relational Database Management System" *Proceedings ACM SIGMOD Conference,* June 1979, pp. 23–34.

SHNEIDERMAN, B., AND THOMAS, G., "An Architecture for Automatic Relational Database System Conversion," *ACM Transactions on Database Systems,* **7** (2) June 1982, pp. 235–257.

SHOSHANI, A., "A Logical-Level Approach to Data Base Conversion" *Proceedings ACM SIGMOD International Conference on Management of Data,* ACM, New York, 1975, pp. 112–122.

SHU, N.C., HOUSEL, B.C., AND LUM, V.Y., "CONVERT: A High Level Translation Definition Langauge for Data Conversion," *Communications of the ACM,* **18** (10), Oct. 1975, pp. 557–567.

SHU, N.C., HOUSEL, B.C., TAYLOR, R.W., GHOSH, S.P., AND LUM, V.Y., "EXPRESS: A Data Extraction, Processing, and Restructuring System" *ACM Transactions on Database Systems,* **2** (2), June 1977, pp. 134–174.

WONG, E., AND YOUSSEFI, K., "Decomposition—A Strategy for Query Processing," *ACM Transactions on Database Systems,* **1**(3), Sept. 1976, pp. 233–241.

8

AUTOMATIC PROGRAM CONVERSION

In Chapter 8 we study the automatic program conversion problem in the context of database logic. We regard old and new databases as database logic views and use an external-to-conceptual mapping as a bridge between the two. In Section 8.1 we illustrate our conversion methodology using two relational databases and the well-known relational SQL DML. In Section 8.2 we extend it to the heterogeneous case using generalized SQL DML, GSQL. In Section 8.3 we study the process of logical optimization of GCALC queries.

8.1 RELATIONAL SQL CONVERSION

In this section we briefly review the relational SQL data manipulation language and show how to convert relational SQL from an old database to a new one. We illustrate the methodology using sample old and new relational databases.

Relational SQL DML

Relational SQL is a quasi-English data manipulation language used for relational databases. We illustrate it by providing some examples on relational view V(Rext) of Figure 8.1. Further details can be found in [Astrahan, et. al.].

Example 8.1.1.

Find the id#'s, names, and dates of admissions of all students who earned the grade of B in Math 103 during the fall 1979 semester.

```
V(Rext): VIEW DEFINITION
  S(Rext): SCHEMA DEFINITION
    TABLE TRANSCRIPT = (STUDID,STUDNAME,SEMESTER,YEAR,DEPT,
      COURSE#,SEC#,TITLE,GRADE,CREDITS)
    TABLE STUDENT = (ID#,NAME,DATEADM)

L(Rext): LANGUAGE DEFINITION
  T(Rext): TYPING DEFINITION
    TYPE SIDTPE = {ID#,STUDID} EBCDIC CHAR(9)
    TYPE NAMTPE = {NAME,STUDNAME} EBCDIC CHAR(20)
    TYPE DATPE = {DATEADM} EBCDIC CHAR(15)
    TYPE SEMTPE = {SEMESTER} EBCDIC CHAR(8)
    TYPE YRTPE = {YEAR} EBCDIC DEC(4)
    TYPE DEPTPE = {DEPT} EBCDIC CHAR(8)
    TYPE CS#TPE = {COURSE#} EBCDIC DEC(4)
    TYPE SEC#TPE = {SEC#} EBCDIC CHAR(10)
    TYPE TTLTPE = {TITLE} EBCDIC CHAR(25)
    TYPE GRDTPE = {GRADE} EBCDIC CHAR(1)
    TYPE CRDSTPE = {CREDITS} EBCDIC DEC(2)

    NONLOGICAL SYMBOLS DEFINITION
      PREDICATES
        TRANSCRIPT:(SIDTPE,NAMTPE,SEMTPE,YRTPE,
          DEPTPE,CS#TPE,SEC#TPE,TTLTPE,GRDTPE,
          CRDSTPE) PREDICATE
        STUDENT: (SIDTPE,NAMTPE,DATPE)
          PREDICATE
          ≤ :(YRTPE,YRTPE) PREDICATE
      FUNCTIONS
        TOTCREDITS:(SIDTPE,SEMTPE,YRTPE;
        CRDSTPE) FUNCTION

C(Rext): CONSTRAINTS DEFINITION
  C(Rext,1):CONSTRAINT TRANSCRIPT:STUDID,
    SEMESTER,YEAR,DEPT,COURSE# →
    STUDNAME,SEC#,TITLE,GRADE,CREDITS
  C(Rext,2):CONSTRAINT TRANSCRIPT:STUDID → STUDNAME
  C(Rext,3):CONSTRAINT TRANSCRIPT:DEPT,COURSE#
    → TITLE,CREDITS
  C(Rext,4):CONSTRAINT STUDENT:ID# → NAME,DATEADM
```

Figure 8.1 Database logic DDL definition of view V(Rext).

Solution A

```
SET W TO
  SELECT UNIQUE ID#,NAME,DATEADM
  FROM TRANSCRIPT,STUDENT
  WHERE SEMESTER = FALL
      AND YEAR = 1979
      AND DEPT = MATH
      AND COURSE# = 103
```

```
AND GRADE = B
AND STUDID = ID# ;
```

This relational SQL query produces a search through the TRANSCRIPT table to find all its rows where the SEMESTER, YEAR, DEPT, COURSE#, and GRADE components are FALL, 1979, MATH, 103, and B, respectively. Then all rows in the STUDENT table are found which have the same ID# as the selected TRANSCRIPT rows. For each such match, the ID#, NAME, and DATEADM values of STUDENT are extracted and stored in W.

An alternative solution is as follows.

Solution B

```
SET W TO
 SELECT UNIQUE ID#,NAME,DATEADM
 FROM STUDENT
 WHERE ID# IN
   SELECT STUDID
   FROM TRANSCRIPT
   WHERE SEMESTER = FALL
     AND YEAR = 1979
     AND DEPT = MATH
     AND COURSE# = 103
     AND GRADE = B;
```

In this example, we are first performing a subquery to find all the STUDIDs of the required rows from TRANSCRIPT. We then find those rows in STUDENT which have an ID# value in the previous subquery execution. The result of execution of this nested query is identical to that of solution A.

Example 8.1.2.

Find the id#'s and names of all the students who earned both a B in Computer Science 103 and Math 103 during the fall 1979 semester.

Solution A

```
SET W TO
 SELECT UNIQUE STUDID FIRST STUDNAME FIRST
 FROM TRANSCRIPT FIRST,TRANSCRIPT SECOND
 WHERE SEMESTER FIRST = FALL
   AND YEAR FIRST = 1979
   AND DEPT FIRST = COMPSCI
   AND COURSE# FIRST = 103
   AND GRADE FIRST = B
   AND SEMESTER SECOND = FALL
   AND YEAR SECOND = 1979
   AND DEPT SECOND = MATH
   AND COURSE# SECOND = 103
   AND GRADE SECOND = B
   AND STUDID FIRST = STUDID SECOND;
```

This query requires two passes through the TRANSCRIPT table. One pass (through TRANSCRIPT FIRST) looks for the Computer Science 103 course; the second pass (through TRANSCRIPT SECOND) looks for the Math 103 course. For each match of STUDID, the STUDID and STUDNAME and stored in W.

Solution B

```
SET W TO
 SELECT UNIQUE STUDID,STUDNAME
 FROM TRANSCRIPT
 WHERE SEMESTER = FALL
   AND YEAR = 1979
   AND DEPT = COMPSCI
   AND COURSE# = 103
   AND GRADE = B
   AND STUDID IN
         SELECT STUDID
         FROM TRANSCRIPT
         WHERE SEMESTER = FALL
                AND YEAR = 1979
                AND DEPT = MATH
                AND COURSE# = 103
                AND GRADE = B;
```

Here, we are again using nested subqueries. The result of execution is identical to that of solution A.

Example 8.1.3.

Find the names of all the students who earned either a B in Computer Science 103 or in Math 103.

Solution

```
SET W TO
 SELECT UNIQUE STUDNAME
 FROM TRANSCRIPT
 WHERE DEPT = COMPSCI
   AND COURSE# = 103
   AND GRADE = B
UNION
 SELECT UNIQUE STUDNAME
 FROM TRANSCRIPT
 WHERE DEPT = MATH
   AND COURSE# = 103
   AND GRADE = B;
```

This is really two subqueries. The first looks for the COMPSCI 103 row of TRANSCRIPT; the second looks for the MATH 103 row.

Example 8.1.4

Insert the information that Robert J. Smith took Biology 103, Introduction, in section 001 during the fall 1979 semester and earned a grade of B.

Solution

```
INSERT INTO TRANSCRIPT
<123456789,ROBERT J. SMITH,FALL,1979,BIO,103,001,INTRO,B,3>;
```

This is a simple insertion of a single row into the TRANSCRIPT table.

Example 8.1.5.

Delete all information about the courses that Robert J. Smith id#, 123456789, took during the fall of 1979.

Solution

```
DELETE TRANSCRIPT
WHERE STUDID = 123456789
  AND SEMESTER = FALL
  AND YEAR = 1979;
```

This operation is actually a query followed by a deletion. The query locates all rows which have, respectively, a STUDID, SEMESTER, and YEAR values of 123456789, FALL, and 1979. The deletion operation removes all such rows.

Example 8.1.6.

Change the grade that Mary T. Jones, id# 361258823, earned in Physics 102 during the spring of 1980 from whatever is recorded to a grade of A.

Solution

```
UPDATE TRANSCRIPT
SET GRADE = A
WHERE STUDID = 361258823
  AND SEMESTER = SPRING
  AND YEAR = 1980
  AND DEPT = PHYSICS
  AND COURSE# = 102;
```

This operation is a query followed by an update. First, all rows of TRANSCRIPT which satisfy the condition are found. Second, they are updated by having their grade values changed to an A.

Conversion Methodology

Induced database structures play a central role in our methodology of program conversion. Intuitively, when one wants to convert old programs, one asks where the old database is "hidden" within the new database. Once this is found, the conversion transforms the old programs to new ones that access the data in the hidden database.

```
   DML on old view
         ↓
    [ STAGE 1 ]
         ↓
  GCALC on old view
         ↓
    [ STAGE 2 ]
         ↓
  GCALC on new view
         ↓
    [ STAGE 3 ]
         ↓
optimized GCALC on new view
         ↓
    [ STAGE 4 ]
         ↓
   DML on new view
```

Figure 8.2 Conversion methodology.

In our approach, the hidden database is precisely the database structure I[M] induced from the new database M via the interpretation I.

Our methodology for converting a DML from an old database to a new one is comprised of four steps (see Figure 8.2). First, we compile the old DML into equivalent GCALC DML. Second, we use an external-to-conceptual mapping of the old database view in the new database view to convert the GCALC to the new database. Third, we optimize the GCALC to "smaller" but equivalent GCALC DML. Fourth, we compile the GCALC DML into an equivalent target DML on the new database.

We illustrate the methodology by showing how to convert relational SQL from V(Rext) of Figure 8.1 to V(Rcon) of Figure 8.3. The interpretation I(Rext;Rcon) is given in Figure 8.4(a) . An operation simulator SIM(DELETE(TRANSCRIPT)) is given in Figure 8.4(b). Notice that the instructions in the simulator are in relational SQL on view V(Rcon), the target language for our conversion.

Converting to GCALC

As mentioned above, the first step in the conversion process is the compilation of relational SQL into GCALC DML. The precise details of this aspect of the conversion methodology requires a formal definition of relational SQL in terms of GCALC DML which is outside the scope of this book. In this section we relegate the presentation of this to illustrations. We refer the interested reader to [Cao and Jacobs] for further details.

Recall solution A to the query given in Example 8.1.1. The equivalent GCALC DML generated is given by the following:

```
GET W (ID#:1,NAME:1,DATEADM:1):
   (E)STUDNAME:1...(E)CREDITS:1
   TRANSCRIPT(ID#:1,STUDNAME:1,FALL,1979,MATH,103,
      SEC#:1,TITLE:1,B,CREDITS:1)
& STUDENT(ID#:1,NAME:1,DATEADM:1);
```

```
V(Rcon): VIEW DEFINITION
  S(Rcon): SCHEMA DEFINITION
    TABLE STUDENT = (ID#,STUDNAME,BIRTHDATE,DATEADM)
    TABLE REGISTRAR = (SEMESTER,YEAR,DEPT,COURSE#,
      SEC#,INSTRUCT,LOCAT,TIMES,STUDID,GRADE)
    TABLE CATALOGUE = (DEPT,COURSE#,TITLE,CREDITS,
      DESCR,PREDEPT,PRECOURSE#)

  L(Rcon): LANGUAGE DEFINITION
  T(Rcon): TYPING DEFINITION
    TYPE IDTPE = {ID#,STUDID} ASCII CHAR(9)
    TYPE NAMTPE = {STUDNAME,INSTRUCT} ASCII CHAR(20)
    TYPE DATPE = {BIRTHDA,DATEADM} ASCII CHAR(15)
    TYPE SEMTPE = {SEMESTER} ASCII CAHR(8)
    TYPE YRTPE = {YEAR} ASCII DEC(4)
    TYPE DEPTPE = {DEPT,PREDEPT} ASCII CHAR(10)
    TYPE CS#TPE = {COURSE#,PRECOURSE#} ASCII DEC(3)
    TYPE SEC#TPE = {SEC#} ASCII CHAR(3)
    TYPE LOCTPE = {LOCAT} ASCII CHAR(30)
    TYPE TIMTPE = {TIMES} ASCII CHAR(20)
    TYPE GRDTPE = {GRADE} ASCII CHAR(1)
    TYPE TTLTPE = {TITLE} ASCII CHAR(25)
    TYPE CRDSTPE = {CREDITS} ASCII DEC(2)
    TYPE DESCR = {DESCR} ASCII CHAR(50)

    NONLOGICAL SYMBOLS DEFINITION
      PREDICATES
        STUDENT: (IDTPE,NAMTPE,DATPE,DATPE)
                         PREDICATE
        REGISTRAR: (SEMTPE,YRTPE,DEPTPE,CS#TPE,
          SEC#TPE,NAMTPE,LOCTPE,TIMTPE,SIDTPE,
          GRDTPE) PREDICATE
        CATALOGUE: (DEPTPE,CS#TPE,TTLTPE,CRDSTPE,
          DESCTPE,DEPTPE,CS#TPE) PREDICATE
        ≤: (YRTPE,YRTPE) PREDICATE
      FUNCTIONS
        TOTCREDITS:(IDTPE,SEMTPE,YRTPE;
          CRDSTPE) FUNCTION

C(Rcon): CONSTRAINTS DEFINITION
  C(Rcon,1):CONSTRAINT STUDENT: ID# → STUDNAME,
    BIRTHDATE,DATEADM
  C(Rcon,2):CONSTRAINT REGISTRAR:SEMESTER,YEAR,DEPT,
    COURSE#,SEC# → INSTRUCT,LOCAT,TIMES
  C(Rcon,3):CONSTRAINT REGISTRAR:SEMESTER,YEAR,DEPT,
    COURSE#,SEC#,STUDID → GRADE
  C(Rcon,4):CONSTRAINT CATALOGUE:DEPT,COURSE#
  → TITLE,CREDITS,DESCR
  C(Rcon,5):CONSTRAINT  REGISTRAR:SEMESTER,YEAR,DEPT,
    COURSE#,STUDID → SEC#
```

Figure 8.3 Database logic DDL definition of view V(Rcon).

```
I(Rext;Rcon): INTERPRETATION DEFINITION
  EXTERNAL VIEW IS V(Rext) = <S(Rext),L(Rext),C(Rext)>
  CONCEPTUAL VIEW IS V(Rcon) = <S(Rcon),L(Rcon),C(Rcon)>

  CODING SECTION
    CODE FOR SIDTPE IS IDTPE;
    CODE FOR NAMTPE IS NAMTPE;
    CODE FOR DATPE  IS DATPE;
    CODE FOR SEMTPE IS SEMTPE;
    CODE FOR YRTPE  IS YRTPE;
    CODE FOR DEPTPE IS DEPTPE;
    CODE FOR CS#TPE IS CS#TPE;
    CODE FOR SEC#TPE IS SEC#TPE;
    CODE FOR TTLTPE IS TTLTPE;
    CODE FOR GRDTPE IS GRDTPE;
    CODE FOR CRDSTPE IS CRDSTPE;

  DEFINING FORMULA SECTION
     PREDICATE: TRANSCRIPT
     ARGUMENTS ARE: (STUDID:1;,STUDNAME:1;,
       SEMESTER:1;,YEAR:1;,DEPT:1;,COURSE#:1;,SEC#:1;,
       TITLE:1;,GRADE:1;,CREDITS:1;)
     IS DEFINED BY:(E)BIRTHDATE:1(E)DATEADM:1
       (E)INSTRUCT:1(E)LOCAT:1(E)TIMES:1(E)DESCR:1
       (E)PREDEPT:1(E)PRECOURSE#:1
         STUDENT(STUDID:1,STUDNAME:1,BIRTHDATE:1,DATEADM:1)
       & REGISTRAR(SEMESTER:1,YEAR:1,DEPT:1,COURSE##:1,
         SEC##:1,INSTRUCT:1,LOCAT:1,TIMES:1,STUDID:1,GRADE:1)
       & CATALOGUE(DEPT:1,COURSE##:1,TITLE:1,CREDITS:1,DESCR:1,
         PREDEPT:1,PRECOURSE##:1)

       PREDICATE: STUDENT
       ARGUMENTS ARE: (ID#:1;,STUDNAME:1;,DATEADM:1;)
       IS DEFINED BY:(E) BIRTHDATE:1
       STUDENT(STUDID:1,STUDNAME:1,BIRTHDATE:1,DATEADM:1)

    PREDICATE: ≤
    ARGUMENTS ARE:(YEAR:1;,YEAR:2;)
    IS DEFINED BY: YEAR:1 ≤ YEAR:2

    FUNCTION: TOTCREDITS
    ARGUMENTS ARE: (ID#:1;,SEMESTER:1;,YEAR:1;,CREDITS:1;)
    IS DEFINED BY: TOTALCREDITS(ID#:1,SEMESTER:1,YEAR:1) = CREDITS:1

    CONSTANT TRANSFORMATION SECTION
            .
            .
            .
```

(a)

```
    PROC SIM(DELETE(TRANSCRIPT))(CW);
      /* CW is a an array of codes where:
         CW(i).STUDID = an SIDTPE code
                      = an ASCII DEC(9) value (IDTPE;),
         CW(i).STUDNAME = a  NAMTPE code
                      = an ASCII CHAR(20) value (NAMTPE;),
```

Figure 8.4 *(cont. next page)*

(continued)

```
            CW(i).SEMESTER = a SEMTPE code
                           = an ASCII CHAR(8) value (SEMTPE;),
            CW(i).YEAR     = a YRTPE code
                           = an ASCII DEC(4) value (YRTPE;),
            CW(i).DEPT     = a DEPTPE code
                           = an ASCII CHAR(10) value (DEPTPE;),
            CW(i).COURSE#  = a CS#TPE code
                           = an ASCII DEC(3) value (CS#TPE;),
            CW(i).SEC#     = a SEC#TPE code
                           = an ASCII DEC(3) value (SEC#TPE;),
            CW(i).TITLE    = a TTLTPE code
                           = an ASCII CHAR(25) value (TTLTPE;),
            CW(i).GRADE    = a GRDTPE code
                             = an ASCII DEC(9) value (GRDTPE;),
            CW(i).CREDITS= a CRDSTPE code
                             = an ASCII DEC(1) value (CRDSTPE;),

   i = 1,...,length(CW) */

     ESTABLISH CHECKPOINT;

  /* If the simulation should fail [e.g., the resultant conceptual database is not
a model of C(Rcon)], we can use this checkpoint to reestablish the old database in-
stance.*/

     FOR i = 1 TO LENGTH(CW);

  /* For each row of CW perform the following operations.*/

     DELETE REGISTRAR
     WHERE SEMESTER = CW(i).SEMESTER
      AND  YEAR = CW(i).YEAR
      AND  DEPT = CW(i).DEPT
      AND COURSE# = CW(i).COURSE#
      AND SEC# = CW(i).SEC#
      AND STUDID = CW(i).STUDID
      AND GRADE = CW(i).GRADE;

  /* Delete from the registrar data pertaining to the student in the i-
th row of CW.*/

      END i;
     IF M(Rcon) |= C(Rcon) THEN RETURN;

  L1: RESTORE TO LAST CHECKPOINT;

  /* If the current conceptual database instance is a model of C(Rcon) then exit;
otherwise, rollback to the instance of the conceptual database prior to execu-
tion.*/
```

(b) END SIM(DELETE(TRANSCRIPT)) ;

Figure 8.4 External-to-conceptual map of view V(Rext) in V(Rcon): (a) interpretation I(Rext;Rcon) of V(Rext) in V(Rcon); (b) SIM(DELETE(TRANSCRIPT)).

The reader can check that the execution of this (as well as the relational SQL above) on the database instance of Figure 1.2 results in placing

{ < 123456789, SEPT 2 1979 > }.

into workspace W. This instruction would also be generated for solution B.

As a second example, consider the deletion given in Example 8.1.5. The corresponding GCALC DML for it is

```
GET W (STUDNAME:1,DEPT:1,COURSE#:1,SEC#:1,
        TITLE:1,GRADE:1,CREDITS:1):
  TRANSCRIPT(123456789,STUDNAME:1,FALL,1979,
     DEPT:1,COURSE#:1,SEC#:1,TITLE:1,GRADE:1,CREDITS:1);
FOR i = 1 TO LENGTH (W);
 DO;
 DELETE(TRANSCRIPT)({ < 123456789,W(i).STUDNAME,
    FALL,1979,W(i).DEPT,W(i).COURSE#,
    W(i).SEC#,W(i),TITLE,W(i).GRADE,
    W(i).CREDITS > });
 END;
```

Note that the deletion operation is "high-level" in the sense that one command represents both a query and a deletion. The reader can check that the result of executing both the relational SQL command or the above on Figure 1.2 results in the deletion of Robert J. Smith's courses for the fall 1979 semester.

Interpreting the GCALC

At this point in the process we have translated the DML into equivalent GCALC DML. We next use the external-to-conceptual mapping to translate the calculus from the old to the new view. The details of this procedure were discussed in Section 2.3.

For example, the GCALC DML on V(Rcon) that corresponds to the query of Example 8.1.1 is given by

```
GET W (DECODE(ID#:1;),DECODE(STUDNAME:2;),DECODE
  (DATEADM:2;) :
  (E)STUDNAME:1...(E)DATEADM:1
   STUDENT(ID#:1,STUDNAME:1,BIRTHDATE:1,DATEADM:1)
& REGISTRAR(FALL,1979,MATH,103,SEC#:1,INSTRUCT:1,LOCAT:1,
       TIMES:1,ID#:1,B)
& CATALOGUE(MATH,103,TITLE:1,CREDITS:1,DESCR:1,
       PREDEPT:1,PRECOURSE#:1)
& STUDENT(ID#:1,STUDNAME:2,BIRTHDATE:2,DATEADM:2);
```

The reader can observe that the execution of the above on the new database instance of V(Rcon) given in Figure 2.2 also results in placing

{ < 123456789, SEPT 2 1979 > }

into W.

Also, recall the GCALC DML for the deletion. The corresponding instructions on V(Rcon) would be

```
GET W (DECODE(STUDNAME:1;),DECODE(DEPT:1;),
     ...,DECODE(CREDITS:1;) ):
  (E)BIRTHDATE:1...(E)PRECOURSE#:1
  STUDENT(123456789,STUDNAME:1,BIRTHDATE:1,DATEADM:1)
& REGISTRAR(FALL,1979,DEPT:1,COURSE#:1,SEC#:1,
  INSTRUCT:1,LOCAT:1,TIMES:1,123456789,GRADE:1)
& CATALOGUE(DEPT:1,COURSE#:1,TITLE:1,CREDITS:1,
  DESCR:1,PREDEPT:1,PRECOURSE#:1);
FOR i = 1 TO LENGTH(W);
 DO;
 SIM(DELETE(TRANSCRIPT))({ <CODE(123456789),
   CODE(W(i).STUDNAME), CODE(FALL),CODE(1979),
   CODE(W(i).DEPT),...,CODE(W(i).CREDITS)> };
END;
```

The reader can also check that the result of the execution of the above will remove from the REGISTRAR table all those rows that correspond to Robert J. Smith's courses during the fall 1979 semester. Hence, the corresponding induced old database will also have such rows removed from TRANSCRIPT.

Optimizing the GCALC

The objective of this stage is to replace the calculus operations by "smaller" but equivalent ones. The operation of reducing queries to ones with smaller formulas is referred to as "logical optimization" and will be considered in more depth in Section 8.3. In this section we simply illustrate the ideas that go into logical optimization.

Notice the translation of the query on V(Rcon) of Example 8.1.1 has two references to the STUDENT table. Since both use the same ID# value, it follows from constraint C(Rcon,1) that both of the rows are identical. Hence, one of them can be eliminated. This results in

```
GET W (DECODE(ID#:1;),DECODE(STUDNAME:1;),DECODE(DATEADM:1;) :
(E)SEC#:1...(E)PRECOURSE#:1
  STUDENT(ID#:1,STUDNAME:1,BIRTHDATE:1,DATEADM:1)
& REGISTRAR(FALL,1979,MATH,103,SEC#:1,INSTRUCT:1,LOCAT:1,
      TIMES:1,ID#:1,B)
& CATALOGUE(MATH,103,TITLE:1,CREDITS:1,DESCR:1,PREDEPT:1,
      PRECOURSE#:1)).
```

The reader can check that the result of execution of this query on Figure 2.2 also results in the placement of

{ <123456789, SEPT 2 1979> }

into W.

The query on V(Rcon) corresponding to the deletion of Example 8.1.5 cannot be made smaller (i.e., it cannot be logically optimized).

Converting to Relational SQL

At this point we take the optimized GCALC DML on the new database and compile it into the target DML for the new database. For an arbitrary DML, this reduces to showing that database logic GCALC DML can be translated into equivalent instructions in the DML. Alternatively, this reduces to being able to build database logic CGALC DML as a "front end" on top of the DML.

In our situation we have to compile GCALC for relational views back into relational SQL. As far as simulators are concerned, this is easy. All one has to do is to write the simulator in relational SQL instead of GCALC DML. The proof that relational GCALC queries can be converted to relational SQL will be left as an exercise.

For example, the relational SQL query corresponding to the query of Example 8.1.1 is

```
SET W
 SELECT UNIQUE DECODE(ID#),DECODE(STUDNAME),DECODE(DATEADM)
 FROM STUDENT,REGISTRAR,CATALOGUE
 WHERE STUDENT.ID# = REGISTRAR.STUDID
   AND SEMESTER = FALL
   AND YEAR = 1979
   AND REGISTRAR.DEPT = MATH
   AND CATALOGUE.DEPT = MATH
   AND REGISTRAR.COURSE# = 103
   AND CATALOGUE.COURSE# = 103;
```

The tables STUDENT, REGISTRAR, and CATALOGUE in the FROM clause represent the tables in the calculus query. The WHERE clause reflects the conditions that are given in the body of the calculus query. The reader can check that the execution of the above on the database of Figure 2.2 also results in placing

$$\{ < 123456789, \text{SEPT 2 1979} > \}$$

into W.

The relational SQL corresponding to the deletion of Example 8.1.5 is

```
SET W TO
 SELECT UNIQUE DECODE(STUDNAME),DECODE(DEPT),...,
      DECODE(CREDITS)
 FROM STUDENT,REGISTRAR,CATALOGUE
 WHERE STUDENT.ID# = 123456789
   AND SEMESTER = FALL
   AND YEAR = 1979
   AND STUDID = 123456789
```

```
    AND REGISTRAR.DEPT = CATALOGUE.DEPT
    AND REGISTRAR.COURSE# = CATALOGUE.COURSE#;
FOR i = 1 TO LENGTH(W);
 DO;
   SIM(DELETE(TRANSCRIPT))({ <CODE(123456789),
     CODE(W(i).STUDNAME), CODE(FALL),CODE(1979),
     CODE(W(i).DEPT),...,CODE(W(i).CREDITS)> };
 END;
```

Recall that the simulator SIM(DELETE(TRANSCRIPT)) is written in relational SQL as opposed to GCALC DML. The reader can check that the execution of the above would also result in the deletion of all of Robert J. Smith's courses for fall 1979 in V(Rcon) and hence in the induced external database.

Exercises

1. Convert the relational SQL query in Example 8.1.2 from V(Rext) to V(Rcon).
2. Convert the relational SQL query in Example 8.1.3 from V(Rext) to V(Rcon).
3. Convert the relational SQL insertion in Example 8.1.4 from V(Rext) to V(Rcon).
4. Convert the relational SQL update in Example 8.1.6 from V(Rext) to V(Rcon).
5. Show that every relational GCALC query of the form

   GET W(<R>):(E)<R'> p1 & p2 & ⋯ & pk (<R>,<R'>);

   can be translated into an equivalent relational SQL query.

8.2 HETEROGENEOUS GSQL CONVERSION

In this section we introduce the data manipulation language GSQL (Generalized SQL) which extends relational SQL to the heterogeneous case. We then show how to convert GSQL DML from an old databases to a new one. We illustrate the methodology using sample old and new heterogeneous databases.

Heterogeneous GSQL DML

Generalized SQL, GSQL, is a quasi-English data manipulation language used for heterogeneous databases. The format of GSQL is the same as relational SQL except that everywhere a "table" name appeared, a "cluster" may now appear. Since table names are special cases of clusters, it follows that relational SQL is a subset of GSQL. We will provide the reader with a brief introduction by way of examples on view V(Dext) of Figure 8.5.

```
V(Dext): VIEW DEFINITION
  S(Dext): SCHEMA DEFINITION
    TABLE TRANSCRIPT = (STUDID,STUDNAME,BIRTHDATE,DATEADM,RECORD)
    TABLE RECORD = (SEMESTER,YEAR,COURSES)
    TABLE COURSES = (DEPT,COURSE#,SEC#,TITLE,GRADE,CREDITS)

L(Dext): LANGUAGE DEFINITION
  T(Dext): TYPING DEFINITION
    TYPE SIDTPE = {STUDID} EBCDIC CHAR(9)
    TYPE NAMTPE = {STUDNAME} EBCDIC CHAR(20)
    TYPE DATPE = {BITRHDATE,DATEADM} EBCDIC CHAR(15)
    TYPE SEMTPE = {SEMESTER} EBCDIC CHAR(6)
    TYPE YRTPE = {YEAR} EBCDIC DEC(4)
    TYPE DEPTPE = {DEPT} EBCDIC CHAR(8)
    TYPE CS#TPE = {COURSE#} EBCDIC DEC(3)
    TYPE SEC#TPE = {SEC#} EBCDIC CHAR(10)
    TYPE TTLTPE = {TITLE} EBCDIC CHAR(25)
    TYPE GRDTPE = {GRADE} EBCDIC CHAR(1)
    TYPE CRDSTPE = {CREDITS} EBCDIC DEC(2)

    NONLOGICAL SYMBOLS DEFINITION
      PREDICATES
        TRANSCRIPT-RECORD-COURSES:
          (SIDTPE,NAMTPE,DATPE,DATPE,RECORD,SEMTPE,
          YRTPE,COURSES,DEPTPE,CS#TPE,SEC#TPE,TTLTPE,
          GRDTPE,CRDSTPE) FULL CLUSTER PREDICATE
        ≤: (YRTPE,YRTPE) PREDICATE
      FUNCTIONS
        TOTCREDITS:(SIDTPE,SEMTPE,YRTPE;
          CRDSTPE) FUNCTION

C(Dext): CONSTRAINTS DEFINITION
  C(Dext,1): CONSTRAINT TRANSCRIPT:
    STUDID → STUDNAME,BIRTHDATE,DATEADM,RECORD
  C(Dext,2):CONSTRAINT TRANSCRIPT-RECORD:
    SEMESTER,YEAR → COURSES
  C(Dext,3):CONSTRAINT TRANSCRIPT-RECORD-COURSES:
    DEPT,COURSE# → SEC#,TITLE,CREDITS,GRADE
```

Figure 8.5 Database logic DDL definition of view V(Dext).

Example 8.2.1.

Find the id#'s, names, and dates of admissions of all students who earned the grade of B in Math 103 during the fall 1979 semester.

Solution.

```
SET W TO
  SELECT UNIQUE STUDID,STUDNAME,DATEADM
  FROM TRANSCRIPT-RECORD-COURSES
```

```
WHERE SEMESTER = FALL
  AND YEAR = 1979
  AND DEPT = MATH
  AND COURSE# = 103
  AND GRADE = B;
```

This GSQL query results in a search through the TRANSCRIPT-RECORD-COURSES cluster to find instances where the SEMESTER, YEAR, DEPT, COURSE#, and GRADE components are FALL, 1979, MATH, 103 and B, respectively. For each such match, the STUDID, STUDNAME, and DATEADM values are extracted.

Example 8.2.2.

Find the id#'s and names of all the students who earned both a B in Computer Science 103 and Math 103 during the fall 1979 semester.

Solution A

```
SET W TO
 SELECT UNIQUE STUDID FIRST,STUDNAME FIRST
 FROM TRANSCRIPT-RECORD-COURSES FIRST,
    TRANSCRIPT-RECORD-COURSES SECOND
  WHERE SEMESTER FIRST = FALL
    AND YEAR FIRST = 1979
    AND DEPT FIRST = COMPSCI
    AND COURSE# FIRST = 103
    AND GRADE FIRST = B
    AND SEMESTER SECOND = FALL
    AND YEAR SECOND = 1979
    AND DEPT SECOND = MATH
    AND COURSE# SECOND = 103
    AND GRADE SECOND = B
    AND STUDID FIRST = STUDID SECOND;
```

This query requires two passes through the TRANSCRIPT-RECORD-COURSES cluster. One pass (through TRANSCRIPT-RECORD-COURSES FIRST) looks for COMPSCI 103; the second pass (through TRANSCRIPT-RECORD-COURSES SECOND) looks for MATH 103. For each match of STUDID, the STUDID and STUDNAME are extracted.

Solution B

```
SET W TO
 SELECT UNIQUE STUDID,STUDNAME
 FROM TRANSCRIPT-RECORD-COURSES
 WHERE SEMESTER = FALL
   AND YEAR = 1979
   AND DEPT = COMPSCI
   AND COURSE# = 103
   AND GRADE = B
```

```
AND STUDID IN
     SELECT STUDID
     FROM TRANSCRIPT-RECORD-COURSES
     WHERE SEMESTER = FALL
       AND YEAR = 1979
       AND DEPT = MATH
       AND COURSE# = 103
       AND GRADE = B;
```

Here, we are using nested subqueries. The result of execution is identical to that of solution A.

Example 8.2.3.

Find the names of all the students who earned a B either in Computer Science 103 or in Math 103.

Solution

```
SET W TO
 SELECT UNIQUE STUDNAME
 FROM TRANSCRIPT-RECORD-COURSES
 WHERE DEPT = COMPSCI
   AND COURSE# = 103
   AND GRADE = B
 UNION
 SELECT UNIQUE STUDNAME
 FROM TRANSCRIPT-RECORD-COURSES
 WHERE DEPT = MATH
   AND COURSE# = 103
   AND GRADE = B;
```

This is really two subqueries. The first looks for the COMPSCI 103 cluster; the second looks for the MATH 103 cluster.

In relational SQL, insertions, deletions, and updates are done in tables. In GSQL, insertion, deletions, and updates are also done in tables. However, clusters used in such instructions must uniquely identify a table at the lowest level. This is illustrated below.

Example 8.2.4.

Insert the information that Robert J. Smith took Biology 103 during the fall 1979 semester and earned the grade of B.

Solution

```
INSERT INTO TRANSCRIPT-RECORD-COURSES
   <BIO,103,001,INTRO,B,3>
WHERE STUDID = 123456789
  AND STUDNAME = ROBERT J. SMITH
  AND SEMESTER = FALL
  AND YEAR = 1979;
```

The cluster TRANSCRIPT-RECORD-COURSES indicates that an insertion is to be done in a COURSES table. This is because COURSES is the "lowest" part of the cluster path. The WHERE clause identifies the specific COURSES table in which the row is to be inserted.

Example 8.2.5.

Delete all information about the courses that Robert J. Smith, id# 123456789, took during the fall of 1979.

Solution

```
DELETE TRANSCRIPT-RECORD-COURSES
WHERE STUDID = 123456789
  AND SEMESTER = FALL
  AND YEAR = 1979;
```

The cluster TRANSCRIPT-RECORD-COURSES indicates that a deletion is to be performed in a COURSES table. The WHERE clause identifies the COURSES tables together with the rows that are to be deleted.

Example 8.2.6.

Change the grade that Mary T. Jones, id# 361258823, earned in Physics 102 during the spring of 1980 from whatever is recorded to a grade of A.

Solution

```
UPDATE TRANSCRIPT-RECORD-COURSES
SET GRADE = A
WHERE STUDID = 361258823
AND SEMESTER = SPRING
AND YEAR = 1980
AND DEPT = PHYSICS
AND COURSE# = 102;
```

The cluster TRANSCRIPT-RECORD-COURSES identifies that the update is to be done on a COURSES table. The WHERE command specifies the COURSES table and the rows that are to be updated. The SET command indicates the changes that are to occur to the rows found.

Conversion Methodology

Our methodology for converting GSQL DML from an old database to a new one is also comprised of four steps. First, we compile the old GSQL into equivalent GCALC DML. Second, we use an external-to-conceptual mapping of the old database view in the new database view to convert the GCALC DML to the new database. Third, we logically optimize the GCALC to smaller, but equivalent GCALC DML. Fourth, we compile the GCALC DML into equivalent GSQL DML on the new database. We illustrate the ideas below by converting GSQL from V(Dext) of Figure 8.5 to V(Dcon)

```
V(Dcon): VIEW DEFINITION
  S(Dcon): SCHEMA DEFINITION
    TABLE SYSTEM = (REGISTRAR,STUDINFO,CATALOGUE)
    TABLE REGISTRAR = (SEMESTER,YEAR,COURSE)
    TABLE COURSE = (DEPT,COURSE#,SECTION)
    TABLE SECTION = (SEC#,INSTRUCT,LOCAT,TIMES,STUDENT)
    TABLE STUDENT = (STUDID,STUDNAME,GRADE)
    TABLE STUDINFO = (ID#,STUDNAME,BIRTHDATE,DATEADM)
    TABLE CATALOGUE = (DEPT,COURSE#,TITLE,CREDITS,DESCR,LINK)
    TABLE LINK = (CATALOGUE)

  L(Dcon): LANGUAGE DEFINITION
    T(Dcon): TYPING DEFINITION
      TYPE SEMTPE = {SEMESTER} ASCII CHAR(8)
      TYPE YRTPE = {YEAR} ASCII DEC(4)
      TYPE DEPTPE = {DEPT} ASCII CHAR(10)
      TYPE CS#TPE = {COURSE#} ASCII DEC(3)
      TYPE TTLTPE = {TITLE} ASCII CHAR(25)
      TYPE CRDSTPE = {CREDITS} ASCII DEC(2)
      TYPE SEC#TPE = {SEC#} ASCII CHAR(10)
      TYPE NAMTPE = {STUDNAME} ASCII CHAR(20)
      TYPE LOCTPE = {LOCAT} ASCII CHAR(30)
      TYPE TIMTPE = {TIMES} ASCII CHAR(20)
      TYPE IDTPE = {STUDID,ID#} ASCII CHAR(9)
      TYPE GRDTPE = {GRADE} ASCII CHAR(1)
      TYPE DATPE = {BIRTHDATE,DATEADM} ASCII CHAR(15)
      TYPE DESCTPE = {DESCR} ASCII CHAR(50)

    NONLOGICAL SYMBOLS DEFINITION
      PREDICATES
        SYSTEM-REGISTRAR-COURSE-SECTION-STUDENT:
          (SEMTPE,YRTPE,COURSE,DEPTPE,CS#TPE,SECTION,
          SEC#TPE,NAMTPE,LOCTPE,TIMTPE,STUDENT,IDTPE,
          NAMTPE,GRDTPE) FULL CLUSTER PREDICATE

        SYSTEM-STUDINFO:
          (IDTPE,NAMTPE,DATPE,DATPE) PREDICATE

        SYSTEM-CATALOGUE-LINK-CATALOGUE:
          (DEPTPE,CS#TPE,TTLTPE,CRDSTPE,DESCTPE,LINK,
          CATALOGUE,DEPTPE,CS#TPE,TTLTPE,CRDSTPE,DESCTPE,
          LINK) PREDICATE

          ≤(YRTPE):(YRTPE,YRTPE) PREDICATE
      FUNCTIONS
        TOTALCREDITS:(IDTPE,SEMTPE,YRTPE;
          CRDSTPE) FUNCTION

  C(Dcon): CONSTRAINTS DEFINITION
    C(Dcon,1):CONSTRAINT SYSTEM-REGISTRAR:SEMESTER,
                YEAR → COURSE
```

Figure 8.6 *(cont. next page)*

(continued)

```
C(Dcon,2):CONSTRAINT SYSTEM-REGISTRAR-COURSE:
  SEMESTER,YEAR,DEPT,COURSE# → SECTION
C(Dcon,3):CONSTRAINT SYSTEM-REGISTRAR-COURSE-
  SECTION:SEMESTER,YEAR,DEPT,COURSE#,SEC#
  → INSTRUCT,LOCAT,TIMES,STUDENT
C(Dcon,4):CONSTRAINT SYSTEM-REGISTRAR-COURSE-
  SECTION-STUDENT:
  SEMESTER,YEAR,DEPT,COURSE#,SEC#,STUDID
  → STUDNAME,GRADE
C(Dcon,5):CONSTRAINT SYSTEM-STUDINFO:ID#
  → STUDNAME,BIRTHDATE,DATEADM
C(Con6):CONSTRAINT SYSTEM-CATALOGUE:DEPT,COURSE#
  → TITLE,CREDITS,DESCR,LINK
C(Dcon,7):CONSTRAINT SYSTEM-REGISTRAR-COURSE-
  SECTION-STUDENT:
  SEMESTER,YEAR,DEPT,COURSE#,STUDID → SEC#
```

Figure 8.6 Database logic DDL definition of view V(Dcon).

of Figure 8.6 using I(Dext;Dcon) of Figure 8.7a and SIM(DELETE(COURSES)) of Figure 8.7(b).

Converting to Calculus

As mentioned above, the first step in the conversion process is the compilation of the GSQL into GCALC DML. The precise details of this aspect would require a formal definition of GQBE in terms of generalized calculus which we do not consider in this book. In this section we relegate the presentation of this to illustrations. We refer the interested reader to [Cao and Jacobs] for further details.

For example, recall the solution to the query given in Example 8.2.2. The equivalent generalized calculus DML for it is given by the following.

```
GET W (STUDID:1,STUDNAME:1):
  (E)BIRTHDATE:1...(E)CREDITS:2
TRANSCRIPT-RECORD-COURSES
    (STUDID:1,STUDNAME:1,BIRTHDATE:1,DATEADM:1,
    RECORD:1,FALL,1979,COURSES:1,COMPSCI,103,
    SEC#:1,TITLE:1,B,CREDITS:1)
& TRANSCRIPT-RECORD-COURSES
    (STUDID:1,STUDNAME:2,BIRTHDATE:2,DATEADM:2,
    RECORD:2,FALL,1979,COURSES:2,MATH,103,
    SEC#:2,TITLE:2,B,CREDITS:2);.
```

The reader can check that the execution of both the GSQL query and the above on the database structure of Figure 1.9 results in placing

{ <123456789, ROBERT J. SMITH> }

into workspace W.

```
I(Dext;Dcon): INTERPRETATION DEFINITION
  EXTERNAL VIEW IS V(Dext) = <S(Dext),L(Dext),C(Dext)>
  CONCEPTUAL VIEW IS V(Dcon) = <S(Dcon),L(Dcon),C(Dcon)>

  CODING SECTION
    CODE FOR SIDTPE IS IDTPE;
    CODE FOR NAMTPE IS NAMTPE;
    CODE FOR DATPE  IS DATPE;
    CODE FOR SEMTPE IS SEMTPE;
    CODE FOR YRTPE  IS YRTPE;
    CODE FOR DEPTPE IS DEPTPE;
    CODE FOR CS#TPE IS CS#TPE;
    CODE FOR SEC#TPE IS SEC#TPE;
    CODE FOR TTLTPE IS TTLTPE;
    CODE FOR GRDTPE IS GRDTPE;
    CODE FOR CRDSTPE IS CRDSTPE;
    CODE FOR RECORD IS IDTPE;
    CODE FOR COURSES IS IDTPE,SEMTPE,YRTPE;

  DEFINING FORMULA SECTION

    PREDICATE:TRANSCRIPT-RECORD-COURSES
    ARGUMENTS ARE: (STUDID:1;,STUDNAME:1;,BIRTHDATE:1,
      DATEADM:1;,STUDID:1;,SEMESTER:1,YEAR:1;,
      STUDID:1,SEMESTER:1,YEAR:1;,DEPT:1;,
      COURSE#:1;,SEC#:1;,TITLE:1;,GRADE:1;,
      CREDITS:1;)
    IS DEFINED BY:(E)COURSE:1(E)SECTION:1
      (E)INSTRUCT:1(E)LOCAT:1(E)TIMES:1(E)STUDENT:1
      (E)LINK:1(E)DESCR:1
        SYSTEM-REGISTRAR-COURSE-SECTION-STUDENT
          (SEMESTER:1,YEAR:1,COURSE:1,DEPT:1,COURSE#:1,SECTION:1,
          SEC#:1,INSTRUCT:1,LOCAT:1,TIMES:1,STUDENT:1,
          STUDID:1,STUDNAME:1,GRADE:1)
    & SYSTEM-CATALOGUE(DEPT:1,COURSE#:1,TITLE:1,CREDITS:1,
          DESCR:1,LINK:1)
    & SYSTEM-STUDINFO(
          STUDID:1,STUDNAME:1,BIRTHDATE:1,DATEADM:1)

    PREDICATE:TRANSCRIPT
    ARGUMENTS ARE: (STUDID:1;,STUDNAME:1;,BIRTHDATE:1,
      DATEADM:1;,STUDID:1;)
    IS DEFINED BY:
      SYSTEM-STUDINFO
        (STUDID:1,STUDNAME:1,BIRTHDATE:1,DATEADM:1)

    PREDICATE: ≤
    ARGUMENTS ARE:(YEAR:1;,YEAR:2;)
    IS DEFINED BY: YEAR:1 ≤ YEAR:2

    PREDICATE: TOTCREDITS
    ARGUMENTS ARE: (ID#:1,SEMESTER:1,YEAR:1;,CREDITS:1;)
    IS DEFINED BY: TOTALCREDITS(ID#:1,SEMESTER:1,YEAR:1) = CREDITS:1
```

Figure 8.7 *(cont. next page)*

(continued)

```
        CONSTANT TRANSFORMATION SECTION
                  .
                  .
                  .
```

(a)

```
          PROC SIM(DELETE(COURSES))(CW);
            /* CW is a an array of codes where:
               CW(i).COURSES.STUDID
                             = an ASCII DEC(9) value (IDTPE),
               CW(i).COURSES.SEMESTER
                             = AN ASCII CHAR(6) value (SEMTPE)
        CW(i).COURSES.YEAR
                      = an ASCII DEC(4) value (YRTPE)
        CW(i).COURSES = a COURSES code

        CW(i).DEPT = a  DEPTPE code
                      = an ASCII CHAR(10) value (DEPTPE;),
        CW(i).COURSE# = a CS#TPE code
                      = an ASCII CHAR(3) value (CS#TPE;),
        CW(i).SEC#    = a SEC# code
                      = an ASCII DEC(3) value (SEC#;),
        CW(i).TITLE = a TTLTPE code
                      = an ASCII CHAR(25) value (TTLTPE;),
        CW(i).GRADE    = a GRDTPE code
                      = an ASCII CHAR(1) value (GRDTPE;),
        CW(i).CREDITS= a CRDSTPE code
                          = an ASCII DEC(2) value (CRDSTPE;),

i = 1,...,length(CW) */

      ESTABLISH CHECKPOINT;

  /* If the simulation should fail [e.g., the resultant conceptual database is
not a model of C(Dcon)], we can use this checkpoint to reestablish the old database
instance.*/

     FOR i = 1 TO LENGTH(CW);

  /* For each row of CW, perform the following operations.*/

  i = 1,...,length(CW) */

        ESTABLISH CHECKPOINT;

    /* If the simulation should fail [i.e., the resultant conceptual database is
not a model of C(Dcon)], we can use this checkpoint to reestablish the old database
instance.*/

        FOR i = 1 TO LENGTH(CW);
```

Figure 8.7 *(cont. next page)*

(continued)

```
   /* For each row of CW, perform the following operations.*/

         DELETE SYSTEM-REGISTRAR-SECTION-STUDENT,
         WHERE SEMESTER = CW(i).COURSES.SEMESTER
          AND  YEAR = CW(i).COURSES.YEAR
          AND  DEPT = CW(i).DEPT
          AND  COURSE# = CW(i).COURSE#
          AND  SEC# = CW(i).SEC#
          AND  STUDID = CW(i).COURSES.STUDID
          AND  GRADE = CW(i).GRADE

     END i;
   IF M(Dcon) |= C(Dcon) THEN RETURN;

 L1: RESTORE TO LAST CHECKPOINT;

 /* If the current conceptual database instance is a model of C(Dcon) then exit;
otherwise, roll back to the instance of the conceptual database prior to exec-
tuion.*/

(b)  END SIM(DELETE(COURSES)) ;
```

Figure 8.7 External-to-conceptual map of view V(Dext) in V(Dcon): (a) interpretation I(Dext;Dcon) of V(Dext) in V(Dcon); (b) SIM(DELETE(COURSES)).

As a second example, consider the deletion operation given in Example 8.2.5. The corresponding GCALC DML for it is given as follows.

```
GET W(COURSES:1,DEPT:1,COURSE#:1,SEC#:1,TITLE:1,
     GRADE:1,CREDITS:1):
  (E)STUDNAME:1...(E)RECORD:1
TRANSCRIPT-RECORD-COURSES
   (123456789,STUDNAME:1,BIRTHDATE:1,DATEADM:1,
    RECORD:1,FALL,1979,COURSES:1,DEPT:1,
    COURSE#:1,SEC#:1,TITLE:1,GRADE:1,
    CREDITS:1);
FOR i = 1 TO LENGTH(W);
    DO;
      DELETE(COURSES)({ <W(i).COURSES,W(i).DEPT,
           W(i).COURSE#,W(i).SEC#,W(i).TITLE,W(i).GRADE,
           W(i).CREDITS)> });
    END;
```

The execution of the GET instruction finds Robert J. Smith's COURSES table for fall 1979 plus all its rows. The execution of the loop results in the removal of these rows from the table. This has the identical effect as the corresponding GSQL DELETE command above.

Interpreting the GCALC

At this point in the process we have translated the DML into equivalent GCALC DML. We next use the external-to-conceptual mapping to translate the calculus from the old to the new database view. The method for doing this was discussed in Section 2.3.

For example, the generalized calculus on V(Dcon) that corresponds to the query of Example 8.2.2 is given by the following.

```
GET W (DECODE(STUDID:1),DECODE(STUDNAME:1)):
    (E)COURSE:1...(E)DATEADM:2
( SYSTEM-REGISTRAR-COURSE-SECTION-STUDENT
   (FALL,1979,COURSE:1,COMPSCI,103,SECTION:1,
   SEC#:1,INSTRUCT:1,LOCAT:1,TIMES:1,STUDENT:1,
   STUDID:1,STUDNAME:1,B)
& SYSTEM-CATALOGUE
     (COMPSCI,103,TITLE:1,CREDITS:1,DESCR:1,LINK:1)
& SYSTEM-STUDINFO
     (STUDID:1,STUDNAME:1,BIRTHDATE:1,DATEADM:1))
& ( SYSTEM-REGISTRAR-COURSE-SECTION-STUDENT
     (FALL,1979,COURSE:2,MATH,103,SECTION:2,
     SEC#:2,INSTRUCT:2,LOCAT:2,TIMES:2,STUDENT:2,STUDID:1,
     STUDNAME:2,B)
& SYSTEM-CATALOGUE
     (MATH,103,TITLE:2,CREDITS:2,DESCR:2,LINK:2)
& SYSTEM-STUDINFO
     (STUDID:1,STUDNAME:2,BIRTHDATE:2,DATEADM:2))
```

The reader can observe that the execution of the above on the instance of V(Dcon) in Figure 2.10 also results in placing

{ <123456789,ROBERT J SMITH> }

in workspace W.

Consider the GCALC DML for the deletion of Example 8.2.5. The corresponding instructions on V(Dcon) are given as follows:

```
GET W (DECODE(123456789,FALL,1979;),
      DECODE(DEPT:1;),DECODE(COURSE#:1;),
      DECODE(SEC#:1;),DECODE(TITLE:1;),
      DECODE(GRADE:1;),DECODE(CREDITS:1;) ):
(E)COURSE:1...(E)DATEADM:1
  SYSTEM-REGISTRAR-COURSE-SECTION-STUDENT
   (FALL,1979,COURSE:1,DEPT:1,COURSE#:1,SECTION:1,
   SEC#:1,INSTRUCT:1,LOCAT:1,TIMES:1,STUDENT:1,123456789,
   STUDNAME:1,GRADE:1)
& SYSTEM-CATALOGUE
     (DEPT:1,COURSE#:1,TITLE:1,CREDITS:1,DESCR:1,LINK:1)
```

```
& SYSTEM-STUDINFO
    (123456789,STUDNAME:1,BIRTHDATE:1,DATEADM:1);
FOR i = 1 TO LENGTH(W);
 DO;
  SIM(DELETE(COURSES))({ <CODE(123456789,FALL,1979;),
    CODE(W(i).DEPT),CODE(W(i).COURSE#),CODE(W(i).SEC#),
    CODE(W(i).TITLE),CODE(W(i).GRADE),CODE(W(i).CREDITS))> });
END;
```

The reader can also check that the result of the execution of the above will remove those rows in STUDENT tables which correspond to Robert J. Smith's courses during the fall 1979 semester. Hence, the corresponding induced old database will have all the rows removed from his fall 1979 COURSES table.

Optimizing the Calculus

In this stage we try to replace the database logic calculus DML with smaller but equivalent calculus. Precise details are given in Section 8.3. Here we just provide some illustrations.

Note the translation of the query on V(Dcon) of Example 8.2.2 has two references to the SYSTEM-STUDINFO cluster. Since both use the same STUDID# value (namely, STUDID:1), it follows from constraint C(Dcon,5) that the clusters are identical. Hence, one of them can be eliminated. At this point no other logical optimization can be performed.

However, suppose that in addition to the constraints C(Dcon), we added some more constraints. The first one says that every course appearing in the REGISTRAR cluster must also be in the CATALOGUE cluster, and vice versa. The second says that every student in the REGISTRAR cluster must also be in the STUDINFO table, and vice versa. This will be explained in more detail in the next section.

With these additions it would follow that the two SYSTEM-CATALOGUE clusters and the remaining SYSTEM-STUDINFO may be removed throughout and still remain logically equivalent. Hence, the result of the logical optimization of the query from Example 8.2.2 would be

```
GET W (DECODE(STUDID:1),DECODE(STUDNAME:1)):
  (E)COURSE:1(E)...(E)LINK:2
  SYSTEM-REGISTRAR-COURSE-SECTION-STUDENT
     (FALL,1979,COURSE:1,COMPSCI,103,SECTION:1,
     SEC#:1,INSTRUCT:1,LOCAT:1,TIMES:1,STUDENT:1,
     STUDID:1,STUDNAME:1,B)
& SYSTEM-REGISTRAR-COURSE-SECTION-STUDENT
     (FALL,1979,COURSE:1,MATH,103,SECTION:2,
     SEC#:2,INSTRUCT:2,LOCAT:2,TIMES:2,STUDENT:2,
     STUDID:1,STUDNAME:2,B);
```

If these were not added, however, the later reduction could not be done.

With the addition of the constraints above, the query corresponding to Example 8.2.5 can have its SYSTEM-STUDINFO predicate removed. Also, the extraneous decoding in the GET, followed by the coding, can be eliminated. The result of both optimizations yields the following.

```
GET W1(COURSES.STUDID:1,COURSES.SEMESTER:1,
     COURSES.YEAR:1,DEPT:1,COURSE#:1,
     SEC#:1,TITLE:1,GRADE:1,CREDITS:1):
(E)COURSE:1...(E)DATEADM:1
  SYSTEM-REGISTRAR-COURSE-SECTION-STUDENT
     (FALL,1979,COURSE:1,DEPT,COURSE#:1,
     SECTION:1,SEC#:1,INSTRUCT:1,LOCAT:1,
     TIMES:1,STUDENT:1,123456789,STUDNAME:1,
     GRADE:1)
& SYSTEM-CATALOGUE
     (DEPT:1,COURSE#:1,TITLE:1,CREDITS:1,
     DESCR:1,LINK:1)
FOR i = 1 TO LENGTH(W);
 DO;
 SIM(DELETE(COURSES))
   ({ <(123456789,FALL,1979;),W(i).DEPT,
       W(i).COURSE#,W(i).SEC#,W(i).TITLE,
       W(i).GRADE,W(i).CREDITS) > });
END;
```

The reader can check that the execution of the above on Figure 2.10 will remove those rows in STUDENT tables which correspond to Robert J. Smith's courses during the fall 1979 semester. Hence, the corresponding induced old database will be changed appropriately.

Converting to GSQL

In this stage we compile the GCALC DML instructions from the last part into equivalent GSQL also on view V(Dcon). The proof that GCALC DML can be converted into equivalent GSQL DML is left as an exercise for the reader.

For example, the GSQL corresponding to Examples 8.2.2 and 8.2.5 are given by

```
SET W TO
 SELECT UNIQUE DECODE(STUDID FIRST),DECODE(STUDNAME FIRST)
 FROM SYSTEM-REGISTRAR-COURSE-SECTION-STUDENT FIRST,
        SYSTEM-REGISTRAR-COURSE-SECTION-STUDENT SECOND
 WHERE SEMESTER FIRST = FALL
   AND YEAR FIRST = 1979
   AND DEPT FIRST = COMPSCI
   AND COURSE# FIRST = 103
   AND GRADE FIRST = B
   AND SEMESTER SECOND = FALL
   AND YEAR SECOND = 1979
```

```
AND DEPT SECOND = MATH
AND COURSE# SECOND = 103
AND GRADE SECOND = B
AND STUDID FIRST = STUDID SECOND;
```

and

```
SET W1 TO
 SELECT UNIQUE DECODE(STUDID,SEMESTER,YEAR;),DEPT FIRST,
      COURSE# FIRST,SEC#,TITLE,GRADE,CREDITS
 FROM SYSTEM-REGISTRAR-COURSE-SECTION,
        SYSTEM-CATALOGUE
 WHERE SEMESTER = FALL
   AND YEAR = 1979
   AND STUDID = 123456789
   AND DEPT FIRST = DEPT SECOND
   AND COURSE# FIRST = COURSE# SECOND ;
FOR i = 1 TO LENGTH(W);
DO;
 SIM(DELETE(COURSES))
  ({ <(W(i).STUDID,W(i).SEMESTER,W(i).YEAR;),W(i).DEPT,
  W(i).COURSE#,W(i).SEC#,W(i).TITLE,
  W(i).GRADE,W(i).CREDITS) > });
END;,
```

respectively. The reader is invited to check that the effect of execution of these correspond to the GCALC DML above on Figure 2.10.

Alternative Approach

Our approach to program conversion is to reduce the DML to GCALC DML, do the transformation there, and return to the original (or other) DML. An alternative approach would be to express the old-to-new mapping in the DML being converted. Then the conversion process might be accomplished by substituting the various definitions in the old queries.

For example, this method can be used to convert relational SQL from V(Rext) to V(Rcon) as follows. One could define the TRANSCRIPT table in V(Rext) by the following relational SQL operation

```
DEFINE TRANSCRIPT
 AS SELECT STUDID,STUDNAME,SEMESTER,YEAR,DEPT,
        COURSE#,SEC#,TITLE,GRADE,CREDIT
   FROM STUDENT,REGISTRAR,CATALOGUE
   WHERE STUDENT.STUDID = REGISTRAR.STUDID
     AND REGISTRAR.DEPT = CATALOGUE.DEPT
     AND REGISTRAR.COURSE# = CATALOGUE.COURSE# ;
```

on the tables of V(Rcon). Then any query on V(Rext) can be converted to V(Rcon) by just substituting this definition for TRANSCRIPT.

We choose not to take the latter approach for three reasons. First, all the theory that was developed for GCALC (e.g., logically implied constraints, solutions to the update problem, etc.) would have to be duplicated for each DML that we wish to convert. Second, our method is DML independent. Namely, no matter what the DML, the person responsible for conversion (i.e., the database admininstrator) need only learn how to construct external-to-conceptual mapping between database logic views. The compilation between the DML and GCALC DML is automatic. Third, our approach allows the situation where the original and the target DMLs are different.

Exercises

1. Convert the GSQL query in Example 8.2.1 from V(Dext) to V(Dcon).
2. Convert the GSQL query in Example 8.2.3 from V(Dext) to V(Dcon).
3. Convert the GSQL insertion in Example 8.2.4 from V(Dext) to V(Dcon).
4. Convert the GSQL update in Example 8.2.6 from V(Dext) to V(Dcon).
5. Show that every GCALC query of the form

$$\text{GET W}(<\text{R}>)\text{:(E)}<\text{R}'>\ \text{p1}\ \&\ \text{p2}\ \&\ \cdots\ \&\ \text{pk}\ (<\text{R}>,<\text{R}'>);$$

can be translated into an equivalent GSQL query.

8.3 LOGICAL OPTIMIZATION

In this section we examine the problem of logical optimization of GCALC queries. We describe a process that can be used to replace GCALC queries with "smaller" but logically equivalent GCALC queries.

Optimization Algorithm

Let V(D) = <S(D), L(D), C(D)> be a database view. The input to the optimization process is a query of the form

$$\begin{aligned}&\text{GET W}\ (<\text{R}>)\text{: Q}(<\text{R}>);\\ &= \text{GET W}\ (<\text{R}>)\text{: (E)}<\text{R}'>\ \text{p1}(<\text{R}>,<\text{c}>,<\text{R}'>)\\ &\qquad\qquad \&\ \cdots\ \&\ \text{pk}(<\text{R}>,<\text{c}>,<\text{R}'>);\end{aligned}$$

where the variables <R> are the free variables, <c> are constants in the language L(D), and <R′> are the existentially quantified variables. This sort of query, called an *existential conjunctive query,* is typical of most of the queries in this book. Each atom pi(-) is called a *conjunct.*

Optimization is performed by applying four rules to the wffs Q(<R>) of the queries. Rule 1 is used to shrink the wff; rules 2 to 4 are used to set up applications of rule 1. For each use of a rule, we get a new wff Q′(<R>), where

$$(*)\ \text{M} \models \text{Q}(<\text{e}>)\ \text{iff}\ \text{M} \models \text{Q}'(<\text{e}>)$$

for all models M(D) of V(D) and constants <e> of L(D). Consequently, their corresponding GCALC queries will yield the same results.

The rules are as follows.

1. Obtain Q′(<R>) from Q(<R>) by removing one occurrence of a subformula that is repeated as a conjunct.
2. Obtain Q′(<R>) from Q(<R>) by renaming some of the existentially quantified variables <R′> of Q(<R>) from either <R>, <R′> or <c>, and getting a wff Q′(<R>) which is comprised totally of conjuncts from the original Q(<R>).
3. Obtain Q′(<R>) from Q(<R>) by replacing variables or constant symbols that are seen to be equal according to some dependency constraint in C(D).
4. Obtain Q′(<R>) from Q(<R>) by replacing wffs that are equivalent according to some constraint in C(D).

The first and second rules satisfy the equivalence property (*) for arbitrary database structures of L(D). The third and fourth satisfy (*) for models of V(D). We leave these verifications as exercises. These rules will be illustrated throughout the remainder of the section.

Optimizing a Relational Query

Consider the following example from Section 8.1.

```
GET W (DECODE(ID#:1;),DECODE(NAME:1;),
     DECODE(DATEADM:1;) :
       (E)STUDNAME:1...(E)DATEADM:2
STUDENT(ID#:1,STUDNAME:1,BIRTHDATE:1,DATEADM:1)
& REGISTRAR(FALL,1979,MATH,103,SEC#:1,
      INSTRUCT:1,LOCAT:1,TIMES:1,ID#:1,B)
& CATALOGUE(MATH,103,TITLE:1,CREDITS:1,
      DESCR:1,PREDEPT:1,PRECOURSE#:1))
& STUDENT(ID#:1,STUDNAME:2,BIRTHDATE:2,DATEADM:2));
```

By rule 3, using the constraint C(Rcon,4)

STUDENT:ID# → STUDNAME,BIRTHDATE,DATEADM,

we can replace STUDNAME:2 with STUDNAME:1, BIRTHDATE:2 with BIRTHDATE:1 and DATEADM:2 with DATEADM:1. Thus we get

```
GET W (DECODE(ID#:1;),DECODE(NAME:1;),
     DECODE(DATEADM:1;) :
   (E)STUDNAME:1...(E)PRECOURSE#:1
   STUDENT(ID#:1,STUDNAME:1,BIRTHDATE:1,DATEADM:1)
& REGISTRAR(FALL,1979,MATH,103,SEC#:1,INSTRUCT:1,
     LOCAT:1,TIMES:1,ID#:1,B)
```

```
    & CATALOGUE(MATH,103,TITLE:1,CREDITS:1,DESCR:1,
        PREDEPT:1,PRECOURSE#:1))
    & STUDENT(ID#:1,STUDNAME:1,BIRTHDATE:1,DATEADM:1));
```

Since we have two identical STUDENT atoms, by rule 1, we can remove one of them.

```
    GET W (DECODE(ID#:1;),DECODE(NAME:1;),
        DECODE(DATEADM:1;) :
      (E)STUDNAME:1...(E)PRECOURSE#:1
      STUDENT(ID#:1,STUDNAME:1,BIRTHDATE:1,DATEADM:1)
    & REGISTRAR(FALL,1979,MATH,103,SEC#:1,INSTRUCT:1,
      LOCAT:1,TIMES:1,ID#:1,B)
    & CATALOGUE(MATH,103,TITLE:1,CREDITS:1,DESCR:1,
    PREDEPT:1,PRECOURSE#:1));
```

Since no further reductions can be made, our optimization process is finished.

Atomic versus Cluster Interpretations

Recall the definition of the cluster TRANSCRIPT-RECORD-COURSES.

```
    TRANSCRIPT-RECORD-COURSES
        (STUDID:1,STUDNAME:1,BIRTHDATE:1,DATEADM:1,
        RECORD:1,SEMESTER:1,YEAR:1,
        COURSES:1,DEPT:1,COURSE#:1,SEC#:1,TITLE:1,
        GRADE:1,CREDITS:1)
⟷ TRANSCRIPT(STUDID:1,STUDNAME:1,BIRTHDATE:1,
        DATEADM:1,RECORD:1)
    & RECORD:1(SEMESTER:1,YEAR:1,COURSES:1)
    & COURSES:1(DEPT:1,COURSE#:1,SEC#:1,TITLE:1,GRADE:1,CREDITS:1).
```

If we interpret the left side by the cluster interpretation and the right side by the atomic interpretations, we get two equivalent wffs. This is what we demonstrate here.

First, using I(Dext;Dcon) of Figure 8.7(a) and renaming variables, we interpret the left side, getting

```
    (E)COURSE:2...(E)LINK:2
    SYSTEM-STUDINFO
      (STUDID:1,STUDNAME:1,BIRTHDATE:1,DATEADM:1).
  & SYSTEM-REGISTRAR-COURSE-SECTION-STUDENT
      (SEMESTER:1,YEAR:1,COURSE:2,DEPT:1,COURSE#:1,SECTION:2,
      SEC#:1,INSTRUCT:2,LOCAT:2,TIMES:2,STUDENT:2,STUDID:1,
      STUDNAME:1,GRADE:1)
  & SYSTEM-CATALOGUE
      (DEPT:1,COURSE#:1,TITLE:1,CREDITS:1,DESCR:2,LINK:2).
```

Second, using I(Dext;Dcon) of Figure 2.11, we interpret the right side with variables renamed:

```
    [TRANSCRIPT interpretation]
  SYSTEM-STUDINFO
    (STUDID:1,STUDNAME:1,BIRTHDATE:1,DATEADM:1)

    [RECORD interpretation]
& (E)STUDNAME:2...(E)STUDENT:2
  SYSTEM-REGISTRAR-COURSE-SECTION-STUDENT
    (SEMESTER:1,YEAR:1,COURSE:2,DEPT:2,COURSE#:2,SECTION:2,
    SEC#:2,INSTRUCT:2,LOCAT:2,TIMES:2,STUDENT:2,STUDID:1,
    STUDNAME:2,GRADE:2)
& SYSTEM-STUDINFO
    (STUDID:1,STUDNAME:2,BIRTHDATE:2,DATEADM:2)

    [COURSES interpretation]
& (E)STUDNAME:3...(E)LINK:3
  SYSTEM-REGISTRAR-COURSE-SECTION-STUDENT
    (SEMESTER:1,YEAR:1,COURSE:3,DEPT:1,COURSE#:1,SECTION:3,
    SEC#:1,INSTRUCT:3,LOCAT:3,TIMES:3,STUDENT:3,STUDID:1,
    STUDNAME:3,GRADE:1)
& SYSTEM-CATALOGUE
    (DEPT:1,COURSE#:1,TITLE:1,CREDITS:1,DESCR:3,LINK:3)
& SYSTEM-STUDINFO
    (STUDID:1,STUDNAME:3,BIRTHDATE:3,DATEADM:3).
```

By moving all variables out, we get

```
  (E)STUDNAME:2...(E)LINK:3
   SYSTEM-STUDINFO
     (STUDID:1,STUDNAME:1,BIRTHDATE:1,DATEADM:1)
& SYSTEM-REGISTRAR-COURSE-SECTION-STUDENT
    (SEMESTER:1,YEAR:1,COURSE:2,DEPT:2,COURSE#:2,SECTION:2,
    SEC#:2,INSTRUCT:2,LOCAT:2,TIMES:2,STUDENT:2,STUDID:1,
    STUDNAME:2,GRADE:2)
& SYSTEM-STUDINFO
    (STUDID:1,STUDNAME:2,BIRTHDATE:2,DATEADM:2)
& SYSTEM-REGISTRAR-COURSE-SECTION-STUDENT
    (SEMESTER:1,YEAR:1,COURSE:3,DEPT:1,COURSE#:1,SECTION:3,
    SEC#:1,INSTRUCT:3,LOCAT:3,TIMES:3,STUDENT:3,STUDID:1,
    STUDNAME:3,GRADE:1)
& SYSTEM-CATALOGUE
    (DEPT:1,COURSE#:1,TITLE:1,CREDITS:1,DESCR:3,LINK:3)
& SYSTEM-STUDINFO
    (STUDID:1,STUDNAME:3,BIRTHDATE:3,DATEADM:3).
```

We can use rule 3 and C(Dcon,5)

SYSTEM-STUDINFO:STUDID → STUDNAME,BIRTHDATE,DATEADM

to identify STUDNAME:2, BIRTHDATE:2, and DATEADM:2 and STUDNAME:3, BIRTHDATE:3, and DATEADM:3 with STUDNAME:1, BIRTHDATE:1 and DATEADM:1. We then use rule 1 to shrink the wff. The result is

```
(E)STUDNAME:1...(E)DESCR:2
 SYSTEM-STUDINFO
    (STUDID:1,STUDNAME:1,BIRTHDATE:1,DATEADM:1)
& SYSTEM-REGISTRAR-COURSE-SECTION-STUDENT
      (SEMESTER:1,YEAR:1,COURSE:2,DEPT:2,COURSE#:2,SECTION:2,
      SEC#:2,INSTRUCT:2,LOCAT:2,TIMES:2,STUDENT:2,STUDID:1,
      STUDNAME:2,GRADE:2)
& SYSTEM-REGISTRAR-COURSE-SECTION-STUDENT
      (SEMESTER:1,YEAR:1,COURSE:3,DEPT:1,COURSE#:1,SECTION:3,
      SEC#:1,INSTRUCT:3,LOCAT:3,TIMES:3,STUDENT:3,STUDID:1,
      STUDNAME:3,GRADE:1)
& SYSTEM-CATALOGUE
      (DEPT:1,COURSE#:1,TITLE:1,CREDITS:1,DESCR:3,LINK:3).
```

We can use rules 2 and 1 to collapse the second SYSTEM-...-STUDENT onto the first. This is done by renaming the existentially quantified variables COURSE:3, SECTION:3, ..., GRADE:3. Following a renaming of the variables, the result is

```
  (E)STUDNAME:2...(E)LINK:2
  SYSTEM-STUDINFO
     (STUDID:1,STUDNAME:1,BIRTHDATE:1,DATEADM:1)
& SYSTEM-REGISTRAR-COURSE-SECTION-STUDENT
      (SEMESTER:1,YEAR:1,COURSE:2,DEPT:1,COURSE#:1,SECTION:2,
      SEC#:1,INSTRUCT:2,LOCAT:2,TIMES:2,STUDENT:2,STUDID:1,
      STUDNAME:2,GRADE:1)
& SYSTEM-CATALOGUE
      (DEPT:1,COURSE#:1,TITLE:1,CREDITS:1,DESCR:2,LINK:2),
```

which is the cluster interpretation.

The above also demonstrates the advantage of cluster interpretations over atomic ones. Namely, if the external programs use atoms, then the translation to the conceptual level may require logical optimization, sometimes a costly process. If, however, the external makes use of clusters, then the interpretation process may not require such optimization. Hence, the translation is "faster" using cluster interpretations.

Optimizing a Heterogeneous Query

Consider the following example from Section 8.2.

```
GET W (DECODE(STUDID:1),DECODE(STUDNAME:1)):
(E)COURSE:1...(E)DATEADM:2
( SYSTEM-REGISTRAR-COURSE-SECTION-STUDENT
    (FALL,1979,COURSE:1,COMPSCI,103,SECTION:1,
    SEC#:1,INSTRUCT:1,LOCAT:1,TIMES:1,STUDENT:1,
    STUDID:1,STUDNAME:1,B)
```

```
& SYSTEM-CATALOGUE
    (COMPSCI,103,TITLE:1,CREDITS:1,DESCR:1,LINK:1)
& SYSTEM-STUDINFO
    (STUDID:1,STUDNAME:1,BIRTHDATE:1,DATEADM:1))
& ( SYSTEM-REGISTRAR-COURSE-SECTION-STUDENT
      (FALL,1979,COURSE:2,MATH,103,SECTION:2,
      SEC#:2,INSTRUCT:2,LOCAT:2,TIMES:2,STUDENT:2,STUDID:1,
      STUDNAME:2,B)
& SYSTEM-CATALOGUE
    (MATH,103,TITLE:2,CREDITS:2,DESCR:2,LINK:2)
& SYSTEM-STUDINFO
    (STUDID:1,STUDNAME:2,BIRTHDATE:2,DATEADM:2));
```

Using C(Dcon,5)

SYSTEM-STUDINFO:STUDID →STUDNAME,BIRTHDATE,DATEADM

we can identify STUDNAME:2, BIRTHDATE:2, and DATEADM:2 with STUDNAME:1, BIRTHDATE:1, and DATEADM:1, respectively. Thus, an application of rule 3 followed by rule 1 results in

```
GET W (DECODE(STUDID:1),DECODE(STUDNAME:1)):
   (E)COURSE:1...(E)LINK:2
    SYSTEM-REGISTRAR-COURSE-SECTION-STUDENT
     (FALL,1979,COURSE:1,COMPSCI,103,SECTION:1,
      SEC#:1,INSTRUCT:1,LOCAT:1,TIMES:1,STUDENT:1,
      STUDID:1,STUDNAME:1,B)
& SYSTEM-CATALOGUE
    (COMPSCI,103,TITLE:1,CREDITS:1,DESCR:1,LINK:1)
& SYSTEM-STUDINFO
    (STUDID:1,STUDNAME:1,BIRTHDATE:1,DATEADM:1)
& ( SYSTEM-REGISTRAR-COURSE-SECTION-STUDENT
      (FALL,1979,COURSE:2,MATH,103,SECTION:2,
      SEC#:2,INSTRUCT:2,LOCAT:2,TIMES:2,STUDENT:2,STUDID:1,
      STUDNAME:1,B)
& SYSTEM-CATALOGUE
    (MATH,103,TITLE:2,CREDITS:2,DESCR:2,LINK:2);
```

Now suppose that we had extra axioms which stated that a DEPT, COURSE# was in SYSTEM-CATALOGUE if and only if it was in SYSTEM-REGISTRAR-COURSE. In formal database logic, these would be expressed as

```
SYSTEM-CATALOGUE
   (DEPT:1,COURSE#:1,TITLE:1,CREDITS:1,DESCR:1,LINK:1)
→ (E)SEMESTER:1(E)YEAR:1(E)COURSE:1(E)SECTION:1
SYSTEM-REGISTRAR-COURSE
   (SEMESTER:1,YEAR:1,COURSE:1,DEPT:1,COURSE#:1,
   SECTION:1)
```

and

```
SYSTEM-REGISTRAR-COURSE
   (SEMESTER:1,YEAR:1,COURSE:1,DEPT:1,COURSE#:1,SECTION:1)
→ (E)TITLE:1(E)CREDITS:1(E)DESCR:1(E)LINK:1
SYSTEM-CATALOGUE
   (DEPT:1,COURSE#:1,TITLE:1,CREDITS:1,DESCR:1,LINK:1).
```

By rule 4, we can change the query to

```
GET W (DECODE(STUDID:1),DECODE(STUDNAME:1)):
   (E)COURSE:1...(E)LINK:2
   SYSTEM-REGISTRAR-COURSE-SECTION-STUDENT
            (FALL,1979,COURSE:1,COMPSCI,103,SECTION:1,
             SEC#:1,INSTRUCT:1,LOCAT:1,TIMES:1,STUDENT:1,
             STUDID:1,STUDNAME:1,B)
   & (E)SEMESTER:3(E)YEAR:3(E)COURSE:3(E)SECTION:3
   SYSTEM-REGISTRAR-COURSE
            (SEMESTER:3,YEAR:3,COURSE:3,COMPSCI,103,SECTION:3)
   & SYSTEM-STUDINFO
            (STUDID:1,STUDNAME:1,BIRTHDATE:1,DATEADM:1))
   & SYSTEM-REGISTRAR-COURSE-SECTION-STUDENT
            (FALL,1979,COURSE:2,MATH,103,SECTION:2,
            SEC#:2,INSTRUCT:2,LOCAT:2,TIMES:2,STUDENT:2,STUDID:1,
            STUDNAME:1,B)
   & (E)SEMESTER:4(E)YEAR:4(E)COURSE:4(E)SECTION:4
     SYSTEM-REGISTRAR-COURSE
            (SEMESTER:4,YEAR:4,COURSE:4,MATH,103,SECTION:4);.
```

Remark. The second of the two wffs ensures that the replacment is reversible, hence providing wff equivalence. We leave this for the reader to verify.

We can use rule 2 and identify SEMESTER:3, YEAR:3, COURSE:3, and SECTION:3 with FALL, 1979, COURSE:1, and SECTION:1. Similarly, we can identify SEMESTER:4, YEAR:4 COURSE:4, and SECTION:4 with FALL, 1979, COURSE:2, and SECTION:2. Then using rule 1 we compact the wff. (Strictly speaking, we first expand the clusters, then apply rules 2 and 1, and then replace the cluster definitions by the cluster predicate.)

```
GET W (DECODE(STUDID:1),DECODE(STUDNAME:1)):
   (E)COURSE:1...(E)LINK:2
   SYSTEM-REGISTRAR-COURSE-SECTION-STUDENT
      (FALL,1979,COURSE:1,COMPSCI,103,SECTION:1,
      SEC#:1,INSTRUCT:1,LOCAT:1,TIMES:1,STUDENT:1,
      STUDID:1,STUDNAME:1,B)
& SYSTEM-STUDINFO
      (STUDID:1,STUDNAME:1,BIRTHDATE:1,DATEADM:1)
& SYSTEM-REGISTRAR-COURSE-SECTION-STUDENT
      (FALL,1979,COURSE:2,MATH,103,SECTION:2,
      SEC#:2,INSTRUCT:2,LOCAT:2,TIMES:2,STUDENT:2,STUDID:1,
      STUDNAME:1,B);
```

Suppose we also had the rule that a name appears in SYSTEM-REGISTRAR-COURSE-SECTION-STUDENT if and only if it is in STUDINFO. That is,

```
SYSTEM-STUDINFO
   (STUDID:1,STUDNAME:1,BIRTHDATE:1,DATEADM:1)
→(E)SEMESTER:1...(E)GRADE:1
SYSTEM-REGISTRAR-COURSE-SECTION-STUDENT
   (SEMESTER:1,YEAR:1,COURSE:1,DEPT:1,COURSE#:1SECTION:1,
   SEC#:1,INSTRUCT:1,LOCAT:1,TIMES:1,STUDENT:1,
   STUDID:1,STUDNAME:1,GRADE:1);
```

and vice versa. Then by rule 4, followed by rules 2 and 1, we have

```
GET W (DECODE(STUDID:1),DECODE(STUDNAME:1)):
   (E)COURSE:1...(E)LINK:2
   SYSTEM-REGISTRAR-COURSE-SECTION-STUDENT
      (FALL,1979,COURSE:1,COMPSCI,103,SECTION:1,
      SEC#:1,INSTRUCT:1,LOCAT:1,TIMES:1,STUDENT:1,
      STUDID:1,STUDNAME:1,B)
& SYSTEM-REGISTRAR-COURSE-SECTION-STUDENT
     (FALL,1979,COURSE:2,MATH,103,SECTION:2,
     SEC#:2,INSTRUCT:2,LOCAT:2,TIMES:2,STUDENT:2,STUDID:1,
     STUDNAME:1,B);
```

Finally, using rule 3 with constraint C(Dcon,1),

SYSTEM-REGISTRAR:SEMESTER,YEAR → COURSE,

we can identify COURSE:1 and COURSE:2, getting

```
GET W (DECODE(STUDID:1),DECODE(STUDNAME:1)):
   (E)COURSE:1...(E)LINK:2
   SYSTEM-REGISTRAR-COURSE-SECTION-STUDENT
    (FALL,1979,COURSE:1,COMPSCI,103,SECTION:1,
    SEC#:1,INSTRUCT:1,LOCAT:1,TIMES:1,STUDENT:1,
    STUDID:1,STUDNAME:1,B)
&  SYSTEM-REGISTRAR-COURSE-SECTION-STUDENT
    (FALL,1979,COURSE:2,MATH,103,SECTION:2,
    SEC#:2,INSTRUCT:2,LOCAT:2,TIMES:2,STUDENT:2,STUDID:1,
    STUDNAME:1,B);
```

This last step tells us that the two parts of the query have a branch (FALL, 1979, COURSE:1) in common. This information can be useful in planning the execution of the query.

Exercises

Translate the following from V(Rext) to V(Rcon) using I′ and logically optimize. Assume that C(Rcon) also has the constraints that a course is in REGISTRAR iff it is in CATALOGUE.

1. The solution to Example 8.1.2.
2. The solution to Example 8.1.3.

Translate the following from V(Dext) to V(Dcon) using I″ and logically optimize. Assume that V(Dcon) also has the constraints mentioned above.

3. The solution to Example 8.2.1.
4. The solution to Example 8.2.3 .

Show that property (*) holds following each applications of

5. Rule 1.
6. Rule 2.
7. Rule 3.
8. Rule 4.

8.4 RELATED READING

AHO, A. V., SAGIV, Y. AND ULLMAN, J. D., "Equivalences among Relational Expressions" *SIAM Journal of Computing,* **8** (2), 1979, pp. 218–246.

ASTRAHAN, M. M., et al., "System R: Relational Approach to Database Management," *ACM Transactions on Database Systems,* **1** (2), June 1976, pp. 97–137.

CAO, D., AND JACOBS, B. E., *On the Automatic Conversion of Generalized Structured English Data Manipulation Language,* Department of Computer Science Technical Report, University of Maryland, College Park, June 1983.

CHANDRA, A. K., AND MERLIN, P. M., "Optimal Implementation of Conjunctive Queries in Relational Databases," *Proceedings Ninth Annual ACM Symposium on Theory of Computing,* Bolder, Colo., May 1977, pp. 77–90.

HOUSEL, B.C., "A Unified Approach to Program and Data Conversion," *Proceedings Third International Conference on Very Large Databases,* ACM, New York, 1977, pp. 327–335.

JACOBS, B. E., *Applications of Database Logic to the Automatic Program Conversion Problem,* Department of Computer Science Technical Report TR-891, University of Maryland, College Park, March 1980.

SAGIV, Y., AND YANNAKAKIS, M., "Equivalences Among Relational Expressions With the Union and Difference Operations" *Journal of the ACM,* **4,** Oct. 1980, pp. 633–655.

SHNEIDERMAN, B., "A Framework for Automatic Conversion of Network Database Programs under Schema Transformation," *Proceedings Jerusalem Conference Information Technology,* North-Holland, Amsterdam, 1978.

SIBLEY, E.B., AND MERTEN, A.G., "Transferability and Translation of Programs and Data," *Information Systems, CONINS IV,* Plenum Press, New York, pp. 291–301.

SU, S.Y.W., "Application Program Conversion Due to Database Changes," *Proceedings of the Second International Conference on Very Large Databases,* Brussels, Belgium, Sept. 1976, pp. 143–158.

SU, S.Y.W., LAM, H., AND LO, D.H., "Transformation of Data Traversals and Operations in Application Programs to Account for Semantic Changes of Databases" *ACM Transactions on Database Systems,* **6** (2), June 1981, pp. 255–294.

TAYLOR, R., FRY, J., SHNEIDERMAN, B., SMITH, D., AND SU, S., "Database Program Conversion: A Framework for Research," *Proceedings of the Fifth International Conference on Very Large Databases,* Rio de Janeiro, Oct. 1979.

YAMAGUCHI, K. AND MERTEN, A.G., "Methodology for Transforming Programs and Data," *Proceedings ACM SIGFIDET Workshop on Data Description, Access and Control,* ACM, New York, 1974, pp. 141–156.

9

EXTERNAL AXIOMATIZATION

In Chapter 9 we investigate the external axiomatization problem. In Section 9.1 we study the problem for the relational case. In dealing with the problem we consider the related notions of implied constraint, onto, invertible, and faithful interpretations. We also look at the situation where the axioms are restricted to special classes of constraints. In Section 9.2 we study the problem for the heterogeneous case using a parallel approach. In Section 9.3 we prove the theorems that are used in the first two sections and show that database logic is different from first-order logic.

9.1 RELATIONAL CASE

In this section we study the external axiomatization problem for the relational case. We will illustrate the ideas using V(Rext) of Figure 9.1, V(Rcon) of Figure 9.2 and I′ = I(Rext;Rcon) of Figure 9.3. Notice that we added to V(Rext) and V(Rcon) extra constraints [i.e., C(Rext,5)-C(Rext,6) and C(Rcon,6)-C(Rcon,9)]. Before we investigate external axiomatization, we first look at the implied constraint problem.

Implied Constraint Problem

Let V(E) = <S(E), L(E), C(E)> and V(C) = <S(C), L(C), C(C)> denote external and conceptual relational views and let I be an interpretation of L(E) in L(C).

Definition. A closed wff Q of L(E) is called an *implied constraint of* V(C) *with respect to* I if for all relational structures M(C) of L(C),

$$M(C) \models C(C) \text{ implies } I[M(C)] \models Q.$$

```
V(Rext): VIEW DEFINITION
  S(Rext): SCHEMA DEFINITION
    TABLE TRANSCRIPT = (STUDID,STUDNAME,SEMESTER,YEAR,DEPT,
     COURSE#,SEC#,TITLE,GRADE,CREDITS)
    TABLE STUDENT = (ID#,NAME,DATEADM)

  L(Rext): LANGUAGE DEFINITION
  T(Rext): TYPING DEFINITION
    TYPE SIDTPE = {ID#,STUDID} EBCDIC CHAR(9)
    TYPE NAMTPE = {NAME,STUDNAME} EBCDIC CHAR(20)
    TYPE DATPE = {DATEADM} EBCDIC CHAR(15)
    TYPE SEMTPE = {SEMESTER} EBCDIC CHAR(8)
    TYPE YRTPE = {YEAR} EBCDIC DEC(4)
    TYPE DEPTPE = {DEPT} EBCDIC CHAR(8)
    TYPE CS#TPE = {COURSE#} EBCDIC DEC(4)
    TYPE SEC#TPE = {SEC#} EBCDIC CHAR(10)
    TYPE TTLTPE = {TITLE} EBCDIC CHAR(25)
    TYPE GRDTPE = {GRADE} EBCDIC CHAR(1)
    TYPE CRDSTPE = {CREDITS} EBCDIC DEC(2)

    NONLOGICAL SYMBOLS DEFINITION
      PREDICATES
        TRANSCRIPT:(SIDTPE,NAMTPE,SEMTPE,YRTPE,
          DEPTPE,CS#TPE,SEC#TPE,TTLTPE,GRDTPE,
          CRDSTPE) PREDICATE
        STUDENT: (SIDTPE,NAMTPE,DATPE)
                          PREDICATE
        ≤:(YRTPE,YRTPE) PREDICATE
      FUNCTIONS
        TOTCREDITS:(SIDTPE,SEMTPE,YRTPE;
          CRDSTPE) FUNCTION

C(Rext): CONSTRAINTS DEFINITION
  C(Rext,1):CONSTRAINT TRANSCRIPT:STUDID,
    SEMESTER,YEAR,DEPT,COURSE#,SEC#
    → STUDNAME,TITLE,GRADE,CREDITS
  C(Rext,2):CONSTRAINT TRANSCRIPT:STUDID → STUDNAME
  C(Rext,3):CONSTRAINT TRANSCRIPT:DEPT,COURSE#
    → TITLE,CREDITS
  C(Rext,4):CONSTRAINT STUDENT:ID# → NAME,DATEADM
  C(Rext,5):CONSTRAINT
    STUDENT(ID#:1,NAME:1,DATEADM:1)
    → (E)SEMESTER:1...(E)CREDITS:1
    TRANSCRIPT(ID#:1,NAME:1,SEMESTER:1,YEAR:1,DEPT:1,
    COURSE#:1,SEC#:1,TITLE:1,GRADE:1,CREDITS)
  C(Rext,6):CONSTRAINT
    TRANSCRIPT(ID#:1,NAME:1,SEMESTER:1,YEAR:1,DEPT:1,
    COURSE#:1,SEC#:1,TITLE:1,GRADE:1,CREDITS)
    → (E)DATEADM:1
    STUDENT(ID#:1,NAME:1,DATEADM:1)
```

Figure 9.1 Database logic DDL definition of view V(Rext).

```
V(Rcon): VIEW DEFINITION
  S(Rcon): SCHEMA DEFINITION
    TABLE STUDENT = (ID#,STUDNAME,BIRTHDATE,DATEADM)
    TABLE REGISTRAR = (SEMESTER,YEAR,DEPT,COURSE#,
      SEC#,INSTRUCT,LOCAT,TIMES,STUDID,GRADE)
    TABLE CATALOGUE = (DEPT,COURSE#,TITLE,CREDITS,
      DESCR,PREDEPT,PRECOURSE#)

  L(Rcon): LANGUAGE DEFINITION
    T(Rcon): TYPING DEFINITION
      TYPE IDTPE = {ID#,STUDID} ASCII CHAR(9)
      TYPE NAMTPE = {STUDNAME,INSTRUCT} ASCII CHAR(20)
      TYPE DATPE = {BIRTHDATE,DATEADM} ASCII CHAR(15)
      TYPE SEMTPE = {SEMESTER} ASCII CAHR(8)
      TYPE YRTPE = {YEAR} ASCII DEC(4)
      TYPE DEPTPE = {DEPT,PREDEPT} ASCII CHAR(10)
      TYPE CS#TPE = {COURSE#,PRECOURSE#} ASCII DEC(3)
      TYPE SEC#TPE = {SEC#} ASCII CHAR(3)
      TYPE LOCTPE = {LOCAT} ASCII CHAR(30)
      TYPE TIMTPE = {TIMES} ASCII CHAR(20)
      TYPE GRDTPE = {GRADE} ASCII CHAR(1)
      TYPE TTLTPE = {TITLE} ASCII CHAR(25)
      TYPE CRDSTPE = {CREDITS} ASCII DEC(2)
      TYPE DESCR = {DESCR} ASCII CHAR(50)

      NONLOGICAL SYMBOLS DEFINITION
        PREDICATES
        STUDENT: (IDTPE,NAMTPE,DATPE,DATPE)PREDICATE
        REGISTRAR: (SEMTPE,YRTPE,DEPTPE,CS#TPE,
          SEC#TPE,NAMTPE,LOCTPE,TIMTPE,SIDTPE,
          GRDTPE) PREDICATE
        CATALOGUE: (DEPTPE,CS#TPE,TTLTPE,CRDSTPE,
          DESCTPE,DEPTPE,CS#TPE) PREDICATE
        ≤: (YRTPE,YRTPE) PREDICATE
        FUNCTIONS
        TOTALCREDITS:(IDTPE,SEMTPE,YRTPE;
          CRDSTPE) FUNCTION

C(Rcon): CONSTRAINTS DEFINITION
   C(Rcon,1):CONSTRAINT STUDENT: ID# → STUDNAME,
     BIRTHDATE,DATEADM
   C(Rcon,2):CONSTRAINT REGISTRAR:SEMESTER,YEAR,DEPT,
     COURSE#,SEC# → INSTRUCT,LOCAT,TIMES
   C(Rcon,3):CONSTRAINT REGISTRAR:SEMESTER,YEAR,DEPT,
     COURSE#,SEC#,STUDID → GRADE
   C(Rcon,4):CONSTRAINT CATALOGUE:DEPT,COURSE# →
     TITLE,CREDITS,DESCR
   C(Rcon,5):CONSTRAINT REGISTRAR:SEMESTER,YEAR,DEPT
     COURSE#,STUDID → SEC#
```

Figure 9.2 *(cont. next page)*

(continued)

```
C(Rcon,6):CONSTRAINT
  STUDENT(STUDID:1,STUDNAME:1,BIRTHDATE:1,DATEADM:1)
  → (E)SEMESTER:1...(E)CREDITS:1
  & REGISTRAR(SEMESTER:1,YEAR:1,DEPT:1,COURSE#:1,SEC#:1,
  INSTRUCT:1, LOCAT:1,TIMES:1, STUDID:1,GRADE:1)
C(Rcon,7):CONSTRAINT
  REGISTRAR(SEMESTER:1,YEAR:1,DEPT:1,COURSE#:1,SEC#:1,
  INSTRUCT:1, LOCAT:1,TIMES:1, STUDID:1,GRADE:1)
    → (E)DATEADM:1
  STUDENT(STUDID:1,STUDNAME:1,BIRTHDATE:1,DATEADM:1)
C(Rcon,8):CONSTRAINT
  CATALOGUE(DEPT:1,COURSE#:1,TITLE:1,CREDITS:1,
    DESCR:1,PREDEPT:1,PRECOURSE:1)
    → (E)STUDID:1...(E)GRADE:1
    REGISTRAR(SEMESTER:1,YEAR:1,DEPT:1,COURSE#:1,SEC#:1,
     INSTRUCT:1, LOCAT:1,TIMES:1, STUDID:1,GRADE:1)
C(Rcon,9):CONSTRAINT
  REGISTRAR(SEMESTER:1,YEAR:1,DEPT:1,COURSE#:1,SEC#:1,
    INSTRUCT:1, LOCAT:1,TIMES:1, STUDID:1,GRADE:1)
    → (E)DESCR:1(E)PREDEPT:1(E)PRECOURSE#:1
    CATALOGUE(DEPT:1,COURSE#:1,TITLE:1,CREDITS:1,
    DESCR:1,PREDEPT:1,PRECOURSE:1)
```

Figure 9.2 Database logic DDL definition of view V(Rcon).

That is, Q is an implied constraint if Q is true on all external databases induced from models of V(C) via I.

For example,

C(Rext,3): CONSTRAINT TRANSCRIPT:DEPT,COURSE#
→ TITLE,CREDITS

of V(Rext) is an implied constraint of V(Rcon) with respect to I′. This is because for any relational structure M(Rcon) that is a model of V(Rcon),

C(Rcon,4): CONSTRAINT CATALOGUE:DEPT,COURSE#
→ TITLE,CREDITS,DESCR

is always true. Thus, any DEPT, COURSE# in CATALOGUE in M(Rcon) uniquely determines its TITLE, CREDITS, and DESCR. But by the details of the interpretation I′ in Figure 9.3, rows that are in TRANSCRIPT all have their DEPT, COURSE#, TITLE, CREDITS and DESCR from CATALOGUE. Consequently,

$$I'[M(Rcon)] \models \text{TRANSCRIPT:DEPT,COURSE\#} \rightarrow \text{TITLE,CREDITS}$$

and C(Rext,3) is an implied constraint.

Definition. The *implied constraint problem* is to determine, given a wff Q of L(E) and an interpretation I of L(E) in L(C), whether or not Q is an implied constraint of V(C) with respect to I.

```
I(Rext;Rcon): INTERPRETATION DEFINITION
  EXTERNAL VIEW IS V(Rext) = <S(Rext),L(Rext),C(Rext)>
  CONCEPTUAL VIEW IS V(Rcon) = <S(Rcon),L(Rcon),C(Rcon)>

  CODING SECTION
    CODE FOR SIDTPE IS IDTPE;
    CODE FOR NAMTPE IS NAMTPE;
    CODE FOR DATPE  IS DATPE;
    CODE FOR SEMTPE IS SEMTPE;
    CODE FOR YRTPE  IS YRTPE;
    CODE FOR DEPTPE IS DEPTPE;
    CODE FOR CS#TPE IS CS#TPE;
    CODE FOR SEC#TPE IS SEC#TPE;
    CODE FOR TTLTPE IS TTLTPE;
    CODE FOR GRDTPE IS GRDTPE;
    CODE FOR CRDSTPE IS CRDSTPE;

  DEFINING FORMULA SECTION
    PREDICATE: TRANSCRIPT
    ARGUMENTS ARE: (STUDID:1;,STUDNAME:1;,
      SEMESTER:1;,YEAR:1;,DEPT:1;,COURSE#:1;,SEC#:1;,
      TITLE:1;,GRADE:1;,CREDITS:1;)
    IS DEFINED BY:(E)BIRTHDATE:1(E)DATEADM:1
      (E)INSTRUCT:1(E)LOCAT:1(E)TIMES:1(E)DESCR:1
      (E)PREDEPT:1(E)PRECOURSE#:1
        STUDENT(STUDID:1,STUDNAME:1,BIRTHDATE:1,DATEADM:1)
      & REGISTRAR(SEMESTER:1,YEAR:1,DEPT:1,COURSE#:1,
          SEC#:1,INSTRUCT:1,LOCAT:1,TIMES:1,STUDID:1,GRADE:1)
      & CATALOGUE(DEPT:1,COURSE#:1,TITLE:1,CREDITS:1,DESCR:1,
          PREDEPT:1,PRECOURSE#:1)

    PREDICATE: STUDENT
    ARGUMENTS ARE: (ID#:1;,NAME:1;,DATEADM:1;)
    IS DEFINED BY:(E) BIRTHDATE:1
      STUDENT(ID#:1,NAME:1,BIRTHDATE:1,DATEADM:1)

    PREDICATE: ≤
    ARGUMENTS ARE:(YEAR:1;,YEAR:2;)
    IS DEFINED BY: YEAR:1 ≤ YEAR:2

    FUNCTION: TOTCREDITS
    ARGUMENTS ARE: (ID#:1;,SEMESTER:1;,YEAR:1;,CREDITS:1;)
    IS DEFINED BY: TOTALCREDITS(ID#:1,SEMESTER:1,
      YEAR:1) = CREDITS:1

  CONSTANT TRANSFORMATION SECTION
                •
                •
                •
```

Figure 9.3 Interpretation I(Rext;Rcon).

The following gives a more syntactic characterization for implied constraints.

Theorem 9.1.1. *A closed wff* Q *of* L(E) *is an implied constraint of* V(C) *with respect to* I *if and only if* C(C) ⊨ I(Q) *in* L(C).

That is, a wff is an implied constraint if and only if its interpretation is a logical consequence [in L(C)] of the constraints in C(C). The proof of Theorem 9.1.1 will be given in Section 9.3.

For example, recall

C(Rext,3) CONSTRAINT TRANSCRIPT:DEPT,COURSE#
→ TITLE,CREDITS

above. In the language L(Rext), this is

(TRANSCRIPT(STUDID:1,STUDNAME:1,SEMESTER:1,
YEAR:1,DEPT:1, COURSE#:1,SEC#:1,TITLE:1,
GRADE:1,CREDITS:1)
& TRANSCRIPT(STUDID:2,STUDNAME:2,SEMESTER:2,
YEAR:2,DEPT:1,COURSE#:1,SEC#:2,TITLE:2,
GRADE:2,CREDITS:2))
→ (TITLE:1 = TITLE:2 & CREDITS:1 = CREDITS:2) .

Interpreting this in I′, we have

I′(C(Rext,3))
= (((E)BIRTHDATE:1...(E)PRECOURSE#:1
STUDENT(STUDID:1,STUDNAME:1,BIRTHDATE:1,DATEADM:1)
& REGISTRAR(SEMESTER:1,YEAR:1,DEPT:1,COURSE#:1,
SEC#:1,INSTRUCT:1,LOCAT:1,TIMES:1,STUDID:1,GRADE:1)
& CATALOGUE(DEPT:1,COURSE#:1,TITLE:1,CREDITS:1,
DESCR:1,PREDEPT:1,PRECOURSE#:1))
& ((E)BIRTHDATE:2...(E)PRECOURSE#:2
STUDENT(STUDID:2,STUDNAME:2,BIRTHDATE:2,DATEADM:2)
& REGISTRAR(SEMESTER:2,YEAR:2,DEPT:1,COURSE#:1,
SEC#:2,INSTRUCT:2,LOCAT:2,TIMES:2,STUDID:2,GRADE:2)
& CATALOGUE(DEPT:1,COURSE#:1,TITLE:2,CREDITS:2,
DESCR:2,PREDEPT:2,PRECOURSE#:2)))
→ (TITLE:1 = TITLE:2 & CREDITS:1 = CREDITS:2),

which is clearly a logical consequence of constraint C(Rcon,4) in L(Rcon).

The reader can check that every constraint in V(Rext) is an implied constraint of V(Rcon) with respect to I′. This was required for the construction of interpretation I′ of view V(Rext) in view V(Rcon). Hence, in the definition in Section 2.1 of interpretation of relational view V(E) in V(C), the condition can be restated as saying that every Q in C(E) is an implied constraint of V(C) with respect to I(E;C).

As a second example, consider the constraint

STUDENT: NAME → ID#,DATEADM

on S(Rext). In the language L(Rext), this is

(STUDENT(ID#:1,NAME:1,DATEADM:1)
& STUDENT(ID#:2,NAME:1,DATEADM:2))
→ (ID#:1 = ID#:2 & DATEADM:1 = DATEADM:2).

Interpreting this in I′, we have

((E) BIRTHDATE:1
STUDENT(STUDID:1,STUDNAME:1,BIRTHDATE:1,DATEADM:1)
& (E) BIRTHDATE:2
STUDENT(STUDID:2,STUDNAME:1,BIRTHDATE:2,DATEADM:2))
→ (STUDID:1 = STUDID:2 & DATEADM:1 = DATEADM:2).

However, it is easy to find a model for V(Rcon) for which this wff is false. For instance, take an M(Rcon) that has only two rows in STUDENT, where each has the same name but has different STUDIDs or DATEADMs. Thus, the wff is not a logical consequence of V(Rcon); hence, by Theorem 9.1.1, Q is not an implied constraint of V(Rcon) with respect to I′.

The question of deciding whether or not a constraint is implied is now reduced to deciding if a wff is a logical consequence of a set of wffs. The latter problem is known as the *decision problem for first-order logic.* A classic result of Godel [see Shoenfield] tells us that the decision problem for first-order logic is *not solvable.* That is, there is no algorithm for deciding whether or not logical consequence between sets of first-order wffs holds. Hence, the implied constraint problem is also not solvable. (We leave this last remark as an exercise.)

However, although the decision problem is, in general, not solvable, there are special cases for which it is solvable. These cases are defined by the quantificational structure of the wffs involved. A survey of the known solvable cases of the decision problem for first-order logic is given in [Dreben and Goldfarb]. Consequently, the solvable cases of the decision problem for first-order logic lead to solvable cases of the implied constraint problem. The latter are considered in [Jacobs, Aronson and Klug].

External Axiomatization Problem

Let V(C) = <S(C), L(C), C(C)> be a relational view, S(E), L(E) a relational schema and language, and I an interpretation of relational language L(E) in L(C).

Definition. A set of wffs C*(E) of L(E) is called an *external axiomatization for* V(C) *and* I if

$$\{ \text{I[M(C)]} \mid \text{M(C)} \models \text{C(C)} \} = \{ \text{M(E)} \mid \text{M(E)} \models \text{C*(E)} \}.$$

That is, C*(E) is a set of wffs of L(E) that completely characterizes the class of external databases obtained from models of V(C) via I.

Definition. The *external axiomatization problem for* V(C) *and* I is that of determining whether or not such an external axiomatization exists, and if so, finding it.

Let V(C), S(E), L(E), and I be as above. Define

$$\text{Co(E)} = \{\text{Q in L(E)} \mid \text{C(C)} \models \text{I(Q) in L(C)}\}.$$

That is, Co(E) is the set of all wffs of L(E) whose interpretations under I are logical consequences of the constraints C(C) in L(C). By Theorem 9.1.1, Co(E) consists of all the implied constraints of V(C) with respect to I.

We show below that whenever an axiomatization exists, it must be equivalent to Co(E). First, a preliminary result is needed.

Claim 9.1.2. Let V(C), S(E), L(E), and I be as above. Let

$$\text{Vo(E)} = <\text{S(E),L(E),Co(E)} >.$$

That is, Vo(E) is the view with S(E) and L(E) whose axioms are the set of all implied constraints of V(C) with respect to I. Then I is an interpretation of view Vo(E) in view V(C).

Proof. We must show that for all Q in Co(E), C(C) $\models$ I(Q) in L(C). But this immediately follows from the definition of Co(E).

We now show that if an external axiomatization exists, then it is equivalent to Co(E).

Theorem 9.1.3. *Let* V(C), S(E), L(E), *and* I *be as above. Suppose that there is an axiomatization* C*(E) *of* L *for*

$$\{\text{I[M(C)]} \quad \mid \text{M(C)} \models \text{C(C)}\}.$$

Then

$$\{\text{M(E)} \mid \text{M(E)} \models \text{C*(E)}\} = \{\text{M(E)} \mid \text{M(E)} \models \text{Co(E)}\}.$$

Proof. Let Vo(E) = <S(E), L(E), Co(E)>; that is, Vo(E) is the external view whose constraints are Co(E). We show that for all Q in L(E),

$$\text{C*(E)} \models \text{Q iff Co(E)} \models \text{Q}.$$

It then follows that since C*(E) and Co(E) have the same logical consequences, they must have the same models M(E).

Suppose that C*(E) $\not\models$ Q. We have to show that Co(E) $\not\models$ Q. Then there is an M(E) where M(E) $\models$ C*(E) but M(E) $\not\models$ Q. Since C*(E) axiomatizes the external databases of V(C) with respect to I, there is an M(C) where M(C) $\models$ C(C) and I[M(C)] $\not\models$ Q. Since I is an interpretation of Vo(E) in V(C), M(C) $\models$ I(Co(E)) (Claim 9.1.2). By the Flipper Theorem, I[M(C)] $\models$ Co(E) and above I[M(C)] $\not\models$ Q. Hence, Co(E) $\not\models$ Q.

Suppose that C*(E) $\models$ Q. We have to show that Co(E) $\models$ Q. By definition of logical consequence, for M(E) of L(E), M(E) $\models$ C*(E) implies that M(E) $\models$ Q. Since C*(E) axiomatizes the external databases of V(C) with respect to I, for all M(C) of L(C), M(C) $\models$ C(C) implies that I[M(C)] $\models$ Q. By the Flipper Theorem, for all M(C) of L(C), M(C) $\models$ C(C) implies that M(C) $\models$ I(Q). Hence, Q is in Co(E), and thus Co(E) $\models$ Q.

To recap, what Theorem 9.1.3 means is that if an external axiomatization exists, then it is equivalent to the set of all implied constraints. We will show below that in the case of finite relational databases (i.e., relational databases with a finite universe U), external axiomatizations always exists.

Onto Interpretations

Let V(E) = <S(E), L(E), C(E)> and V(C) = <S(C), L(C), C(C)> be two relational views and I an interpretation of view V(E) in V(C). By Theorem 2.1.2, the inducing map I[M(C)] maps the class of models of V(C) into the class of models of V(E).

Definition. Interpretation I of V(E) in V(C) is called an *onto* interpretation if

$$\{I[M(C)] \mid M(C) \models C(C)\} = \{M(E) \mid M(E) \models C(E)\}.$$

That is, I is an onto interpretation of V(E) in V(C) if not only is the inducing map into, but it is also *onto* the class of models of C(E).

Onto interpretations are related to the external axiomatization problem. For if I is an onto interpretation, then the external constraints C(E) form an external axiomatization. In the following, we study two properties- "invertibility" and "faithfulness" which can be used to demonstrate ontoness and consequently, external axiomatizability.

Theorem 9.1.4. *Let* V(E), V(C), *and* I *be as above. Suppose that there is an interpretation* I^{-1} *of* V(C) *in* V(E), *where for all atoms* A(<R>) *of* L(E)

$$C(E) \models A(<R>) \longleftrightarrow I^{-1} \circ I(A(<R>)).$$

Then I *is onto.*

That is, I of V(E) in V(C) is onto if there is an "inverse" interpretation I^{-1} of V(C) in V(E). The proof of Theorem 9.1.4 is given in Section 9.3.

For example, consider the interpretation I′ = I(Rext;Rcon) of V(Rext) in V(Rcon) in Figure 9.3. An inverse interpretation I'^{-1} = I(Rcon;Rext) of V(Rcon) in V(Rext) is given of Figure 9.4. The symbols -; in the interpretation I'^{-1} represent fixed constant symbols of L(Rext). They are used to represent data in V(Rcon) that does not exist in V(Rext). For any relational structure M(Rext) of L(Rext), the induced

```
I(Rcon;Rext): INTERPRETATION DEFINITION
  EXTERNAL VIEW IS V(Rcon) = <S(Rcon),L(Rcon),C(Rcon)>
  CONCEPTUAL VIEW IS V(Rext) = <S(Rext),L(Rext),C(Rext)>

  CODING SECTION
    CODE FOR IDTPE IS SIDTPE;
    CODE FOR NAMTPE IS NAMTPE;
    CODE FOR DATPE IS DATPE;
    CODE FOR SEMTPE IS SEMTPE;
    CODE FOR YRTPE  IS YRTPE;
    CODE FOR DEPTPE IS DEPTPE;
    CODE FOR CS#TPE IS CS#TPE;
    CODE FOR SEC#TPE IS SEC#TPE;
    CODE FOR LOCTPE IS LOCTPE
    CODE FOR TIMTPE IS TIMTPE;
    CODE FOR GRDTPE IS GRDTPE;
    CODE FOR TTLTPE IS TTLTPE;
    CODE FOR CRDSTPE IS CRDSTPE;
    CODE FOR DESTPE IS DESTPE;

  DEFINING FORMULA SECTION
    PREDICATE: REGISTRAR
    ARGUMENTS ARE:(SEMESTER:1;,YEAR:1;,DEPT:1;,COURSE#:1;,
      SEC#:1;,-;,-;,-;,STUDID:1;,GRADE:1;)
    IS DEFINED BY:
      (E)STUDNAME:1(E)TITLE:1(E)CREDITS:1
      TRANSCRIPT(STUDID:1,STUDNAME:1,SEMESTER:1,YEAR:1,DEPT:1,
         COURSE#:1,SEC#:1,TITLE:1,GRADE:1,CREDITS:1)

    PREDICATE: STUDENT
    ARGUMENTS ARE:(STUDID:1;,STUDNAME:1;,
      -;,DATEADM:1;)
    IS DEFINED BY:
      STUDENT(STUDID:1,STUDNAME:1,DATEADM:1)

    PREDICATE: CATALOGUE
    ARGUMENT ARE:(DEPT:1;,COURSE#:1;,TITLE:1;,
      CREDITS:1;,-;,-;,-;)
    IS DEFINED BY:
      (E)STUDID:1...(E)GRADE:1
      TRANSCRIPT(STUDID:1,STUDNAME:1,SEMESTER:1,YEAR:1,DEPT:1,
         COURSE#:1,SEC#:1,TITLE:1,GRADE:1,CREDITS:1).

    PREDICATE: ≤
    ARGUMENTS ARE:(YEAR:1;,YEAR:2;)
    IS DEFINED BY: YEAR:1 ≤ YEAR:2

    FUNCTION: TOTCREDITS
    ARGUMENTS ARE: (ID#:1;,SEMESTER:1;,YEAR:1;,CREDITS:1;)
    IS DEFINED BY: TOTALCREDITS(ID#:1,SEMESTER:1,YEAR:1) = CREDITS:1

  CONSTANT TRANSFORMATION SECTION
    PROC CODE(SIDTPE)(STUDID:1) RETURNS(ID#:1);
     .
     .
     .
    END;
```

Figure 9.4 Interpretation I(Rcon;Rext).

I'^{-1}[M(Rext)] will have these values in the columns indicated by the definition I'^{-1}. We leave it for the reader to check to see that I'^{-1} is an interpretation of view V(Rcon) in V(Rext).

To see that the rest of the hypothesis of Theorem 9.1.4 holds, consider the atom TRANSCRIPT of L(Rext). Then

I′(TRANSCRIPT(STUDID:1,...,CREDITS:1))

= (E)BIRTHDATE:1...(E)PRECOURSE#:1
STUDENT(STUDID:1,STUDNAME:1,BIRTHDATE:1,DATEADM:1)
& REGISTRAR(SEMESTER:1,YEAR:1,DEPT:1,COURSE#:1,
SEC#:1,INSTRUCT:1,LOCAT:1,TIMES:1,STUDID:1,GRADE:1)
& CATALOGUE(DEPT:1,COURSE#:1,TITLE:1,CREDITS:1,DESCR:1,
PREDEPT:1,PRECOURSE#:1).

By the definition of I'^{-1}

I^{-1} o I′(TRANSCRIPT(STUDID:1,...,CREDITS:1))

= STUDENT(STUDID:1,STUDNAME:1,DATEADM:1)
& (E)STUDNAME:2...(E)CREDITS:2
TRANSCRIPT(STUDID:1,STUDNAME:2,SEMESTER:1,YEAR:1,DEPT:1,
COURSE#:1,SEC#:1,TITLE:2,GRADE:1,CREDITS:2).
& (E)STUDID:3...(E)GRADE:3
TRANSCRIPT(STUDID:3,STUDNAME:3,SEMESTER:3,YEAR:3,DEPT:1,
COURSE#:1,SEC#:3,TITLE:1,GRADE:3,CREDITS:1).

By the logical optimization operations of Chapter 8, we can show that

C(Rext) ⊨ TRANSCRIPT(STUDID:1,...,CREDITS:1)
⟷ I'^{-1} o I′(TRANSCRIPT(STUDID:1,...,CREDITS:1)).

We leave it as an exercise to check that the condition of Theorem 9.1.4 holds for the other atomic predicates of L(Rext). Consequently, I′ is an onto interpretation and C(Rext) is an external axiomatization for V(Rcon) and I′.

Definition. Interpretation I of V(E) in V(C) is called *faithful* if for all wffs Q of L(E),

C(C) ⊨ I(Q) iff C(E) ⊨ Q.

That is, I is faithful if for all wffs Q of L(E), Q is an implied constraint of C(C) with respect to I [i.e., C(C) ⊨ I(Q)] if and only if Q is itself a logical consequence of the constraints C(E). The implication from right to left holds for all interpretations between relational views. (We leave this as an exercise for the reader.) The left-to-right implication says, essentially, that the external constraints C(E) are as strong as the conceptual constraints with respect to wffs in L(E).

A relationship between ontoness and faithfulness is given by the following result.

Theorem 9.1.5. *If* I *is onto, then* I *is faithful.*

For example, suppose that the constraint

C(Rcon,10) CONSTRAINT STUDENT:STUDNAME $\rightarrow$ ID#

was added to the set C(Rcon). Then I′ is still an interpretation of view V(Rext) in the new view V′(Rcon) = <S(Rcon), L(Rcon), C(Rcon) $\cup$ {C(Rcon,10)}>. We will show that I′ is not an onto interpretation by showing that I′ is not faithful. Let Q be the wff of L(Rext) that says

STUDENT: NAME $\rightarrow$ ID#.

It is easily seen that

$$\{C(Rcon,10)\} \models I'(Q).$$

It is also easily seen that

$$C(Rext) \not\models Q,$$

since one can readily construct a model M(Rext) such that Q is false in M(Rext). Since I′ is not faithful, I′ cannot be onto.

Theorem 9.1.6. *If* I *is faithful then*

$$\{I[M(C)] \mid M(C) \models C(C) \textit{ and } M(C) \textit{ is finite}\}$$
$$= \{M(E) \mid M(E) \models C(E) \textit{ and } M(E) \textit{ is finite}\}.$$

Theorems 9.1.5 and 9.1.6 essentially tell us that for finite databases, faithfulness is equivalent to ontoness. These two results are proven in Section 9.3.

Our next result tells us that if we deal only with finite databases, then axiomatizations always exist. By Theorem 9.1.3, any such axiomatization is equivalent to Co(E).

Theorem 9.1.7. *Let* V(C) , Vo(E) = <S(E), L(E), Co(E)> *and* I *be as above. Then*

$$\{I[M(C)] \mid M(C) \models C(C) \textit{ and } M(C) \textit{ finite}\}$$
$$= \{M(E) \mid M(E) \models Co(E) \textit{ and } M(E) \textit{ finite}\}.$$

Proof. We prove that the interpretation I of Vo(E) in V(C) is faithful. The result follows by Theorem 9.1.6.

Let Q be a wff of L(E). We must show that

$$C(C) \models I(Q) \text{ iff } Co(E) \models Q.$$

If I(Q) is logically implied by C(C), then Q is in Co(E), hence, Co(E) $\models$ Q. To show the opposite implication, suppose that C(C) $\not\models$ I(Q). We have to show Co(E) $\not\models$ Q. Then, for some model M(C) of V(C), M(C) $\not\models$ I(Q); hence, by the Flipper Theorem,

I[M(C)] $\not\models$ Q. By Claim 9.1.2 and the Flipper Theorem, I[M(C)] $\models$ Co(E). But then, I[M(C)] is a witness to the fact that Co(E) $\not\models$ Q.

Restricted External Axiomatization

Let CL(E) and CL(C) be, respectively, classes of wffs of relational languages L(E) and L(C). For example, CL(E) [CL(C)] could be all the functional dependencies expressible in L(E) [L(C)]. Given a relational view V(C) = $<$S(C), L(C), C(C)$>$, where C(C) is contained in CL(C), relational schema S(E), relational language L(E), and interpretation I of L(E) in L(C), a variation of the external axiomatization problem is as follows.

Definition. A set of wffs C*(E) contained in CL(E) is called an *external axiomatization for* V(C) *and* I *resticted to classes* CL(C) *and* CL(E) *if*

$$\{ I[M(C)] \mid M(C) \models C(C) \} = \{ M(E) \mid M(E) \models C^*(E) \}.$$

Definition. The *external axiomatization problem for* V(C) *and* I *restricted to classes* CL(C) *and* CL(E) is that of determining whether or not such an external axiomatization exists, and if so, finding it.

The following result immediately follows from our earlier observations.

Theorem 9.1.8. *Let* V(C), S(E), L(E), I, CL(E) *and* CL(C) *be as above. If there exists an axiomatization* C*(E) *in* CL(E), *then*

$$\{M(E) \mid M(E) \models C^*(E)\} = \{M(E) \mid M(E) \models (Co(E) \textit{ intersect } CL(E))\}.$$

That is, if such a resticted axiomatization exists, it is equivalent to the set of Q in CL(E) that are implied constraints of C(C) with respect to I.

We illustrate the restricted axiomatization problem for the relational case in which the interpretation represents the projection operator. We show that when CL(C) and CL(E) are functional dependencies, an axiomatization within CL(E) may not exist. In other words, in the case of projection, axiomatizations based solely on functional dependencies are not adequate.

Let

$$S(Eo) = \{S = (A,B,C,D)\}$$

be a relational schema and L(Eo) be some relational language for S(Eo) which has only one zero-order type and one predicate symbol S. Let

$$S(Co) = \{T = (A,B,C,D,E)\}$$

be a relational schema, L(Co) be some relational language for S(Co) with the same type as L(Eo) and only one predicate symbol T. Let

$$C(Co) = \{T{:}B \rightarrow E,\ T{:}D \rightarrow E,\ T{:}C,E \rightarrow A\}$$

be a set of constraints on L(Co). Let I(Eo;Co) be an interpretation of L(Eo) in L(Co) which captures the fact that S(Eo) is a projection of S(Co) over column E. That is, I(Eo;Co) has

PREDICATE S
ARGUMENT ARE (A:1;,B:1;,C:1;,D:1;)
IS DEFINED BY
(E)E:1 T(A:1,B:1,C:1,D:1,E:1).

Since the types in L(Eo) are the same as in S(Co) and L(Co), the codings are identities.

Claim. 9.1.9. *Let*

$$\text{Co(Eo)} = \{\text{Q } in \text{ L(Eo)} \mid \text{C(Co)} \models \text{I(Eo;Co)(Q)}\}$$

and let FDo(Eo) *be the set of all functional dependencies in* Co(Eo). *Then*

$$\{\text{M(Eo)} \mid \text{M(Eo)} \models \text{Co(Eo)}\} \textit{ is a proper subset of } \{\text{M(Eo)} \mid \text{M(E)} \models \text{FDo(Eo)}\}.$$

It will then follow by Theorem 9.1.3 that FDo(Eo) cannot be an external axiomatization of

$$\{\text{I(Eo;Co)[M(Co)]} \mid \text{M(Co)} \models \text{C(Co)}\}.$$

It will also follow that in the case of CL(E), CL(C) being functional dependencies, an axiomatization of functional dependencies is not sufficient to capture the class of external databases obtained via the projection operator.

Proof. (of Claim). Since FDo(Eo) is a subset of Co(Eo), it follows that if M(Eo) is a model of Co(Eo), it must also be a model of FDo(Eo). Hence, the set of models of Co(Eo) is contained in the set of models of FDo(Eo). The remainder of the argument shows that the containment is proper.

Since the set of all functional dependencies in L(Eo) is finite, we can use Theorem 9.1.1 to generate the set

$$\text{FDo(Eo)} = \{\text{S:B,C} \rightarrow \text{A, S:D,C} \rightarrow \text{A, S:B,C,D} \rightarrow \text{A}\}.$$

For example, notice that

I(Eo;Co)(S:B,C → A)
= ((E)E:1 T(A:1,B:1,C:1,D:1,E:1)
& (E)E:2 T(A:2,B:1,C:1,D:2,E:2))
→ A:1 = A:2

is a logical consequence of T:B → E and T:C,E → A. The others are left as exercises for the reader.

S			
A	B	C	D
1	1	1	1
0	1	0	0
0	0	1	0

Figure 9.5 Relational structure M(Eo).

Let Q be the wff of L(Eo):

$$(\text{S(A:1,B:1,C:1,D:1)} \ \& \ \text{S(A:2,B:1,C:2,D:2)} \ \& \ \text{S(A:2,B:2,C:1,D:2)}) \rightarrow \text{A:1} = \text{A:2}\ .$$

Then

$$\begin{aligned} &\text{I(Eo;Co)(Q)} \\ &\quad = ((\text{E})\text{E:1 T(A:1,B:1,C:1,D:1,E:1)} \\ &\quad \& \ (\text{E})\text{E:2 T(A:2,B:1,C:2,D:2,E:2)} \\ &\quad \& \ (\text{E})\text{E:3 T(A:2,B:2,C:1,D:2,E:3))} \\ &\qquad \rightarrow \text{A:1} = \text{A:2}, \end{aligned}$$

and the reader can check that C(Co) $\models$ I(Eo;Co)(Q). Hence, Q is in Co(Eo). However, Figure 9.5 is a relational structure M(Eo) for L(Eo) such that M(Eo) $\models$ FDo(Eo), but M(Eo) $\not\models$ Q. Hence, it follows that the set of models of FDo(Eo) is strictly larger that the set of models of Co(Eo).

Exercises

1. Show that the nonsolvability of the decision problem for first-order logic implies the nonsolvability of the implied constraint problem for relational databases.

2. Show that if I is an interpretation of relational view V(E) in V(C), then for any wff Q of L(E)

$$\text{C(E)} \models \text{Q implies C(C)} \models \text{I(Q)}.$$

3. Show that I'^{-1} = I(Rcon;Rext) is an interpretation of relational view V(Rcon) in V(Rext).

4. Show that I'^{-1} = I(Rcon;Rext) satisfies the conditions of Theorem 9.1.4.

5. Find the set of all functional dependencies on L(Eo). Show that

$$\text{FDo(Eo)} = \{\text{S:B,C} \rightarrow \text{A, S:D,C} \rightarrow \text{A, S:B,C,D} \rightarrow \text{A}\}.$$

9.2 THE HETEROGENEOUS CASE

In this section we study the external axiomatization problem for the heterogeneous case. We will illustrate the ideas using V(Dext) of Figure 9.6, V(Dcon) of Figure 9.7, and I″ = I(Dext;Dcon) of Figure 9.8. However, as before, we first investigate implied constraints.

```
V(Dext): VIEW DEFINITION
  S(Dext): SCHEMA DEFINITION
    TABLE TRANSCRIPT = (STUDID,STUDNAME,BIRTHDATE,DATEADM,RECORD)
    TABLE RECORD = (SEMESTER,YEAR,COURSES)
    TABLE COURSES = (DEPT,COURSE#,SEC#,TITLE,GRADE,CREDITS)

  L(Dext): LANGUAGE DEFINITION
  T(Dext): TYPING DEFINITION
    TYPE SIDTPE = {STUDID} EBCDIC CHAR(9)
    TYPE NAMTPE = {STUDNAME} EBCDIC CHAR(20)
    TYPE DATPE = {BITRHDATE,DATEADM} EBCDIC CHAR(15)
    TYPE SEMTPE = {SEMESTER} EBCDIC CHAR(6)
    TYPE YRTPE = {YEAR} EBCDIC DEC(4)
    TYPE DEPTPE = {DEPT} EBCDIC CHAR(8)
    TYPE CS#TPE = {COURSE#} EBCDIC DEC(3)
    TYPE SEC#TPE = {SEC#} EBCDIC CHAR(10)
    TYPE TTLTPE = {TITLE} EBCDIC CHAR(25)
    TYPE GRDTPE = {GRADE} EBCDIC CHAR(1)
    TYPE CRDSTPE = {CREDITS} EBCDIC DEC(2)

    NONLOGICAL SYMBOLS DEFINITION
      PREDICATES
        TRANSCRIPT-RECORD-COURSES:
          (SIDTPE,NAMTPE,DATPE,DATPE,RECORD,SEMTPE,
          YRTPE,COURSES,DEPTPE,CS#TPE,SEC#TPE,TTLTPE,
          GRDTPE,CRDSTPE) FULL CLUSTER PREDICATE
          ≤ :(YRTPE,YRTPE) PREDICATE
      FUNCTIONS
        TOTCREDITS:(SIDTPE,SEMTPE,YRTPE;
          CRDSTPE) FUNCTION

C(Dext): CONSTRAINTS DEFINITION
  C(Dext,1) CONSTRAINT TRANSCRIPT:
    STUDID → STUDNAME,BIRTHDATE,DATEADM,RECORD
  C(Dext,2):CONSTRAINT TRANSCRIPT-RECORD:
    STUDID,SEMESTER,YEAR → COURSES
  C(Dext,3):CONSTRAINT TRANSCRIPT-RECORD-COURSES:
    STUDID,SEMESTER,YEAR,DEPT,COURSE#
    → SEC#,TITLE,CREDITS,GRADE
```

Figure 9.6 Database logic DDL definition of view V(Dext).

```
V(Dcon): VIEW DEFINITION
  S(Dcon): SCHEMA DEFINITION
    TABLE SYSTEM = (REGISTRAR,STUDINFO,CATALOGUE)
    TABLE REGISTRAR = (SEMESTER,YEAR,COURSE)
    TABLE COURSE = (DEPT,COURSE#,SECTION)
    TABLE SECTION = (SEC#,INSTRUCT,LOCAT,TIMES,STUDENT)
    TABLE STUDENT = (STUDID,STUDNAME,GRADE)
    TABLE STUDINFO = (ID#,STUDNAME,BIRTHDATE,DATEADM)
    TABLE CATALOGUE = (DEPT,COURSE#,TITLE,CREDITS,DESCR,LINK)
    TABLE LINK = (CATALOGUE)

  L(Dcon): LANGUAGE DEFINITION
  T(Dcon): TYPING DEFINITION
    TYPE SEMTPE = {SEMESTER} ASCII CHAR(8)
    TYPE YRTPE = {YEAR} ASCII DEC(4)
    TYPE DEPTPE = {DEPT} ASCII CHAR(10)
    TYPE CS#TPE = {COURSE#} ASCII DEC(3)
    TYPE TTLTPE = {TITLE} ASCII CHAR(25)
    TYPE CRDSTPE = {CREDITS} ASCII DEC(2)
    TYPE SEC#TPE = {SEC#} ASCII CHAR(10)
    TYPE NAMTPE = {STUDNAME} ASCII CHAR(20)
    TYPE LOCTPE = {LOCAT} ASCII CHAR(30)
    TYPE TIMTPE = {TIMES} ASCII CHAR(20)
    TYPE IDTPE = {STUDID,ID#} ASCII CHAR(9)
    TYPE GRDTPE = {GRADE} ASCII CHAR(1)
    TYPE DATPE = {BIRTHDATE,DATEADM} ASCII CHAR(15)
    TYPE DESCTPE = {DESCR} ASCII CHAR(50)

    NONLOGICAL SYMBOLS DEFINITION
      PREDICATES
        SYSTEM-REGISTRAR-COURSE-SECTION-STUDENT:
          (SEMTPE,YRTPE,COURSE,DEPTPE,CS#TPE,SECTION,
          SEC#TPE,NAMTPE,LOCTPE,TIMTPE,STUDENT,IDTPE,
          NAMTPE,GRDTPE) FULL CLUSTER PREDICATE

        SYSTEM-STUDINFO:
          (IDTPE,NAMTPE,DATPE,DATPE) PREDICATE

        SYSTEM-CATALOGUE-LINK-CATALOGUE:
          (DEPTPE,CS#TPE,TTLTPE,CRDSTPE,DESCTPE,LINK,
          CATALOGUE,DEPTPE,CS#TPE,TTLTPE,CRDSTPE,DESCTPE,
          LINK) FULL CLUSTER PREDICATE
          ≤ :(YRTPE,YRTPE) PREDICATE
      FUNCTIONS
        TOTALCREDITS:(IDTPE,SEMTPE,YRTPE;
          CRDSTPE) FUNCTION
C(Dcon): CONSTRAINTS DEFINITION
  C(Dcon,1):CONSTRAINT SYSTEM-REGISTRAR:SEMESTER,
    YEAR → COURSE
  C(Dcon,2):CONSTRAINT SYSTEM-REGISTRAR-COURSE:
    SEMESTER,YEAR,DEPT,COURSE# → SECTION
```

Figure 9.7 *(cont. next page)*

(continued)

```
C(Dcon,3):CONSTRAINT SYSTEM-REGISTRAR-COURSE-
  SECTION:SEMESTER,YEAR,DEPT,COURSE#,SEC#
  → INSTRUCT,LOCAT,TIMES,STUDENT
  C(Dcon,4):CONSTRAINT SYSTEM-REGISTRAR-COURSE-
    SECTION-STUDENT:
    SEMESTER,YEAR,DEPT,COURSE#,SEC#,STUDID
  → STUDNAME,GRADE
  C(Dcon,5):CONSTRAINT SYSTEM-STUDINFO:
    ID# → STUDNAME,BIRTHDATE,DATEADM
  C(Dcon,6):CONSTRAINT SYSTEM-CATALOGUE:
    DEPT,COURSE# → TITLE,CREDITS,DESCR,LINK
  C(Dcon,7) = CONSTRAINT SYSTEM-REGISTRAR-
    COURSE-SECTION-STUDENT:
    SEMESTER,YEAR,DEPT,COURSE#,STUDID → SEC#
```

Figure 9.7 Database logic DDL definition of view V(Dcon).

```
I(Dext;Dcon): INTERPRETATION DEFINITION
  EXTERNAL VIEW IS V(Dext) = <S(Dext),L(Dext),C(Dext)>
  CONCEPTUAL VIEW IS V(Dcon) = <S(Dcon),L(Dcon),C(Dcon)>

  CODING SECTION
    CODE FOR SIDTPE IS IDTPE;
    CODE FOR NAMTPE IS NAMTPE;
    CODE FOR DATPE  IS DATPE;
    CODE FOR SEMTPE IS SEMTPE;
    CODE FOR YRTPE  IS YRTPE;
    CODE FOR DEPTPE IS DEPTPE;
    CODE FOR CS#TPE IS CS#TPE;
    CODE FOR SEC#TPE IS SEC#TPE;
    CODE FOR TTLTPE IS TTLTPE;
    CODE FOR GRDTPE IS GRDTPE;
    CODE FOR CRDSTPE IS CRDSTPE;
    CODE FOR RECORD IS IDTPE;
    CODE FOR COURSES IS IDTPE,SEMTPE,YRTPE;

  DEFINING FORMULA SECTION
    PREDICATE:TRANSCRIPT-RECORD-COURSES
    ARGUMENTS ARE: (STUDID:1;,STUDNAME:1;,BIRTHDATE:1,
      DATEADM:1;,STUDID:1;,SEMESTER:1,YEAR:1;,
      STUDID:1,SEMESTER:1,YEAR:1;,DEPT:1;,
      COURSE#:1;,SEC#:1;,TITLE:1;,GRADE:1;,
      CREDITS:1;)
    IS DEFINED BY:(E)COURSE:1(E)SECTION:1
      (E)INSTRUCT:1(E)LOCAT:1(E)TIMES:1(E)STUDENT:1
      (E)LINK:1(E)DESCR:1
        SYSTEM-REGISTRAR-COURSE-SECTION-STUDENT
          (SEMESTER:1,YEAR:1,COURSE:1,DEPT:1,COURSE#:1,SECTION:1,
          SEC#:1,INSTRUCT:1,LOCAT:1,TIMES:1,STUDENT:1,STUDID:1,
          STUDNAME:1,GRADE:1)
```

Figure 9.8 *(cont. next page)*

(continued)

```
      & SYSTEM-CATALOGUE
          (DEPT:1,COURSE#:1,TITLE:1,CREDITS:1,DESCR:1,LINK:1)
      & SYSTEM-STUDINFO
          (STUDID:1,STUDNAME:1,BIRTHDATE:1,DATEADM:1)

    PREDICATE:TRANSCRIPT
    ARGUMENTS ARE: (STUDID:1;,STUDNAME:1;,BIRTHDATE:1,
      DATEADM:1;,STUDID:1;)
    IS DEFINED BY
      SYSTEM-STUDINFO
        (STUDID:1,STUDNAME:1,BIRTHDATE:1,DATEADM:1)

    PREDICATE: ≤
    ARGUMENTS ARE:(YEAR:1;,YEAR:2;)
    IS DEFINED BY: YEAR:1≤ YEAR:2

    PREDICATE: TOTCREDITS
    ARGUMENTS ARE: (ID#:1,SEMESTER:1,YEAR:1;,CREDITS:1;)
    IS DEFINED BY: TOTALCREDITS(ID#:1,SEMESTER:1,
      YEAR:1) = CREDITS:1

  CONSTANT TRANSFORMATION SECTION
              .
              .
              .
```

Figure 9.8 Interpretation I(Dext;Dcon) of L(Dext) in L(Dcon).

Implied Constraint Problem

Let V(E) = <S(E), L(E), C(E)> and V(C) = <S(C), L(C), C(C)> denote external and conceptual database views and let I be an interpretation of L(E) in L(C).

Definition. A closed wff Q of L(E) is called an *implied constraint of* V(C) *with respect to* I if for all database structures M(C) of V(C),

$$M(C) \models C(C) \text{ implies } I[M(C)] \models Q.$$

That is, Q is an implied constraint if Q is true on all external databases induced from models of V(C) via I.

For example,

C(Dext,3):CONSTRAINT TRANSCRIPT-RECORD-COURSES:
STUDID,SEMESTER,YEAR,DEPT,COURSE#
→ SEC#,TITLE,CREDITS,GRADE

of V(Rext) is an implied constraint of V(Rcon) with respect to I″. This is because for any database structure M(Dcon) that is a model of V(Dcon),

C(Dcon,4):CONSTRAINT SYSTEM-REGISTRAR-COURSE-
SECTION-STUDENT:
SEMESTER,YEAR,DEPT,COURSE#,SEC#,STUDID
→ STUDNAME,GRADE,

C(Dcon,6):CONSTRAINT SYSTEM-CATALOGUE:
DEPT,COURSE#
→ TITLE,CREDITS,DESCR,LINK

and
C(Dcon,7):CONSTRAINT SYSTEM-REGISTRAR-COURSE-
SECTION-STUDENT:
SEMESTER,YEAR,DEPT,COURSE#,STUDID
→ SEC#

is always true. But by the details of I″ in Figure 9.8, in particular, by the way cluster TRANSCRIPT-RECORD-COURSES is defined, we must have

I″[M(Rcon)] ⊨ TRANSCRIPT-RECORD-COURSES:
STUDID,SEMESTER,YEAR,DEPT,COURSE#
→ SEC#,TITLE,CREDITS,GRADE

and C(Dext,3) is implied.

Definition. The *implied constraint problem* is to determine, given a wff Q of L(E) and an interpretation I of L(E) in L(C), whether or not Q is an implied constraint of V(C) with respect to I.

Theorem 9.2.1. *A closed wff* Q *of* L(E) *is an implied constraint of* V(C) *with respect to* I *if and only if* C(C) ⊨ I(Q) *in* L(C).

That is, a wff is an implied constraint if and only if its interpretation is a logical consequence [in L(C)] of the constraints in C(C). The proof of Theorem 9.2.1 (and consequently, Theorem 9.1.1) will be given in Section 9.3.

For example, recall

C(Dext,3):CONSTRAINT TRANSCRIPT-RECORD-COURSES:
STUDID,SEMESTER,YEAR,DEPT,COURSE#
→ SEC#,TITLE,CREDITS,GRADE

above. In the language L(Dext), this is

(TRANSCRIPT-RECORD-COURSES(STUDID:1,STUDNAME:1,
BIRTHRTHDATE:1,DATEADM:1,RECORD:1,SEMESTER:1,YEAR:1,
COURSES:1,DEPT:1,COURSE#:1,SEC#:1,TITLE:1,GRADE:1,
CREDITS:1)
& TRANSCRIPT-RECORD-COURSES(STUDID:1,STUDNAME:2,
BIRTHDATE:2,DATEADM:2,RECORD:2,SEMESTER:1,YEAR:1,
COURSES:2,DEPT:1,COURSE#:1,SEC#:2,TITLE:2,GRADE:2,
CREDITS:2))
→ (SEC#:1 = SEC#:2 & TITLE:1 = TITLE:2
& GRADE:1 = GRADE:2 & CREDITS:1 = CREDITS:2)

Interpreting this in I″, we have

I″(C(Dext,3))
= ((E)COURSE:1(E)SECTION:1...(E)DESCR:1
SYSTEM-REGISTRAR-COURSE-SECTION-STUDENT
(SEMESTER:1,YEAR:1,COURSE:1,DEPT:1,COURSE#:1,
SECTION:1,SEC#:1,INSTRUCT:1,LOCAT:1,TIMES:1,
STUDENT:1,STUDID:1,STUDNAME:1,GRADE:1)
& SYSTEM-CATALOGUE
(DEPT:1,COURSE#:1,TITLE:1,CREDITS:1,DESCR:1,LINK:1)
& SYSTEM-STUDINFO
(STUDID:1,STUDNAME:1,BIRTHDATE:1,DATEADM:1))
& ((E)COURSE:2(E)SECTION:2...(E)DESCR:2
SYSTEM-REGISTRAR-COURSE-SECTION-STUDENT
(SEMESTER:1,YEAR:1,COURSE:2,DEPT:1,COURSE#:1,
SECTION:2,SEC#:2,INSTRUCT:2,LOCAT:2,TIMES:2,
STUDENT:2,STUDID:1,STUDNAME:2,GRADE:2)
& SYSTEM-CATALOGUE
(DEPT:1,COURSE#:1,TITLE:2,CREDITS:2,DESCR:2,LINK:2)
& SYSTEM-STUDINFO
(STUDID:1,STUDNAME:2,BIRTHDATE:2,DATEADM:2))
→ (SEC#:1 = SEC#:2 & TITLE:1 = TITLE:2
& GRADE:1 = GRADE:2 & CREDITS:1 = CREDITS:2),

which is clearly a logical consequence of constraint C(Dcon,4), C(Dcon,6), and C(Dcon,7) in L(Dcon).

The reader can check that every constraint in V(Dext) is an implied constraint of V(Dcon) with respect to I″. This was required for the construction of interpretation I″ of view V(Dext) in view V(Dcon). Hence, in the definition in Section 2.2 of interpretation of database view V(E) in V(C), the condition can be restated as saying that every Q in C(E) is an implied constraint of V(C) with respect to I(E;C).

As a second example, consider the constraint

TRANSCRIPT:STUDNAME → STUDID,BIRTHDATE,DATEADM

on S(Dext). In the language L(Dext), this is

(TRANSCRIPT(STUDID:1,STUDNAME:1,BIRTHDATE:1,DATEADM:1,
RECORD:1)
& TRANSCRIPT(STUDID:2,STUDNAME:1,BIRTHDATE:2,DATEADM:2,
RECORD:2))
→ (STUDID:1 = STUDID:2 & BIRTHDATE:1 = BIRTHDATE:2
& DATEADM:1 = DATEADM:2).

Interpreting this in I″, we have

(SYSTEM-STUDINFO
(STUDID:1,STUDNAME:1,BIRTHDATE:1,DATEADM:1)
& SYSTEM-STUDINFO
(STUDID:2,STUDNAME:1,BIRTHDATE:2,DATEADM:2))

$\rightarrow$ (STUDID:1 = STUDID:2 & BIRTHDATE:1 = BIRTHDATE:2 & DATEADM:1 = DATEADM:2).

However, it is easy to find a model for V(Dcon) for which this wff is false. For instance, take an M(Dcon) that has only two rows in STUDINFO, where each has the same STUDNAME but has different STUDIDs or BIRTHDATEs or DATEADMs. Hence, the wff is not a logical consequence of V(Dcon) and by Theorem 9.2.1, Q is not an implied constraint of V(Dcon) with respect to I″.

The question of deciding whether or not a constraint is implied is now reduced to deciding if a wff is a logical consequence of a set of wffs. This latter is called the *decision problem for database logic.* Since first-order logic is a special case of database logic, it follows from Godel's result that the decision problem for database logic is not solvable. Hence, the implied constraint problem for database logic is also not solvable. An open research topic is to find classes of formulas in database logic for which the decision problem is solvable. This will lead to solvable cases of the implied constraint problem for database logic. Initial steps on this problem have been taken in [Aronson].

External Axiomatization Problem

Let V(C) = <S(C), L(C), C(C)> be a database view, S(E), L(E) a database schema and language, and I an interpretation of database language L(E) in L(C).

Definition. A set of wffs C*(E) of L(E) is called an *external axiomatization for* V(C) *and* I, if

$$\{ \ I[M(C)] \mid M(C) \models C(C) \ \} = \{ \ M(E) \mid M(E) \models C^*(E) \ \}.$$

That is, C*(E) is a set of wffs of L(E) that completely characterizes the class of external databases obtained from models of V(C) via I.

Definition. The *external axiomatization problem for* V(C) *and* I is that of determining whether or not such an external axiomatization exists, and if so, finding it.

Let V(C), S(E), L(E) and I be as above. Define

$$Co(E) = \{Q \text{ in } L(E) \mid C(C) \models I(Q) \text{ in } L(C)\}.$$

That is, Co(E) is the set of all wffs of L(E) whose interpretations under I are logical consequences of the constraints C(C) in L(C). By Theorem 9.2.1, Co(E) consists of all the implied constraints of V(C) with respect to I.

Claim 9.2.2 . *Let* V(C), S(E), L(E), *and* I *be as above. Let*

$$Vo(E) = \ <S(E),L(E),Co(E)>.$$

That is, Vo(E) is the view with S(E) and L(E) whose axioms is the set of all implied constraints of V(C) with respect to I. Then I is an interpretation of view Vo(E) in view V(C).

Proof. This follows from the definition of Co(E).

Theorem 9.2.3. *Let* V(C), S(E), L(E), *and* I *be as above. Suppose that there is an axiomatization* C*(E) *of* L *for*

$$\{I[M(C)] \mid M(C) \models C(C)\}.$$

Then

$$\{M(E) \mid M(E) \models C^*(E)\} = \{M(E) \mid M(E) \models Co(E)\}.$$

Proof. The same as the proof of Theorem 9.1.3 except that relational structures and relational views are replaced by database structures and database views.

To recap, what Theorem 9.2.3 tells us is that if an external axiomatization exists, then it is equivalent to the set of all implied constraints. We will show below that in the case of finite heterogeneous databases, external axiomatizations always exists.

Onto Interpretations

Let $V(E) = \langle S(E), L(E), C(E)\rangle$, $V(C) = \langle S(C), L(C), C(C)\rangle$ be two database views and I an interpretation of view V(E) in V(C). By Theorem 2.2.2, the inducing map I[M(C)] maps the class of models of V(C) into the class of models of V(E).

Definition. Interpretation I of V(E) in V(C) is called an *onto* interpretation if

$$\{I[M(C)] \mid M(C) \models C(C)\} = \{M(E) \mid M(E) \models C(E)\}.$$

That is, I is an onto interpretation of V(E) in V(C) if not only is the inducing map into, but it is also *onto* the class of models of C(E).

As in the relational case, if I is an onto interpretation, then the external constraints C(E) form an external axiomatization. We also study the two properties "invertibility" and "faithfulness," which can be used to demonstrate ontoness and consequently an external axiomatizability.

Theorem 9.2.4. *Let V(E), V(C), and* I *be as above. Suppose that there is an interpretation* I! *of* V(C) *in* V(E), *where for all atoms* $A(\langle R\rangle)$ *of* L(E),

$$C(E) \models A(\langle R\rangle) \longleftrightarrow I^{-1} \circ I(A(\langle R\rangle)).$$

Then I *is onto.*

That is, I of V(E) in V(C) is onto if there is an "inverse" interpretation I^{-1} of V(C) in V(E). Theorem 9.2.4 is an obvious generalization of Theorem 9.1.4 .The proof of Theorem 9.2.4, and, hence, Theorem 9.1.4, is given in Section 9.3.

For example, consider the interpretation $I'' =$ I(Dext;Dcon) of V(Dext) in V(Dcon) in Figure 9.8. An inverse interpretation $I''^{-1} =$ I(Dcon;Dext) of V(Dcon) in

```
I(Dcon;Dext): INTERPRETATION DEFINITION
  EXTERNAL VIEW IS V(Dcon) = <S(Dcon),L(Dcon),C(Dcon)>
  CONCEPTUAL VIEW IS V(Dext) = <S(Dext),L(Dext),C(Dext)>

  CODING SECTION
    CODE FOR SEMTPE IS SEMTPE;
    CODE FOR YRTPE IS YRTPE;
         .
         .
         .
    CODE FOR DESCTPE IS DESCTPE;
    CODE FOR COURSE IS SEMTPE,YRTPE;
    CODE FOR SECTION IS SEMTPE,YRTPE,DEPTPE,CS#TPE;
    CODE FOR STUDENT IS SEMTPE,YRTPE,DEPTPE,CS#TPE,SEC#TPE;
    CODE FOR CATALOGUE IS DEPTPE,CS#TPE;
    CODE FOR LINK IS DEPTPE,CS#TPE;

  DEFINING FORMULA SECTION
    PREDICATE: SYSTEM-REGISTRAR-COURSE-SECTION-STUDENT:
    ARGUMENTS ARE:(SEMESTER:1;,YEAR:1;,SEMESTER:1,YEAR:1;,
      DEPT:1;,COURSE#:1;,SEMESTER:1,YEAR:1,DEPT:1;,COURSE#:1;,
      SEC#:1;,-;,-;,-;,SEMESTER:1,YEAR:1,DEPT:1,COURSE#:1,SEC#:1;,
      STUDID:1;,STUDNAME:1;,GRADE:1;)
    IS DEFINED BY:
      (E)RECORD:1,(E)COURSES:1(E)TITLE:1(E)CREDITS:1
         TRANSCRIPT-RECORD-COURSES(STUDID:1,
             STUDNAME:1,BIRTHDATE:1,DATEADM:1,RECORD:1,SEMESTER:1,YEAR:1,
             COURSES:1,DEPT:1,COURSE#:1,SEC#:1,TITLE:1,GRADE:1,CREDITS:1)

    PREDICATE: SYSTEM-STUDINFO
    ARGUMENTS ARE:(STUDID:1;,STUDNAME:1;,
      BIRTHDATE:1;,DATEADM:1;)
    IS DEFINED BY:
      (E)RECORD:1
        TRANSCRIPT(STUDID:1,STUDNAME:1,BIRTHDATE:1,
            DATEADM:1,RECORD:1)

    PREDICATE: SYSTEM-CATALOGUE-LINK-CATALOGUE
    ARGUMENTS ARE:(DEPT:1;,COURSE#:1;,TITLE:1;,
      CREDITS:1;,-;,DEPT:1,COURSE#:1;,DEPT:1,COURSE#:1;,
      -;,-;,-;,-;,-;,-;,-;)
    IS DEFINED BY:
      (E)STUDID:1...(E)GRADE:1
        TRANSCRIPT-RECORD-COURSES(STUDID:1,
            STUDNAME:1,BIRTHDATE:1,DATEADM:1,RECORD:1,SEMESTER:1,YEAR:1,
            COURSES:1,DEPT:1,COURSE#:1,SEC#:1,TITLE:1,GRADE:1,CREDITS:1)

    PREDICATE: ≤
    ARGUMENTS ARE:(YEAR:1;,YEAR:2;)
    IS DEFINED BY: YEAR:1 ≤ YEAR:2

    PREDICATE: TOTALCREDITS
    ARGUMENTS ARE: (ID#:1;,SEMESTER:1;,YEAR:1;,CREDITS:1;)
    IS DEFINED BY: TOTCREDITS(ID:1,SEMESTER;1,
      YEAR:1) = CREDITS:1

  CONSTANT TRANSFORMATION SECTION
                 .
                 .
                 .
```


Figure 9.9 Interpretation I(Dcon;Dext).

V(Dext) is given in Figure 9.9. The symbols -; in the interpretation I''^{-1} represent fixed constant symbols of L(Dcon). They are used to represent data in V(Dcon) that does not exist in V(Dext). For any database structure M(Dext) of L(Dext), the induced I''^{-1}[M(Dext)] will have these values in the columns indicated by the definition I''^{-1}. We leave it for the reader to check to see that I''^{-1} is an interpretation of view V(Dcon) in V(Dext).

To see that the rest of the hypothesis of Theorem 9.2.4 holds consider the cluster TRANSCRIPT-RECORD-COURSES of L(Dext). Then by I″,

I″(TRANSCRIPT-RECORD-COURSES(STUDID:1,...,CREDITS:1))
= (E)COURSE:1...(E)DESCR:1
SYSTEM-REGISTRAR-COURSE-SECTION-STUDENT
(SEMESTER:1,YEAR:1,COURSE:1,DEPT:1,COURSE#:1,SECTION:1,
SEC#:1,INSTRUCT:1,LOCAT:1,TIMES:1,STUDENT:1,STUDID:1,
STUDNAME:1,GRADE:1)
& SYSTEM-CATALOGUE
(DEPT:1,COURSE#:1,TITLE:1,CREDITS:1,DESCR:1,LINK:1)
& SYSTEM-STUDINFO
(STUDID:1,STUDNAME:1,BIRTHDATE:1,DATEADM:1).

By the definition of I''^{-1},

I''^{-1} o I″(TRANSCRIPT-RECORD-COURSES(STUDID:1,...,CREDITS:1))
= (E)RECORD:1,(E)COURSES:1(E)TITLE:1(E)CREDITS:1
TRANSCRIPT-RECORD-COURSES(STUDID:1,
STUDNAME:1,BIRTHDATE:1,DATEADM:1,RECORD:1,SEMESTER:1,
YEAR:1,
COURSES:1,DEPT:1,COURSE#:1,SEC#:1,TITLE:1,GRADE:1,
CREDITS:1)
& (E)STUDID:2...(E)GRADE:2
TRANSCRIPT-RECORD-COURSES(STUDID:2,
STUDNAME:2,BIRTHDATE:2,DATEADM:2,RECORD:2,SEMESTER:2,
YEAR:2,
COURSES:2,DEPT:1,COURSE#:1,SEC#:2,TITLE:2,GRADE:2,
CREDITS:1)
& (E)RECORD:3
TRANSCRIPT(STUDID:1,STUDNAME:1,BIRTHDATE:1,
DATEADM:1,RECORD:3).

By the logical optimization operations of Chapter 8, we can show that

C(Dext) $\models$ TRANSCRIPT-RECORD-COURSES(STUDID:1,...,CREDITS:1)
$\longleftrightarrow$ I''^{-1} o I″(TRANSCRIPT-RECORD-COURSES(STUDID:1,...,CREDITS:1)).

Remark. Notice that we did not have to add new constraints to either V(Dext) or V(Dcon) as we did for V(Rext) and V(Rcon) in Section 9.1.

We leave it as an exercise to check that the condition of Theorem 9.2.4 holds for the other atomic predicates of L(Dext). Consequently, I″ is an onto interpretation and C(Dext) is an external axiomatization for V(Dcon) and I″.

Definition. Interpretation I of V(E) in V(C) is called *faithful* if for all wffs Q of L(E),

$$C(C) \models I(Q) \text{ iff } C(E) \models Q.$$

That is, I is faithful if for for all wffs Q of L(E), Q is an implied constraint of C(C) with respect to I [i.e., $C(C) \models I(Q)$] if and only if Q is itself provable from the constraints C(E). The implication from right to left holds for all interpretations between database views. (We leave this as an exercise for the reader.) The left to right implication says, essentially, that the external constraints C(E) are as strong as the conceptual constraints with respect to wffs in L(E).

Theorem 9.2.5. *If* I *is onto, then* I *is faithful.*

For example, suppose that the constraint

C(Dcon,8): CONSTRAINT SYSTEM-STUDINFO:STUDNAME → ID#

were added to the set C(Dcon). Then I″ is is still an interpretation of view V(Dext) in the new view V′(Dcon) = <S(Dcon), L(Dcon), C(Dcon) ∪ { C(Dcon,11)}>. We will show that I″ is not an onto interpretation by showing that I″ is not faithful. Let Q be the wff of L(Dext) that says

TRANSCRIPT: STUDNAME → STUDID.

It is easily seen that

$$\{C(Dcon,8)\} \models I''(Q).$$

It is also easily seen that

$$C(Dext) \not\models Q,$$

since one can readily construct a model M(Dext) such that Q is false in M(Dext). Since I″ is not faithful, I″ cannot be onto.

Theorem 9.2.6. *If* I *is faithful then*

$$\{I[M(C)] \mid M(C) \models C(C) \textit{ and } M(C) \textit{ is } \text{finite}\}$$
$$= \{M(E) \mid M(E) \models C(E) \textit{ and } M(E) \textit{ is finite}\}.$$

Theorems 9.2.5 and 9.2.6 essentially tell us that for finite databases, faithfulness is equivalent to ontoness. These two results generalize Theorems 9.1.5 and 9.1.6. These two results are proven in Section 9.3.

Our next result tells us that if we deal only with finite databases, then axiomatizations always exist. By Theorem 9.2.3, any such axiomatization is equivalent to Co(E).

Theorem 9.2.7. *Let* V(C) , Vo(E) = < S(E), L(E), Co(E) > , *and* I *be as above. Then*

$$\{I[M(C)] \mid M(C) \models C(C) \textit{ and } M(C) \textit{ finite }\}$$
$$= \{M(E) \mid M(E) \models Co(E) \textit{ and } M(E) \textit{ finite }\}.$$

Proof. The proof of Theorem 9.2.7 is identical to the proof of Theorem 9.1.7 except that database structures and views replace relational structures and views.

Exercises

1. Show that the nonsolvability of the decision problem for first-order logic implies the nonsolvability of the implied constraint problem for database logic.
2. Show that if I is an interpretation of database view V(E) in V(C), then for any wff Q of L(E).

$$C(E) \models Q \text{ implies } C(C) \models I(Q).$$

3. Show that I''^{-1} = I(Dcon;Dext) is an interpretation of database view V(Dcon) in V(Dext).
4. Show that I''^{-1} = I(Dcon;Dext) satisfies the conditions of Theorem 9.2.4.

9.3 SOME THEOREMS

In this section we prove the theorems used in Sections 9.1 and 9.2. We also show that database logic is mathematically different from first-order logic.

Implied Constraints

Let V(E) = < S(E), L(E), C(E) > and V(C) = < S(C), L(C), C(C) > denote external and conceptual database views and let I be an interpretation of L(E) in L(C).

Definition. A closed wff Q of L(E) is called an *implied constraint of* V(C) *with respect to* I if for all database structures M(C) of V(C),

$$M(C) \models C(C) \text{ implies } I[M(C)] \models Q.$$

Theorem 9.2.1. *A closed wff* Q of L(E) *is an implied constraint of* V(C) *with respect to* I *if and only if* C(C) ⊨ I(Q) *in* L(C).

Proof. Suppose that C(C) ⊨ I(Q). To show that Q is implied, let M(C) be a model of V(C). We have to show that I[M(C)] ⊨ Q. Since M(C) is a model of V(C), M(C) ⊨ C(C). Since C(C) ⊨ I(Q), M(C) ⊨ I(Q). By the Flipper Theorem, I[M(C)] ⊨ Q.

Suppose that C(C) ⊭ I(Q). We have to show that Q cannot be an implied constraint. Then there is a model M(C) of V(C) where M(C) ⊨ C(C) but M(C) ⊭ I(Q). By the Flipper Theorem, M(C) is a model of V(C) but I[M(C)] ⊭ Q. Hence, Q cannot be implied.

Invertability

Let V(E) = < S(E), L(E), C(E) > and V(C) = < S(C), L(C), C(C) > be two database views and I an interpretation of view V(E) in V(C).

Definition. Interpretation I of V(E) in V(C) is called an *onto* interpretation if

$$\{I[M(C)] \mid M(C) \models C(C)\} = \{M(E) \mid M(E) \models C(E)\}.$$

Theorem 9.2.4. *Let* V(E), V(C), *and* I *be as above. Suppose that there is an interpretation* I^{-1} *of* V(C) *in* V(E), *where for all atoms* A(< R >) *of* L(E)

$$C(E) \models A(<R>) \longleftrightarrow I^{-1} \circ I(A(<R>)).$$

Then I *is onto.*

Proof. Let M(E) be a model of V(E). By the definition of interpretation of views, I^{-1}[M(E)] is a model of V(C), and I[I^{-1}[M(E)]] is a model of V(E). Our proof is complete if we show that I[I^{-1}[M(E)]] is M(E). For then we can take I^{-1}[M(E)] to be the model of V(C) whose image under I is M(E).

Let Q be any variable-free atom of L(E). Then Q must be of the form

$$p(<t>),\ t1 = (Tj)\ t2, \text{ or } t1(<t>),$$

where < t >, t1, and t2 are variable-free terms in L(E). We have to show that

$$I[I^{-1}[M(E)]] \models Q \text{ iff } M(E) \models Q.$$

By the Flipper Theorem,

$$I[I^{-1}[M(E)]] \models Q \text{ iff } I^{-1}[M(E)] \models I(Q).$$

By the Flipper Theorem, again,

$$\text{iff } M(E) \models I^{-1}(I(Q)).$$

By the definition of composition of interpretations,

$$\text{iff } M(E) \models I^{-1} \circ I(Q).$$

It follows from the hypothesis of the theorem,

$$\text{iff } M(E) \models Q.$$

Faithfulness

Definition. Interpretation I of V(E) in V(C) is called *faithful* if for all wffs Q of L(E),

$$C(C) \models I(Q) \text{ iff } C(E) \models Q.$$

Theorem 9.2.5. *If* I *is onto, then* I *is faithful.*

Proof. Let Q be any wff of L(E). Suppose that C(E) $\models$ Q. We have to show that C(C) $\models$ I(Q). By definition of interpretation I of view V(E) in V(C), C(C) $\models$ I(C(E)). If C(E) $\models$ Q, then it is easily seen that I(C(E)) $\models$ I(Q). For suppose that M(C) is a database structure for L(C) and that M(C) $\models$ I(C(E)) but M(C) $\not\models$ I(Q). By the Flipper Theorem, I[M(C)] $\models$ C(E) and I[M(C)] $\not\models$ Q. But this contradicts the fact that C(E) $\models$ Q. Since C(C) $\models$ I(C(E)), and I(C(E)) $\models$ I(Q), we have that C(C) $\models$ I(Q). [Note that this part of the proof holds for any interpretation of V(E) in V(C), not only onto ones.]

Suppose that C(E) $\not\models$ Q. We have to show that C(C) $\not\models$ I(Q). Then for some model M(E) of V(E), M(E) $\models$ C(E) and M(E) $\not\models$ Q. Since I is onto, let M(E) = I[M(C)] for some model M(C) for V(C). Thus, M(C) $\models$ C(C) and I[M(C)] $\not\models$ Q. Since M(C) $\models$ C(C), and by the Flipper Theorem, M(C) $\not\models$ I(Q), we conclude that C(C) $\not\models$ I(Q).

Before we prove Theorem 9.2.6 we introduce the following definition. Let L(D) be a a database language.

Definition. A database structure M(D) for L(D) is called *finitely describable in* L(D) if there exists a wff Q(M(D)) of L(D) such that for all database structures M′(D) of L(D),

$$M'(D) \models Q(M(D)) \text{ iff } M'(D) = M(D).$$

That is, a database structure M(D) is finitely describable in L(D) if there is a formula of L(D) for which the only database structure that satisfies it is M(D) itself. We leave it as an exercise to show that if M(D) represents a finite database, then M(D) is finitely describable in L(D).

Theorem 9.3.1. *Suppose that* I *is a faithful interpretation of* V(E) *in* V(C). *Then for all finitely describable* M(E) *in* L(E) *that are also models of* V(E), *there exists a model* M(C) *of* V(C) *such that* I[M(C)] = M(E).

Proof. Suppose that there is a finitely describable M(E) in L(E) that is also a model of V(E) but is not the interpretation of any model of V(C). We show that I cannot be faithful. By finite describability, there exists a wff Q(M(E)) of L(E) such that for all database structures M′(E) of L(E),

$$M'(E) \models Q(M(E)) \text{ iff } M'(E) = M(E).$$

Thus, for all database structures M(C) for L(C),

$$M(C) \models C(C) \text{ implies } I[M(C)] \models \sim Q(M(E)).$$

By the Flipper Theorem, for all database structures M(C) for L(C),

$$M(C) \models C(C) \text{ implies } M(C) \models I(\sim Q(M(E))).$$

Hence, by the definition of logical implication,

$$C(C) \models I(\sim Q(M(E))).$$

But since $M(E) \not\models \sim Q(M(E))$, we have that

$$C(E) \not\models \sim Q(M(E)).$$

Hence, I cannot be faithful.

Theorem 9.2.6. *If* I *is faithful then*

$$\{I[M(C)] \mid M(C) \models C(C) \text{ and } M(C) \text{ is finite}\}$$
$$= \{M(E) \mid M(E) \models C(E) \text{ and } M(E) \text{ is finite}\}.$$

Proof. Theorem 9.2.6 follows from Theorem 9.3.1 and the fact that finite databases are always finitely describable.

Database Logic versus First-Order Logic

We conclude this chapter and the book by showing that database logic is intrinsically different from first-order logic. This is done in two ways. First, we show that since database logic allows quantification over sets, we get full "second-order" logic. Second, we show that even if we tried to "fake" set membership by defining it in a first-order way, we still cannot fully embed database logic in first-order logic.

One of the important properties of first-order logic is the Compactness Theorem. Let L(R) be a first-order (i.e., relational) language.

Theorem. 9.3.2 *(Compactness). A set of wffs* DEL *of* L(R) *has a model if and only if every finite subset of* DEL *has a model.*

The implication from left to right is immediate. The implication from right to left represents a fundamental property of first-order logic. The proof of the Compactness Theorem can be found in any standard logic text [Shoenfield].

Claim 9.3.3. *There is a database language* L(D) *and a set of wffs in* L(D) *which has no models but every finite subset has a model.*

As a consequence of the Claim, database logic is different from first-order logic.

Proof. Let

$$S(D) = \{A = (B), B = (C1,C2)\}$$

and let L(D) be a database language with typing {A,B, {C1,C2}}, no function symbols, no predicate symbols, and the constant symbols

$$\{e(A)\}, \{e(B){:}i\}, \text{ and } \{e(C){:}i\}.$$

MBR		
A	B	A
A	e(B):1	e(A):1
A	e(B):4	e(A):4
e(A):1	e(B):2	e(A):2
e(A):2	e(B):3	e(A):3

(a)

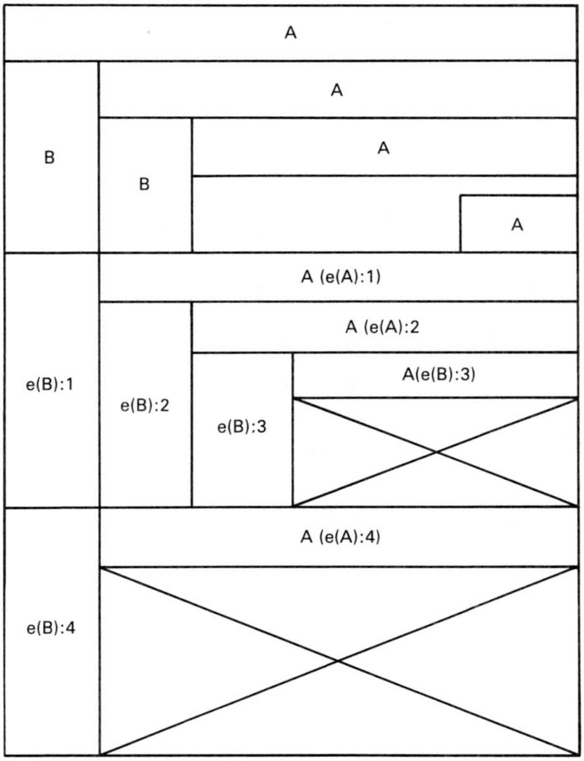

(b)

Figure 9.10 (a) Relational structure M(R(N*)); (b) database structure I[M(R(N*))].

We will show that there is a set of wffs of L(D) for which compactness fails.

For each k > 1, we have a wff Qk in L(D) which says that "there are at least k objects." For example, Q3 is

(E)C:1(E)C:2(E)C:3
~C:1 = C:2 & ~C:1 = C:3 & ~C:2 = C:3.

For arbitrary k, Qk is

(E)C:1(E)C:2...(E)C:k
~C:1 = C:2 & ··· & ~C:1 = C:k
& ~C:2 = C:3 & ··· & ~C:2 = C:k ···
& ~C:k-1 = C:k.

Another wff, called Q*, says that "there are an infinite number of objects." This wff is

(E)B:1
((A)C:1(A)C:2(A)C:3
((B:1(C:1,C:2) & B:1(C:2,C:3)) → B:1(C:1,C:3))
& (A)C:1 ~B:1(C:1,C:1)
& (A)C:1(E)C:2 B:1(C:2,C:1)).

The wff says that there is a set B:1 (first line) which is a "transitive" (third line) "antireflexive" (fourth line) in which every element has a predecessor (fifth line). Thus, any model of this wff must have an infinite number of elements.

Consider the infinite set of wffs

{~Q*, Q1, Q2, ...}.

From the meanings of these wffs the entire set has no model. However, every finite subset has a model.

One of the reasons compactness fails is because database logic has set quantification and "true" set membership. An alternative approach is to change the semantics of database logic so as to have a "fake" set membership. We can do this by interpreting arbitrary database views in relational (or first-order) views. The relational views will have tables which represent the set membership on the database view.

For example, consider a database schema

S(N*) = {A = (B,A)}

and database language L(N*) with types {A,{B}}, no nonlogical function or predicate symbols and the constant symbols:

{e(A):i} and {e(B):i}.

Corresponding to this is a relational schema

S(R(N*)) = { MBR = (A,B,A)}.

Here the MBR table will contain information on the membership relation of A tables in L(N*). Also, there is relational language L(R(N*)) with types {A, {B}}, no nonlogical function and predicate symbols, and the constant symbols

{MBR}, {e(A):i}, and {e(B):i}.

We can define an interpretation I of L(N*) in L(R(N*)) as follows. The coding section is the identity since the types in the two languages are the same. The defining formulas for row predicate is

PREDICATE A(A,B)
ARGUMENTS ARE (A:1;,B:1;,A:2;)
IS DEFINED BY MBR(A:1,B:1,A:2).

Notice that a relational structure M(R(N*)) for L(R(N*)) induces database structures for L(N*). In particular, the rows in the MBR tables of M(R(N*)) indicate the rows of the A tables in I[M(R(N*))]. For example, the relational structure in Figure 9.10(a) induces the database structure of Figure 9.10(b).

Definition. We say that a database view V(E) is *embeddable* in database view V(C) if there is an onto interpretation I of V(E) in V(C). In such a case we call I an *embedding of* V(E) in V(C).

In our next theorem, we show that there is a database view that is not embeddable in any relational view. Consequently, we see that database logic is not "embeddable" in first-order logic.

Theorem 9.3.4. *There is a database view* V(D) *in which the set of constraints is empty such that for any relational view* V(R), *there is no embedding of* V(D) *in* V(R).

Proof. Let

V(N*) = <S(N*),L(N*),C(N*)>,

where S(N*) and L(N*) be as defined above and let C(N*) be the empty set of wffs of L(N*). Suppose that there exists a relational view V(R) = <S(R), L(R), C(R)> and some interpretation I such that the inducing map sends the class of models of V(R) onto the class of models of V(N*).

Consider the infinite set of wffs

DEL(N*)
= {e(A):1(e(B):1,e(A):2),
e(A):2(e(B):1,e(A):3), ...}

of L(N*) and

I(DEL(N*))
= {I(e(A):1(e(B):1,e(A):2)),
I(e(A):2(e(B):1,e(A):3)), ...}

of L(R).

Claim 9.3.5. C(R) ∪ I(DEL(N*)) *has a model* M^+(R) *in* L(R).

Proof. (of Claim). We show that every finite subset of C(R) ∪ I(DEL(N*)) has a model. Hence, by the Compactness Theorem for First-Order Logic, C(R) ∪ I(DEL(N*)) has a model in L(R). Let I(DEL) be a finite subset of I(DEL(N*)) to show C(R) ∪ I(DEL) has a model in L(R). Let DEL be the set of wffs in L(N*) whose image under I is in DEL. Clearly, DEL has a model M(N*) in L(N*). Since I is onto, let M(R) be a model of C(R) where I[M(R)] = M(N*). By the Flipper Theorem, M(R) ⊨ I(DEL). Hence, C(R) ∪ I(DEL) has a model.

By the Flipper Theorem, I[M^+(R)] is a model for DEL(N*) which contains an **infinite descending chain.** Since database structures are not permitted such chains, we arrive at a contradiction.

Since the relational views subsume first-order predicate logic, it follows that the database view V(N*) is not embeddable in any first-order theory. Consequently, database logic cannot be "embedded" within first-order logic.

Exercises

1. Show that every finite database represented by a database structure is finitely describable in its language.
2. Construct a relational view V(R(Dext)) and an interpretation I(Dext;R(Dext)) of V(Dext) in V(R(Dext)).
3. Show that I(Dext;R(Dext)) of Exercise 2 is an embedding.
4. Show that hierarchical views are always embeddable in relational views.
5. Construct a relational view V(R(Dcon)) and an interpretation I(Dcon;R(Dcon)) of V(Dcon) in V(R(Dcon)).
6. Suppose that the depth of nesting on V(Dcon) is at most three. Show that I(Dcon;R(Dcon)) of Exercise 5 is an embedding.
7. Show that for any database view for which the depth of nesting is bounded by some fixed finite number is embeddable in a relational view.

9.4 RELATED READING

ARONSON, A. R., *Solvable Cases of the Decision Problem For Database Logic,* Ph.d Thesis, Department of Computer Science, University of Maryland, June 1980.

DREBEN, B. AND GOLDFARB, W., *The Decision Problem: Solvable Classes of Quantificational Formulas,* Addison-Wesley, Reading, Mass., 1979.

ENDERTON, H. B., *A Mathematical Introduction to Logic,* Academic Press, New York, 1972.

FAGIN, R., "Horn Clauses and Database Dependencies," *Journal of the ACM,* **29** (4), Oct. 1982, pp. 952–985.

GINSBURG, S., AND ZAIDDAN, S. M., *Properties of Functional Dependency Databases,* Computer Science Report, University of Southern California, Los Angeles, Jan. 1981.

GRANT, J. AND JACOBS, B. E., "On the Family of Generalized Dependency Constraints," *Journal of the ACM,* **29** (4), Oct. 1982, pp. 986–997.

JACOBS, B. E., ARONSON, A.R., AND KLUG A.C., "On Interpretations of Relational Languages and Solutions to the Implied Constraint Problem," *ACM Transactions on Database Systems,* **7** (2), pp. 291–315.

KLUG, A. C., "Calculating Constraints on Relational Expressions," *ACM Transactions on Database Systems,* **5** (3), Sept. 1980, pp. 260–290.

KLUG, A. C., *Theory of Database Mappings.* Department of Computer Science Technical Report TR CSRG-98, University of Toronto, 1978.

SHOENFIELD, J., *Mathematical Logic.* Addison-Wesley, Reading, Mass., 1967.

INDEX OF NOTATIONS

Notation	Meaning	Defined on Page:
R:A,B → C	Functional dependency	14
S, or S(–)	Schema:	
	heterogeneous	27, 99
	relational	16
R0=(R1,...,Rn)	R0-rule:	
	heterogeneous	27, 99
	relational	16
Ri	Name:	
	heterogeneous	27, 99
	relational	16
L, or L(–)	Language:	
	heterogeneous	28, 100
	relational	16
T, or T(–)	Typing:	
	heterogeneous	28, 100
	relational	16
Tj	Type:	
	heterogeneous	28, 100
	relational	16
p	Predicate symbol:	
	heterogeneous	28, 100
	relational	16

Notation	Meaning	Defined on Page:
R0( )	Row predicate symbol	100
f	Function symbol:	
	heterogeneous	28, 100
	relational	16
e(Tj):i	Constant symbol:	
	heterogeneous	28, 100
	relational	16
E	Existential quantifier:	
	heterogeneous	29, 100
	relational	18
A	Universal quantifier:	
	heterogeneous	29, 100
	relational	18
&	And:	
	heterogeneous	29, 100
	relational	18
V	Or:	
	heterogeneous	29, 100
	relational	18
~	Not:	
	heterogeneous	29, 100
	relational	18

Notation	Meaning	Defined on Page:
Q(<R1;>,..., <Rn>;<R0;>)	Defining formula for a function:	
	heterogeneous	72, 105
	relational	51
CODE(Tj)(−)	Code function:	
	heterogeneous	72, 106
	relational	51
DECODE(Tj)(−)	Code function:	
	heterogeneous	72, 106
	relational	51
I(Q)	Interpretation of a wff:	
	heterogeneous	77, 107
	relational	51
I({Q})	Interpretation of a set of wffs:	
	heterogeneous	
	relational	186
I[M], or I(−;−)[M(−)]	Induced structure:	
	heterogeneous	78, 108
	relational	52
CODE(W)	CODE function applied to W:	
	heterogeneous	81
	relational	57
DECODE (<R;>)	DECODE function applied to <R;>:	
	heterogeneous	89
	relational	89
O(Ri)(W) or O(Ri)(W,M)	Operator:	
	heterogeneous	91, 152
	relational	91, 121
SIM(O(Ri))(CODE(W)) or SIM(O(Ri))(CODE(W),M)	Operation simulator:	
	heterogeneous	91, 155
	relational	91, 122
O*(Ri)(W)	Constraint-free operator:	
	heterogeneous	156
	relational	132
SIM*(O(Ri))(CODE(W),M)	Constraint-free operation simulator:	
	heterogeneous	156
	relational	132

Notation	Meaning	Defined on Page:
U	Union	104
dtk(<R1;>,..., <Rn;>)	Defining terms	105
<t;>	Code for term t	106
X<R> Q1<R>	Prenex normal form	107
DEF(R0)(−)	Defining formula for row predicate R0(−)	107
delta(O(R))(W)	Formulas for operation O(R):	
	heterogeneous	152
	relational	121
C ⊨ C' over STR	Logically implies over STR:	
	heterogeneous	157
	relational	134
STR (SIM*(O(R)))	Image of SIM*(O(R)):	
	heterogeneous	157
	relational	135
I(A;B) o I(B;C)	Composition of interpretations:	
	heterogeneous	191
	relational	186
SIMi	Set of operation simulators	192
PHI(Ei)	External-to-conceptual map	192
pHp	Positive Horn preserving interpretation	207
c(CART)	Cardinality of Cartesian product	244
c(Ci)	Number of rows in cluster Ci	244
rf(WFF)	Reduction factor for the wff	244
size (SUBRESULT)	Size of subresult	245
length(ROW)	Length of row	245
DOPR	Directory of previous results	245
C*(E)	External axiomatization:	
	heterogeneous	312
	relational	297

Notation	Meaning	Defined on Page:
Co(E)	Implied constraints:	
	heterogeneous	312
	relational	298
I^{-1}	Inverse interpretation:	
	heterogeneous	313
	relational	299
CL(−)	Classes of relational language L(−)	303
Qk	Wff that says there are exactly k elements	322
Q*	Wff that says there are an infinite number of elements	322

INDEX